THE STAMP COLLECTOR'S
ENCYCLOPAEDIA

STAMP-PRINTING PROCESSES

Plate	Paper	Enlargement	Image	Process
STEEL or COPPER PLATE			B	**LINE ENGRAVING** Also known as: Recess, Direct plate, in copper as Taille douce or Intaglio Characteristics: Raised, granular inked image above paper surface. Back of paper slightly depressed, especially if printed on dampened paper
STONE or Grained Metal			B	**LITHOGRAPHY** Also known as: Litho: offset photo-litho, or planographic Characteristics: Homogenious inked image resting on surface with soft outlines. May be 'screened'-dots, or in a lattice or other pattern
ZINC or TYPE METAL			B	**LETTERPRESS** Also known as: Typo (typography), 'surface' or relief (relievo) Characteristics: Inked image depressed into paper with piled-up ink on edges. Back of the paper sometimes shows 'bump' or impress
COPPER Cylinder or Plate			B	**PHOTOGRAVURE** Also known as: 'Gravure, intaglio, helio-gravure or roto (rotogravure) Characteristics: Surface image. Usually screened cross-line, dots or in mosaic with edges slightly irregular or ragged

Reproduced from Practical Philately *by R. J. Sutton (Hutchinson)*

THE
STAMP COLLECTOR'S
ENCYCLOPAEDIA

Compiled by
R. J. SUTTON

Sixth edition revised by
K. W. ANTHONY

PHILOSOPHICAL LIBRARY

This edition published by Bonanza Books,
a division of Crown Publishers, Inc.,
by arrangement with Philosophical Library

J K L M N O P Q R S

Manufactured in the United States of America

Preface to the Sixth Edition

The late R. J. Sutton, who originally compiled this book, was a prolific writer whose death in a road accident, shortly before the appearance of the last edition in 1959, was a sad loss to philatelic literature. Now it has fallen to me to produce a new edition of the Encyclopaedia which for nearly fifteen years had been perhaps his best-known work.

In the past six years the rapid march of world events has had so many repercussions on philately that the task of revision this time has been a particularly heavy one. Among many other changes a number of new names have entered the stamp album for the first time since 1959, and will be found duly recorded in the following pages.

Numerous new items have been added; many more have been revised, amplified where necessary, and brought up to date. In the result a substantial part of the book has been entirely rewritten.

In its new form I hope it will prove a helpful guide to those taking up the fascinating hobby of stamp-collecting for the first time and a useful quick-reference volume for more experienced collectors, as well as providing in some measure a memorial to the original compiler. Observations and suggestions from readers for the further improvement of future editions will be welcome and will receive careful consideration.

K. W. ANTHONY

How to use this book

For stamp identification. If the name of the issuing authority (e.g. country of origin) is not on the specimen, then look for some distinguishing detail—or even a postmark—as a clue. The coinage may help. Look it up under (say) 'rupee' or whatever is the key word. Stamps of the East—China, Japan, Manchuria, etc.—nearly all have a national emblem prominently displayed. Thus China shows the 'Rising Sun'; Japan the 'Chrysanthemum'; Manchuria the 'Orchid' (see page 184), etc. Communist countries may show the 'Hammer and Sickle'. From there it is easy. Where a foreign word appears try to determine what language it is. If it is Cyrillic, then the stamp may be Russian, Bulgarian, or Yugoslav, and reference to the foreign notes at the end of each letter section may solve the problem.

Overprints can usually be identified immediately, upon reference to the first word or letter. Many of them have separate headings in this work. Appendix IV, an illustrated 'Stamp Recognition' section, should render identification of difficult specimens much easier.

Appendix III presents in one consolidated form all the identification details of British stamps used abroad, brought as up to date as the information available allows. Many place names have altered since first this list was published, but most of them have been successfully traced and given their present nomenclature.

Appendix V is as complete a stamp currency guide as possible, and should prove to be a most valuable addition. Rates of exchange given are those notified and accessible as this book goes to press, but, of course, they fluctuate and alter from time to time.

THE STAMP COLLECTOR'S
ENCYCLOPAEDIA

A.M.G.   ABYSSINIA   A.R.

A

'A'. On the stamps of Colombia the capital letter 'A' has three distinct meanings. Inscribed on the early Registration stamps it stands for 'Anotación'. As an overprint on the SCADTA semi-official airmails it is a control letter indicating that the stamp is a consular overprint sold in Germany. Overprinted on the airmail issue of 1950–1 it stands for AVIANCA, an airline, q.v. On the stamps of South Australia the 'A' overprint indicates departmental use by the Government Architect.

The capital letter also occurs as two watermarks. 'A' surmounted by the Imperial Crown was the standard watermark of Australia from 1913 to 1926. An outline letter (the initial of Amic, the papermaker) was the watermark in the one-lira issue of Modena, 1852.

A.E.F. Afrique Equatoriale Française (French Equatorial Africa, q.v.).

A.G. Overprinted on stamps of South Australia for official use in the Attorney General's Department.

A.H.PD. From 1906 to 1910 stamps of Portugal were overprinted with these initials for use in the Azores. The overprint stands for Angra, Horta, and Ponta Delgada, q.v.

A.I.F. Australian Imperial Forces (1940 set for Australia).

A.M. Overprint or inscription on stamps of Greece, 1900–2, standing for Axia Metallike (Gr.) = Value in gold. They were used mainly on overseas parcels, on which postage had to be paid in gold currency.

A.M.G.-F.T.T. Overprint on Italian stamps issued by Allied Military Government, Free Territory of Trieste, between 1947 and 1954.

A.M.G.-V.G. Overprint on Italian stamps issued by Allied Military Government, Venezia Giulia, from 1945 to 1947, prior to the Trieste area being made a free territory by the U.N.

A.M. Post/Deutschland. Stamps inscribed thus were issued by the Allied Military Government in Germany, 1945–6.

A.O. Afrique Orientale (East Africa). O/p on 1918 Red Cross stamps of Congo State for German East Africa. O/p on stamps of South Australia = 'Audit Office'.

A.O.F.   Afrique Occidentale Française. (French West Africa.)

A.P.S.   American Philatelic Society.

A.R.   (Span.). Aviso de Recepción = Advice (acknowledgment) of receipt. Chile, Montenegro, Salvador, etc., issued stamps as a prepayment fee for an acknowledgment of receipt of a registered package. In Colombia's first such issues the service covered was indicated by two stamps, one bearing the letter 'A' (Spanish: anotación or anotado); the other the initial 'R' (Spanish: registro) signifying 'Registered'; one fee covering the registration and the other the notification of receipt. It is a service recognised by the Universal Postal Union (q.v.).

A.S.   Punctured in 2, 5, or 10 mill. stamps of Sudan means 'Army Service'.

A.S.D.A.   American (or Australian) Stamp Dealers' Association.

A.T.A.   American Topical Association.

AT.   Army Telegraphs. O/p on stamps of Orange Free State. See also: 'TF', 'Telegraph Stamps', etc.

A.U.   Control letters overprinted on the semi-official SCADTA issues of Colombia, indicating 'Sold in Argentina or Uruguay'.

A.Z.   Ahmed Zogu (later King Zog I). O/p on 1925 stamps of Albania, with wreath and surcharged new value 1928.

A. and T.   Annam and Tonquin (q.v.).

Abnormals.   In the Queen Victoria G.B. surface-printed issues, the practice was to print six preliminary sheets for each plate as it was completed. One sheet was kept for record purposes in the archives (imprimatur, q.v.), and the others were often perforated and issued. In many cases these stamps differed in either colour, paper, watermark or perforation from the subsequent regular issues, and were consequently 'abnormals' and became prized rarities.

Abu Dhabi.   One of the Trucial States on the Persian Gulf, where a British postal agency was opened on 30 March, 1963. Initially the agency employed British stamps surcharged for use in Muscat; in 1964 Abu Dhabi's own first stamps appeared.

Abutshi.   Niger Coast. One of the catalogued Royal Niger Co.'s official rubber-stamp obliterators. See 'Niger Coast'.

Abyssinia.   Ethiopia (q.v.).

Acambaro.   District of Mexico which issued revolutionary provisionals in 1914.

Acaponeta.   District of Mexico which issued a revolutionary provisional in 1914.

Accessories.   A wide range of accessories is available to aid the modern collector, including hinges and mounts of various kinds, magnifiers, tweezers, perforation and measurement gauges, colour guides, etc. In the

AÇORES   ADEN   'ADMIRALS'

stamp trade other goods such as albums, catalogues, and philatelic books are not usually looked on as 'accessories' but are more frequently considered 'departments' on their own!

Acknowledgment of Receipt Stamps. See 'A.R.' above.

Açores. The Azores. Portuguese Atlantic islands. First issues were Portuguese general issues o/p in 1868, followed by colonial key-types. Since 1931 uses general issues of Portugal. Area: 922 sq. m.; pop. (1930): 253,935; capital: Ponta Delgada; currency: 1853: 1,000 reis = 1 milreis; 1912: 100 centavos == 1 escudo.

Adams & Co.'s Express. U.S.A. Pacific coast local issues of 1854–5. There was also an Adams City Express Post operating in New York in 1850, and was possibly the Atlantic coast affiliation of the Californian company.

Additional Halfpenny. From 1813 to 1839 hand-struck markings of this type were applied, in certain circumstances, to mail passing from England to Scotland. They denoted that an extra ½d. postage was chargeable. The additional charge was authorised to reimburse the Post Office for tolls paid by mailcoaches on Scottish turnpike roads.

Adelie Land. French possession in Antarctica, first discovered by Dumont Durville in 1840. In 1948 a French expedition established a base in Adelie Land, and in January 1950 a Madagascar stamp was overprinted 'Terre Adelie–Dumont Durville 1840' for use there. Since 1955 Adelie Land has used the stamps of the French Southern and Antarctic Territories, q.v.

Aden. British colony and protectorate in South Arabia. First annexed to British India in 1839, Aden used Indian stamps until it became a separate Crown Colony on 1 April, 1937. On the same day Aden's first distinctive stamps were issued, a set of pictorials in the famous Dhow design. Area of colony and protectorate: about 112,000 sq. m. Pop. (est. 1960): 660,000. Colony only: 75 sq. m. Pop. (est. 1964): 210,000. Indian currency was in use until 1951; thereafter East African currency—100 cents = 1s. Since 1963 the colony of Aden has formed part of the South Arabian Federation (q.v.).

Aden States. Only two of the sultanates of the Aden Protectorate issue their own stamps—Kathiri State of Seiyun and Qu'Aiti State of Shihr and Mukalla, otherwise known as Qu'Aiti State in Hadhramaut. In philatelic literature these two states, which together make up the Eastern Aden Protectorate, are usually referred to as Aden (Kathiri) and Aden (Qu'Aiti). Stamps first issued 1942.

Adhesive. Stamp-collecting is usually taken to imply the collecting only of adhesive postage stamps. The term adhesive is used (frequently as a noun) to distinguish such stamps from other postal material, particularly stamps printed or embossed on postal stationery.

'Admirals'. Colloquial name for three sets of British Commonwealth stamps, the 1912–18 issue of Canada, 1926 New Zealand, and 1913 Rhodesia, all of which show King George V in naval uniform.

Admiralty Official. Stamps of Great Britain overprinted for Official use.

'Adson' stamps of New Zealand of 1893 are the stamps carrying advertisements on their backs. Messrs. Truebridge, Miller & Reich of Wellington were the agents, and the ads. were on the 1882–97 series of Q.V. Many of the products given publicity are well known in G.B. and even today are household names: Sunlight Soap, Fry's and Cadbury's chocolate, 'Flag' sauces, etc. Others were local firms. They have unabated interest for the collector today.

Advertisements on Stamps. For advertising purposes some sheets of the Great Britain 1d. lilac of 1881 and ½d. vermilion of 1887 were printed on the backs, over the gum, with the legend 'Pear's Soap', in double-lined lettering in orange, blue, or mauve. A number of unused copies have survived, but their postal use was vetoed by the Postmaster-General. The 1893 stamps of New Zealand carried advertising on the reverse; see 'Adson' above. Some cases are known in which labels printed se-tenant with stamps to make up booklet panes have been used for advertising. Over many years the stamp booklets of Great Britain and some other countries have been interleaved with advertising pages.

Advertising by Postmarks. The idea of using cancellations to put across an advertising message first caught on in the First World War. Since then many 'slogan cancellations' have been used for Government publicity. France has actually used a cancellation to advertise the attraction of stamp-collecting! In 1963 the British Post Office announced a scheme offering pictorial or slogan cancellations (for a fee) to local authorities wishing to advertise their towns. Holiday resorts in particular were quick to show interest in the scheme.

Aegean Islands. See 'Dodecanese.'

Aer-Phost. (Erse). Air Post.

Aereo. (Span.). Airborne, or by air.

Aerogramme (also Aerogram). Official U.P.U. name for an airletter sheet. These lightweight sheets with gummed flaps, and usually with a stamp printed on them, are carried by air at less than normal airmail rates. The first example was issued by Iraq as early as July 1933, but it was

AFFRANCHTS   AFGHANISTAN   AIRMAILS

the extensive use of Forces' airletters, introduced during the last war, that led to their adoption all over the world. In recent years this branch of postal stationery has become a recognised philatelic sideline and at least one British dealer runs a New Issue Service for them. The outstanding publication on the subject is *Kessler's Catalog of Aerograms* in two loose-leaf volumes (published in New York).

Aero-philately. The collection and study of postage stamps for use on airborne mail has now become an intensive specialised branch of the hobby, with its own literature, sources of supply and exchange, and its own peculiar and particular phraseology. See also 'Airmail', 'Zeppelin', and allied subjects.

Affixing Machines, Stamp. Special semi-automatic machines designed to affix ordinary postage stamps to large departmental or office mails. The stamps are in coils, automatically dampened, and pressed into position on to envelopes or wrappers by applied pressure. Not to be confused with **vending** machines (q.v.) or with metered mail (q.v.). The rolls or coils are especially made and are listed by the British G.P.O. under stock key letters: M, N, O, P, S, and T. The stamps are attached by their long sides—those for vending machines are short-side attached—and this results in their being watermarked sideways, which in the case of current G.B. stamps make a major variety. See also 'Sideways Watermarks', etc.

Affranchts. Abbreviation for Affranchissements (literally, 'exempted from payment'); a pre-cancel marking found on French stamps used on Official mail or on bulk postings of business mail.

Afghanes. See 'Afghanistan' below.

Afghanistan. Asian kingdom situated between Pakistan and Persia. Stamps first issued, 1870. The early issues, with their curious circular designs, are a complex study for specialists; no cancellations were available and to prevent re-use a piece was torn or cut from the stamp by the issuing clerk, with the result that few unmutilated copies have survived. All the stamps of Afghanistan were imperf. until 1907. Currency: 1868, 12 shahi = 6 Sanar = 3 abasi = 2 kran = 1 rupee; 1921, 100 pouls or 66 paises = 1 Afghani. Area: about 250,000 sq. m. Capital: Kabul. Est. pop.: 13,800,000.

Africa correios. Inscription on the 1898 general issue for all the Portuguese territories in Africa.

Africa Occidental Española. Spanish West Africa, q.v.

Africa Orientale Italiana. Italian East Africa, q.v.

Afrique Equatoriale Française. French Equatorial Africa, q.v.

Afrique Occidentale Française. French West Africa, q.v.

Agency. This term has two meanings in philately.

1. A postal agency operated by the Post Office of one country in the territory of another, by arrangement with the latter—for example the British postal agencies in the Persian Gulf area.

2. An organisation of either public or private enterprise handling and promoting sales of new issues to the stamp trade on behalf of the issuing governments. The outstanding example is the Crown Agents Stamp Bureau, with headquarters in London and an American bureau in Washington, currently supplying dealers with the stamps of more than sixty territories of the British Commonwealth.

See also 'Clandestine Agency'.

Aguascalientes. District of Mexico which issued revolutionary provisionals in 1914.

Aguera, La. See 'La Aguera.'

Aguinaldo. Local stamps of doubtful status issued by the Aguinaldo revolutionary government of the Philippines in 1898.

Airgraph. Forces' mail introduced in 1941 to reduce the load carried by aircraft. Letters written on special forms were photographed on to microfilm and carried to their destination where they were photographically enlarged and forwarded to the addressee. In this way a ton of ordinary mail could be reduced to slightly more than 17 lb. in weight. The service was withdrawn in 1945.

A somewhat similar system was adopted during the Franco-Prussian War of 1870 for flying messages into besieged Paris by pigeon.

Airmail. The carriage of mail by air goes back much further in time than many collectors realise. The first government-sponsored airmail flight took place in the United States on 17 August 1859, when Professor John Wise's balloon *Jupiter* carried mail from Lafayette to Crawfordsville, Indiana. The destination was intended to be New York, but contrary winds obliged the balloonist to descend. The centenary of this flight was marked by a commemorative American stamp.

This was, however, only an isolated flight. The first service to be conducted over a period with some degree of regularity was arranged during the Siege of Paris in the Franco-Prussian War of 1870. The beleaguered city kept in touch with the rest of France by dispatching mail by balloon, inward mail being received by means of pigeons. Items carried by this service, particularly those marked *'Par Ballon Monte'* ('By Piloted Balloon'), are greatly prized by collectors. See also under 'Balloon Post'.

The first time letters were carried by powered aircraft appears to have been a flight from Paris to St. Nazaire, France, in August 1908. The first

British flight was by Claude Graham White from Blackpool to Southport two years later.

The first government-sponsored airmail flight by powered aircraft took place between Allahabad and Naini in India in February 1911. The first such regular service was the 'Coronation Airmail' between London and Windsor in September of that year, when some 130,000 letters and postcards, postmarked 'First United Kingdom Aerial Post', were carried.

Many further experimental airmail flights, both official and private, took place in the succeeding years. The first international service, between Austria and the Ukraine, started in 1918. In the following year regular airmail facilities were provided between London and Paris, and thereafter the system was gradually extended to most parts of the world.

In some cases mail is carried by air without extra charge. The outstanding example was the Empire Air Mail Scheme, popularly known as the 'All-Up Service', introduced in 1937, by which all first-class mail between Britain and the Commonwealth was carried by air. This service was discontinued on the outbreak of war.

It remains true, however, that postage on airmail usually costs more than by surface post, and over the years many stamps have been issued specifically or mainly for airmail use. Such stamps are known as airmails, air stamps, or simply airs. The earliest airmail stamp was a semi-official inscribed 'Balloon Postage', issued in the United States in 1877 in connection with balloon flights by Samuel Archer King, of which only two copies are known used on flown cover. The first government-issued air stamp was an Italian Express issue overprinted in 1917 for an experimental service between Rome and Turin.

The collection of airmail stamps and covers has become an extremely popular branch of the hobby. The Sanabria catalogue, published in America, is devoted exclusively to them.

Air Covers. Envelopes or other postal wrappers bearing cachets or airmail stamps or other evidence of their having been airborne. See 'Aerophilately' above, 'Aerogramme', etc.

Air Labels or 'Etiquettes'. Member countries of the Universal Postal Union adopt a standardised blue label for affixing to airborne correspondence to expedite such mail by affording ready recognition. The label is worded in the official U.P.U. language (French) 'Par Avion' and in the language of the issuing country, is supplied gratis, and is to be affixed to the top left of the address panel. Their collection is an interesting sideline in aero-philately.

Airletter Sheet. See 'Aerogramme'.

Air Stamp. See under 'Airmail'.

Aitutaki. Cook Islands, Southern Pacific, a British dependency administered by New Zealand. It had its own o/p and surcharged issues of New Zealand from 1903 to 15 March 1932, since when it has used stamps of the Cook Islands. Is an atoll 9 miles by 21 miles, encircling a lagoon, and with a land area of 7 sq. m.; pop. (1961): 2,582. N.Z. currency.

| ALBANIA | AIR LABELS | ALAOUITES |

'Ajl' or 'Ajahlas'. (Magyar). Registered letter. O/p on 1946 inflation issues of Hungary.

Ajman. One of the Trucial States of Arabia. Stamps first issued, 1964. Currency: 100 naye paise = 1 rupee.

Akahi. (Hawaiian). One.

Akassa. One of the Royal Niger Company's official cancellers on stamps of G.B. 1895–9. See 'Niger Coast Protectorate'.

Alaouites. Coastal territory of Syria, formerly part of the Ottoman Empire, using Turkish stamps to the end of World War I. Under French mandate 1920–41, but formed into a separate province 1924, renamed Latakia (q.v.) in 1930, and reabsorbed into the Republic of Syria from 1920 to 1925, when stamps of France (and then Syria) were o/p 'Alaouites' until the change of name in 1930. Area: 2,500 sq. m.; pop. (est. 1930): 278,000; capital: Latakia.

Alaskan (U.S.A.) Mail often bears sets of numbers, the first of which is the number of the Judicial District (there are four), then the chief town in brackets, thus: the S.E. district is No. 1 (Juneau); the Western, No. 2 (Nome); the Middle West, No. 3 (Anchorage); and N.E. to S.E., No. 4 (Fairbanks). The second and third numbers are the latitude and longitude so that even small places are easily pin-pointed on a map. (S.C.F., December 1951.)

Alava. The Basque Provinces of Northern Spain—Alava, Biscay, Guipuzcoa, and Navarre issued their own Carlist stamps, bearing Don Carlos' portrait in 1873. They were suppressed after the defeat of the party in 1876.

Albania. This Adriatic country (variously inscribed on the stamps as Shqipenia, Shqyptare, Shqipni, Shqiperija, etc.) was formerly part of the Ottoman Empire, using Turkish stamps. Greece, Italy, and Austria all maintained post offices there, Greece from 1861 to 1881, and Italy from 1902 to 1916 (using Italian stamps overprinted). Austria had offices in the principal towns until 1915, using stamps of the Austrian Levant.

The country achieved a precarious independence in 1912, and the first Albanian stamps appeared in the following year. A short-lived attempt to introduce a monarchy was made in 1914, but during the First

World War the central government ceased to function, various parts of the country being occupied by the Serbs, Greeks, Italians, Bulgarians, Austrians, and French. During this period local regimes issued their own stamps for Valona, Central Albania, Scutari, and Koriza.

Independence was regained after the war, though an Allied council continued to govern at Scutari until February 1920 (issuing its own stamps), and the Yugoslavs occupied the northern part of the country until 1921. A republic was proclaimed in 1918, but this was replaced by a regency in 1920 and by a kingdom in 1928, the first monarch being King Zog. He was deposed in 1939 when Italy invaded and quickly occupied the country, at first overprinting Albanian stamps and then issuing their own after the Italian pattern.

In 1940 Italy used Albania as a base for the invasion of Greece, but the Greeks drove the Italians back and occupied southern Albania in 1941-2, this resulting in yet further occupation issues, overprinted on Greek stamps. The Greeks were repulsed by the Germans who took over Albania from the Italians in 1943.

By November of the following year, however, the Albanian guerrilla forces had regained control of most of the country and the present republic was established.

Area: 11,097 sq. m.; pop. (est. 1961): 1,665,000. Capital: Tirana. Currency: Turkish to 1913, then 100 qind = 1 franc (with a temporary change to 100 centimes = 1 franc in 1917); 1947, 20 qidars = 1 lek, 5 lek = 1 franc ar (gold franc); 1958, 100 qintars = 1 lek. See also under 'Epirus', 'Durazzo', 'Saseno' and 'Scutari.'

Albanie Centrale. Stamps issued for Central Albania by the local regime of Essad Pasha in 1915.

Albino. Without colour. An impression made by a cliché or other printing plate or die, bearing a design from which all colour (ink) is missing, either by accident through the printing surface failing to take up ink, or—more usual—two sheets of paper passing through the machine at once, thus masking one sheet. A loose scrap of paper, a wide crease or turned-in corner would create a similar effect, partially or wholly masking one or more stamps. Albino varieties are rare and are, strictly speaking, printers' waste accidentally included in bulk consignments.

Album. Literally a blank book. Stamp albums are normally blank books, or are partially printed, but with blank spaces designed to hold and display a collection of postage stamps. There are two main types: a bound book of blank, grilled, or partially illustrated and printed pages; and the other, a loose-leaf construction comprising a cover, containing leaves or pages as described above, held by spring action, or by pegs, screws, laces or thongs, or other securing device. The so-called album 'standard page' measures $9\frac{7}{8}$ in. by $11\frac{1}{8}$ in., but there are many sizes available from quite small pocket editions to large tomes for library use. The first recorded album designed for the collection of postage stamps was published in Paris, by Lallier in 1862, there being three editions in French, German, and English. Edward A. Oppen published the first album in

ALEXANDRIA   ALGERIA   ALFONSO XIII

England shortly afterwards. W. S. Lincoln and Stanley Gibbons were, however, the pioneers of mass-produced albums for the popular new hobby. See also 'Arrangement', 'Hinges', 'Writing up', etc.

'Album Weeds'. Title of one of the best-known early works on forged stamps, by the Rev. R. Brisco Earée. The last edition of the original work appeared in 1906, but in recent years parts have been reprinted. The work summarises a long series of articles entitled 'The Spud Papers' which were published in a periodical, *The Philatelist*, beginning in 1871. The term 'Album Weeds' is also applied to forgeries in general.

Alende. District of Mexico which issued a revolutionary provisional in 1914.

Alerta. Peruvian district with one stamp with handwritten surcharge, in 1884.

Alexandretta. See 'Hatay'.

Alexandria, Egypt. French stamps o/p 'Alexandrie' were in use in French post offices in Egypt 1899–1931. Stamps of G.B. used abroad (q.v.) bore cancellation 'BO1' 1860–80, and stamps of France (1852–99), Austria, Greece, Italy, and Russia, who all had offices there, can be found and identified by postmarks.

Alexandria, Kherson, Russia. One of the 'Zemstvos' (local government issues) of Russia. Its 1870 stamp bore a curious and coincidental resemblance to the U.S.A. typeset stamp (noted below) for the town of the same name. See 'Locals', 'Zemstvos', etc.

Alexandria, Virginia. A circular typeset 'Postmasters' ' stamp came from this U.S.A. town in 1846.

Alfonso XII. King of Spain 1875–86, portrayed on his country's general and keytype stamps during his reign.

Alfonso XIII. King of Spain from birth 1886 to 1931, and shown from babyhood to manhood on Spain's stamps until the revolution.

Algeria (Algérie). Former French territory in North Africa, since 1962 an independent republic. Stamps first issued, 1924. Prior to this date, and again from 1958 to 1962, ordinary French stamps were used. Area: 847,522 sq. m.; pop. (1960): 10,786,000; capital: Algiers; currency: as France.

ALLIED	ALSACE AND	ALWAR	AMTLICHER
OCCUPATION	LORRAINE		VERKEHR
ISSUES			

Allen's City Dispatch. Local stamp issued in Chicago, U.S.A., in 1882.

Allenstein. Former district of East Prussia, Germany, occupied by an Allied Commission until 1920. In that year a plebiscite resulted in the area's return to Germany. German stamps were overprinted for use there during the plebiscite period. Now part of Poland, known as Olsztyn.

'Alpha' and 'Beta' flaws. Name given to characteristic flaws found on the bicoloured stamps of Denmark, 1870–85.

'Alphabetizacion' also Alphabetisation. Inscription on tax stamps issued by Mexico and Haiti to raise funds for a campaign against illiteracy.

Alsace and Lorraine. French border provinces twice invaded and occupied by Germany—in 1870 and again in 1940. In the Franco-Prussian War Germany issued special occupation stamps with values in French currency. These are catalogued under Alsace and Lorraine, but although used in these two provinces they were also used throughout occupied France until the end of the war. Thereafter they were valid only in Alsace and Lorraine until these areas were incorporated in the German Empire and German stamps came into use.

After the First World War Alsace and Lorraine were returned to France, only to be occupied again in 1940 when German issues were separately overprinted for Alsace and for Lorraine. Since 1945 the territories have again formed part of France.

Alwar. As a feudatory state of Rajasthan, British India, issued its own 'locals' 1877–99; in 1901 was given convention status and from then up to partition used stamps of British India. Now in the Republic of India. Area: 3,158 sq. m.; pop. (1941): 823,055.

Amadeus, or **Amadeo.** King of Spain 1870–3. There were several portrait stamp issues during his short reign.

Ambulante. Travelling. Thus 'Poste Ambulante' used on stamps of France and Belgium means a travelling or mobile vehicle used for purely postal purposes, and may define a mail-van used on rail or road. See 'Mobile Post Offices'.

America. Used colloquially in Great Britain, normally implies the U.S.A., but the continents of North and South Americas contain a number of stamp-issuing countries and authorities, dealt with separately in this work.

American Bank Note Company. Messrs. Rawdon, Wright, Hatch & Edson, a famous New York firm of printers of postage stamps, incorporated as the American Bank Note Company on 1 May 1858. One of the first contracts was to produce the 1859 issues for Canada. It still flourishes and has been responsible for many of the finest stamp issues for the Americas and elsewhere.

American Express Company. Stamps so inscribed were short-lived locals issued by Smith & Dobson in the U.S.A. in 1857.

American Letter Mail Co. Locals of Boston, U.S.A., issued by Lysander Spooner in 1844.

American Topical Association (A.T.A.). Leading organisation, based in the United States, for thematic collectors. (Thematics, q.v., are known as topicals in the U.S.A.) The Association publishes its own journal and handbooks on thematic subjects.

Amoy. Treaty port of Southern China. British post office opened 1844 using stamps of Hong Kong with postmark A1. Closed December 1922.

Amtlicher Verkehr. (Ger.). Official Communication. Inscription on the 'Officials' (Dienst) stamps of Württemberg 1881–1919.

Amur Province. In February 1920 a People's Revolutionary Committee set up an autonomous administration at Blagovestchansk which ended when the Far Eastern Republic (q.v.) was established. Stamps issued in 1920 bore Russian inscription 'Amur Province—Postage stamp'.

Anatolia. Greek name for Asia Minor—otherwise known as Anatolia-Roumelia, or (formerly) Turkey in Asia.

Ancachs. Postal district of Haurez, Peru. A provisional stamp o/p 'Franca' was in use in 1884.

Anchal, or **Anchel.** Native Indian internal postal service. Applied to the limited service within its confines, as distinct from the British Indian or Government coverage. Example: stamps of Cochin.

Anchor. Watermark used in certain issues of Great Britain and Colonies, i.e.: G.B. 1867–74; Cape of Good Hope triangulars 1853–64. A 'fouled' anchor is one with a length of cable around the shank, as shown in many stamp papers, notably the fiscals of Q.V. 1853–60.

Andaman Islands. Group in the Indian Ocean used as a penal settlement until 1926. Came under Burmese postal administration until 1937, when it was transferred to Indian control. There are about 200 islands covering 2,260 sq. m. and had at one time a convict pop. of 10,000, but the penal settlement closed in 1945. Pop. (1951), excl. aborigines: 18,939; capital: Port Blair. Is now a province of the Indian Republic.

Andorra (Andorre). Tiny independent state in the Pyrenees, between France and Spain, placed under the joint suzerainty of the Bishop of Urgel in Spain and the Count of Foix in France by a treaty of 1278. The interest of the Counts of Foix later passed to the kings of Navarre and of

ANGOLA   ANDORRA   ANJOUAN

France, and eventually to the president of the French Republic. A Spanish postal service was established in 1928, and a French post office three years later. The two services issue their own stamps concurrently. Andorra is the only country in the world which handles internal mail free of postage. Area: 191 sq. m.; pop. (1957): 6,439; capital: Andorra la Vella, or la Vieja.

Angola. Portuguese territory in south-west Africa. Stamps first issued, 1870. Area: 481,351 sq. m.; capital: formerly Loanda, now Nova Lisboa (New Lisbon); currency; 1870, 1,000 reis = 1 milreis; 1913 and again 1960: 100 centavos = 1 escudo; 1928–60, 100 centavos = 1 angolar; pop. (1961): 4,832,677.

Angora, Ankhara or Ankara. Headquarters of Kemal's National Government in 1919, and now capital of the Turkish Republic. Had an issue of fiscal and other Turkish stamps o/p in 1921, followed by special issues in 1922 and general issues for the whole of Turkey after the occupation of Constantinople (Istanbul) in 1923.

Angra. Angra do Heroísmo. Seaport and chief town of the Açores, Portuguese island territories. It stands on the south coast of Terceira Island. Used colonial keytypes 1892–1906. Now uses stamps of Açores. Area: 275 sq. m.; pop. (1950): 86,577.

Anguilla. Northernmost island of the Lesser Antilles, now postally linked with St. Kitts-Nevis. Area: 50 sq. m.; pop. (1960) 5,592. Alternatively known as Snake Island.

Anhyphenate. Without hyphen. (See 'Hyphenated'.) Sometimes applied to the early issues of the Union of South Africa.

Aniline. The accepted philatelic meaning is a water-soluble and fugitive ink, with a dye base that runs when wetted, and fluoresces under the quartz lamp (ultra-violet ray). The Q.V. 1900 1s. green and carmine, K.E. VII 1911 1d. aniline pink, both of G.B., and some modern Netherlands issues are examples. In August 1949 the Expert Committee, Royal Philatelic Society, London, made a lengthy decision in regard to 1d. aniline scarlets of G.B., K.G. V, in which they laid down that 'it has now been decided to reserve certificates in respect of aniline stamps for specimens which show unusual translucence, unusual brilliance of tone on the

21

surface and extreme reaction to the quartz-ray lamp'. Stanley Phillips, writing in *G.S.M.* of March 1949, defined a true 'aniline' as one with 'a peculiar quality of brightness coupled with a suffusion of colour on the surface of the stamp, and the colour showing through to a marked degree on the back'. Where the use of such inks is suspected, stamps on paper should be most carefully 'floated off' (q.v.), and the surfaces protected from rubbing—even when dry. Strictly speaking, most modern inks have an aniline (coal-tar) base, but the colours in question were developed and used designedly to prevent erasure of post- and penmarking, and to prevent re-use. In the Scott catalogue there is quite a useful list of such susceptible stamp issues.

Anjouan. One of the Comoro Islands, a French territory off the east coast of Africa, which used French colonial types inscribed Sultanat d'Anjouan from 1892 to 1914, when the Comoro Islands were incorporated in Madagascar. Stamps of Madagascar were then used until 1950, when the first issue for Comoro Islands appeared. Area: 89 sq. m.

Ankhara, or Ankara. See 'Angora'.

Anna. Former Indian currency unit, and valid in Red Sea ports = 1/16th of a rupee.

Annam and Tonquin. French Indo-China, now part of Viet-Nam (q.v.). 'Commerce' keytypes o/p 'A. & T.' and surcharged with new value were in use 1888. Used stamps of Indo-China after 1892. Area: Annam, 39,758 sq. m.; Tonquin (Tonkin), 40,530 sq. m.; pop. (1930): Annam, 4,820,000; Tonquin, 8,182,962; currency: 100 cents = 1 piastre. Indo-China produced one separate issue for Annam in 1936.

Annapolis (Maryland, U.S.A.). One of the 'Postmasters' Provisionals', a rare stamped envelope issued in 1846.

Annigoni Portrait. The portrait of Queen Elizabeth II by Italian artist Pietro Annigoni has been adapted for stamp designs on many occasions, notably by Hong Kong and Fiji.

Annobon. See 'Elobey, Annobon and Corisco'.

Annule. (Fr.). Cancelled.

Anotado. (Span.). Noted or authorised. Obsolete stamps of Mexico were so o/p to render them again valid for temporary use pending arrival and release of delayed new issues, *vide* Gibbons, but Pemberton records that they were 'undoubtedly for registered letters'. They have been extensively forged. See also 'Habilitado'.

Antananarivo. See 'Madagascar'.

Antarctic Expedition Stamps. See 'King Edward VII Land', 'Victoria Land' and 'Byrd (U.S.A.)', etc.

Antigua. One of the Leeward Islands group in the British West Indies. Stamps first issued, 1862. Prior to this, British stamps were in use in Antigua between 1858 and 1860, being distinguished by the 'A 02'

A PAYER   ANTIGUA   A PERCEVOIR

cancellation (St. John's) or 'A 18' (English Harbour). Area: 171 sq. m.; capital: St. John's; currency: Sterling to 1951, now B.W.I. decimal.; pop. (1962): 65,100.

Anti-Malaria. Term used to describe the stamps issued by numerous countries in 1962 to mark the U.N. Malaria Eradication Campaign.

Antioquia. Department of Colombia which issued its own stamps from 1868 until 1906, when they were superseded by Colombian issues. Area: 25,516 sq. m.; capital: Medellin (q.v.); currency: 100 centavos = 1 peso; pop. (1962): 1,971,710.

'Any.': O/p on inflated pengo issues of Hungary 1946 indicates use for prepayment by sample post.

A Payer—Te Betalen. (Fr. and Flemish). To pay. Inscribed on the postage due stamps of Belgium.

À Percevoir. (Fr.). To collect. Inscription on 'dues' of Canada, France, Monaco and Egypt.

Approvals, also approval sheets, approval books: priced selections of stamps sent out by dealers to collectors on approval.

Apurimac. Peruvian department with a 'revolutionary' issue 1881–5.

Arabia. Contains a number of stamp-issuing authorities, e.g. Saudi Arabia, Aden, Aden Protectorate States, Bahrain, Kuwait, Yemen, etc., all of which see. The Arab Postal Union was inaugurated in July 1954.

ᐯ ᒥ ᒣ Ɛ ⵔ ᐭ � ᐱ ໑ ✦ ᐯ••

| 1 | 2 | 3 | 4 | 5 | 6 | 7 | 8 | 9 | 0 | 100 |

Arabic script and numerals (see above) appear on many of the stamps of the Near Eastern countries.

Arab Union. A short-lived political linking of Iraq with Jordan which was marked by the issue of a special stamp in early 1958.

Arad. The Arad issues of Hungary appeared during the French occupation 1919, and were current Hungarian issues o/p 'Occupation Française'.

It is an important railway and trading town with a population of (1956) 106,457, now a part of Roumania.

Arbe. Adriatic island and town. See under 'Fiume.'

'Arch' Set of Canada. The K.G. V portraits of 1930–1. So called (to differentiate them from the previous series) on account of the design.

Archer Perfs. Term applied to the trial separations carried out on the G.B. Penny Red between 1848 and 1850 by Henry Archer, inventor of the first practical perforating machine. Some of these were rouletted 12, others perf. 16. These trials were undertaken privately but with the consent of the Post Office, the stamps being distributed in the normal way. They were followed by Government trial perforations. In June 1853 Archer was awarded £4,000 by the Treasury for his machine and his patent rights, and from the beginning of the following year all British stamps (except the 6d. embossed) were perforated.

Archipel des Comores. Comoro Islands, q.v.

Arc Piercing. See 'Percé en arc', 'Rouletting', etc.

Arctische Post. Local issue of Spitzbergen by Captain W. Bade about 1897. It had a presumed value of 10 pfennig.

Arequipa. Peruvian city and centre of resistance to the Chilean invasion after the fall of Lima in 1881. Was captured by Chile in 1883 but evacuated with other Peruvian cities after the peace treaty of October 1883. Civil war followed, and stamps were again issued at Arequipa 1884–5 by the forces opposing the Lima government. Many of these issues were overprinted with controls identified with various cities, fully listed in most catalogues. See also: 'Cuzco', 'Moquegua', 'Ayacucho', 'Piura', etc.

Argentina. Republic of South America, a confederation until 1862. Stamps first issued 1858, but two constituent states, Corrientes and Buenos Aires, had prior issues. Area: 1,153,119 sq. m.; capital: Buenos Aires; currency: 100 centavos = 1 peso; pop. (est. 1962): 21,247,420.

Armenia. Soviet republic of Trans-Caucasia, now part of the U.S.S.R. Was temporarily independent 1918–23, and had its own issues which were superseded by the stamps of the Trans-Caucasian Federation (q.v.). Area: 11,945 sq. m.; pop. (1923): 1,214,391; capital: Erivan; Russian currency.

Armenwet (Ned. = Poor Law): O/p on stamps of the Netherlands 1913. Official use for Poor Law Administration.

Arms Types. Stamps bearing coats of arms, armorial and heraldic devices, are commonly known as 'Arms' types. France, Luxembourg, Russia, Jamaica, Mauritius, Papal States, St. Vincent, Andorra and many South American states, and others have issued such stamps. They form a most interesting 'subject' (q.v.) collection.

Army Frank. Inscription on a privately produced label in the U.S.A. in 1898, purporting to be an 'official' of the War Department. It is a close

ARMS TYPES   ARMENIA   ARMY POST STAMPS

copy of the 1869 10 **c.** with the added legend 'Official Business Only', and issued without official sanction.

Army Official. See 'Officials'.

Army Post. Egyptian stamps with this inscription were used from 1936 to 1951 by British forces stationed in Egypt, who enjoyed a concessionary rate of postage on their mail to England.

Arrangement. The interest and value of any collection are greatly enhanced by careful and artistic presentation in the album. Each page should be arranged to present the collection to its best advantage. An excellent book on the subject which can be recommended is *How to Arrange and Write-up a Stamp Collection*, by Stanley Phillips and C. P. Rang (published by Gibbons).

Arrow Block. A block of stamps bearing on the attached margin or selvedge the broad arrow or similar device to indicate point of cleavage into panes or blocks of predetermined values, on certain sheets of G.B., for instance. See 'Blocks', 'Margins', etc.

Art Paper. A superfine 'calendered' (ironed) paper with a surface of china clay, or kaolin, giving it a highly enamelled finish for the printing of fine-screen half-tone blocks. Has occasionally been employed for stamp printing. The issues of Kishangarh are examples.

Aruba. Dutch West Indian island, now part of the Netherlands Antilles (q.v.). Area: 190 sq. km.; pop. (1956): 56,050.

Ascension. British island colony in the South Atlantic, and a dependency of St. Helena. Stamps of G.B. were in use 1867–1922. First definitives appeared in 1922. Area: 34 sq. m.; pop. (1960): 429; capital: Georgetown; British coinage.

Asch. Sudeten town and district of Czechoslovakia, with its own surcharged issues 1938. Now known as As. See 'Sudetenland', etc.

Ash, John. Printing manager to Thos. De La Rue of London 1907–27; appointed banknote and stamp printer to the Commonwealth Bank of Australia 1927, planned, equipped and supervised new modern machinery for the Melbourne printing works, and his rotaries printed for most of Australasia. Retired in favour of W. C. McCracken 1941, died 1947.

ASISTENTA SOCIALA   ASCENSION   AUSTRALIA

Asia Minor Steamship Company. Two local stamps were issued in 1868 to frank letters carried from Smyrna to Cyprus and Constantinople. Less than a dozen copies genuinely used are known.

'As is'. Against an item in an auction catalogue indicates that the stamps are sold without guarantee or promise of refund. (Inspection before bidding is advisable.)

Asistenta Sociala. Charity stamps of Roumania.

Assistencia. (Port.). Assistance or charity. Portugal has colonial stamps so inscribed, the receipts of which are used to combat tuberculosis.

At Betale. (Nor.). To pay. Inscribed on 1889–1927 postage due stamps of Norway.

Athens. Georgia, U.S.A. Had a Confederate 'Postmasters' ' stamp in 1861.

Athens Prints. The first issues of Greece were printed by Meyer in Paris, but later printings from November 1861 were made in Athens. Not only do the Athens prints vary in colour, but there are line shading differences in the plates known to collectors and illustrated or detailed in all good catalogues.

Atlantis. When the U.S.A. took over the former Danish West Indies (now the U.S. Virgin Islands) malcontents are said to have set up their own government on several of the smaller islands, and to have published a set of stamps for the proposed new country of Atlantis. They had no postal validity and were probably entirely bogus.

Auctions. The first recorded stamp auction was held in Paris 29 December 1865. J. W. Scott organised one in New York in May 1870 and Sotheby one in London 18 May 1872. They are now a widely used method of buying and selling stamps, particularly the great rarities and stamps in wholesale quantities.

Auner's Despatch Post. A local issued in Philadelphia, U.S.A., by A. W. Auner in 1851.

Aunus, or Olenetz. On the N.E. shore of Lake Ladoga, North Russia. Captured by Finnish troops 1919, an issue of Finnish stamps o/p 'Aunus' (the Finnish name for the district) appeared. It was later recaptured and retained by the Russians.

AUSTRIA   AUSTRIAN MILITARY POST   AYTONOMOΣ

Ausserkurs. (Ger. Ausserkurssetzung). Withdrawal or demonetisation. O/p diagonally in black on remaindered stamps of Switzerland.

Australia. The Commonwealth of Australia, an island continent between the Indian and Pacific oceans, is an independent member of the British Commonwealth, formed in 1901 from the former colonies of New South Wales, Queensland, South Australia, Victoria, Western Australia, and Tasmania. Each colony continued to issue its own stamps until 1913, when the first issue for all Australia appeared in the famous Kangaroo design (q.v.). The first all-Australian postage dues, however, appeared in 1902. Australia now administers Papua and New Guinea, the Cocos Islands, Norfolk Island, Nauru and Christmas Island, all of which have their own stamps.

Area of Australia: 2,974,581 sq. m.; capital: Canberra; currency: Sterling less 20 per cent—£1 Australian = 16s. sterling; pop. (est. 1962): 10,603,936. Decimal currency, 100 cents. = 1 dollar (8s. sterling) introduced Feb. 1966.

Australian Antarctic Territory. The Australian sector of Antarctica. Stamps first issued, 1957. The Territory's stamps are also valid for postage in Australia itself, where they are put on sale for a short time when first issued.

Austria (Österreich). State of central Europe, centre of the Austro-Hungarian Empire until 1918, thereafter a republic. Stamps first issued, 1850. From 1938 to 1945 Austria was absorbed into Greater Germany, and in this period German stamps and currency were used. Area: 32,369 sq. m.; capital: Vienna (Wien); currency: 1850, 60 kreuzer = 1 gulden; 1858, 100 kreuzer = 1 gulden; 1899, 100 heller = 1 krone; 1925 and again 1945, 100 groschen = 1 schilling; pop. (1961): 7,067,000. (Prior to the First World War, the Austro-Hungarian empire had an area of 261,259 sq. m. and a population of 51,000,000.)

Austrian Italy. The northern provinces of Lombardy (capital: Milan) and Venice (Venezia Tridentina), administered by Austria after the Napoleonic Wars. Lombardy was ceded to Sardinia in 1859, and Venice to Italy in 1866. Stamps first issued, 1850; currency: 100 centesimi = 1 lira.

27

Austrian Levant. Issues for use at the Austrian post offices in the Ottoman Empire. Stamps first issued, 1867. The offices were closed and the stamps withdrawn in 1914–15. Currency: 1867, 100 soldi = 1 gulden; 1886, 40 para = 1 piaster.

Austrian Military Post. Stamps inscribed or overprinted 'K.U.K. Feldpost' were for use by the Austrian forces during the First World War, and also in the Austrian occupation of parts of Italy, Montenegro, Roumania, and Serbia. Austrian issues for Bosnia and Herzegovina were inscribed 'K.U.K. Militarpost' from 1912 to 1918.

Austrian Occupation Issues, 1914-18. See above.

Austrian Post Offices in Crete. General Austrian stamps were surcharged in 1903–8 in centimes or francs for use in these establishments, with a commemorative issue also valued in French coinage in 1908. The island was handed over to Greece in 1913, and foreign post offices closed.

Authenticity. See under 'Expertising'.

Automatic Machines for vending, affixing, and/or meter marking in lieu of postage stamps are dealt with under their appropriate headings, i.e.: 'Metered Mail', 'Affixing Machines, Stamp', 'Stamp Vending Machines', etc.

Average Copy. A stamp in average condition for the issue concerned. Not superb, but a sound copy, of moderately pleasing appearance and good colour and usually, if used, not too heavily postmarked.

AVIANCA. Colombian airline (successor to SCADTA, q.v.), responsible for the 'A' overprints on Colombia airmail issues of 1950 and 1951. The initials stand for Aerovias Naciónales de Colombia, Cia. Anonima.

Avion. (Fr.) Airplane. See 'Par Avion'.

Avion Messre Tafari. On 1931 air stamps of Ethiopia (q.v.). Literally 'Royal airmail'.

Avisporto Mærke. Literally: Prepaid Information Stamp. The inscription on the newspaper, journal, or printed papers stamp of Denmark.

Avo. Basic Portuguese monetary unit, on stamps of Macao and Timor.

Ayacucho. Peru. One of the Arequipa issues (q.v. above) with special o/p in use 1881.

Aytonomoϵ. (Gr.). Autonomous. Inscription on the 1914 war issues for the Epirus (q.v.).

Ayuntamiento de Barcelona. Local obligatory tax stamp of the Corporation of Barcelona, Spain, with no other postal validity.

Azad Hind. (Free India). Inscription on Nazi-German emissions, printed in Vienna, 1942, in anticipation of the conquest of India, and designed for use by the puppet-ruler elect, Subhas Chandra-Bose. Never officially issued, they have a curiosity value only.

Azemar Machine. An early cancelling machine named after J. G. Azemar who introduced it to the British Post Office in 1869. It appears, however, that the machine was invented by Wilhelm Ree of Hamburg, and that Azemar merely acted as his agent. After various trials the machine was discarded as unsatisfactory in 1873. Its distinctive postmark consisted of seven horizontal bars with a central diamond bearing a letter and number.

Azerbaijan. North-western province of Persia (Iran). Persian stamps were overprinted 1945–6 by the short-lived autonomous communist government during the Russian occupation. Arms-type stamps of Russia overprinted 'Occupation Azirbaydejan' were connected with the earlier Russian occupation of 1915–18; formerly listed in the catalogues, these overprints are now regarded as bogus. For the present Soviet republic of Azerbaijan (which was also part of Persia until 1828), see below.

Azerbaijan. U.S.S.R. One of the Soviet republics west of the Caspian Sea. Formerly part of the Trans-Caucasian Federation (q.v.) and temporarily independent 1917–23, during which time it issued its own stamps. Not to be confused with Azerbaijan, Iran (q.v. above). Area: 32,686 sq. m.; pop. (1956): 3,400,000; capital: Baku; Russian currency.

Azores. See 'Açores'.

Azuay. Province of Ecuador, for which a control o/p was in use on the 1901 set of Ecuador as a check on the misuse of suspected stolen stocks of stamps.

Cyrillic

АВИО-ПОЧТОВАЯ: Avio-pochtovayah = Air postage, or airmail.
АВИОПОЧТА C.C.C.P.: Airpost U.S.S.R. = Russian airmail stamp.
АСОБНЫ АТРАД: Asobnoui Atrad   = White Russian stamps of
                (see below)   1920 were so inscribed.

Greek: The Alpha (A).

ΑΝΑΤΟΛΙΚΗ ΡΩΜΥΛΙΑ: Anatolia Roumelia = Eastern Roumelia.
                                 = Asia Minor.

ΑΥΤΟΝΟΜΟΣ Autonomous

B.C.O.F.   'B' (BELGIUM)   'BABY'   BACKSTAMP

B

'B'. Overprinted on stamps of the Straits Settlements, 'B' indicates use at the British post office in Bangkok, capital of Siam. On stamps of Belgium 'B' within an oval indicates use on railway parcels. On the SCADTA semi-official airmails of Colombia, an overprinted 'B' indicates that the stamp is a consular overprint sold in Belgium.

'B Blank'. Plate No. 77 of G.B.'s 1d. reds of 1858–64 originally had an impression (first stamp, second row) with a blank check letter square at the bottom right, where the letter 'B' should have been punched in. This made the 'variety' known as 'B blank'. It was corrected on 12 January 1858, and the plate renumbered 77b—this being the elusive plate from which so few stamps were ever printed and put into circulation.

B.A.   British Administration. On 1950 issues for Eritrea and Somaliland.

B.C.   British Columbia, or British Colonies (or Commonwealth).

B.C.A.   British Central Africa.

B.C.M.   British Consular Mail (q.v.).

B.C.O.F.   British Commonwealth Occupation Force. Stamps of Australia were o/p 'B.C.O.F.' for use by Australian troops stationed in Japan. The ½d., 1d., and 3d. values were first issued 11 October 1946. They were withdrawn two days later, but were reissued with the 6d., 1s., 2s., and 5s. values on 8 May 1947. Withdrawn 12 February 1949, and remainders officially burnt.

B.E.A.   British East Africa. See 'Kenya, Uganda, and Tanganyika'.

B.E.F.   British Expeditionary Force.

B.G.   Bollo Gazzette. (Ital.).   Newspaper stamp.

B.I.   British India.

B.I.E.   O/p on a stamp of Switzerland (S.G. 465) indicates use by the Bureau International d'Éducation, 1946.

B.I.T.   (Fr.). Bureau International du Travail—International Labour Office, Geneva, Switzerland. O/p on 1930 stamps of Belgium, and 1938 issues of Switzerland.

B.L.P. (Ital.). Buste Lettere Postali.

B.M.A. Overprint denoting British Military Administration, found on British stamps issued for use in Eritrea, Somalia, and Tripolitania in 1948–9; also on stamps of Burma, North Borneo, Sarawak, and Straits Settlements (the latter for use throughout Malaya) immediately following the Second World War.

B.N.A. British North America. (Canada, Newfoundland, etc.).

B.N.F. Castellorizo. (Base navale Française, Castelrosso). O/p on stamps of French Levant in 1920 for the naval occupation of Castelrosso in the Aegean. See also: 'O.N.F.' and 'O.F.'.

B.P.A. British Philatelic Association (q.v.).

B.R.A. British Railway Administration. O/p on stamps of China, and surcharged for railway express postal charges during the 1901 Boxer campaign.

B.T. surmounted by a crown. Punch-perforated on stamps of G.B. signifies 'Board of Trade'. Now discontinued.

B.W. & Co. Bradbury, Wilkinson & Co., British stamp printers.

B.W.A. British West Africa.

B.W.I. British West Indies.

'Baby'. The name collectors give to the early issues (1886–1900) of King Alfonso XIII of Spain and her colonies, and which names a keytype.

Backprint. Any printing on the back of a stamp. A preferable term to underprint, often used in this connection but better reserved for printing on the front of the stamp but beneath the main design.

Backstamp. A postmark applied to the back of any item of mail. The backstamping of all inward mail received by a post office is a practice which was formerly widely followed in many countries, but is now seen only rarely. In Britain a backstamp of a plain diamond, seen from time to time, is used for statistical purposes, being applied by a machine which counts the mail.

Baden. Former grand duchy of Germany, which had its own stamps from 1851 until absorbed into the German Empire in 1871. In 1947, as part of the French Occupation Zone, Baden again received its own separate issues until incorporated in the West German Federal Republic in 1949. Area: 58,193 sq. m.; capital: Karlsruhe; currency: 1851–71, 60 kreuzer = 1 gulden; afterwards, as Germany.

Baghdad. City of Iraq. Turkish pictorial stamps were o/p 1917 (during World War I) 'Baghdad in British Occupation'. They have been extensively forged. See also: 'Persian Gulf Agencies'.

Bahamas. Island group of the British West Indies. The first issue of 1859 consisted of a 1d. value for 'Interinsular Postage', inter-island mail within the group. The first regular issue for general, overseas use followed

BADEN (RURAL POST)   BAHAWALPUR   BAHAMAS

in 1861. Prior to this, from 1858, British stamps were used at the capital of Nassau, being distinguished by the 'A 05' cancellation. The group consists of about 700 islands and islets, extending from the coast of Florida to Haiti, but only twenty-two of these are inhabited. Land area: 4,404 sq. m.; currency: sterling; pop. (est. 1962): 112,556.

Bahawalpur. Former Indian state, now part of West Pakistan. Official stamps were first issued in 1945, but Indian stamps continued to be used for ordinary postage purposes until 1948, when Bahawalpur produced its own first issue. The stamps of Pakistan have been used since 1950. Area: 32,443 sq. m.; pop. (1961): 3,205,000.

Bahrain (Bahrein). Independent sheikhdom in the Persian Gulf, under British protection since 1861. For many years the postal service was administered by India, and Indian stamps, distinguishable only by the postmarks, were in use from 1884 to 1933. In that year Indian stamps overprinted for use in Bahrain were first provided. In 1948 the Bahrain postal agency was taken over by Great Britain, and from then until 1960 British stamps were provided overprinted and surcharged for use in Bahrain.

In 1953 Bahrain's first distinctive stamps appeared—a set of three values valid for internal postage only. In 1966 the British postal agency was ended and the Bahrain Government set up its own postal administration and issued its own stamps. Area: 213 sq. m.; capital: Manama; currency: As India; pop. (1959): 143,213.

Baja California. District of Mexico which had its own revolutionary and civil war provisionals in 1914–15.

Bajar Porto. Postage due, Indonesian Republic.

Baker's City Express Post. A local of Cincinnati, U.S.A., for use in 1849.

Bakker Express. Local stamps issued by mail-contractor F. M. Bakker in 1887 for franking letters carried to Nylstroom, Pretoria, and Marabstad and covering services to outlying farms in the Transvaal. He also issued a halfpenny postage due.

Baku. See 'Azerbaijan, U.S.S.R.'.

'Balay'. French colonial keytype 1906–12. So called because it bore the portrait of Dr. N. Eugene Balay.

Balbo's mass Transatlantic formation air flight on 20 May 1933 was commemorated by a special Italian issue of that year.

Balek. Or Balex, o/p on Russian stamps by German occupation troops in Great Alexandrovka (Bolshoi ALEXandrovka) 1941–2.

Ballon Monté. Fr. 'Piloted Balloon'. The term is used particularly for letters dispatched by balloon during the Siege of Paris in 1870. See under 'Airmail'.

Balloon Post. See 'Ballon Monté' above. In 1877 Professor Archer King made a balloon trip in his 'Buffalo' gasbag from Nashville, Tennessee, to Galatin, about 26 miles, and carried mail franked with semi-official 'Balloon Postage' stamp valued at five cents, and printed in blue. The first recorded G.B. post by balloon was the *Daily Graphic* attempt 14–25 October 1907. The balloon left the Crystal Palace, London, and was vacated over Sweden. The mail was recovered near Tosse, from where it was posted. See also under 'Airmail'.

Baltimore (U.S.A.). American city which had its own postmaster's stamps and prepaid envelopes in 1945–6, and local carriers' stamps issued 1850–7.

Bamra. Indian Native State which issued its own stamps (for internal use only) from 1888 to 1894. Since then Indian stamps have been used. Area: 1,988 sq. m.; pop. c. 280,000.

Bánát-Bácska. Formerly a district of Hungary, its capital was Temesvar (q.v.), and was a frontier district ruled by a Bán. It was divided between Roumania and Yugoslavia in 1919. Stamps of Hungary were o/p during the Roumanian occupation. Area was 11,260 sq. m.

Bandelette. Alternative name for dominical tablet on stamps of Belgium. See 'Dominical'.

Bangkok. Siamese (Thailand) city and seaport. Stamps of the Straits Settlements were o/p 'B' for use in the Bangkok British post office 1882–5.

Bank Mixture. Stamps, usually on paper, gathered from incoming mail of banking houses, whose international contacts and insured registered post may be presumed to have exceptional philatelic interest.

Bank & Insurance City Post. Inscribed on the 'locals' issued in New York, U.S.A., by Hussey's Post (q.v.).

'Banknote' Issues of U.S.A. 1870–87: Stamps printed by the National, Continental, and American Banknote Companies.

Banknotes Used as Stamps. In 1919–21 Latvia used paper, prepared for use as Bermondt (German) and Bolshevik (Russian) five-rouble notes, on which to print certain of their stamps.

Bantams. The miniature, war-economy and war-effort stamps of the Union of South Africa were so nicknamed on account of their size.

BANTAMS   BASUTOLAND   BARBADOS

Baranya. Hungary. Stamps of Hungary were o/p by occupying Serbian troops from 1919 until they withdrew in August 1921.

Barbados, also Barbadoes. The most easterly of the Windward Islands in the British West Indies. Stamps first issued, 1852. Area: 166 sq. m.; capital: Bridgetown; currency: sterling to 1950, thereafter B.W.I. decimal; pop. (est. 1962): 241,706.

Barbuda. Northernmost of the Leeward Islands, British West Indies, and a dependency of Antigua. In 1922 Barbuda had its own series of stamps, overprinted on those of Leeward Islands, but at other times the stamps of Antigua (and of Leeward Islands up to 1956) have been used there. Area (with Redonda): 63 sq. m.; capital: Codrington.

Barcelona. Spain. Had revolutionary issues in 1931, e.g. regular stamps o/p 'REPUBLICA'. See also: 'Ayuntamiento de Barcelona'.

Barnard's Cariboo Express. A carrier service of British Columbia which had affiliations with the Wells Fargo Co., and which issued adhesive local stamps *circa* 1850.

Barnard's City Letter Express. A Boston, U.S.A., local of 1845–7, established by Morris H. Barnard.

Barre, Jean Jacques. Born 1793. Engraver to the Paris Mint 1849–60.

Barre, Désiré Albert: 1818–78. Son of the above, whom he succeeded at the Paris Mint. Engraved dies for French 1863–70 stamp issues; first 'Hermes' design for Greece, and first issues for Persia.

Barred. Stamps overprinted with black bars or rules are usually remainders sold to the stamp trade at cut prices. As a rule they are therefore worth much less than either mint or postally used copies, though in certain cases, notably North Borneo, they are separately priced by the catalogues. Barred stamps of this kind should not be confused with precancels, particularly those of the U.S.A., in which the town of origin is printed between black bars. An entirely different case of barred stamps occurred in the 1953 issue of Egypt, where black bars were adopted to disfigure the portrait of ex-king Farouk. Bars have also been used frequently in conjunction with overprints in cases where it has been desired to change the face value or other details of a stamp.

Barr's Penny Dispatch. A local letter service established in Lancaster, Penn., U.S.A., by Elias Barr, for which two stamps were issued in 1855.

Barwani. Former feudatory native state of central British India, which first issued its own internal stamps in 1921. Area: 1,189 sq. m.; pop. (1952): 176,666; capital of same name; Indian currency. Independent issues ceased 1 July 1948. Now uses stamps of the Republic of India.

Base Atlantica. See 'Italia Repubblicana Fascista'.

Basle, Bâle or Basel. Northern Swiss city and canton with its own stamp issues from 1 July 1845 to 5 April 1850, when Swiss Federal issues replaced them.

Basra. Chief port of Iraq. See 'Persian Gulf Agencies'.

Basutoland. British protectorate in South Africa, entirely surrounded by the South African Republic. The first stamps were issued in December 1933. Prior to this the postal service in this remote and mountainous territory was practically non-existent except in the case of Maseru, the capital, whose postal needs were supplied first by Cape of Good Hope and subsequently by South Africa. Area: 11,716 sq. m.; currency: sterling to 1961, thereafter as South Africa. Pop. (est. 1960): 888,000.

Bâton Rouge. Louisiana, U.S.A. One of the Confederate 'Postmasters' ' issues emanated from here in 1861.

Bâtonné. Thin 'bank' letter paper, designed for lightweight foreign correspondence, and watermarked with parallel lines to facilitate neatness in writing. Has often been used for stamp printing. Basically, it may be either laid or wove, its chief characteristic being the guide lines, which are normally horizontal, but may be found vertical. See 'Laid', 'Wove', 'Paper', etc.

Batum. A town and port of the Soviet Republic of South Georgia on the S.E. coast of the Black Sea. It issued its own stamps in 1919, and also o/p arms types of Russia. British troops in occupation from 1 December 1918 to 7 July 1920 also o/p current Russian issues 'British Occupation', with and without surcharges, when control then passed to Georgia.

Bavaria. (Ger. Bayern). Until 1918 a kingdom in South Germany (since 1871 as part of the German Empire) and a stamp-issuing authority from 1 November 1849 to 1920, when it transferred its postal rights to the Reichpost for the sum of 620 million marks, since when it has used stamps of Germany. Area: 30,562 sq. m.; pop. (1963): 9,731,200; capital: Munich (München); currency: 1851, 60 kreuzer = 1 gulden; 1876, 100 pfennig = 1 mark. See: 'Retourbrief'.

Bayern. Bavaria (q.v. above).

Bayonne City Dispatch. A local mail service of Bayonne City, New Jersey, U.S.A., which issued a stamp in 1883.

'Bears'. See 'St. Louis'.

Beaufort House Essays. Elaborate engine-turned designs submitted by Charles Whiting in the G.B. Treasury Competition for designs for the

BAVARIA   BECHUANALAND PROTECTORATE   'BEARS'

first stamp in 1840. Copies of the essays in various colours are in many collections.

Beaumont. Texas. One of the Confederate 'Postmasters' ' of 1861.

'Beaver'. Name applied to the early stamps of Canada, the 3d. value first issued in 1851 and the 5¢. value of 1859 from the animal portrayed on them. The design, by Sir Sandford Fleming, was the first to feature an animal. It was reproduced on the 15¢. value of the Stamp Centenary set in 1951.

Bechuanaland. Name of two territories in Southern Africa, which should not be confused. One was British Bechuanaland, a colony which was annexed to Cape of Good Hope in 1895 and now forms part of the Republic of South Africa. The other is the Bechuanaland Protectorate, which adjoins South Africa on the north. British Bechuanaland (area: 51,524 sq. m.; principal town: Vryburg (q.v.)) issued its own stamps from 1885 to 1897, some of which were overprinted on the issues of Cape of Good Hope and Great Britain.

The first stamps for Bechuanaland Protectorate appeared in 1888. Most of the Protectorate issues consisted of overprints on British stamps until 1932, when the first pictorials were issued in the well-known 'Baobab tree and cattle drinking' design, which with changes of royal portrait lasted until 1961. Area of the Protectorate: approx. 222,000 sq. m.; capital: Serowe; currency: sterling to 1961, thereafter as South Africa; pop. (1956): 320,000.

Beirut. See 'Beyrouth'.

Belgian Congo. See under 'Congo'.

Belgian Occupation of German East Africa. Stamps of the Belgian Congo were overprinted 'Est Africain Allemand Occupation Belge' in 1916 for use in those parts of German East Africa occupied by Belgian forces during the First World War. The area became a Belgian mandate in 1924 and was renamed Ruanda-Urundi (q.v.).

Belgian Occupation of Part of Germany was responsible for the Eupen and Malmedy stamps (q.v.), 1919–20, and for the 'Allemagne/Duitschland'

36

BELGIAN CONGO

BELGIAN
OCCUPATION
OF PART OF
GERMANY

BELGIUM:
GERMAN
OCCUPATION OF

o/ps for use by troops occupying part of the left bank of the Rhine 1919–21. These latter stamps are usually postmarked 'Poste Militaire'.

Belgisch Congo. Belgian Congo (q.v.).

Belgium. Independent kingdom of Europe, a constitutional monarchy, the present monarch being King Baudouin. First stamps appeared on 1 July 1849. It was overrun in both world wars. German occupation stamps appeared 1914–18. Area: 11,775 sq. m.; pop. (1962): 9,200,000; capital: Brussels (Bruxelles); currency: 100 centimes = 1 franc Belge. See also: 'Roll Cancel'.

Belgium, German Occupation of. See 'German occupation'.

Belize Relief Fund Stamps. Stamps of British Honduras were o/p and surcharged in 1932.

Benaders. (Persian) Ports. O/p on 1922 stamps of Persia for use in the ports of the Persian Gulf. On the increase of postal rates in that year, the old rates were retained in these ports to compete with the Indian Postal Agencies (q.v.) which had not altered their charges.

Benadir. See 'Italian Somaliland'.

Benghazi, also **Bengasi.** Capital of Cyrenaica, North Africa, now part of Libya. Stamps of Italy overprinted BENGASI were in use at the Italian post office there from 1901 to 1911. These were replaced by Libyan issues in 1912 after the Italian conquest.

Benin. Territory of French West Africa. Stamps first issued, 1892. Incorporated in Dahomey (q.v.) from 1899.

Benjamin & Sarpy. Alfred Benjamin and Julian Sarpy were notorious dealers in forged and faked stamps, active in the late 1880s. With George Kirke Jeffryes, the engraver who produced the forgeries, they formed the 'London Gang'. Their fraudulent career ended in 1892 when Benjamin and Sarpy were each sentenced to six months' hard labour and Jeffryes to four months. At one time this audacious pair had a trade card which read: 'Dealers in all kinds of facsimiles, faked surcharges, and fiscal postals—1 Cullum Street, London, E.C.—Fakes of all descriptions supplied on the shortest notice.'

Bentley's Dispatch. A local stamp was issued in 1856 by H. W. Bentley, who operated a local mail service (later acquired by Swarf's (q.v.)), in New York City, U.S.A.

Benzine. Colourless volatile liquid used to clarify and render legible the watermarks on stamps. It is conveniently dispensed by means of a dropping bottle, and used in conjunction with a watermark detector tray or tile. Is highly inflammable, should not be used near a naked flame, and must **not** be used on modern stamps printed by photogravure or rotogravure—it is a solvent of the inks used for these processes. Modern G.B. are examples, and Scott gives a short list of stamps susceptible. See also 'Carbon tetrachloride', 'Watermark detector', etc.

Berford & Co.'s Express. Local stamps were issued in 1851 for a service organised by Berford and Lombard, conveying mail from New York to Panama by steamer and thence to west-coast ports of North and South America.

Bergedorf. A town belonging to the free cities of Lübeck and Hamburg, and since 1867 has been part of the latter. From 1861 to 1867 it issued its own stamps. Pop.: about 15,000.

Berlin. Pre-war capital city of Germany, divided into four occupation zones in 1945. West Berlin (comprising the American, British and French zones) has had its own stamps since 1948. Stamps inscribed 'Stadt Berlin' were issued in the Russian zone in 1945–6; they were for use throughout Brandenburg as well as in East Berlin. The latter is now capital of East Germany (German Democratic Republic). See also under 'West Berlin.'

Berlin City Post. See 'Stadt Berlin'.

Bermuda. Also known as the Somers Islands, the Bermudas are a British colony in the western part of the North Atlantic. Though a long way from the West Indies, the stamps of Bermuda are frequently collected as part of the B.W.I. group. In 1848 the postmaster, W. B. Perot, produced his own unauthorised stamps, adding the value and his own signature to an impression of the postmark of Hamilton. These remained in use until 1854, and have become great rarities. The first regular stamps appeared in 1865. Area: 19 sq. m.; capital: Hamilton; currency: sterling; pop (est. 1962): 45,900.

Besa. (1) Albanian overprint, indicating 'True' or 'Genuine', applied to 1921 issues to defeat forgers who had circulated large quantities of spurious stamps. (2) Unit of currency in Italian Somaliland.

Beyrouth, or Beyrout or Beirût. Chief seaport of Syria (Levant). Obliterator 'G 06', and a panel-capped circular pmk. were in use on stamps of G.B. 1873–1914. The French issued an o/p provisional in 1905; and Russian o/p issues were in use in 1909. Now part of Lebanon. Pop. (est. 1957): 400,000.

Bhopal or Bhopaul. Former feudatory native state of British Central India, it had its own internal stamp issues from 1876 to 1908, and its own Official Stamps from 1908 to 1950. Area: 6,921 sq. m.; pop. (1951):

BERMUDA   BILINGUAL PAIRS   BHOPAL

838,107; Indian currency. From 1844 to 1926 the throne of the Begum descended in the female line.

Bhor. Former feudatory native state in the Bombay Presidency, British India. Issued its own anchal stamps from 1879 to 1902. Area: 928 sq. m.; pop. (1941): 155,961; Indian currency.

Bhutan. Independent princely state in the Himalayas, lying between Tibet and India, under the protection of the Indian Republic. The first stamps were a set of four fiscals authorised for postal use late in 1954. The first regular definitives appeared in 1962. Until 1963 Bhutan stamps were valid only on internal mail; they are now accepted internationally. Area: about 16,000 sq. m.; capital: Thimphu; currency: 100 chetrum = 1 ngultrum or rupee; pop. about 700,000.

Bicentennial. 200th anniversary.

Bi-coloured Stamps. Stamps printed in two colours. It is usual for the frame to be in one colour and the central motif—either portrait or landscape or other design—to be in the other. The central design is usually vignetted (q.v.).

Bicycle Mail. Several local posts are on record which made use of bicycles. The first of these appear to have been established in 1894—one in Australia and the other in America. The former was the Coolgardie Cycle Express, which issued local stamps on a service between the goldfields and Kalgoorlie. The latter was formed by Arthur C. Banta, agent for a cycle manufacturer, who issued local stamps in diamond format for a bicycle post which he organised in San Francisco during the rail strike. See also under 'Coralit'.

Bigelow's Express. Local stamps were issued in Boston, U.S.A., to frank mail carried by this service 1848–51.

Bijawar. Former Indian native state which had its own internal issues from 1935 to 1939. Area: 973 sq. m.

Bilingual Pair. Two joined stamps which are identical except that the inscriptions on one stamp are in one language, and on the second in another. The outstanding examples are South Africa and South-West Africa, many of whose stamps between 1926 and 1954 were inscribed alternately in English and Afrikaans throughout the sheet. Bilingual pairs

39

should not be confused with bilingual stamps, in which inscriptions in two languages appear on the same stamp—for example Belgium (French and Flemish), Canada (English and French), South Africa (English and Afrikaans), etc.

Billig's Philatelic Handbooks. Are advanced specialist reference works published by F. Fritz Billig, 168-39 Highland Avenue, Jamaica 3, N.Y., U.S.A., covering practically the whole field of philatelic study.

Bisect. A stamp cut into two parts (diagonally, vertically or horizontally), each part paying postage to the amount of half the face value of the complete stamp. Numerous cases are known in which this practice has been authorised to overcome a temporary shortage of certain denominations; on many occasions it has been resorted to unofficially. Generally only authorised bisects are of any value; they should be collected preferably on complete cover to prove their authenticity, or at least on piece with tied postmark.

Bishop Mark. The earliest postmark, devised by Henry Bishop, the first Restoration Postmaster-General, to indicate the day and month that a letter was received at the post office. The exact date on which it was introduced is not known; but the earliest surviving examples date from May 1661. Bishop himself wrote: 'A stamp is invented that is putt upon every letter shewing the day of the moneth that every letter comes to the office, so that no Letter Carryer may dare detayne a letter from post to post; which before was usual.'

Bishop's City Post. Organised in Cleveland, U.S.A., by the 'Penny Postman', Henry S. Bishop, 1848–51. He issued two local stamps.

Bit. Has two philatelic connotations; (a) unit of currency in the Danish West Indies, 1855–1917; and (b) a design or device reproduced in bent wire or flat metal for attachment to the dandy-roll of a paper-making machine, to produce a watermark (q.v.).

Bizonia. Combined British-American Zones of Occupied Germany, 1947–9.

'Black Flag' Republic. See 'Formosa'.

'Black Jack'. Name given to the 1862 U.S.A. 2 ¢. black bearing the portrait head of Andrew Jackson, reproduced from a miniature by J. W. Dodge.

'Black-out' Cancel. (Canada). Machine-cancel town marks with name removed as a security measure in World War II. Measure applied to localities near coast to conceal location and movements of service personnel. See 'Dumb Postmarks'.

'Black' Plates. Plates originally made for the 'Penny Black' of 1840 which were later used for the early printings of the 1d. 'Red' stamps. They were plates numbers 1b, 2, 5, 8, 9, 10, and 11. See also: 'Married pairs'.

BISECTS   'BLUENOSE'   'BLANC'

'Blanc'. The basic design for a French stamp designed by Joseph Blanc in 1900, which became a colonial keytype extensively o/p and used for the smaller outposts of the French Colonial Empire.

Bleuté. (Fr.). Tinged with blue, blueish. Applied to the early issues of G.B. and other early issues printed by Perkins Bacon. This characteristic colouring of the paper base is said to be due to the presence of prussiate of potassium, either as a constituent of the printing ink, latent in the paper, or by a chemical combination of impurities in each. It caused dyeing of the paper fibres when it was dampened previous to printing. See also 'Ivory Head', 'Perkins Paper', etc.

'Blitz' Perfs. Applied to the perforation variations of the 1940–1 printings of New Zealand and various British colonies. So named because they were produced by Waterlow when De La Rue's works were 'blitzed'.

Block. Four or more unsevered stamps, and less than a whole 'pane' (q.v.) or sheet. Thus, four stamps in one row are known as a strip, but if 2×2 forming a rectangle, they are a 'block'. An 'imprint' block is a marginal one bearing the official imprint or name of the printer on the selvedge. A control block includes the marginal control number, while an arrow block shows the arrow indicator. It is the modern philatelic fashion to collect in blocks of four or more, control blocks being usually six marginal stamps 2×3. The word is also correctly applied to the mounted zincos or copper half-tones from which 'typo' (q.v.) stamps are printed, but to obviate confusion, the French 'Cliché' is more often employed.

Block Letter. Plain squared printers' type, without ornament or serifs (q.v.), e.g. san serif. See 'Type', etc.

Blood's. See 'City Despatch Post', and 'Phila. Despatch Post'. Blood & Co. of Philadelphia, U.S.A., issued a number of local stamps from 1841 to about 1860 with various inscriptions.

Bluefields. Nicaragua. See 'Zelaya'.

'Blue Gibbons'. Colloquial term in common use for *Stanley Gibbons Catalogue*, Part III, which covers stamps of foreign countries except those of Europe and Colonies, and is published every two years.

'Bluenose'. The fishing smack pictured on the 50 ¢. blue of the 1928–9 series of Canada. This now famous schooner was built in 1901, held many

| BOHEMIA AND MORAVIA | BOOKLET STAMPS (TRIMMED PERFS.) | BOLIVAR |

racing records, and was lost off Haiti in 1946. The stamp has become a minor rarity. See 'Ships on Stamps'.

Bo. On the SCADTA semi-official airmails of Colombia, these letters indicate that the stamp is a consular overprint sold in Bolivia.

Board of Education. G.B. 'officials' (q.v.).

'Board-walk' Margins (U.S.A.). Extra wide margins.

Bogota. Colombia. Had its own local issues 1889–1903.

Bohemia and Moravia. (Böhmen and Mähren). These ancient kingdoms, the western and central portions of Czechoslovakia, were given separate status and autonomy within the German Reich 1939–45, and became a new stamp-issuing authority with a first o/p issue of current Czech stamps in 1939, speedily followed by a most attractive landscape series of definitives. The final stamp was issued in 1945. It now again uses the stamps of Czechoslovakia. Area: Bohemia 20,102 sq. m.; Moravia 8,616 sq. m.; pop.: approx. 9 million; capital: Prague (Praha); currency: 100 heller = 1 krone.

Bogus. A bogus stamp is a complete impostor, a fraudulent production made only to deceive collectors, which has never existed in genuine form. For example, stamp-like labels have been printed for non-existent countries, or countries which had no genuine stamps or postal service. In other cases bogus values have been added to genuine sets before sale to collectors. Bogus stamps (also known as phantoms or fantasies) should not be confused with fakes (which are genuine stamps 'doctored' in some way to make them appear what they are not) nor with forgeries (which are fraudulent imitations of genuine stamps). Bogus postmarks, overprints, and even perforations are also known.

Boiling a stamp in *pure* or distilled water may seem a drastic step, but is often recommended as a 'kill or cure' treatment for an old copy very badly soiled. A few seconds immersion are usually sufficient to loosen the obstinate accretions of dirt and paper, etc. See 'Cleaning stamps', etc.

Boîte Mobile. See under 'Moveable Box'.

42

Boka Kotarska, also Cattaro. Bay of Kotor, a Yugoslav province occupied by Italy and Germany during the Second World War, for which overprints in Italian and German currency were provided in 1944.

Bolivar. Department of Colombia which had its own internal issues from 1863 to 1904, the first issue being among the smallest stamps in the world. Named after Simon Bolivar, the Liberator, who played a leading part in the struggle to secure South American independence from Spain in the early nineteenth century, and whose portrait appears frequently on the stamps of many South American countries.

Bolivia. South American republic, also named after Simon Bolivar (see above). The first Bolivian stamps were produced by Justiniano Garcia, under the terms of an extremely short-lived postal contract, in 1863; very few are known used. The first regular Government issue appeared in 1866. Area: 424,000 sq. m.; chief town: La Paz; constitutional capital: Sucré; currency: 1863, 8 cuartos = 1 real; 1866, 100 centavos = 1 boliviano; pop. (1962): 3,509,000.

Bollo. (Ital.). Stamp; 'franco bollo' = prepaid postage stamp.

Bond Paper. A thin crisp paper with a hard surface, usually wove, and sometimes 'bàtonne' (q.v.). Some of the early stamps of the U.S.A. were printed on bond.

Bonny River. One of the Royal Niger Company's rubberstamp cancellers, in use on stamps of G.B. 1892.

Booklets. Luxemburg was the first country to adopt the practice of selling stamps in handy booklets in 1895, and the idea was soon taken up in many other countries. In Great Britain booklets were introduced in 1904; they were the first to be interleaved with pages of commercial advertising. Nowadays booklet collecting has become a popular philatelic sideline; some of the early booklets have become items of considerable rarity, and fetch high prices.

British stamps intended for booklets come from special printings in a make-up of opposed panes, one of which is inverted in relation to the other. In cases of faulty assembly this has occasionally resulted in tête-bêche varieties. It also means that half the stamps from booklets have inverted watermarks. The process of manufacture often results in the outer edges of booklet panes having trimmed perforations, giving certain stamps the appearance of being imperf. along one side. See also 'Advertisements on Stamps', 'Exploded', and 'Pane'.

An earlier production than any of the above was an advertising booklet with a Penny Lilac inserted through a slot in the cover, prepared in England by a private company with Post Office approval in 1891. It was intended for sale from vending machines fixed to pillarboxes, but the experiment was short-lived. This has been claimed as the world's first booklet, but it was not a true stamp booklet in the accepted meaning of the term, which implies panes of stamps bound into the booklet by stapling or stitching.

Borneo (Indo.: Kalimantan). Large island in the South China Sea, the major portion of which is now in Indonesia (former Netherlands East Indies). Sarawak, Brunei, and British North Borneo occupy the rest of the island. All of which see.

Boscawen, New Hampshire, U.S.A., had one of the 'Postmasters'' issues *circa* 1846.

Bosnia and Herzegovina. Bosnien Hercegovina. Two former Turkish provinces in the Balkans which were occupied by Austria in 1878 and annexed in 1908, and which have formed part of Yugoslavia since 1918. Bosnia and Herzegovina had their own stamps from 1879 to 1918. Prior to this period Turkish stamps were in use; afterwards, those of Yugoslavia. Area: 19,900 sq. m.; capital: Sarajevo (scene of the assassination of Archduke Ferdinand which precipitated the First World War, the Archduke being commemorated on Bosnian stamps of 1917). Currency: 1879, 100 novcica = 1 florin; 1900, 100 heller = 1 krone; pop. (1961): 3,277,948.

Boston. Massachusetts, U.S.A., was responsible for the issue of two semi-official 'Carriers' (q.v.) stamps 1849.

Boten. Term applied to the local stamps of Hamburg of a century ago— from their inscription, 'Institut Hamburger Boten'. Those of C. Hamer & Co. (first issued in 1861) have the best claim to genuine postal use. The rest of the 'Botens' are of doubtful status; there are many bogus items and forgeries. (Boten = 'Messenger'.)

Bougainville. Former German possession, and largest of the Solomon Islands (q.v.). Politically it is mandated to New Guinea under Australian supervision, and it uses Australian stamps, and not those of the archipelago. Area: 3,880 sq. m.; pop.: 49,071; administrative centre is Sohano; Australian currency.

Bourse. An arranged, and organised, meeting of dealers or of collectors at which stamps change hands on a cash or a barter basis.

Bouton. John W. Bouton of New York, U.S.A., organised the Franklin City, Manhattan Express, and the City Despatch posts in 1847–8, for which various 'locals' were issued.

Bouvet Oya. (Bouvet Island). O/p on 'Post-horn' and 'Lion' stamps of Norway. Marked the visit of Vice-Admiral E. R. G. Evans, R.N. ('Evans of the *Broke*'—later Lord Mountevans), flying his flag in H.M.S. *Milford*, to Bouvet Island, Antarctica, in February 1934. Discovered in the South Atlantic in 1739 by Pierre Bouvet, recognised as a dependency of Norway in 1930. In 1955 the S.A.S. *Transvaal* brought back mail postmarked 'Bouvet Island Expedition—Jan.–Feb. 1955'.

Boyacá. Department of Colombia, with its own stamps 1899–1904. Area: 24,934 sq. m.; pop. (est. 1950): 791,300.

Boyce's City Express Post. A U.S.A. local of 1852.

Boyd's City Express. A local post service for the handling of printed matter organised in New York, U.S.A., by John T. Boyd in 1830, for

BOY SCOUT ISSUES   BOSNIA AND HERZEGOVINA   BRASIL

which a number of local stamps were issued between 1844 and 1880. There are numerous forgeries.

Boy Scout Issues. The periodic international 'Jamboree' of the Boy Scout Association is often commemorated by a special set of the country giving hospitality. Thus Roumania 1936; Netherlands 1937; Lithuania 1938; France 1947; Australia 1948–9 (Pan-Pacific 1959); and the Centenary Moot at Sutton Coldfield in 1957, can be quoted at random. Other youth organisations have been similarly honoured, e.g. the Hitler Youth 1935 (Germany); Hlinka (Czechoslovakia) 1942; Greek Youth Organisation 1940; Hungarian Girl Guides (Pax Ting) 1939; U.S.S.R. 'Pioneers' 1929 and 1936, are a few such issues. A section of the *Catalogue General Timbres Sportifs et Scouts*, published by Guy Depolier, 25 Rue Henri-Barbusse, Levallois-Peret (Seine), France, lists them in some detail.

Br. On the SCADTA semi-official airmails of Colombia, these letters indicate that the stamp is a consular overprint sold in Brasil.

Brăc. An island near Split, Yugoslavia, for which a German panzer (tank) unit o/p 1939 Yugoslavian stamps 'Brac' or 'Brac Franco' in 1943.

Bradbury, Wilkinson & Co., Ltd. A British firm of printers who have been associated with stamp production over many years.

Bradway's Despatch. A local stamp to frank mail carried between Philadelphia and Millville, U.S.A., was issued in 1857.

Brady & Co. Stamps so inscribed were 'locals' issued in New York, U.S.A., in 1857–8. One bearing the Chicago inscription is not authenticated.

Brainard & Co. A privately owned American local post, with headquarters in New York, which issued its own local stamps in 1844.

Brasil (Brazil). The only Portuguese-speaking country in South America, Brasil was formerly a vast Portuguese colony. It was an independent empire from 1822 to 1889, when a republic was established. Brasil was the second country in the world to introduce adhesive postage stamps, the first issue of 1843 being known to collectors as the 'Bull's Eyes'. Area: 3,289,440 sq. m.; capital: Rio de Janeiro until 1960, now Brasilia. Currency: 1843, 1,000 reis = 1 milreis; 1942, 100 centavos = 1 cruzeiro; pop. (est. 1963): 77,500,000.

BRAUNSCHWEIG   BRITISH GUIANA   BREMEN

Brattleboro. Vermont, U.S.A. Postmasters' stamp issued 1846. Scott lists eleven varieties.

Braunschweig. Brunswick (q.v.).

Brazil. Brasil (q.v.).

Bremen. One of Germany's former free cities of the Hanseatic League, with its own stamp issues 1855–67, when it joined the North German Confederation, later absorbed into the German Empire. Currency: 72 grote = 60 silbergroschen = 1 thaler.

Bridgeville. Alabama, U.S.A. One of the Confederate civil war towns with its own postmaster's provisional in 1861.

Briefmarken. (Ger.). Letter stamps, e.g. postage stamps.

Briefpost. (Ger.). Letter post.

Brigg's Despatch. Various 'locals' so inscribed were in use in Philadelphia, U.S.A., in 1848.

Brilliant Mint. Term used to describe a stamp in immaculate unused condition, exactly as issued by the post office—unmarked, unfaded and undamaged. It is applied usually to the older issues where mint condition may be something less than perfect.

'Britannia' Types. Early British colonial design engraved by Perkins, Bacon & Co., and used, suitably inscribed, for Barbados, Mauritius, and Trinidad, 1851–83.

British Antarctic Territory. Comprising the British sector of Antarctica (including Graham Land), the South Shetlands, and the South Orkneys, previously forming part of the Falkland Island Dependencies (q.v.). Stamps first issued, February 1963.

British Bechuanaland. See 'Bechuanaland'.

British Caribbean Federation. See 'West Indies Federation'.

British Central Africa. Former name for Nyasaland (q.v.), by which it was known until 1908.

British Colonials. A term somewhat loosely used in philately to denote all the stamps of the British Commonwealth and Empire, including protectorates and mandated territories, and frequently also those of other countries which were under British influence in the past, such as Egypt, Iraq, Eire, etc.

British Columbia. Former British colony on the Pacific coast of North America, now part of Canada. The first stamp, a 2½d. value which appeared in 1860, was inscribed 'British Columbia and Vancouver's Island'. The two territories (the latter place then known as Vancouver Island) received their own separate stamps in 1865, but in the following year they were consolidated into one under the name of British Columbia, and the stamps of both were valid throughout the combined colony until a new issue appeared in 1868–9. Canadian stamps have been in use since 1871. Area: 366,255 sq. m.; currency: 1860, sterling; 1868, 100 cents = 1 dollar.

British Consular Mail. Stamps issued between 1884 and 1887 for a consular postal service organised for the benefit of British subjects in Madagascar. A similar system operated in 1895; see 'British Inland Mail'.

British East Africa. Former name for Kenya. The territory was administered by the British East Africa Company (whose name appears on the early stamps) until 1895, when the Imperial administration took over. Stamps of British East Africa, first issued in 1890, were replaced in 1903 by those for the combined administration of East Africa and Uganda (q.v.). Currency: as India.

British Forces in Egypt. This inscription appears on the so-called 'postal seals', issued between 1932 and 1936 for use on forces' mail to England, which enjoyed a concessionary rate of postage. Though described as seals, they are genuine postage stamps recognised and listed by the leading catalogues. They were superseded in 1936 by Egyptian stamps inscribed 'Army Post'.

British Guiana. British colony on the north-east coast of South America. The first stamps, issued in 1850, were typeset productions printed locally in a circular design. As a safeguard against forgery each stamp was initialled by the issuing postmaster or clerk. These stamps, nicknamed 'cotton reels', are now great rarities; but an even greater rarity is the famous 1 ¢. black on magenta of the 1856 issue (also typset locally) of which only one copy is known and which for many years held the record for the highest price paid for a single stamp. British stamps were in use in British Guiana between 1856 and 1858, and may be distinguished by the cancellations: A 03 for Georgetown or Demerara, A 04 for New Amsterdam or Berbice. Area: 83,000 sq. m.; capital: Georgetown; currency: 100 cents = 1 B.W.I. dollar; pop. (1962): 602,660.

British Honduras. British Crown Colony on the east coast of Central America. Stamps of G.B. in use 1858–60 (canceller 'A 06'). First definitive issue in January 1866. Guatemala laid philatelic claim to the territory in its map issues of 1939, and despite diplomatic representations no official correction was made. (See 'Map Stamps'.) Area: 8,867 sq. m.; pop.

(1960): 90,019; capital: Belize (with a specially o/p relief issue 1933); currency: decimal—100 cents = one British Honduras dollar.

British India. See 'India'.

British Inland Mail. Stamps issued at Antananarivo (Tantanarive) in Madagascar while the French fleet was blockading the port of Tamatave between January and September 1895. Mail franked by these stamps was carried by runner to Vatomandry, where it was collected by a British steamer. The post was suppressed when the French entered Antananarivo, and in the following year Madagascar became a French colony.

British Levant. British stamps overprinted Levant were issued for use at British post offices in the Middle East, particularly Turkey, Syria, Palestine, and Egypt, between 1885 and 1914. There was a special issue of Levant stamps for Salonica in 1916—and a further issue in 1921 for use during the British occupation of certain parts of the old Ottoman Empire. They were finally withdrawn in 1923. Currency: Sterling and Turkish.

British New Guinea. Former name for Papua (q.v.), by which name it was known until 1906.

British North America. Philatelic group of countries comprising Canada, all the old Canadian provinces, and Newfoundland. Geographically Bermuda may be considered part of this group, but its stamps are more often collected as part of the British West Indies group.

British North Borneo. See 'North Borneo'.

British Philatelic Association. 446 Strand, London, W.C.2. Membership open to collectors, dealers, societies, exchange clubs, auctioneers, journalists and publishers.

British Post Offices in China. Stamps of Hong Kong have been used in many of the ports and postal agencies in China. See 'Hong Kong'. In 1917 a special o/p 'China' was applied for use in Wei-Hai-Wei in Shantung province and other treaty ports. Issue ceased on 1 October 1930 when the concessions concerned were returned to China. See 'Hong Kong' for further details.

British Post Offices in Crete. Stamps were issued in 1898–1900 in the British sphere of the joint administration by France, Britain, Italy, and Russia, prior to the setting up of an autonomous government in Crete.

British Post Offices in Morocco. See 'Morocco Agencies'.

British Post Offices in Siam. See 'Bangkok'.

British Post Offices in the Turkish (Ottoman) Empire. See 'British Levant'.

British Solomon Islands. British protectorate in the Pacific. Stamps first issued, February 1907. Until September of that year they paid postage only as far as Australia, the stamps of New South Wales being necessary for onward transmission. The postal system ceased to operate during the Japanese occupation of 1942, but was re-established by July 1943. American, Australian and New Zealand field post offices operated during the

BRITISH P.O.'S
IN CHINA

BRITISH INLAND
MAIL

BRITISH
SOLOMON IS.

re-conquest. Land area: 11,500 sq. m.; capital: Tulagi until 1942; now Honiara on Guadalcanal; currency: Australian (£1 = 16s. sterling); pop. (est. 1965): 130,000.

British Somaliland. See 'Somaliland Protectorate'.

British South Africa Company. Chartered company which formerly administered the territory of Rhodesia. The name appears on all the stamps of Rhodesia from the first issue of 1890 until 1924, when control passed to the Crown and the territory was divided into Northern and Southern Rhodesia.

British West Africa. Philatelic group comprising Gambia, Gold Coast and Nigeria; also Southern and Northern Nigeria, Lagos, Niger Coast and Southern Cameroons; and the occupation issues for Cameroons and Togo.

British West Indies. Archipelago between the continents of North and South Americas partially in the Gulf of Mexico, and comprising a number of stamp-issuing communities, the following of which have their place in our modern albums and stamp catalogues: Antigua, Bahamas, Barbados, Barbuda, Bermuda (not actually and geographically in B.W.I., but conveniently bracketed thus by philatelists), Cayman Islands, Dominica, Grenada, Jamaica, Leeward Islands, Montserrat, Nevis, St. Christopher, St. Kitts-Nevis, St. Lucia, St. Vincent, Tobago, Trinidad (Trinidad and Tobago), Turks Islands, Turks and Caicos Islands, and the Virgin Islands. See 'West Indies Federation'. British or British West Indian currency: 100 cents = one B.W.I. dollar = 4s. 2d. British currency. The West Indies also includes Cuba, Curaçao, former Danish West Indies (now U.S.A. territory), Dominican Republic, Guadeloupe (Fr.), Republic of Haïti, Martinique (Fr.), Puerto Rico (U.S.A.).

Broadway Post Office. A New York, U.S.A., 'local' issued by J. C. Harriot in 1848.

Bronson & Forbes City Express Post. A Chicago, U.S.A., 'local' of 1855-8.

Brooklyn City Express Post. Several local stamps so inscribed were issued in Brooklyn, U.S.A., from 1951 to 1864.

49

Browne (also **Brown**) **& Co.'s City Post.** Local stamps were issued in Cincinnati, U.S.A., by J. W. S. Brown, 1852-5.

Browne's Easton Despatch Post. Typeset 'locals' were issued by William J. Browne to frank locally carried mail in 1857.

Brown's City Post. A local New York, U.S.A., post established by William P. Brown, a Nassau Street stamp dealer, in 1876.

Brunei. Sultanate of North Borneo under British protection. The first stamps of 1895 were for long thought to be bogus, but are now recognised as genuine locals which prepaid postage on mails carried to and from Labuan in the Sultan's yacht. The first regular issue consisted of overprints on Labuan stamps and appeared in 1906; the first definitives followed in 1907. During the Japanese occupation of 1942-5 Brunei stamps were overprinted in Chinese characters 'Imperial Japanese Government'. Brunei was reoccupied by British forces in 1945, and stamps of North Borneo and Sarawak overprinted B.M.A. (British Military Administration) were used until Brunei stamps reappeared in 1947. Area: 2,226 sq. m; currency: 100 cents = 1 Malayan dollar; pop. (1962): 91,816.

Brunswick (Braunschweig). German duchy which issued its own stamps from 1852 until incorporated in the North German Federation in 1868. Area: 1,417 sq. m.; currency: 30 silbergroschen = 24 gutegroschen 1 thaler.

Brunswick Star. Edinburgh postmark in use 1863-73 and much sought after by collectors. It is a star of lines radiating from the number '131'. (See p. 53).

'Buccleuch' Find. Consisted of mint blocks of 48 twopenny blues of 1840 from Plate 2, and 55 penny reds of 1841, Plate 16. Found in an old writing set, the property of the Duke of Buccleuch, in 1946. See also 'Mayfair Find'.

Buchanan. See 'Harper' and 'Liberia'.

Buenos Aires, also Buenos Ayres. Province and capital city of Argentina which issued its own stamps from 1858 to 1864. Buenos Aires seceded from the Argentine Confederation in 1853 and was a separate republic until 1859. A British post office operated in the city from 1860 to 1873, using British stamps with a 'B 32' cancellation.

Buiten Bezit. (Ned.) = **Buitenbezittingen.** O/p on stamps of Netherlands Indies of 1908 means 'Outer possessions'. These issues were for use in islands other than Java and Madura in what was then known as the Dutch East Indies.

Bulgaria. Former Turkish province in the Balkans, which after a long struggle for independence secured autonomy, as a principality under nominal Turkish suzerainty, in 1878. Complete independence was declared in 1908, and in the following year Prince Ferdinand assumed the title of Tsar. In 1946 the monarchy was replaced by a republic. Stamps first issued, 1879. Area: 42,796 sq. m.; capital: Sofia; currency: 1879, 100 centimes = 1 franc; 1881, 100 stotinki = 1 leva; pop. (1963): 8,100,000.

BULGARIA   BRUNEI   BURÉLAGE
                                                 (STAMP WITH)

Bulgarian Occupation of Romania. As an ally of Austria and Germany, in 1916 Bulgaria o/p her stamps for use in the occupation of Romania.

'Bulls'. See 'Moldavia'.

'Bull's Eyes'. Nickname given to the first issue of Brasil, 1843. A 'socked-on-the-nose' cancellation (q.v.) is also often known as a bull's eye.

Bundesrepublik Deutschland. German Federal Republic (West Germany), (q.v.).

Bundi. Former Indian native state which had its own internal issues from 1894 to 1948. From 1948 to 1950 it formed part of Rajasthan, Bundi stamps continuing to be used with a special overprint. Since 1950 Bundi has used Indian stamps. Area: 2,200 sq. m.; est. pop.: 250,000.

Bureau International d'Education, or Bureau International du Travail, o/p on stamps of Switzerland indicate use by the International Boards of Education, and of Labour, respectively.

Bureau Prints. (U.S.A.). Stamps printed by the Bureau of Engraving & Printing, Washington, or precancellations applied there.

Burélage, Burelé. A fine pattern or network of lines or dots printed either on the face of the stamp but beneath the main design, or on the back of the stamp, either to discourage forgery or to prevent tampering with the design or postmark. The outstanding example of burélage on the face of the stamp is the early issues of Denmark, 1851–64. A more modern example is the 1932 Air Stamps of Venezuela, printed on 'Winchester' security paper (q.v.).

Burin. Steel engraver's stylus.

Burma. Formerly part of the British Indian Empire, it had a separate status in 1937 within the British Commonwealth of Nations, and stamps of British India were o/p 'Burma'. In 1938 first definitives appeared. During the Japanese invasion 1943–5 there were various o/p and occupation issues, followed by the 'B.M.A.' o/p issues. In 1946 it declared its intention of assuming complete independence, and in October 1947 an interim government o/p appeared on the current stamps. On 5 January

BURMA   BY-POST STAMPS   BUSSAHIR

1948 it became an independent republic. Area: 261,789 sq. m.; pop. (est. 1963): 23,735,000; capital: Rangoon; currency: Formerly Indian; since July 1952: 100 pyas (or cents) = 1 kyat, which equals former rupee.

'Buros'. (U.S.A.). Bureaus. See 'Bureau Prints', above.

Burr. The uneven raised edge of surplus metal resulting from the passage of the engraver's burin (q.v. above), or letter punch, which, if not removed, prints as a flaw.

Burundi. Independent kingdom of central Africa, established in 1962 when the first stamps were issued. Formerly part of the Belgian mandated territory of Ruanda-Urundi (q.v.). Area: 10,747 sq. m.; capital: Usumbura; currency: 100 centimes = 1 franc.; pop. (est. 1964): 2,750,000.

Burutu. A Royal Niger Company's station with its own rubber-stamp canceller for use on stamps of G.B. 1897–9.

Bury's City Post. A New York 'local' stamp of 1857.

Bush's Brooklyn City Express. A hand-stamped U.S.A. 'local' of 1848.

Bushire. (Bshehr). Iranian (Persian) seaport occupied by British troops 8 August 1915. Stamps of the country were o/p 'Bushire Under British Occupation', and were in use from 15 August to 16 October 1915. Pop. (1940): 27,317. See also: 'Persian Gulf Agencies'.

Bussahir. (Bashahr). Former feudatory native state in the Punjab, British India, with its own internal issues from 20 June 1898 to 1901, since when Indian stamps have been used. There have been numerous reprints, and forged o/p remainders exist. Collectors are especially warned against forged cancelled copies bearing Rampur pmks. and dated 19 May 1900. Area: 3,651 sq. m.; pop. (1951): 116,305; capital: Rampur; Indian currency.

'Butterfly' Postmarks. Name given to the curious cancellations used on the first issues of the state of Victoria, consisting of a double concaved, lined device reminiscent of the insect's wings, with a post office number forming the 'head' and the letter 'V' as a 'tail'. Eagerly sought varieties.

Buu-Chinh = North Viet-Nam. See 'Viet-Nam'.

By-Posts. In modern parlance, these were the 'feeder services' to the six great Post Roads in Britain in the latter half of the seventeenth and the eighteenth centuries, the mails being carried on horseback or on foot between a convenient place on the main post road and the towns in the vicinity.

By-Post Stamps. Local issues of Scandinavia.

Byrd. The Byrd Antarctic Exploration II stamp of the U.S.A. issued in 1933 commemorates his unique flights over and around the South Polar regions. In imperf. edition it was issued at the New York National Philatelic Exhibition, in sheets of six ungummed—a true 'souvenir' sheet (q.v.). It was also re-issued in 1934, perforated and without gum. See 'Antarctic Exploration Stamps'.

Cyrillic: Б *or* б

БУЛГАРИЯ	= Bulgaria.
БАКУ	= Baku.
БАТУМ	= Batum or Batoum.

В in Cyrillic is the equivalent of the English 'V', thus:

ВЕНДЕНСКАЯ = Vendenskaya = Wenden (q.v.).
ВОСТОЧНАЯ
КОРРЕСПОНДЕНЦIЯ = Vostochnayah correspondentsia—literally 'East Mail'. On stamps of Russian Levant.

B. The Beta, in Greek, used as in English.

BRUNSWICK STAR

C

'C'. In catalogues the capital letter is frequently used as an abbreviation indicating chalky paper; in tables of relative value it stands for 'Common'. The small letter is universally used as an abbreviation for cents, centimos, etc., in decimal currency systems. The capital overprinted on the 1922 stamps of Paraguay stands for 'Campaña'—country or rural; on the SCA-DTA semi-official airmails of Columbia it indicates that the stamp is a consular overprint sold in Cuba. As a cancellation it was used at Constantinople (Istanbul), and with the addition of various figures on British stamps used abroad.

CA. Initials appearing in the watermark of innumerable British Colonial stamps, in conjunction with a crown or Royal Cipher. It was first introduced in 1882 as a single watermark, commencing to appear in multiple form in 1904. At various times the initials have appeared in block capital or script form. The letters stand for Crown Agents—the Crown Agents for Oversea Governments and Administrations, known until 1954 as the Crown Agents for the Colonies. On the SCADTA semi-official airmails of Colombia, the same letters indicate that the stamp is a consular overprint sold in' Canada.

CC. Crown Colonies. Used in conjunction with, or over a crown, was the watermark that preceded the 'CA' device (see above), and was in use from about 1863 to 1882. Also the initials of the Collectors' Club, a thriving philatelic community in the U.S.A., with Headquarters at 22 East 35th Street, New York 16, N.Y.

C.C.C.P. U.S.S.R. See 'Russia'.

C.Ch. (Fr.). Cochin Chine. French Cochin China.

c.d.s. Circular date stamp (postmark).

C.E.F. Cameroons Expeditionary Force; or China Expeditionary Force, the former o/p on the 1915 German colonial 'Yacht' (q.v.) keytypes; and the latter on stamps of India for various Chinese campaigns in three reigns: 1900, 1904, 1909, and 1913–21.

C.F.A. and C.F.P. See 'Franc C.F.A. and C.F.P.' 'C.F.A.' o/p on French issues for Reunion in March, 1952, revalues them to C.F.A. currency.

C.G.H.S. Commission de Gouvernment Haute Silésie. See 'Upper Silesia'.

C.G.R. Cape Government Railways. O/p on stamps used on mail carried by train from Caledon, Cape Province, 1911–12.

CH. Overprinted on the SCADTA semi-official airmails of Colombia, the letters indicate that the stamp is a consular overprint sold in Chile.

C.I. Channel Islands.

C.I.H.S. Commission Interalliée Haute-Silésie. O/p or hand-stamped on stamps of Germany for Upper Silesia (q.v.).

C.M.T. (Romanian) = Comandamentul Militar Teritorial. O/p (with surcharges) on general issues of Austria for the occupation of part of Romania and of Galicia in 1919.

C.N.C. Chinese National Currency (1948).

C of A. Commonwealth of Australia. Multiple watermark (with crown) introduced 1931.

C.O.R.O.S. Collectors of Religion on Stamps (U.S.A.). See also 'Guild of St. Gabriel'.

C.R. Cacabau (or Cakobau) Rex. Native king of Fiji whose monogram, complete with regal crown, appeared on the 1871–4 issues. (Described by the late E. L. Pemberton as 'The gentlemanly cannibal'.)

C.R. Overprinted on the SCADTA semi-official airmails of Colombia, the letters indicate that the stamp is a Consular overprint sold in Costa Rica.

Cs. (Magyar: Csomag). Parcel. O/p on 1946 inflation stamps of Hungary indicating validity and usage.

C.S.A.R. Central South African Railways. See 'Transvaal'.

c.t.o. Cancelled to order.

C/V. Catalogue value.

c.w.o. Cash with order.

C.X.C. (Cyr.). Serbia, Croatia, Slovenia. Yugoslavia (q.v.).

Cabo. (Span.). Cape. Cabo Gracias à Dios = Thanks to God Cape. O/p on stamps of Nicaragua 1904–9. See 'Zelaya'.

Cabo Juby. or Jubi. See 'Cape Juby'.

Cabo Verde. See 'Cape Verde'.

Cachet. (Fr.) Literally, a stamp or seal. In philately, an addition to the cover in the form of a printed, embossed, impressed, or hand-struck inscription or device to authenticate, date, or give publicity to an event or exceptional philatelic circumstance connected with the the mailing of that particular cover or card. In particular, a cachet is frequently employed for First Day covers (q.v.), philatelic exhibitions, first or special airmail flights, commemorations, etc.

Caisse d'Amortissement. (Fr.). Sinking Fund (q.v.).

Calf of Man. Small island off the southern tip of the Isle of Man, for which stamp-like publicity labels were produced in 1962. They are of no

CABO VERDE   CAMEROONS   'CAMELS'

postal validity. The only resident is a warden appointed by the Manx National Trust.

California City Letter Express Co.; California Penny Post Co. Two local mail services from San Francisco and other towns, for which 'locals' were issued in the 1850s and 1860s.

Calino, or Calimno.   See under 'Dodecanese'.

Callao.   See 'Lima'.

Cambodia (Cambodge).   Former French protectorate in Indo-China, since 1955 an independent kingdom. Stamps first issued, 1951; prior to this date the stamps of Indo-China were in use. Indo-China also issued a separate set of stamps for Cambodia in 1936. Area: 71,000 sq. m.; capital: Pnompenh; currency: 1951, 100 cents = 1 piaster; 1955, 100 cents = 1 real; pop. (1962): 5,748,842.

Camel Postman.   Famous stamp design of the Sudan, introduced with the first definitives in 1898. It is one of the few designs to remain in regular use (with changes of inscription, colour, and size) for more than fifty years. The jubilee of the design was marked by a special stamp in 1948, and even in the 1951 series the Camel Postman motif was retained for the top 50 p. value. It appeared again on the Self-Government issue of 1954.

Cameroons, also Cameroun (Fr.) and Kamerun (Ger.).   Former German colony in West Africa, later mandated to France and Britain, and now an independent republic. The first stamps were German issues introduced in 1887, distinguishable only by the Kamerun postmark. The first Cameroons issue was a set of six overprints on German stamps in 1897, followed by the standard German Colonial designs from 1900.

On the outbreak of war in 1914, the country was quickly invaded by Anglo-French forces. A supply of the German Colonial stamps, found on board a captured German steamer, was in 1915 overprinted C.E.F. (Cameroons Expeditionary Force) for use during the British occupation. At the same time the French produced their own occupation issues by overprinting the stamps of Gaboon, French Congo, and Middle Congo.

After the war by far the greater part of the country was mandated to France and had its own stamp issues. A much smaller zone, adjoining Nigeria, was allocated to Britain. This area was administered as part of

56

Nigeria, and used Nigerian stamps, though the postmarks indicated that the zone was a British mandate, and not part of Nigeria proper.

In 1958 an autonomous government was set up in the French Cameroons, and in 1960 the country became an independent republic. Also in 1960 a plebiscite was held in the British zone, as a result of which the people of the Southern Cameroons decided to join the new Cameroons Republic. In October 1960 Nigerian stamps were overprinted 'Cameroons U.K.T.T.' (United Kingdom Trust Territory) for use in this region prior to its incorporation in the republic in the following year. Area: 200,600 sq. m.; capital : Yaoundé; pop. about 4,000,000.

Campbell Island. Barren Antarctic island about 400 miles south of New Zealand, established as a N.Z. civil aviation meteorological service station in 1941, with its own post office.

Campbell Paterson Catalogue of the stamps of New Zealand is a complete and detailed listing in loose-leaf and ring binding. Publishers: Campbell Paterson Ltd., Epsom, S.E.3, Auckland, N.Z.

Campeche. State and city of Mexico, with local provisionals issued in 1876, during the revolution.

Campione. Campione d'Italia, an enclave, and isolated fragment of Italy within Swiss territory, on Lake Lugano. The Commune issued its own pictorial set of provisionals of five values on 20 May 1944, followed by a definitive set of seven values printed heliogravure by Courvoisier on 7 September 1944, which were in use until 30 June 1952, as part of the Swiss P.O. administration, and purchasable with Swiss currency. Both Swiss and Italian issues are now valid and available at the post office.

Canada. Independent nation of the British Commonwealth in North America, combining the former independent stamp-issuing colonies of Canada, Nova Scotia, New Brunswick, Prince Edward Island, British Columbia, and Vancouver's Island. First Canadian colonial issues appeared on 23 April 1851, the values being in English coinage and known as the 'Pence' issues. After 1859 the decimal system and coinage was introduced. Canada was given Dominion status in 1867, absorbing the above-mentioned colonies. Area: 3,851,113 sq. m.; pop. (est. 1963): 18,896,000; capital: Ottawa: currency: 100 cents = 1 dollar. Newfoundland was absorbed on 30 March 1949.

Canadian 'Locals'. Apart from semi-official modern air issues, there were no really genuine locals issued, and the following 'stamps' are bogus: Baldwin's Railway Postage; Bancroft's City Express; Bell's Dispatch; Corbeil's Private Post; Ker's City Post; M'Lachlan's Post; and Winslow & Co.'s Express. Most of these were probably S. A. Taylor's (q.v.) productions.

Canadian Republic. (Fr. Republique Canadienne). In 1869 Louis Riel's insurgent provisional government in the Red River district planned a stamp issue which never came into use owing to the failure of the revolt. It is believed that only two copies survived the destruction of the stock and the scrapping of the plates.

CANADA CANAL ZONE CAPE OF
GOOD HOPE

Canal Maritime de Suez. See 'Suez Canal'.

Canal Zone. Panama. Central America, a strip of territory either side of the Panama Canal, leased to the U.S.A. 1903. Panama Republican stamps o/p 'Canal Zone' first appeared June 1904, followed by similar issues alternating with current U.S.A. issues also o/p until 1928 when portrait and pictorial sets of definitives appeared. Area: 648·01 sq. m.; pop. (1960): 42,122. U.S.A. currency.

Cancellation. A postmark designed to cancel or deface the stamp to render re-use impossible, often combining this purpose with an indicaton of the time and place of posting.

'Cancelled'. The word overprinted on stamps indicates either remainders or printers' 'samples'. In 1861 Perkins, Bacon and Co. supplied various classic stamps, cut from sheets of printers' waste and hand-stamped 'CANCELLED' in a barred oval, without proper authority, to members of Sir Rowland Hill's family.

Cancelled/V-R-I. See 'Wolmaransstad'.

Cancelled to Order. Term used to describe stamps cancelled, usually in quantity, by the issuing postal authority, for sale to the stamp trade, without the stamps having passed through the post.

Candia, or Heraklion. See 'British P.O.s in Crete', and 'Crete'.

Canna. Hebridean island for which a stamp-like charity label was issued in 1958 by the laird, John Lorne Campbell. It is not a local, having no postal validity whatever.

Canton. City of Southen China, one of the Treaty Ports. A British Post Office opened in 1844, using stamps of Hong Kong. (Identifying postmark 'C 1'.) It was closed 1922. The French issued stamps of Indo-China o/p in French and Chinese 1901–22 for use of their post offices in Canton. Pop. (1950): 1,496,000.

Canton Island. Phoenix Group, S.W. Pacific. A trans-Pacific International airport, a G.B. and U.S.A. condominium by an agreement of 1939. See 'Phoenix Islands'.

Cantonal Stamps. Issues of the Swiss cantons (provinces) of Zürich, Geneva, and Basle (Basel) prior to the first issue for the whole of Switzerland in 1850.

Cape Gracias à Dios. Nicaragua, South America. Had its own local issues 1904–9 to counteract currency anomalies. See also 'Zelaya'.

Cape of Good Hope. Former British colony, later a province of the Union (and now Republic) of South Africa. The first issue of 1853 consisted of the famous 'Cape Triangulars'. These were the world's first triangular stamps, the format being adopted so that the postal clerks and sorters (many of whom were then illiterate) could distinguish the colony's outgoing mails at a glance from the incoming mails from England. South African stamps have been in use at the Cape of Good Hope since 1910. Area: 276,995 sq. m.; capital: Cape Town; currency: sterling; pop. (1911): 2,564,965.

Cape 'Triangulars'. See 'Cape of Good Hope' above, 'Woodblocks', etc.

Cape Juby. (Span. Cabo Juby or Jubi). Spanish possession in North-West Africa. Stamps of Rio de Oro (1914 types), o/p and surcharged 1916, were followed by other o/p issues until 1940, when it became a part of Spanish Western Sahara (q.v.).

Cape Verde (Cabo Verde). Group of Portuguese islands in the Atlantic, off the west coast of Africa. Stamps first issued, 1877. Area: 1,557 sq. m.; capital: Praia; currency: Portuguese; pop. (1960): 201,549.

Carbon Tetrachloride. A volatile fluid (usually sold under proprietary names and trade marks) used as a non-inflammable substitute for benzine (q.v.) for the detection of watermarks, and for cleaning soiled stamps. Must *not* be used on modern issues printed by photogravure, as it has a solvent action on the inks normally employed. **Warning:** Has a toxic effect upon many and the vapour should not be inhaled. See 'Watermark detector', etc.

Carchi (Charki, or Karki). See 'Dodecanese Is.'

'Cardiff' Penny. Applied to any copy from the imperforate sheet of the G.B. penny red, from Plate No. 116, inadvertently issued to the Cardiff Post Office in January 1870.

Carelia. See 'Karelia'.

Carinthia. Austrian province for which a League of Nations plebiscite issue of Austrian stamps o/p 'Karnten Abstimmung'; and of Yugoslav o/p 'K.G.C.A.' appeared in 1920. It passed back to Austria. Area: 3,680 sq. m.; pop.: (1951) 474,764; capital: Klagenfurt (Celovec).

Caritas. (Lat.). Charity. Inscribed on Luxembourg's special issues.

Carlist issues of Spain were authorised in 1873–5 by Don Carlos, who proclaimed himself King Carlos VII in 1872, in the Northern Provinces: Biscay, Navarre, Guipuzcoa, and Alava. See also: 'Catalonia' and 'Valencia'.

'Carlos'. The name given to a Portuguese keytype, bearing the portrait of King Carlos, who reigned 1889–1908.

'CARLOS'   CARINTHIA   'CARRIERS'

Carn Iar. Small Scottish island for which local stamps were prepared in 1961 but not issued. Afterwards some were overprinted and used on a privately operated parcel delivery service in London during the work-to-rule of Post Office employees in January 1962. This 'London Delivery Service' was in operation in competition with the better-known service of the People's League (q.v.).

Carnes' City Letter Express. A local mail service established in San Francisco, U.S.A., in 1864, by G. A. Carnes, an ex-post office clerk. His stamps bore a drawing of a bear. Similar stamps, with Carnes' name erased, were used in 1868 by Wm. E. Loomis.

Carnets de Timbres. (French). Stamp booklets.

Caroline Islands, also Karolinen (Ger.). Former German colony in the Pacific, occupied by Japan from 1914 to 1945, and now under United States trusteeship. The only separate stamp issues for the Caroline group were those under the German regime from 1899 to 1914. Japanese stamps were then used until the end of the Second World War, and American stamps are now in use. Area: 390 sq. m.

Carriers' Stamps. Locals issued in the United States in the 1842–60 period, when the ordinary United States stamps prepaid postage only from one post office to another. Carriers' stamps paid the delivery fee from the post office to the addressee, or the postage on local letters, from one address to another in the same city. Some carriers' stamps were officially issued by the United States Post Office, for example the New York City Despatch and the Philadelphia U.S.P.O. issues. Others were semi-officials—issued by private companies but with Post Office recognition. These included Honour's City Express and Kingman's, Martin's, Beckman's, and Steinmeyer's City Posts at Charleston (South Carolina); Williams' City Post at Cincinnati (Ohio); Bishop's City Post at Cleveland (Ohio); Whartons, and Brown & McGill's Despatch at Louisville (Kentucky).

Cartagena. Colombia. Which issued its own provisionals 1899–1900, during the Civil War.

G. Carter's Despatch. Labels so inscribed are 'locals' of the U.S.A. issued in Philadelphia 1849–51.

Carto-Philately. (U.S.A.). The collection and study of stamps incorporating maps in their designs. A branch of thematic or Topical Collecting (q.v.).

'Cartwheel' Cancellations. Circular numeral types used by Spain 1858–64. There are sixty-five numbers listed for the major towns, from Madrid (No. 1) to San Roque (No. 63) and two un-numbered—San Marta Ortigueira en Corogne, and Arzua, the latter bears the town name instead.

Carúpano. Caribbean coast town of Venezuela with its own provisional issues in 1902.

Cashmere, Kashmir. See 'Jammu and Kashmir'.

Caso. (Kasos). See under 'Dodecanese Islands'.

Caspary Collection. The vast stamp collection of Alfred H. Caspary, an American millionaire banker, was disposed of in the U.S.A. and England in sixteen auction sales extending over three years (1955–8) and realised the record sum of £1,033,840. Many items established new prices much in excess of standard catalogue quotations.

Castelrosso, or Castellorizo. Island off the south coast of Asia Minor, occupied by the French in 1915. Stamps of France o/p 'O.N.F.' (Occupation Navale Français), 'B.N.F.' (Base Navale Français), and 'O.F. Castelloriso' in 1920. It was transferred to Italy in Jan. 1921 and Italian issues were o/p 'Castelrosso'. Ceded to Greece in 1947 with the Dodecanese Islands.

Cat. Accepted abbreviation for 'Catalogue'.

Catalogues. A stamp catalogue is more than an illustrated price-list; it is the collector's principal work of reference, listing and describing each stamp in order and giving much valuable information on the purpose and date of issue, etc. Without a catalogue to identify his stamps it is almost impossible for a collector to arrange a collection in an orderly and sensible manner. The first such list on record was *Timbres Poste*, published in Strasbourg in 1861. Shortly afterwards another catalogue appeared in Paris. April 1862 saw the first English catalogue, published by Frederick Booty of Brighton. (This was the first to have illustrations.) Many others followed; some were soon forgotten, but others remain famous names to the present day.

Today the leading catalogues published in Britain are Stanley Gibbons (which first appeared in 1865, making it the oldest continuously published catalogue in the world), and the Commonwealth—the latter dealing only with stamps of the reigns of King George VI and Queen Elizabeth II. In America the leading catalogues are the old-established Scott, and the comparative newcomer Minkus. The principal Continental catalogues are Yvert (French), Michel (German), and Zumstein (Swiss, printed in German), all three of which were first published in the same year, 1874. All the above famous publications are accorded world-wide recognition. But there are many more, too numerous to mention individually, published in various other countries and languages.

There are, too, many excellent specialised catalogues, dealing in much more detail than the general catalogues with one particular country or group. Any collector taking up a specialised interest is well advised to consult his dealer first on the specialised catalogues and other literature available. Sanabria, published in America, is the best-known catalogue dealing only with airmail issues of the world, and Kessler, another American publication, is the authority on aerogrammes.

Catalogue Value. The price quoted for a stamp in a recognised catalogue —not to be confused with market value. Some catalogues—Stanley Gibbons is the outstanding example—are also the price-list of their publishers; others, for example Scott, are published by firms which are not stamp-dealers at all, and give an entirely independent opinion on what the compilers consider to be fair buying prices. In the former case catalogue value is the price at which the publisher is prepared, at the time of publication, to sell you a single copy of the stamp in question, in top-class condition, if in stock. Many stamps are obtainable at considerably less than catalogue value. A dealer can usually sell a complete issue of stamps, even more a large collection, at less cost than the same stamps sold one at a time, because the time and trouble involved are so much less. The state of the dealer's stock and of the stamp market generally, and the popularity or otherwise of the stamps concerned, are other factors which help to determine the selling price. Thus terms such as 'half cat.', 'third cat.', etc., are often seen to describe a stamp offered at the quoted proportion of catalogue value.

Catalonia. (Cataluña). Carlist stamps of Spain (see above) were issued for this province 15 April 1874. See also 'Valencia'.

Catapult Mail. Mail carried by an aircraft catapulted from a ship at sea. By the late 1920s aircraft had undergone considerable development, but were not yet powerful enough to fly non-stop across the oceans. Experiments were therefore carried out by mounting aircraft on the decks of passenger liners, and dispatching them by catapult several hundred miles before the ship reached her destination. In this way it was possible to deliver the mail at the terminal port rather more rapidly. The first catapult mails were those flown from the French liner *Île de France*, on the North Atlantic run, in 1928 and 1929. But the best known were those from the German liners *Bremen* and *Europa* introduced in 1929–30. In 1933–4 the German Government experimented with an airmail service across the South Atlantic, using a ship, the *Westfalen*, as a halfway refuelling base. Planes were catapulted from this vessel on several occasions. Most items of catapult mail can be identified by special cachets applied prior to the flight.

Cattaro. See 'Boka Kotorska'.

Cauca. Department of Colombia, with its own local issues 1879 and 1903.

Cavalle. (Kavalla). French stamps were o/p for use in this former Turkish seaport 1893–1912. Occupied by Bulgaria in 1912, and in 1913 by Greece—the Greeks o/p Bulgarian stamps. Now Greek territory.

CENTRAL
LITHUANIA

CAYMAN ISLANDS

'CERES'

Cayman Islands. Group of three islands in the British West Indies, and a dependency of Jamaica. First issues were Q.V. keytypes on 19 February 1901. Area: 93 sq. m.; pop. (1960): 8,800; capital: Georgetown on Grand Cayman; British currency.

Čechy a Morava. (Czech). Bohemia and Moravia.

Cent. Cents, centimes, centimos, centavos, are all coinage or currency names indicating that their value is 100th of the standard currency unit.

Centenary. Or centennial. 100th anniversary. A favourite excuse for a commemorative stamp issue.

Central African Federation. See under 'Rhodesia and Nyasaland.'

Central African Republic (Republique Centrafricaine). The French territory formerly known as Oubangui-Chari (q.v.) became an autonomous republic within the French Community in 1958 under the style of Republique Centrafricaine, and stamps inscribed with the new name were first issued in 1959. Area: 238,000 sq. m.; capital: Bangui; pop. (1960): 1,200,000.

Central Lithuania. Issued stamps during its transient independence 1920-2. Later absorbed by Poland, and now under Russian dominance. Area was approx. 10,000 sq. m.; pop. figures not available; currency: 100 fenigow = 1 mark.

Centred. Stamps printed centrally between the perforations leaving an equal margin all round are said to be well centred, and are always preferred by discriminating collectors. Stamps not so centrally printed are said to be 'off-centre'.

Cephalonia. Largest of the Ionian Islands. Area: 260 sq. m.; chief town: Argostoli. Stamps of Greece were o/p by the Italian occupying forces 'Italia/Occupazione Militare/Italiana isole/Cefalonia e Itaca' in April 1941. Modern Greek name: Kephallenia.

'Ceres'. Goddess of grain (or harvest), gives her name to a keytype design of Portugal introduced in 1912. There are nearly 200 'Ceres' stamps in the parent country's issues alone, and as the colonies have had inscribed sets also, this keytype has distinct possibilities for the specialist.

CERTIFICADO CEYLON 'CHAIN-
BREAKERS'

'Ceres' also names the 1849, 1870–2, and 1944 sets of France, and the 1856 issues of Corrientes—all of which depict the head of the goddess.

Certificado. (Span.). Certificated, or certified. Registered.

Certified Mail. Mail for which a receipt is given to the sender and required from the addressee, but for which no compensation is given in the event of loss. In 1955 the United States issued a special 15 ¢. stamp for Certified Mail. In Britain the system is called Recorded Delivery.

Česko-Slovensko. Czechoslovakia.

Ceskych Skautu. 'Czech Scouts'—the inscription on the first issue of Czechoslovakia in October 1918, produced by the Revolutionary Committee in Prague. The distribution of the first mails carried under the auspices of the new republic was undertaken by Boy Scouts.

Ceylon. Island off the south of India, a former British colony which was granted dominion status in 1948. Stamps first issued, 1857. Modern issues share with Cyprus the distinction of having tri-lingual inscriptions—the name of the country being given in Sinhalese, Tamil, and English. Area: 25,332 sq. m.; capital: Colombo; currency: 1857, Sterling (the early stamps are known as the Pence issues); 1872, 100 cents = 1 rupee; pop. (1961): 10,168,000.

Chachapoyas. Peruvian town with its own o/p issue in 1884.

Chad. See 'Tchad'.

'Chain-breakers'. Popular name for the 1919 issues of Yugoslavia, so called from the design which shows a symbolic figure breaking his chains. With numerous printing and other varieties, they have been widely studied by specialists. The name is also applied to the 1920–5 issue of Czechoslovakia.

Chala. Peru. Had its own temporary issue 1884.

Chalky paper. A highly surfaced, chalk-coated paper introduced for stamp-printing purposes in 1902 and still used from time to time. It is designed to deter any attempt at the fraudulent re-use of stamps by making it impossible to clean off the postmark without removing the stamp design as well. Chalky paper can be distinguished from ordinary by touching it with silver, when a dark pencil-like mark is left. An interesting variant of the idea was the diamond-latticed lines of chalk on the Arms type of Russia of 1909. Stamps on chalky paper should not be immersed in water, and great care should be taken when 'floating off'. In catalogues chalky paper is usually indicated by the capital letter 'C'. When the letters 'C–O' appear together, it means the stamp exists on both chalky and ordinary paper.

Chalmers, James. Publisher and bookseller of Dundee (1772–1853) was a claimant to the invention of the adhesive postage stamp. His family claim that he designed and used such a label in 1834.

Chalon Portrait. Famous full-face portrait of Queen Victoria, painted by Alfred Edward Chalon in 1837, on the occasion of the Queen's first visit to the House of Lords after her accession. It was used for many of the classic issues of the British Empire, the first being the 12d. black stamp of Canada issued in 1851. A notable occasion in the present century on which the Chalon portrait has appeared on stamps was the high values of the Turks and Caicos Islands issue of 1948, marking the centenary of the islands' separation from the Bahamas.

Chamba. Former Indian convention state which used overprinted Indian stamps from 1886 to 1950. Since that date Indian stamps have been used. Area: 3,216 sq. m.

Changes of Colour. Postal authorities introduce colour changes in their stamp issues for various reasons. In the past many changes took place to accord with the regulations of the U.P.U., which sought to ensure that for easy identification stamps used for particular postal charges were printed in specified colours. Other changes have occurred to avoid confusion with another stamp of a different value. In 1941–2 certain low-value British stamps were printed in lighter colours as a wartime economy measure. The exposure of stamps to excessive heat, damp or sunlight can lead to unwanted colour changes; faded stamps not only spoil the appearance of the collection—they are generally worthless. See also 'Colour Changeling'.

Changeling. See 'Colour Changeling'. The term is also used to denote an inferior copy of a stamp substituted for a better one by an unscrupulous member of an exchange club.

Channel Islands. During the German occupation of 1940–5, stocks of British stamps were soon depleted; bisects were authorised to overcome the shortage temporarily. In 1941, with the approval of the occupying power, both Guernsey and Jersey started issuing their own stamps. These remained valid for postage after the liberation, until 19 April 1946. In 1948 Great Britain issued two stamps to celebrate the third anniversary of Channel Islands liberation; they were sold only in the Channel Islands and at certain major towns of Britain, but were valid for postage throughout the United Kingdom. In 1958 3d. Regional stamps were issued for both Jersey and Guernsey, followed by corresponding 2½d. values in 1964. See also 'Chausey', 'Herm', 'Jethou', and 'Commodore Shipping'.

CHANNEL ISLANDS   CHARITY STAMPS

Charity Stamps. Issues sold at a surcharge over face value in aid of charitable purposes. Typical examples are the New Zealand Health and the Swiss 'Pro Juventute' issues. In some countries, particularly America, charity stamps are often referred to as semi-postals.

Charkhari. Former Indian native state which had its own internal issues from 1894 to 1950. Since that date Indian stamps have been used. Area: 880 sq. m.; pop.: 150,000.

Charleston. South Carolina city and seaport, which issued its own 'Postmasters' ' series as a Confederate town in the American Civil War.

Charleston. City of West Virginia, U.S.A., from which came the semi-official 'Honour's, Martin's, Steinmeyer's and Beckman Posts'—'Carriers' ' stamps of 1849–60. See 'Carriers' Stamps'.

Chausey. Les Îles Chausey—the French Channel Islands—comprise a group of 50-odd islets 8 miles from Granville and 28 from Jersey. La Grande Île is the only one permanently inhabited. There is a letter-box but no post office. Mail is usually stamped with a cachet in blue, but cancellation is done at Granville.

Cheap Stamps are available from stamp dealers in a wide range of all-different packets. They are a useful means of starting a collection on a small outlay, or of augmenting it quickly in sections where it is weakest. Such stamps are obtainable in good condition so easily that there is no excuse for the torn, creased, dirty, faded, or damaged copies which spoil the appearance of some beginners' collections.

Check Letters. Letters in the corners of the early issues of G.B., inserted as a precaution against forgery and re-use.

Cheever & Towle. A mail-carrying firm of Boston, U.S.A., who issued 'local' stamps 1846–50, which have since been reprinted on various colour-ed papers, other than the original blue ink on white.

Chemical Cleaning. It is considered legitimate to clean the accumulated dirt, adhesions of unwanted paper, and old hinges off a stamp by any means that will restore it to some semblance of its pristine condition, but 'chemical cleaning' in its philatelic sense usually implies the sinister practice of removing postmarks, pen, and other fiscal cancellations, with a view to enhancing values illegitimately. See 'Boiling', 'Changes of Colour', 'Changeling', etc.

| CHECK LETTERS | CHINA | CHILE |

Chemins de Fer. Iron road; railroad or railway (Fr.). Parcel Post issues of Belgium are so inscribed as they prepay postage on parcels carried by rail. They are, however, official productions of the Post Office, not of the railways. The Flemish term is Spoorwegen, which also appears on the stamps.

Cheque Stamp. The only example of a cheque stamp pressed into service for postage occurred in Nyasaland (then known as British Central Africa) in 1898. An acute shortage of the 1d. stamp developed when further supplies expected from England failed to arrive. A provisional 1d. surcharge on the 3s. value did not last long, and the cheque stamp (on which in those days the duty was only 1d.) was adapted to its new role by surrounding it with rectangular frame lines and applying the overprint 'Internal Postage'. They were not sold direct to the public but were affixed to letters by the postal clerks in exchange for cash; they are therefore practically unknown mint. At first the postmaster authenticated each copy with his initials; later, control numbers or letters were printed on the back. The cheque stamps were in use for about eight months before fresh supplies of the normal 1d. stamp arrived, and altogether about 30,000 were issued.

Cherifien Posts. Local service of Morocco organised by the Cherifien Administration in September 1911 by French consent, linking most of the chief towns. A set of stamps, values one to fifty monzouma, was issued in May 1912. (Should apparently be 'Shereefian'.)

Chiapas. Mexican state with its own local provisional during the 1867–8 revolution.

Chicago Penny Post. A very scarce U.S.A. local of 1862–3.

Chiclayo. Peru. It had a provisional control o/p 'Franca' issued in April 1884.

Chiffre Taxe. (Fr.). Amount, or total, due. Postage dues of France, French colonies, Monaco, etc., are so inscribed.

Chihuahua. District of Mexico which issued its own revolutionary stamps in 1914.

Chile. South American republic. Stamps first issued, 1853. Up to 1910 (with the exception of a Telegraph stamp overprinted for postage) the

'CHOPS' CHINA: POST OFFICES IN: CILICIA
KIRIN SINKIANG
HEILUNGCHANG

only portrait to appear on Chilean stamps was that of Columbus; the word 'Colon', boldly inscribed on the early issues, is Columbus's name in Spanish. Area: 286,396 sq. m.; capital: Santiago; currency: 1853, 100 centavos = 1 peso; 1960: 1,000 milesimos = 100 centimos = 1 escudo; pop. (1960): 7,339,546.

Chilean Occupation of Peru. Peruvian stamps were overprinted with the arms of Chile in 1881, during the Chilean occupation of Lima in the War of the Pacific (1879–83). Victorious Chile gained Antofagasta from Bolivia (depriving that country of her outlet to the sea) and Arica from Peru.

Chimarra. Port and district of Epirus, now part of Albania. The provisional Epirus government issued stamps here in 1914, followed by further issues for Chimarra during the Greek occupation of 1914–16. See under 'Epirus'.

Chimborazo. Province of Ecuador, which had stamps o/p with a control mark in 1902 as a deterrent to the use of stocks suspected as stolen.

China. British Post Offices. See 'Hong Kong'.

China. Ancient Cathay, a Manchu Empire until 1912, now an Asian republic, with a stamp history dating back to the Imperial Maritime Customs Post issues of 1878. Civil and world wars, and Japanese infiltration, resulted in a complex medley of local, sectional, inflation, and occupation issues most difficult to disentangle, but making it a fascinating country for the specialist collector. Various 'Treaty Port' and other issues made by the Western powers and America and Japan add to the complexity and interest, while issues for territories over which China claims suzerainty must also be noted, e.g. Tibet and Mongolia. Currency difficulties have also resulted in separate issues for Szechwan and Yunnan (q.v.), and financial crises have resulted in stamps of fantastic values, many of doubtful origin and status. Area: 3,380,692 sq. m.; pop. (est. 1964): 735,000,000; former capital: Nanking, now at Peking or Peiping; currency: 1878, 100 candereen = 1 tael; 1897, 100 cents = 1 Chinese dollar, now the 'People's Bank' dollar, or yuan (10 fen = 1 chaio; 10 chiao = 1 yuan) (revalued 1955, $1 = 10,000 old dollars). Examples of Chinese figures are given below.

CENT	DOLLAR	HALF	ONE	TWO	THREE	FOUR	FIVE

SIX	SEVEN	EIGHT	NINE	TEN	25 CENTS	500

See also: British, French, German, Italian, Japanese, Russian, and United States Post Offices in China, and Chinese local posts, Shanghai, and the various foreign settlements, under their various place names in this work.

Simplified modern characters

ONE	TWO	THREE	FOUR	FIVE	TWO	ONE	DOLLAR SIGNS
STYLE 1				STYLE 2			

Since 1950 the situation has been further complicated by the existence of the Nationalist Government in Formosa, with its own stamp issues which are usually listed under 'China' in the catalogues.

China Expeditionary Force. Stamps of India o/p 'C.E.F.' were issued for the use of British and Indian troops in North China (Boxer Rebellion) 1900, 1904, 1909, and 1913–21.

Chinese Local Posts. Were established in various Treaty Ports: Amoy (1895), Chefoo (1893), Chinkiang (1894), Chungking (1894), Foochow (1895), Hankow (1893), Ichang (1895), Kewkiang (1894), Nanking (1896), Wuhu (1894), and Shanghai (1865). All were closed after establishment of the Imperial Post in 1897.

Chios. Former Turkish island in the Aegean, part of Greece since 1912. In May 1913 a Greek stamp was overprinted for use there.

'Chops'. Ideographs, or native Japanese characters o/p, hand-stamped, or handwritten on stamps of temporarily occupied territories by the Japanese troops during World War II.

Chorrillos. See 'Lima'.

Chosen or Tyosen. Corea (Korea). Japanese name for the country.

Christmas Mail. In the early years of the century the British Post Office operated in certain towns a scheme by which mail could be posted in advance for delivery on Christmas Day. Special postmarks were applied to explain the delay in delivery. The scheme began at Rochdale in 1902, spread to various other Lancashire towns, found its way north to Glasgow and south to Reading, but came to a sudden end after 1909 and was never repeated. The reason for abandoning it is believed to be that the scheme was too successful; that it was becoming physically impossible to deliver all the mail on Christmas Day. In recent years Christmas Day deliveries have themselves been abandoned.

Special cancellations are applied to Christmas mail at two American post offices—Christmas, Florida, and Santa Claus, Indiana.

Christmas Island. Island in the Pacific, one of the Ellice group—not to be confused with the island of the same name in the Indian Ocean, see below. Annexed by Great Britain in 1888, the island has been included in the Gilbert and Ellice Islands protectorate since 1918. But for many years there was no official post office, and about 1916 the Central Pacific Coconut Plantations Ltd., who leased the island for its copra, introduced local stamps. These were used to collect a fee for the carriage of letters by the company's schooner *Ysabel* to the nearest port of call, where the mail was handed over to the postal authorities for onward transmission; the stamps remained in use until 1938. In 1939 the first official post office was opened, using Gilbert and Ellice stamps. During the Second World War the island was temporarily occupied by the Americans. In 1956 the island was chosen as a nuclear testing site, the first tests being carried out by Britain in the following year. British Army and American post offices have functioned there for the benefit of personnel employed on the tests, using British and American stamps respectively. Christmas Island is an atoll with a lagoon 100 miles wide, but the land area is only 222 sq. m.

Christmas Island. Island in the Indian Ocean—not to be confused with the island of the same name in the Pacific, see above. A former dependency of Singapore, the island was transferred to Australian administration in 1958. A post office was first opened in 1900, the stamps of Straits Settlements and later those of Singapore being used. In 1958 Christmas Island received its own stamps for the first time, the first issues being provisionals in an Australian design, suitably overprinted and surcharged in Malayan currency. The first definitives followed in 1963. Area: 62 sq. m.; chief settlement: Flying Fish Cove; currency: 100 cents = 1 Malayan dollar; pop. (1963): 3,277.

Christmas Seals. Adhesive labels of no postal validity sold at Christmas time in aid of various charities; often seen affixed to the backs of envelopes.

Cigarette revenue tax stamps. Were used as provisional postage dues at Durban and Fordsburg in the Union of South Africa in August and December 1922.

Cilicia. Turkish Asia Minor. During 1918–21 was occupied by the French who o/p various Turkish and French stamps 'Celicie', 'T.E.O. Cilicie', 'T.E.O.', and 'O.M.F.' (Occupation Militaire Française), etc. Now again part of South Asiatic Turkey.

Circuit. (U.S.A.). An exchange club.

Circular Delivery Companies. For thirty years after the great postal reforms of 1840, the British Post Office turned a deaf ear to appeals for a reduced rate of postage for printed papers and circulars. And so private enterprise stepped in. In 1865 Robert Brydone formed the first of the Circular Delivery Companies, undertaking to deliver circulars within the boundaries of Edinburgh and Leith for a farthing each. The service was successful, but when Brydone started extending his operations to London and other cities, and there was even a hint of a National Circular Delivery Company, the Post Office instituted legal proceedings as a result of which the companies' activities were suppressed as an infringement of the State postal monopoly. In their four-year career the companies issued various local stamps; these are an interesting specialist study but in genuine used condition, especially on cover, are rare. As a direct result of the companies' enterprise, the Post Office heeded the demand for cheaper postage in 1870, and in that year the first ½d. stamp was issued to meet the new reduced rate for printed papers.

Cirenaica, also Cyrenaica.   Former Turkish territory in North Africa, an Italian colony from 1911 to 1941, and now part of the kingdom of Libya. Turkish stamps were used until 1911, but prior to this an Italian post office was opened in the capital of Benghazi (q.v.) in 1901. With the Italian occupation Cirenaica was incorporated in the colony of Libya, using Libyan stamps, but from 1923 to 1939 also had its own stamps which were in use concurrently with Libyan issues. From 1942 onwards British stamps were used overprinted M.E.F. After the war Cirenaica secured independence and in 1950 again had its own stamps for a time. In 1951 the country was embodied in the kingdom of Libya, and since that time Libyan stamps have been in use. Area: 330,000 sq. m.; capital: Benghazi; currency: 1923, as Italy; 1942, Sterling; 1950, 1,000 milliemes = 1 pound; pop. about 320,000.

City Despatch, City Despatch Post, City Post, City Express.   Inscriptions on various Carriers' stamps and locals of the United States. See 'Carriers' Stamps'.

Ciudad Juarez.   District of Mexico which issued its own revolutionary overprints in 1914.

Clandestine Agency.   Term devised by the B.P.A. and P.T.S. Joint Standing Committee on New Issues and Stamps of Doubtful Status; used to describe any organisation of trade interests which arranges new stamp issues for an overseas country but does not openly advertise itself as the agent, with a view to manipulating the issue to obtain an enhanced price from collectors.

Clark & Co.   Issued a one-cent 'local' in New York, U.S.A., in 1857.

Clark & Hall's Penny Post.   A St. Louis, U.S.A., 'local' of 1851.

Clarke's Circular Express.   Was established to carry printed matter in New York, U.S.A., by Marion M. Clarke, in 1863–8.

Classic.   Early issues which by reason of their history, rarity, or beauty have earned a position of distinction in philately. The term is not easy to define exactly; some collectors would say that no stamp issued after 1875 qualifies as a classic, but others apply the term, relatively speaking, to more modern stamps.

Cleaned. In philately the term usually implies a stamp from which a marking has been removed for fraudulent purposes.

Cleaning Stamps. The cleaning of a soiled specimen is an operation usually for an expert, and trial should always be made on one of small value. Benzine, petrol, or carbon tetrachloride can be used upon stamps *not* printed by one of the photogravure processes. Distilled water, cold or boiling (q.v.) may be employed, but not on aniline (q.v.) prints. Detergents have been recommended for the rather drastic treatment of stained specimens. Peroxide of hydrogen will often restore the clean white of a faded or yellowish paper, but is liable to alter the colour of the ink. Refer to the items mentioned above under their separate headings for more detail. See also 'De-sulphurisation'.

Cliché. (Fr.). A stereo or electro. Strictly speaking, a replica of a plate or die, or a block made by direct or indirect casting, but loosely applied by philatelists to all individual components of a printing plate.

'Clippers'. U.S.A. 'China Clipper' design Trans-Pacific airmail stamps of 1935 and 1937.

Clipperton Island. A S.E. Pacific guano island worked by the Oceanic Phosphate Company for which a dubious set of 'local' stamps of 10 values was produced in 1895. Part of French Oceania since 1930.

Clubs, Stamp. See under 'Stamp Exchange Clubs and Philatelic Societies'.

Coamo. Town in the province of Ponce, Puerta (Porto) Rico, West Indian island ceded to the U.S.A. by Spain in 1898. Had a typeset 5-cent black provisional of that year. See also 'Puerto Rico'.

Coated Paper. See 'Art Paper' and 'Chalky Paper'.

Cochin. Former Indian native state, which had its own internal issues from 1892 to 1949, although the State's Official stamps were still being issued up to 1951. For ordinary postage Cochin stamps were replaced in 1949 by those of Travancore-Cochin (q.v.). All Cochin stamps carry an 'Anchal' inscription (q.v.). Area: 1,493 sq. m.; capital: Ernakulam; currency: early issues valued in puttans; 1898, 11 pies = 1 puttan; 1909, As India.

Cochin China. Former French territory in Indo-China, which used the general French Colonies issues until these were replaced by those of Indo-China in 1892. The only stamps specifically listed under Cochin China are some surcharges applied locally in 1886–8. The modern territory corresponding to Cochin China is South Viet-Nam (q.v.).

Cocos, or Cocos-Keeling, Islands. Group of islands in the Indian Ocean, annexed to Singapore in 1903. A postal agency functioned from 1933 to 1937, using Straits Settlements stamps. At other times, from 1909 onwards, the population had to rely on a 'barrel mail' (inwards) and a 'tin can mail'

COCHIN   'COILS'   CO-EXTENSIVE LINE

(outwards). Passing ships slowed down to deposit a barrel containing the Cocos mail in the sea, whence it was picked up by a launch from the islands. The same launch brought out a sealed tin canister containing the outward mail, and this was hauled aboard the ship by line. At the end of 1951 the Royal Australian Air Force sent a party of men to reconstruct a wartime airstrip, and for them and their families a service post office was set up, using Australian stamps; this functioned until January 1954. From 1952 most of the Cocos mail was sent by air. In September 1952 the Singapore postal agency was reopened for the civilian population, using Singapore stamps, and this lasted until October 1954, when the islands were transferred to Australia. Thereafter Australian stamps were again used until the Cocos Islands received their own first definitive issue in 1963. Area: about 5 sq. m.; pop. (1963): 664.

Co-extensive Line. When the 'Jubilee' line (q.v.) on the selvedge or margins of a sheet of stamps of G.B. is intermittent and interrupted so that short lengths accompany each individual stamp, it is known as a co-extensive line, but when unbroken it is 'continuous'.

Cog-Wheel Punch. Fletcher's patent, which comprised eight punches arranged in a circle, and which 'blind' punched (cut into without removing any paper) the stamp, was a protective device used experimentally on the 1873 issues of the U.S.A. It was a security device designed to prevent chemical cleaning, or the removal of post or pen marking. See also 'Grill'.

'Coils'. Are stamps wound in the form of reels, rolls, or coils for insertion and use in stamp-vending or affixing machines. Their manufacture usually results in such departure from the normal as to render them distinct and collectable varieties. See 'Interrupted perfs.', etc.

Colima. District of Mexico which issued its own revolutionary overprints in 1914.

Colis Postal. (Fr.). Parcel Post (q.v.).

Collateral Material. Related auxiliary matter: maps, book, or other illustrations, newscuttings, etc., exhibited with a stamp collection or display to help 'tell the story'.

COLOMBIA   COLIS POSTAL   'COMMERCE'

College Stamps. Colleges at Oxford and Cambridge, England, issued stamps for their messenger services 1871–86. They were discontinued at the request of the P.M.G. In U.S.A. and Canada are 'labels' used in business training colleges to teach mailing methods. See also: 'O.U.S.', 'Private Postage Stamps', etc.

Colombia. South American republic, formerly known as the Granadine Confederation and the United States of New Granada; the name of Colombia was introduced in 1861. Stamps first issued, 1859. In addition to the national issues, various Colombian states (known as departments) had their own stamps from the 1860's, in some cases up to 1904. These states were Antioquia, Bolivar, Cauca, Cundinamarca, Santander, and Tolima, all of which are separately mentioned in this book. Another Colombian state with its own stamps was Panama, which seceded in 1903 and became an independent republic; its departmental issues, inscribed 'Colombia', are usually listed under Panama. Colombia is also noted for its unusual semi-official airmail stamps of SCADTA and AVIANCA (q.v.). Area: 455,335 sq. m.; capital: Bogota; currency: 100 centavos = 1 peso; pop. (1962): 14,768,510.

Colon. (Span.). Columbus. Inscribed on Chile's first issues.

Colonia. (Ital.). Colony.

Colour changeling. A stamp whose colour has been altered, either accidentally or deliberately, by chemical means, or by excessive exposure to sunlight, heat, or damp.

Colour Guide. Identification of the many colours used in stamp printing, particularly the minor shades, can be a problem for beginners. To assist in overcoming this the colour guide has been devised; its usual form is a folding card on which all the principal philatelic colours are shown and named. This useful accessory readily shows some of the differences between philatelic colour-naming and that adopted in other spheres. A study of a philatelic colour guide and, for example, a paint manufacturer's colour card will provide some interesting contrasts!

Colours, Universal Postal Union. At Washington, 1898, it was recommended that stamps of all member countries should be partially standardised as regards colours of the three most-used values in use for international services, as follows: Green for the international single printed matter rate (1 ¢. in the U.S. and Canada, ½d. in sterling countries, 5 centimes, centisimi, centimos, lepta, or leu in Latin Monetary Union lands). Red for international postal card rate (2 ¢. in North America, 1d. sterling, 10 centimes, lepta, etc., in L.M.U. lands). Dark blue for international single letter rate (5 ¢. in North America, 2½d. sterling, 25 centimes, lepta, etc., in L.M.U. lands). This ruling accounted for a number of colour changes throughout the world, but owing to departures from the gold standard, and fluctuations in international currency after two world wars, fell into disuse. In late years G.B. reverted to rule but, following agreement reached at the Brussels U.P.U. meeting in 1952, the colour rule lapsed as from 1 July 1953. See 'Universal Postal Union'.

Colour Trials. Proof impressions of a stamp design, taken in various colours, from which the final selection is made as to the colour or colours in which the stamp will be printed.

Coloured Cancellations. Do not invariably indicate fiscal or revenue usage as they are used by many postal administrations, and stamps so obliterated should be treated with discretion.

Columbia, British. See 'British Columbia'.

Columbus. Christopher Columbus, or Christophé Colón, appears on many of the stamps of the Americas, and one of the first commemorative sets was in honour of his discovery of America—the famous 1893 U.S.A. Columbian Exposition set. Chile would allow no portrait but that of Columbus upon her stamps until 1910, and the 1899 set of the Dominican Republic was devoted to the portrayal of scenes from his life. G.B. has not been behind in honouring him on many of its colonial issues, and perpetuated the amusing error on the Colony's seal, in allowing him to be shown on the 1903–23 issues of St. Kitts-Nevis using a spy-glass or telescope, which history says was not invented until about 100 years later.

Column. A complete vertical row of stamps from the sheet.

Combination Cover. One bearing stamps of two stamp-issuing authorities. One for internal transmission to the frontier, and the other for franking to an overseas, or extra-territorial, final destination. Necessary only in the case of U.P.U. non-members. See also 'Mixed Postage'.

Comb Perforation. Machine punch-plate perforation which consists of one full line right across a sheet of stamps, attached to which are short lengths of punches at right angles, corresponding to the length of one stamp, and which then has a rough resemblance to a comb with widely-spaced teeth. See 'Perforation'.

Commando Brief. (Afrik.). Unofficial Boer issue used in the second South African War. Printed in black on yellow surface-coloured (enamelled) paper measuring 40 × 30 mm., the 'stamp' was inscribed 'Commando Brief/O.V.S./Franko' within an ornamental typeset border. One in the compiler's possession is postmarked 'Modder River/Oc 24/99/CGH', indicating postal use of some kind.

Commat. (U.S.A.). Postmark. Said to derive from '*comma*', Greek for mark or impression. Thus 'Machine commat' means a machine-applied postmark cancellation.

Commemorative. A stamp issued, usually for a limited period, to mark a particular event or anniversary, as distinct from a definitive, intended for normal, everyday postal use for an indefinite period. The question of which issue can rightly be described as the first commemorative has been the subject of much debate. Peru issued a stamp in 1871 on the twentieth anniversary of the first railway in South America, and to this issue the honour is usually accorded. The 'Laureated' types of France, showing the head of Napoleon III crowned with a laurel wreath, which were first issued in 1862, have been claimed as the first commemoratives, since the laurel wreath celebrated the Emperor's victories in Italy; but they were really definitive in purpose, and lasted until 1870. The New South Wales series of 1888, issued on the centenary of the first British settlement in Australia, may be regarded as the first British Empire commemoratives; these too were used as definitives, but each design included the words 'One Hundred Years'—the first commemorative inscription.

'Commerce'. Name given to the French colonial general issues of May 1881, which depict the allegorical figure that gave rise to the title. There is also a 'Peace and Commerce' design and keytype (15 April 1876) which has been largely imprinted and used for French colonies, and which is often confused with the 'Tablet' type, a very similar grouped design. Designed by J. A. Sage, and engraved by E. Mouchon.

Commission Für Retourbriefe. This inscription, with a town name, appears on the returned letter stamps of Bavaria. As these issues do not prepay postage, British and American catalogues do not list them.

Commodore Shipping. Pictorial stamps thus inscribed were first issued in 1961 by the Commodore Shipping Co. Ltd. to prepay charges on parcels carried by the company's vessels on the cargo and passenger service between Guernsey, Sark, and Alderney in the Channel Islands.

Commonwealth Stamp Catalogues. Published by the Commonwealth Stamp Co. of Liverpool, these are semi-specialised catalogues dealing with the King George VI and Queen Elizabeth II issues of the British Commonwealth only. The Elizabethan volume is published annually; that dealing with King George VI issues, every two years. The first Commonwealth catalogue appeared in 1951. In October 1965 it was announced that the King George VI Catalogue would henceforth be published by Bridger and Kay Ltd. of 86 Strand, London, W.C.2.

Commonwealths. The Dominions of Great Britain were re-named Commonwealths of the British Commonwealth of Nations by statute in 1947.

Comoro Islands or Archipelago. (Archipel des Comores). Group of French islands off the east coast of Africa. Anjouan, Grand Comoro, Mayotte, and Moheli all had their own stamps prior to 1914, when the islands were attached to Madagascar. Stamps of Madagascar were then

COMMEMORATIVE   CONDOMINIUM   COMPANHIA DE
MOÇAMBIQUE

used until 1950, when the first Comoro stamps appeared. Area: 838 sq. m.; capital: Moroni; pop. (1958): 183,133.

Companhia de Moçambique. See 'Mozambique Company'.

Companhia do Nyassa. See 'Nyassa'.

Compound perf. Where more than one gauge of perforation exists on different sides of the same stamp. Thus a stamp with perforation measuring 14 on the two horizontal sides and 15 on the two vertical, is said to be perf. 14 × 15.

Compre ud. Cafe de Costa Rica. A plea to taste and buy Costa Rican coffee which, in 1923, was overprinted on the 1910 5 ¢. orange stamp of Costa Rica.

Comunicaciónes. (Span.). Communications, but postal services are implied and understood.

Condition. The state of the stamp as measured against the finest examples of the issue concerned. Condition applies to the state of the paper, the nature and colour of the printing, the perforation (if perf.) or margins (if imperf.), the gum (if mint) or cancellation (if used). Condition is the all-important factor in determining the value of a stamp, particularly in the case of the older issues, while modern stamps in anything less than fine condition are usually practically worthless. Descriptions applied to condition range from 'superb' and 'very good' to 'good', 'average', 'fair' and 'poor'.

Condominium. A territory jointly ruled by two powers. The two outstanding examples in philately are the stamps of Sudan, which prior to independence was an Anglo-Egyptian condominium, and of New Hebrides, an Anglo-French condominium.

Confed. Granadina. Former name of Colombia (q.v.).

Confederate States of America. The states which seceded from the Union in the American Civil War of 1861–5 issued their own stamps during that period. In the early months of the war various postmasters' provisionals appeared. These were replaced in September 1861 by the first regular issue of the Confederate States. A number of these C.S.A. issues depicted Jefferson Davis, first and only president of the Confederate States, who was the only American ever to be portrayed on his country's stamps during his lifetime.

Confederatio Helvetica. Switzerland. (Confederated Helvetia).

Congo. Vast area of Central Africa which remained largely unexplored until the nineteenth century, the first European settlement being established in 1880. In 1885 the Congo was recognised as a sovereign state (État Independant du Congo) under King Leopold II of Belgium. In 1908 it became a Belgian colony, known as the Belgian Congo (Congo Belge), and in 1960 an independent republic. Stamps first issued, 1886. Special care should be taken in distinguishing the modern issues from those of Congo Republic, see below. Area: 895,348 sq. m.; capital: Leopoldville; currency: Congolese franc; pop.: about 13,750,000.

Congo Français. French Congo (q.v.).

Congo Free State. See Congo above.

Congo, Portuguese. See 'Portuguese Congo'.

Congo Republic. Former French territory in Central Africa, known as Middle Congo before being incorporated in French Equatorial Africa in 1936. In 1958 it was proclaimed an independent republic within the French Community. Stamps first issued, 1959. Collectors should be careful not to confuse this country with the former Belgian Congo (listed above under 'Congo'), especially as both of them are now issuing stamps inscribed 'Republique du Congo'. Area: 132,012 sq. m.; capital: Brazzaville; pop. (1961): 900,000.

Congreso de los Disputados. (Span.). Stamps for Spain's members of parliament, 1895–8.

Congress. When used alone the word can be taken to refer to the Philatelic Congress of Great Britain (q.v.).

Connell, the Hon. Charles. Postmaster-general of New Brunswick, whose portrait appeared, without adequate authority or explanation, upon the 5 ¢. stamp of 1860—the value with the largest postal use. It was withdrawn and the bulk destroyed, but copies are extant. The new replacement bore the head of Queen Victoria. See 'New Brunswick'. A unique pair of the Connell stamp was sold in London in November 1963 for £1,400.

Consommation. Papier de Grande Consommation. A rather poor grey 'granite' type of paper used for the French war-time issues 1917–20.

Constant. A variety which occurs regularly in the same position on the sheet throughout one or more printings of a stamp is said to be 'constant'. See under 'Varieties'.

Constanta. See 'Küstendje'.

Constantinople (Stamboul). Former capital city of the Ottoman Empire, now known as Istanbul. Several European nations formerly operated post offices there—Britain from 1857, using British stamps (with 'C' and

'S' cancellations) to about 1885, then stamps of British Levant to 1914; Italy from 1908 to 1923, using Italian stamps overprinted Costantinopoli; Roumania from 1896 to 1919 using Roumanian stamps surcharged or overprinted Constantinopol; Russian stamps were overprinted Constantinople in 1909–10 for use at the Russian post office in the city.

'Constitution' Sets. Have been issued in a number of territories to mark the granting of new constitutions within the framework of the British Commonwealth of Nations.

Consular Overprints. Semi-official stamps issued in 1921–3 by SCADTA, the Colombian airline, were sold at various Colombian consulates in Europe, Latin America, etc., to prepay airmail postage within Colombia on letters sent from abroad. For identification and control purposes overprints were applied to the stamps to indicate in which country they had been sold. Thus an 'A' overprint indicates Germany, A-U = Argentina or Uruguay, B = Belgium, Bo = Bolivia, Br = Brazil, C = Cuba, C.R = Costa Rica, Ca = Canada, Ch = Chile, D = Denmark, E = Spain, EU = United States, F = France, G.B = Great Britain, I = Italy, H = Netherlands, P = Panama, PE = Peru, Su = Sweden, S = Switzerland, and V = Venezuela.

Continente. (Port.). Continent, or mainland. Inscribed on the stamps of Portugal 1880, 1892, 1925. This latter issue (Marquis de Pombal commems.) were intended for colonial use, but the nameplate was also inscribed 'Continente' to make them valid for use in Portugal. They were in the nature of a compulsory tax, their use in addition to ordinary postage being obligatory on certain days. Failure to conform was penalised by the affixing of 'Postage Due' stamps, the amounts of which were collected from the addressee.

Continuous Line. See 'Co-Extensive Line' and 'Jubilee Line'.

Controle 1922. O/p on 1911 issues of Persia in 1922 in pursuit of a measure to regulate the sale and postal use of certain pictorial postcards.

Control Overprints, also Control Letters and Numbers. It was common practice in some South American states to o/p a distinctive device upon stamps issued to major cities and to departments, as a check upon misuse.

Controlled Mail. (U.S.A.). Large trading concerns with many branches or depots use selected and high-value stamps for inter-communicating mail, which (often by arrangement) are lightly and philatelically cancelled. Receiving offices send these stamps to a central depot or company head office, where they are sorted, packaged, and diverted to the stamp trade.

Controls. Marginal control letters and/or numbers appeared on sheets of British stamps from 1881 (the first stamp to be so treated being the Penny Lilac) until 1947, when they were superseded by cylinder numbers (q.v.). Stamps with the marginal control attached have an added value to specialists. Controls were references for accounting purposes, the figures being the last two of the year of issue and preceded by an index letter. On

'CONSTITUTION' SETS   CONTROLS

photogravure issues controls had bars below, to left and right, or all round, representing progressive periods during the year. These too are studied and collected.

Convention States. Indian states formerly in convention status with the Indian Empire: Chamba, Faridkot, Gwalior, Jind, Nabha, and Patiala, all of which are mentioned separately in this book. From 1884–7 onwards, each convention state had its own overprints on Indian stamps, which were valid for postage throughout the whole of India, as distinct from the native states which produced stamps in original designs valid only within the state of issue. In 1950 all the convention states' issues were replaced by normal Indian stamps without overprint.

Coo, also Cos.   See under 'Dodecanese Islands'.

Cook Islands.   Group of Pacific islands named after the explorer Captain James Cook, who discovered them in 1773; a native kingdom until 1901, when the islands were annexed to New Zealand. Stamps first issued, 1892. From 1919 to 1932 Cook Islands stamps were inscribed Rarotonga (the name of the principal island) though they continued to be used throughout the group. Two other islands, Aitutaki (from 1903) and Penrhyn (from 1902), had their own stamps until 1932. Niue, a further island in the group, used Cook Islands stamps until 1902, since when it has had its own issues. Area: 90 sq. m.; currency: Sterling; pop. (1961): 18,378.

Cook's Dispatch.   A local stamp of Baltimore, U.S.A., of 1853.

'Coralit'.   (Ital.). Corrièri Alta Italia. This railway express company organised a bicycle mail operating in northern Italy in 1944–5, and in May 1945 issued 'local' stamps sanctioned by the Allied Military Government.

Cordoba, also Cordova.   Province of Argentina which issued its own stamps from 1858 to 1865.

Corea.   See 'Korea'.

Corfu.   One of the Ionian Islands, part of Greece since 1864. Corfu has twice been occupied by Italy—in 1923, during a dispute with Greece, when Italian stamps were overprinted for use in the island, and again in 1941, when Greek stamps were overprinted. The latter were superseded later the same year by the Italian occupation issue for all the Ionian Islands. Greek stamps were re-introduced in 1943.

COOK ISLANDS   COREA   CORREOS

Corisco. See under 'Elobey, Annobon, and Corisco'.

Cork Cancellers. Have been used by many early postal administrations, U.S.A., Canada, St. Helena, etc. The applied end of the corks were cut into fanciful designs, initials, figures, stars, etc., or simply incised with straight cuts. More durable types were cut from wood, hard rubber, and metal.

CORK CANCELLERS: FROM U.S.A.   FROM ST. HELENA

Corner Letters. See 'Check letters'.

Cornwell/Post Office, Madison Square. Inscription on a New York 'local' of 1856.

Coroco. Stamps so inscribed are said to be publicity labels to advertise Arthur Bray's fantasy 'The Clue of the Postage Stamp' in the nineties.

Coromina. Bartolomeo Coromina is credited with having inscribed the famous 1850 6 cuartos black of Queen Isabella of Spain direct on to the litho stone from which it was printed. He engraved the dies of the subsequent 1851, 1852 stamps of Spain.

Coros. Collectors of Religion on Stamps. U.S.A. organisation centred on Davenport, Iowa.

Corps Expéditionnaire Franco-Anglais Cameroun. See 'Cameroons'.

Correos. (Span.). Posts; Correos franco = post paid.

Correo Interior. (Span.). Inland posts. 1853 issue of Spain, bearing the arms of Madrid. Issues bearing the head of Isabella II, 1859–63, were for use in the Philippine Islands.

Correios. (Port.). Posts.

Correspondencia Urgente. (Span.). Urgent correspondence. On Express Letter stamps of Spain.

CÔTE D'IVOIRE   COSTA RICA   CÔTE FRANÇAISE
                                          DES SOMALIS

Corrientes. Province of Argentina with its own locals 1856–80. The design chosen was a close copy of the early 'Ceres' stamps of France. See 'Plagiarism'.

Cos, or **Coo.** See 'Dodecanese Islands'.

Costa Atlantica. (Span.). The Atlantic coast. O/p on stamps of Nicaragua 1907. See 'Cabo', and 'Zelaya' also.

Costa Rica. Central American republic. Its first stamps appeared in 1863. Area: 19,695 sq. m.; pop. (1962): 1,302,829; capital: San José; language: Spanish; currency: 1852, 8 reales = 1 peso; 1881, 100 centavos = 1 peso; 1900, 100 centimos = 1 colón.

Côte d'Ivoire. (Fr.). Ivory Coast (q.v.).

Côte Française des Somalis. French Somali Coast (q.v.).

'Cotton Reels'. The first (1850) circular typeset issues of British Guiana were so nicknamed on account of their similarity to the conventional labels on reels of sewing cotton.

Counani. Bogus issues of an Amazonian 'republic' formed by the self-styled 'President' in 1886, and who issued these stamps for a non-existent postal service.

Counterfeit Stamps are those that have been unofficially and fraudulently imitated and copied, with a view to their being passed off as genuine. They are usually referred to as forgeries (q.v.).

Counterfoil. Stamps with counterfoils, as distinct from coupons (see below), have been issued. The Kotelnich (Russia) and Drammen (Norway) locals had them, and the modern parcel post issues of Italy and San Marino can also be classed as stamps with counterfoils.

Coupon. A label attached to a postage stamp carrying a slogan, propaganda matter, or related device to the design on the stamp, or other feature, and which in itself has no postal validity. They have been used by Austria, Czechoslovakia, Italy, etc.

Courbould, Edward Henry, R.I. Son of Henry Courbould (above). 1815–1905. Designer of some of the early British Colonial stamps, including the 'Britannia' types for Mauritius.

Courbould, Henry, F.S.A., 1787–1844, whose drawing of the head of Queen Victoria from the 'Wyon' (q.v.) medal, was the basis of design for G.B.'s 1d. black of 1840. Perkins is reputed to have paid him £12 for the finished drawing.

Cour Permanente de Justice Internationale. (Fr.). The Permanent Court of International Justice, The Hague, Netherlands. O/p on stamps of the Netherlands (when the Court is sitting) for use on its official mail since 1934. Later amended to 'Cour Internationale De Justice'. See also 'League of Nations'.

Courier Mail. East Germany issued four stamps in 1947 for sealing confidential official correspondence. Mauve, with large white letters 'DDR' they are o/p 'Zentraler Kurierdienst'. Departments receiving them must destroy the stamps. Collectors cannot buy them, and possession renders one liable to five years' imprisonment—in Eastern Germany! Both mint and used copies have been seen in London.

Courrier De La Société Des Nations. See 'League of Nations'.

Court Bureau. A series of 'locals' printed in red with values from 1d. to 6s. was issued in London in 1890 to prepay services rendered by a limited company which undertook to collect Sunday mail from London clubs and hotels to terminal railroad stations, or for posting in suburban offices so as to effect delivery first post on Mondays. The company ceased operations in 1891, and the stamps are rare—even in unused condition.

Cover. Any type of covering for any kind of matter sent through the post; in practice, usually an envelope. The meaning is often extended to include newspaper wrappers and letter-sheets.

Cowries. Small seashells (*Cyproea moneta*) used from time immemorial as currency in India and Africa. The first stamps of Uganda Protectorate in 1895 were typewritten, and values were expressed in the local 'coinage' —cowries.

Crash cover. A cover salvaged after an air crash, usually with an appropriate endorsement indicating the circumstances.

Crawford, K.T., The Earl of. President of the Royal Philatelic Society, London, 1910, a famous collector whose U.S.A. and British fully annotated collections (in particular) made philatelic history. His philatelic library was extensive and unique.

Crawford Medal. Silver-gilt medal awarded by the Royal Philatelic Society, London, for the most valuable and original contribution to the study and knowledge of philately published during the two years preceding the award. The period of two years to run from January 1st to December 31st. Such contribution may consist of: (*a*) a book, article, or

CRETE   CROATIA   CROWN WATERMARKS

series of articles on the stamps of a country, group of countries, one or more issues of a country, or a single stamp. (*b*) a book, article, or series of articles on any subject of philatelic interest. This medal is open to world-wide competition, and shall be awarded annually if, in the opinion of the Council, there has been during such period of two years any contribution which merits such recognition. In the case of joint authorship the Council shall award a medal to each author.

Creased Stamps. Have a depreciated value. If the paper fibres are unbroken and intact, a crease may be rendered almost invisible and even completely removed by dampening and ironing with a moderately warm iron.

Cressman & Co.'s Penny Post. Was established in Philadelphia, U.S.A., in 1856 for which one-cent 'locals' were issued.

Crete. Mediterranean island, formerly Turkish. In the nineteenth century a movement sprang up in favour of union with Greece. Greek forces landed on the island in 1897, but the leading European powers intervened and occupied Crete with an international force. Both British and Russian occupying forces issued stamps between 1898 and 1900. An autonomous government was then set up under nominal Turkish suzerainty, producing its own stamps from 1900. In 1908 union with Greece was proclaimed, and Cretan stamps overprinted *ΕΛΛΑΣ*, but this was not finally achieved until 1913. Since that year Greek stamps have been in use. See also under 'British Post Offices in Crete'. Area: 3,235 sq. m.; capital: Canea; currency: as Greece; pop. (1961): 483,258.

Crevichon. See under 'Jethou'.

Crimea. South Russian peninsula. During the Crimean campaign of 1854–7 special Army Field Post cancellers were in use on the stamps of G.B. used to frank the mail of the British troops. It is now a soviet republic within the U.S.S.R., but the anti-Bolshevik Kuban Government o/p 'Arms' types of Royalist Russia for use in the Crimea 1918–20. The scene of very heavy fighting in World War II. Area: 23,312 sq. m.; pop. (est. 1950): 1,127,000.

Croatia (Hrvatska). A region of the Austro-Hungarian Empire until 1918, now part of Yugoslavia. There was a series of overprints for Croatia

84

on Hungarian stamps in 1918, but these are listed among the eaily issues of Yugoslavia. The only distinctive issues for Croatia were those of the puppet government set up under the German occupation of 1941–5. Apart from these, Yugoslav stamps, have been in use. At intervals since 1951 bogus Croatian stamps, produced by a group of exiles, have appeared on the market. Area: 16,920 sq. m.; capital: Zagreb; currency: 1941, 100 para = 1 dinar; 1941–4, 100 banica = 1 kuna; pop. (1961): 4,159,696.

Crociera Italiana 1924. O/p on stamps of Italy used on an Italian cruiser, on a South American trade and propaganda tour 1924.

Croissant Rouge Turc. (Fr.). Turkish Red Cross.

Crosby's City Post. A local post in New York City 1870–1, for which 2 ¢ carmine imperf. stamps were issued.

Cross Posts. The introduction of cross posts, under an Act of 1711, was the first great reform in the history of the British Post Office. In the seventeenth century the postal system was organised in six great post roads, each administered separately with its own by-posts. At this time cross-country posts did not exist; a letter for a destination not in the network of the post road on which it started had to go into London and then out again on the other road. Even a letter from Bristol to Plymouth, for example, had to travel via London instead of direct. To overcome this, cross posts were set up to provide direct cross-country links between one road and another, designed to speed up the mails by avoiding London. Letters carried by the cross posts were known as 'cross road letters'.

Crown Agents. The full title is the Crown Agents for Oversea Governments and Administrations (formerly known as the Crown Agents for the Colonies), of 4 Millbank, London S.W.1. The Crown Agents act for the governments of numerous territories of the British Commonwealth in selling current stamps to dealers in many parts of the world. They also operate a sales bureau in Washington. The Crown Agents publish a monthly stamp bulletin giving details of new and forthcoming issues.

'Crown' Keytypes. A Portuguese colonial stamp design with a crown as its central motif, was issued for Angola in 1870; was amended for Cape Verde 1877; and inscribed for other colonies.

Crown Watermarks. Many of the monarchical countries have used this regal emblem as a watermark, and the very first adhesive stamp of them all, the 1d. black of G.B., bore it. There have been at least six distinct variations of design of this G.B. watermark: the 'small' crown of 1840; the 'large' of 1855 in two designs; the 'Imperial' of 1880; the 'formal' (with Royal Cipher) of 1912 and on, the 'Tudor' and 'St. Edward', and the present design. The crown of St. Stephen, showing the bent cross, was a watermark of Hungary 1898–1908. Italy used the crown of Savoy as a mark 1863–1915; Greece had a simple crown over initials 1901–5; the letter 'A' over a crown has been used by Australia; it appears in conjunction with the letters 'CC' and 'CA' on British Colonial stamps;

and even Sarawak used what is known as the 'Oriental' crown in its 1932 issues. A collection of crown watermarks could be very interesting indeed.

Cruz Roja Española. Spanish Red Cross.

Cruz Vermelha Portuguesa. Portuguese Red Cross.

Cuba. Island in the West Indies, a former Spanish colony under United States administration 1898–1902 and since then an independent republic. Stamps were first issued in 1855, the early issues being for use also in Puerto Rico. The 1873 issue was the first for use in Cuba alone, although the stamps continued to be inscribed 'Ultramar' ('Overseas') until 1877, when stamps inscribed 'Cuba' appeared for the first time. During the Spanish-American War of 1898 Cuba was occupied by the United States, and American stamps overprinted for use in Cuba were issued for a time in 1899. Area: 44,206 sq. m.; capital: Havana; currency: 1855, 8 reales de plata fuerte = 1 peso; 1866, 100 centesimos = 1 escudo (or peseta from 1871); 1881, 1,000 milesimas = 100 centavos = 5 pesetas = 1 peso; 1898, 100 cents = 1 dollar; 1899, 100 centavos = 1 peso; pop. (est. 1961): 6,900,000.

Cubierta. Large label affixed to certain South American insured letters. Not strictly a postage stamp, and therefore not generally listed.

Cúcuta. Colombia, South America. It had its own provisionals for local use 1900–6. Pop. about 50,000.

Cuernavaca. District of Mexico which had a local provisional issue in 1867. Genuine examples are among the rarest of Mexican provisionals.

Cumming's City Post. Operated in New York, U.S.A., in 1845 and issued local stamps.

Cundinamarca. Department of Colombia, which issued its own stamps 1870–1904. Area: 8,674 sq. m.; pop. (est. 1962): 2,121,680; capital: Bogota; currency: 100 centavos = 1 peso.

Curaçao. Dutch island colony in the West Indies. Stamps thus inscribed, first issued in 1873, were used throughout the Dutch West Indies, comprising Curaçao, Bonaire, and Aruba (off the Venezuela coast), and Saba, St. Eustatius, and part of St. Martin in the Leeward Islands. In 1948 the group became an autonomous part of the Netherlands, and was renamed Netherlands Antilles (Nederlandse Antillen), stamps thus inscribed replacing those of Curaçao in 1950. Area: 366 sq. m.; capital: Willemstad on Curaçao Island; currency: as Netherlands; pop. (1963): 199,607.

'Curly Head'. Spanish Colonial keytype depicting the youthful King Alfonso XIII in 1898 (then about 12 years old), his curly locks being responsible for the title.

Current Issues. Those at present in use.

Cut-out. An impressed or embossed stamp cut from the item of postal

CURAÇAO   CZECHOSLOVAKIA   CYPRUS

stationery or other material of which it formed part. The word is used as a noun.

Cut Square.   Imperforate stamps of any design other than rectangular or square, cut from the sheets with the corners of the paper left intact; i.e. not cut to the shape of the design. Cut-square stamps are worth more than stamps cut to shape. The term is sometimes wrongly used to denote a cut-out, see above.

Cutting's Despatch Post.   A local mail delivery, and stamp, of Baltimore, U.S.A., 1847.

Cuzco.   District of Peru which overprinted Arequipa revenue stamps for postage 1881–5.

Cylinder Numbers.   Photogravure (or rotogravure) rotary cylinders are each numbered as they are put into use, and the numbers record themselves on the margins of sheets of stamps of G.B. Two sheets are normally printed side by side, one of which has a dot (or full stop) after the number.

Cyprus.   Mediterranean island, formerly Turkish, administered by Great Britain from 1878 to 1960, and now an independent republic within the British Commonwealth. The first Cyprus stamps were British issues overprinted, which appeared in 1880; they were followed in 1881 by the first definitives. Prior to this, however, the stamps of Austrian Levant were used at the Austrian post office at Larnaca, opened in 1845 and closed following the establishment of a British protectorate. British stamps without overprint were used at various towns in Cyprus between 1878 and 1881. Area: 3,572 sq. m.; capital: Nicosia; currency: 1880–1, sterling; 1881, 40 paras = 1 piastre, 180 piastres = £1; 1955, 1,000 mills = £1; pop. (est. 1962): 584,000. Since 1960 Cyprus stamps have been unusual in showing the name of the country in three languages—Greek, Turkish, and English.

Cyrenaica.   'See Cirenaica'.

Cyrillic.   The Cyrillic alphabet was adapted from the ancient Greek by St. Cyril, apostle to the Slavs, who is shown on three stamps issued by Czechoslovakia on 21 July 1935 (S.G. Nos. 342–4), with St. Methodius.

With modifications the alphabet is used by Russia, Bulgaria, and Yugoslavia (formerly by Serbia and Montenegro) and their stamps have Cyrillic inscriptions.

Cyrillic		English equivalents	Cyrillic		English equivalents
А	а	A a	Р	р	R r
Б	б	B b	С	с	S s
В	в	V v	Т	т	T t
Г	г	G g	У	у	U u
Д	д	D d	Ф	ф	Ph, ph, F f
Е	е	E e, Ye ye	Х	х	Kh kh
Ж	ж	Zh zh	Ц	ц	Ts ts
З	з	Z z	Ч	ч	Ch ch
И	и	I i	Ш	ш	Sh sh
І	і	I i	Щ	щ	Shch shch
Й	й	I i	Ы	ы	Y y
К	к	K k	Э	э	E e
Л	л	L l	Ю	ю	Yu yu
М	м	M m	Я	я	Ya ya
Н	н	N n	Ѳ	ѳ	Th th, F f
О	о	O o			
П	п	P p			See also Appendix II

Czechoslovakia (Cesko-Slovensko). Formerly part of the Austro-Hungarian Empire, an independent republic from 1918 to 1939 and again since 1945. Prior to independence Austrian issues were in use (in Slovakia those of Hungary from 1871). The first issue of the republic was the Scouts' Post stamps of October 1918, issued by the Revolutionary Committee in Prague and so called because Boy Scouts acted as postmen to deliver the first mails. The first definitives followed in December of the same year. In 1939 the country was invaded by Nazi Germany and divided into two puppet states—Bohemia and Moravia, and Slovakia—each of which had its own issues until 1945 when the Czechoslovak republic was re-established. Area: 49,381 sq. m.; capital: Prague (Praha); currency: 100 haleru = 1 koruna; pop. (est 1963): 13,970,000. The Czechoslovak army in Siberia had its own stamps in 1919–20.

Czechoslovak Army in Siberia. This epic trek has its place in philately by reason of the stamps issued by this army in 1919–20, and which have been accorded recognition and catalogue status.

Czernavoda. See 'Kustendje'.

Cyrillic

'C' is the equivalent of the English letter 'S', thus:

C.C.C.P.: = S.S.S.R., which we translate as U.S.S.R. = Russia
СРБИЈА = Serbia

88

C.X.C.   = S.H.S. (Serbs, Croats and Slovenes) on 1918 issues
          of Yugoslavia
СТОТИНКИ   = Stotinki—unit of Bulgarian currency
САНТ or САНТИМ = Cent, or Centime (Bulgaria 1879).

 There is no letter C in Greek—the K or hard 'C', and the X (chi).

A 'CUT SQUARE'

DANMARK   'DEATH MASK'   DANZIG

D

'D'. Overprinted on the SCADTA semi-official airmails of Colombia, the capital letter indicates that the stamp is a consular overprint sold in Denmark.

D.B.P. In script monogram was the o/p on Russian 'Arms' types of stamps of the Far Eastern Republic 1919–20.

D.B.S.R. Danube and Black Sea Railway. See 'Kustendje'.

D.D.R. Deutsche Demokratische Republik (East Germany).

D.E.I. Dutch (Netherlands) East Indies.

DJ. Djibouti. O/p on stamps of Obock, 1894.

D.M. (Dienst Marke). O/p on official stamps of Danzig, 1921–2.

D.O.X. See 'DO-X' below.

D.R.L.S. Despatch rider letter service.

D.Y. Demir Yol (Turk.). Railroad.

Dahomey. Former French territory in West Africa, originally known as Benin. Dahomey's first stamps appeared in 1899, replacing the earlier Benin issues. From 1945 to 1959 Dahomey used stamps of French West Africa (q.v.), but in 1960 became an independent republic within the French Community and issued its own stamps once more. Area: 44,290 sq. m.; capital: Porto Novo; currency: French C.F.A.; pop. (1961): 2,050,000.

Dai Nippon. Empire of Japan. Occupation stamps of conquered territories in the Pacific and Malaya, etc., were frequently o/p with these words and the year in Japanese notation, with or without 'chops' (q.v.), thus: Dai Nippon 2602 = 'Japanese Empire 1942'.

Dala. (Hawaiian). Dollar.

Dalmatia (Zara region). Former Italian enclave in Yugoslavia, occupied by Italy 1921–2 when a set of surcharges on Italian stamps was issued. Now part of Yugoslavia. Area: 4,916 sq. m.; chief town: Sibenik; currency: 100 centesimi = 1 corona.

Dandy Roll. Trade designation of the wire-gauze roller which bears upon the paper pulp as it leaves the vats, and which gives to the finished product its impressed design or characteristics, which are called 'wove' or 'laid' according to the roller's pattern. It is upon this roll that the 'bits' which form the watermarks are woven or soldered. See 'Bits', 'Laid', 'Wove', 'Watermarks', etc.

Danish West Indies. The islands of St. Thomas, St. Croix, and St. John, former Danish territories which issued stamps from 1855 to 1917, when they were purchased by the United States of America, whose stamps and currency are now used. They are now known as the United States Virgin Islands. Area: 133 sq. m.; pop. (1950): 26,665; capital: Charlotte Amalie on St. Thomas; currency: 1855 and since 1917, 100 cents = 1 dollar; 1905–17, 100 bit = 1 franc.

Danmark. See 'Denmark'.

Dansk Vestindien. Danish West Indies. (See above.)

Danube Steam-Packet Company. An Austrian company which handled mail for the Levant before the Danubian states organised their own posts. Local stamps were issued from 1866 to 1871, which were reprinted in 1877 and are found imperf. and perf. 10. Originals were perf. 12 and 9½.

Danville. Virginia, U.S.A. One of the Confederate towns with a 'Post-masters' ' issue during the American Civil War.

Danzig. Former Free State, under the League of Nations, on the Baltic, comprising the seaport and its immediate district. First stamp issues were German o/p 'Danzig' in 1920, with definitives following in 1921 to 1939, when the territory was again re-absorbed into Germany. The Polish post office issued stamps o/p 'Port Gdansk' 1925–39, and a definitive set commemorating the 20th anniversary of Polish independence in 1938. Area: 754 sq. m.; pop. (1939): about 407,000; currency: 1920, 100 pfennige = 1 mark; 1923, 100 pfennige = 1 gulden.

Dardanelles. Entrance to the Sea of Marmora from the Mediterranean. Russia o/p stamps for use in her post offices there in about 1910.

Darmstadt Label. Name given to a proof of South Africa's 1d. Riebeeck's Ship stamp made on paper watermarked with a floral design; made by a German firm to demonstrate a new process to the South African government. In some manner, copies have appeared on the market, but are accepted as authorised.

'Dateds . See 'Precancels'.

Datia. Duttia. (q.v.).

Davis's Penny Post. A Baltimore, U.S.A., 'local' of 1852.

Day of the Stamp. F.I.P. (Federation Internationale de Philatelie) at its 1936 Luxembourg conference decided that any affiliated country should celebrate 'The Day of the Stamp' on one Sunday each year. Several countries do so, with exhibitions, special issues, and cachets. Switzerland, for example, has chosen the first Sunday in December each year.

Dealers. See 'Stamp Dealers'.

'Death Mask' Stamps. Name given to the Serbian commemorative series of 1904 marking the centenary of the Karageorgevich dynasty and the coronation of King Peter I. They are so called because when the stamp is turned upside down the sombre features of the previous monarch, King Alexander Obrenovich V, are revealed between those of Karageorge and Peter. Alexander, last ruler of the Obrenovich faction, had been assassinated in the previous year; it was his death that cleared the way for the return of the Karageorgevich dynasty. In the turbulent Balkans of the time the stamps caused a political sensation. The stamp design was engraved by the famous French designer, Eugéne Mouchon. He strenuously denied that the effect was intentional, and it is hard to believe that he could have been involved in Serbian political intrigue. But if indeed the effect was accidental, it was certainly an extraordinary coincidence.

Debreczin (Debrecen). Hungary. Romania occupied it and issued o/p Hungarian occupation stamps for this important city and railway junction in 1919–20, when they overthrew the Bolshevik government established by Bela Kun in 1919.

Deccan. India. See 'Hyderabad'.

Decimal provisionals. This term is usually taken to refer to the provisional surcharges applied to the stamps of Basutoland, Bechuanaland, and Swaziland on the introduction of decimal currency on the South African pattern in 1961.

Deckle-Edged. A wavy, thinned, and often voluted edge, a characteristic of hand-made paper, but also found on the two outer edges of some machine-made papers, being caused by the 'deckle' straps which confine the pulp within bounds.

Dedeagatch, also Dedegatz, Dédéagh. Former Turkish seaport, now part of Greece. A French post office was opened there in 1874 and continued to operate until August 1914. At first ordinary French stamps were in use, but from 1893 stamps overprinted or inscribed Dédéagh were provided. In 1912 the town was occupied by the Bulgarians, but they were driven out in the following year by the Greeks, who issued their own occupation stamps, mostly Greek stamps overprinted. The town was subsequently restored to Bulgaria, but was ceded to Greece after the First World War.

Deficit. (Span.). Postage dues of Peru are so endorsed.

Definitive. A stamp intended for normal everyday postal use, usually put on sale for an indefinite period, as distinct from a provisional, commemorative, or charity stamp.

D'Haïti. Of Haïti or Hayti. The Republic of Haïti. See 'Haïti'.

De la Ferté. Jean Ferdinand Joubert, 1810 (Paris)–1884. Engraver to De La Rue & Co., London. Engraved dies for G.B., British Columbia, Vancouver Island, Belgium (1865), Ceylon, Hong Kong, India, Italy, etc.

De La Rue. Messrs. De La Rue & Co., Ltd., of London, England. A famous stamp printing and publishing firm.

De León. See 'León'.

Deming's Penny Post. Local stamps so inscribed were used by a mail service operating in Frankford, Penn., U.S.A., in 1854.

Demonetised. A stamp is said to have been demonetised when the issuing authority has declared that it is no longer valid for the prepayment of postage. In some cases, for example certain modern commemoratives, the period of validity is announced in advance at the time of issue, but usually stamps remain postally valid long after they have been withdrawn from sale at the post offices. Thus all the Queen Victoria stamps of Great Britain were demonetised as from 30 June 1915, and those of King Edward VII as from 31 March 1930.

Denikin. General Denikin's Volunteer Army issues. See: 'South Russia'.

Denmark (Danmark). North European kingdom. Stamps first issued, 1851. For the first thirteen years all Denmark's stamps were square in shape, and are noted for their burelage (q.v.). Area: 16,577 sq. m.; capital: Copenhagen (København). currency: 1851, 96 rigsbank skilling (R.B.S.) = 1 rigsbank daler; 1854, 92 skilling = 1 rigsdaler; 1875, 100 øre = 1 krone; pop. (est.' 1962): 4,636,700. See also under 'Faröe Islands'.

Denomination. The inscribed value of a stamp.

Departmental Stamps. Official stamps designated for use by one particular government department only, as distinct from general Official use. Among the countries which formerly issued them are Great Britain, United States, and South Australia.

Derechos de firma. (Span.). Duty on acknowledgments. Fiscal stamps so inscribed did postal duty in the Philippine Islands under Spanish rule.

Des. Design, or Designed by.

Despatch Post. Several U.S.A. 'locals' are so inscribed, notably: Hampton's, Harris's, Johnson's, Mearis's, Mills', all of which see.

De-sulphurisation. Some of the inks used in stamp printing tend to become iridescent, or darkened by being sulphurised or oxydised with age and exposure to gas or other fumes. To de-sulphurise, immerse the specimen in clean water until limp, then treat with dilute hydrogen peroxide, applying the chemical with a brush, the stamp being first laid on damp, clean white blotting paper. When the desired result has been achieved, wash thoroughly to remove all traces of the peroxide. This treatment tends to render the paper flabby and cannot be applied to 'anilines', or to 'mint' specimens without risk of damaging the gum. See also 'Cleaning stamps', 'Boiling', etc.

Deutsche Bundespost. Inscription on issues of the German Federal Republic (West Germany) and of West Berlin (q.v.).

Deutsche Demokratische Republik. German Democratic Republic— East Germany under Russian domination.

DEUTSCHES REICH   'DIADEM'   DIENST

Deutsche Post. Inscription on various post-war German issues. At various times it has appeared on stamps of West Germany, East Germany, and West Berlin.

Deutsches Reich. 'The German State'. Inscription on most German stamps up to 1945.

Deutsch Militärverwaltung Kotor. German Military Government, Kotor. See 'Boka Kotorska'.

Deutsch-Neu-Guinea. German New Guinea. See 'New Guinea'.

Deutsch-Ostafrika. German East Africa.

Deutsch-Österreich. German Austria. See 'Austria'.

Deutsch-Sudwestafrika. German South West Africa (q.v.).

Dhar. Former feudatory native state of British India, with its own internal issues 1897–1901. It then used stamps of British India. Area: 1,798 sq. m.; pop. (1952): 253,210; Indian currency.

Diadem. The circlet of gold and jewels forming Queen Victoria's head-dress on many of the earlier stamp issues of her reign, and on many of the portrait issues of Queen Elizabeth II. The 1897 Jubilee issues of Canada illustrate the distinction between the diadem of 1837 and the crown of 1897.

Diamond Roulette. See 'Lozenge roulette'.

Dickinson Paper. John Dickinson, founder of the famous British paper-making firm, patented in 1830 a security banknote paper containing long silk transverse threads which could be so arranged and devised that one or more ran through each individual note. This was adapted for stamp printing, and was used also for the 1841 G.B. embossed envelopes as well as for the 1847–54 embossed Somerset House 10d. and 1s. stamps; and by Switzerland and Bavaria. The invention was rejected by the British Post Office for the other issues of G.B. as it was contended that partition by cutting with scissors, etc., would result in the withdrawal of the threads, and thus defeat the object aimed at.

Die. The piece of metal or other material on which the original design of the stamp is engraved or otherwise applied, and which is subsequently multiplied to form the plate from which the stamps are printed. When more than one die is used to produce a particular issue, the differences are often sufficiently noticeable to become collectable varieties. For example the Queen Victoria colonial head-plate is catalogued from two dies; the King George V colonial head-plate from four.

Die Proof. A proof or trial impression taken directly from the die (q.v.).

Diégo Suarez. Former French colony on the coast of Madagascar, which had its own stamps from 1890 until 1896, when they were replaced by the issues of Madagascar.

Dienst. (Ger. and Dutch). Official (or municipal) service. Dienstmarke = Official stamp; dienstsache = official matter.

Diligencia. A type of mail or stage coach (Spanish). The word appears on the first stamps of Uruguay to indicate the means by which the mail was carried.

Dinero. Early Peruvian coin. Value expressed on 1858–62 issues of Peru.

Disinfected Mail. From the fourteenth to the early nineteenth century it was common practice in many parts of Europe to disinfect mail which had originated in or passed through an area considered to be disease-infested, particularly the Middle East. This was done by fumigating the letters through slits cut in them, or by splashing or even immersion in vinegar. Each country had its quarantine stations through which all mail from abroad had to pass. The system was in use in Britain from about 1671 to 1850. Various disinfection markings were applied to mail thus treated, but these are not postal markings in the true sense since they were the responsibility of the public health authorities and not the Post Office. In the light of modern medical knowledge the practice of disinfecting mail in this manner is now known to have been almost completely point-less, but letters which show signs of disinfection are keenly studied and collected by postal history enthusiasts.

Distinguished Philatelists, Roll of. See 'R.D.P.'.

Dividing Marks. Circular floral ornaments on Perkins, Bacon plates in 1851. Placed marginally between rows J and K, they were to facilitate halving the sheets of penny reds then in use. Modern stamps of G.B. have an arrow for the same purpose.

Djibouti. Red Sea port and capital of French Somali Coast. Stamps of Obock were overprinted for Djibouti in 1894, and the name of the port appeared on French Somali Coast issues from 1894 until 1902, and reap-peared on the 1938 issue.

Doar Ivri. (Heb.). Hebrew Post. Inscribed on Israel's first stamps.

Dockwra's London Penny Post. In 1680 William Dockwra, a merchant, set up as a private venture a postal service covering London and its suburbs. It was the first post to use postmarks indicating that postage had been prepaid. With its cheap, flat rates of postage and frequent deliveries

DJIBOUTI   DOMINICAL   DOPLATA (POLAND)
                   LABEL

it was a remarkable precursor of the postal systems of today. In 1682, when the service was becoming a commercial success, an action was brought against the proprietor for infringing the postal monopoly of the state. As a result the service was taken over by the Government. The early triangular 'Penny Post Paid' markings used by Dockwra's post and its state-operated successor are keenly sought by postal history enthusiasts.

Doctor-blade Flaws. In high-speed modern printing machines surplus ink is removed from the printing surface by a flexible steel blade, known as the doctor (or ductor) blade. This process can cause characteristic flaws on the printed stamps. For example, a piece of fine grit in the ink may be picked up by the blade, scratching a fine line on the cylinder. Until worked out this can cause a semi-constant flaw.

Documentary Stamps. Fiscals (q.v.) applied to official and business documents, or impressed thereon.

Dodecanese Islands. Island group in the Aegean (the name means 'Twelve Islands'). Formerly Turkish, they were occupied by Italy from 1912 to 1945, and are now part of Greece. In the Turkish-Italian war of 1912 the local Greek population assisted the Italian invasion in return for a promise of union with Greece, and stamps were prepared locally in anticipation of this event. These were, however, suppressed by the Italians, who issued their own stamps for the group instead. Most were Italian stamps overprinted 'Isole Italiane dell'Egeo' (Italian Aegean Islands), under which name they are usually catalogued. In addition, in the 1912–32 period, there were separate overprints for each of the following islands: Calimno (Calino), Carchi (Karki), Caso, Coo (Cos), Lero (Leros), Lipso (Lisso), Nisiro (Nisiros), Patmo (Patmos), Piscopi, Scarpanto, Simi, and Stampalia. Rhodes (Rodi), the largest island of the group, also had its own issues at various times between 1912 and 1935. In 1944–5 a German garrison was stationed in the Dodecanese, and Inselpost stamps were issued for their use. British forces then took over, and British stamps overprinted M.E.F. were in use until April 1947, when the islands were ceded to Greece who issued special overprinted stamps to mark the occasion. Since then the normal Greek stamps have been in use. The population of the group in 1961 was 122,346.

'Dom Pedros'. Name given to certain of the early issues of Brazil with the portrait of Emperor Dom Pedro, especially the issues of 1866–79.

Dominica. Island of the British West Indies, not to be confused with the Dominican Republic (see below). Stamps first issued, 1874. From 1890 to 1903 stamps of Dominica were replaced by those of the Leeward Islands. In the latter year Dominica started issuing its own stamps once more, but Leeward Islands issues continued in use concurrently until 1940, when the island was transferred to the Windward Islands administration. Between 1858 and 1860 British stamps were used at Roseau, being distinguishable by the 'A 07' cancellation. Area: 289 sq. m.; capital: Roseau; currency: 1874, Sterling; 1951, 100 cents = 1 B.W.I. dollar; pop. (1960): 59,916.

Dominical Label or Tablet. A small label attached by perforation to the foot of all Belgian stamps issued between 1893 and 1914, inscribed in French and Flemish 'Do not deliver on Sunday'. The label was part of a campaign to reduce the amount of postal work done on Sundays. These stamps should always be collected complete with label. By leaving the label intact the sender could indicate that Sunday delivery was not desired.

Dominican Republic (Republica Dominicana, also San or Santo Domingo). West Indian republic occupying the eastern two-thirds of the island of Hispaniola, not to be confused with the British West Indian colony of Dominica, see above. Originally achieving independence in 1844, the Dominican Republic became a Spanish colony again from 1861 to 1865, and in this period the stamps of Spanish Cuba were in use. In the latter year the Spanish withdrew, independence was restored, and the country issued its own first stamps. British stamps were in use at Puerto Plata from 1868 to 1871, distinguishable by the 'C 86' cancellation, and again at Santo Domingo from 1876 to 1880 with the 'C 87' cancellation. Area: 18,700 sq. m.; capital: Santo Domingo (otherwise known as Ciudad Trujillo during the Trujillo dictatorship, 1936–61); currency: 1865, 8 reales = 1 peso; 1880 and since 1885, 100 centavos = 1 peso; 1883–5, 100 centimos = 1 franco, 5 franco = 1 peso; pop. (1960): 3,013,525.

Dominions. See 'Commonwealths'.

Don Government. See 'South Russia'.

Doplata. (Cyr. or Russian). To pay, or to collect. In Czech it takes the form of 'Doplatné'.

'Douane'. (Fr. and Afrik.). Customs. A revenue o/p on stamps of South Africa, to collect small sums payable as Customs duty on certain advertising matter. They are thus often found postally cancelled. Early issues can also be found o/p in red 'Customs Duty'.

'Double Genevas'. The 1843 cantonal issue of Geneva, Switzerland, so called because it consisted of 10 ¢. stamps printed in a curious double design, each half being usable as a 5 ¢. stamp.

Double-lined. Term applied to outline figures or letters, particularly those appearing as watermarks, in which the character is delineated in double lines.

Double Impression. A stamp in which some small part (or in rare cases the whole) of the design has been doubly printed.

Double Paper. A type of paper invented and patented by C. F. Steel in the U.S.A. about 1870, and consists of two thin sheets of differing character, substance, tint, or colour, cemented together. Designed to prevent forgery, erasure, and tampering, e.g. a 'security' paper (q.v.). It was (*vide* Gibbons) used for the printing of some of the 1873 issues of the U.S.A. There is a modern tendency to use the term for a double-*thick* paper, which makes for confusion.

Douglas' City Despatch. Stamps were issued by George H. Douglas of Broadway, New York, U.S.A., in 1879, in connection with his local mail service.

'Doves'. The famous Bâle (Basel or Basle) Swiss cantonal stamp issue of 1845.

DO-X. International registration mark or 'number' of the German Dornier, the first multi-engined plane to fly the Atlantic from West to East, in 1932. Newfoundland issued a specially o/p stamp to mark the occasion, in May 1932.

'Drop' Letter. (U.S.A.). One delivered from the same office where originally posted.

Dropped Letters. A typeset (letterpress) o/p in which one or more letters or pieces of type have dropped below the level of the remainder.

Drzava S.H.S. See 'Yugoslavia'. Territory of the Serbs, Hrvats (Croats), and Slovenes.

Dubai. Sheikhdom of Trucial Oman, on the Arabian coast south of the Persian Gulf. An Indian post office, opened in 1909 and using Indian stamps, provided the only postal service for many years. In 1948 the office became a British postal agency, employing British stamps surcharged with values in Indian currency which were also used in Muscat. In January 1961 these were replaced at Dubai by a new series of stamps inscribed 'Trucial States'. In June 1963 the British postal agency came to an end, the Trucial States stamps were withdrawn, and Dubai took over its own postal service, issuing its own stamps. Currency: As India; pop.: About 45,000.

Duc di Parma. Dukedom of Parma. See 'Parma'.

Due. (Ital.). Two. (Port.). Owing. Catalogue name given by Gibbons to Portuguese keytype used for colonial postage dues.

'Dues'. Postage due stamps.

Duitsch Oost Afrika/Belgische Bezetting. (Flem.). German East Africa/ Belgian Occupation.

DRZAVA SHS   DUPLEX POSTMARK   'DUES'

Dulac, Edmund. Born in Toulouse in 1882, became a British subject in 1912. His sculptured head portrait of King George VI was the basis of design for the 1937–52 stamps of G.B. He was also the artist responsible for the design of G.B.'s 1936 and 1953 1s. 3d. Coronation stamps, the Free French colonials, the 1944 French 'Marianne' design, and many others. He died in London in May 1953.

'Dumb'. A stamp or postmark is said to be 'dumb' when it bears no outward indication of the country or place of origin. Sometimes the term is extended to include stamps which bear no indication of the face value.

Duplex Postmarks. British double (or dual) obliterators which were in use from 1853 to 1906, usually consisted of an oval of bars, with or without an office number—the 'killer' (q.v.)—and the circular postmark bearing the name of the office of origin, the time and date of collection. They were devised to obliterate the stamp and yet to provide a legible postmark of origin—both on the one handstamp.

Duplicates. Copies identical with those already in one's collection. Such specimens should be carefully examined to ensure that they *are* duplicates in every respect as regards watermark, perforations, colour, or design. Such close inspection often reveals subtle differences which may prove of interest, and entitle the specimen to a place in the album as a major or minor variety.

Dupuy & Schenk Penny Post. 'Locals' issued in New York, U.S.A., 1846–8.

Dutch Guiana. See 'Surinam'.

Dutch East Indies. See 'Netherlands East Indies'.

Dutch New Guinea. See 'Netherlands New Guinea'.

Duttia (or Datia). Former feudatory native state of Central British India, with its own internal issues 1893–1921. Issued specimens were obliterated in blue by a circular canceller, a replica of the Maharajah's seal, with a figure of the Hindu divinity 'Ganesh' surrounded by a native inscription. Area: 846 sq. m; pop.: 174,072. Since 1921 Indian stamps have been used.

Duty Plate. Printing plate used for applying the inscriptions (name of country, face value, etc.) in the case of stamps partly printed from a keyplate (q.v.).

Cyrillic

Д: = The English 'D'.
ДРЖАВА СХС: Drzava S.H.S. (see above).
ДОПЛАТА: Doplata = Postage due.

Greek: The Delta (Δ).

ΔΡΑΧΜΑ: Drachma, Greek unit of currency = 100 lepta (ΛΕΠΤΑ).

E (ESCUDO)   E.E.F.   EAST AFRICA   EAST INDIA

E

'E'. Abbreviation for escudo, currency unit of Portugal and other countries. Preceded by the £ sign it indicates the Egyptian pound. Overprinted on Bavarian stamps of 1908 it signifies 'Eisenbahn behorden' (for the use of railway officials). On the SCADTA semi-official airmails of Colombia the capital letter indicates that the stamp is a consular overprint sold in Spain (España).

E.A.F. East African Forces. Stamps of G.B. thus o/p were in use by British troops in Somalia, and were first issued on 15 January 1943. They were superseded by B.M.A. o/ps in 1948.

E.C.A.F.E. Economic Commission for Asia and the Far East.

E.E.F. Egyptian Expeditionary Force. Stamps thus inscribed were first issued in February 1918 for use in the British-occupied parts of the Ottoman Empire in the Middle East. From 1920 they remained in use, suitably overprinted, under the civil administration in Palestine. They were not replaced until the first Palestine definitives appeared in 1927.

E.L.S. Express letter service.

E.U. Abbreviation for Estados Unidos (Spanish), meaning United States. The initials appear as part of the full country name on the stamps of certain Spanish-American countries. On the SCADTA semi-official airmails of Colombia, the letters indicate that the stamp is a consular overprint sold in the U.S.A.

Eagle City Post. Local stamps so inscribed were issued in Philadelphia, U.S.A., by W. Stait, 1848–50.

East Africa and Uganda. Stamps thus inscribed, first issued in 1903, superseded separate issues for British East Africa and for Uganda. They were in turn replaced in 1922 by stamps inscribed Kenya and Uganda.

East India. Stamps thus inscribed were for use throughout India. The apparently misleading inscription, introduced in 1855, was due to the fact that the territories concerned were administered up to 1858 by the Honourable East India Company. The practice continued until the 1882 issue, the first to appear after Queen Victoria assumed the title of Empress of India in 1877.

East Indies. See 'Netherlands East Indies'.

East River P.O. Local stamps issued by Clark & Wilson in New York, U.S.A., 1854–65.

East Silesia. A former Austrian crownland, was the subject of a League of Nations plebiscite in 1920, and issues of Czechoslovakia and of Poland were o/p 'S.O. 1920' during the interim period. The territory was eventually divided between Poland and Czechoslovakia through Teschen. Area: 1,987 sq. m.; pop. (1920): 680,422; the old capital was Troppau—now known as Opava.

Eastern Karelia. During the Finnish occupation, 1941–3, stamps of Finland were in use o/p 'ITA—KARJALA/Sot hallinto' = East Karelia Military Occupation. See 'Karelia'.

Eastern Roumelia. Former Turkish province, now part of Bulgaria. Turkish stamps o/p 'R.O.' and/or inscribed 'Roumelia Orientale' were issued 1880–5, when they were superseded by South Bulgarian issues, which in 1886, in turn, were replaced by those of Bulgaria. See 'South Bulgaria'.

Ecuador. South American republic. Stamps first issued, 1865. At the port of Guayaquil the stamps of Great Britain were used on overseas mail from 1865 to 1880 (with the 'C 41' cancellation) and from 1868 to 1875 French stamps also. Area: 116,270 sq. m.; capital: Quito; currency: 1865, 8 reales = 1 peso; 1881, 100 centavos = 1 sucre; pop. (est. 1963): 4,650,000.

Edwardian. Appertaining, in particular, to the stamps of the reign of King Edward the Seventh of Great Britain—22 January 1901 to 6 May 1910.

Eesti. Esthonia, or Estonia.

Efterporto. (Danish). After-paid. Postage due, Denmark.

Egeo. Aegean Islands (Italian); see 'Dodecanese Is'.

Egypt. Country of North Africa, formerly ruled by a khedive under nominal Turkish suzerainty. It became a British protectorate from 1914 to 1922, then an independent kingdom until a republic was established in 1953. Stamps were first issued in 1866. Succeeding issues, from 1867 to 1914, showed the Sphinx and Great Pyramid, and have been described as the first stamps to feature an historical subject. In 1958 Egypt joined with Syria to form the United Arab Republic (U.A.R.), each country continuing to issue its own stamps. In 1962 Syria left the U.A.R., but Egypt has retained the title and the initials continue to appear on Egyptian stamps. From 1860 to 1885 stamps of Great Britain were used at the British post offices at Alexandria (cancellation B 01) and Suez (cancellation B 02), and by the British Army Post Office in Egypt. French stamps were formerly

ECUADOR   EGYPT   EIRE

overprinted for use at the French post offices at Alexandria and Port
Said (q.v.). In its early days the Suez Canal Company (q.v.), also issued its
own local stamps. Area: 386,198 sq. m.; capital: Cairo; currency: 1866,
40 paras = 1 piastre; 1888, 1,000 milliemes (mills) = 100 piastres = £E1.
pop. (1960): 26,065,000.

Egyptian Occupation of Palestine. See 'Palestine'.

Egyptian Post Offices Abroad. Egypt formerly operated post offices in
various parts of the Ottoman Empire, in Ethiopia, Somaliland, and the
Sudan. They used the normal Egyptian stamps which can be identified only
by the postmarks. The earliest such offices, at Constantinople, Smyrna, and
Gedda (Djeddah, Saudi Arabia), were opened as early as 1865. All had
been closed by 1885.

Egyptiennes. Egyptian.

Eighth Avenue Post Office. A local stamp issued by James Price, New
York, U.S.A., 1852.

Eire. Republic comprising all Ireland except most of Ulster (Northern
Ireland). Formerly part of the United Kingdom (using British stamps)
it was granted dominion status as the Irish Free State in 1922. Since 1949
the official title has been Republic of Ireland. The first stamps issued in
February 1922 were British issues overprinted, followed later in the year
and in 1923 by the first definitives. Area: 27,137 sq. m.; capital: Dublin;
currency: sterling; pop. (1961): 2,818,341.

Electro. Electrotype. A copper-faced printing block, duplicated from an
original line or half-tone block.

Elima. (Hawaiian). Five.

Elobey, Annobon, and Corisco. Spanish island colonies off the west coast
of Africa, which had their own stamps from 1903 to 1909. Previous to this
they used the stamps of Fernando Poo from 1868; from 1909 the stamps
of Spanish Guinea were in use. Elobey and Corisco now use the stamps of
Rio Muni; Annobon those of Fernando Poo. Area: 13¼ sq. m.; pop.
(1910): 2,950.

El Parlamento Español a Cervantes. Stamps issued on tercentenary of
death of Cervantes, for use by members of the Spanish Parliament.

El Salvador. See 'Salvador'.

Elsaz. (Ger.). Alsace.

Elua. (Hawaiian). Two.

Elusive. Term often used to denote a stamp not regarded as rare or expensive, but which seems difficult to find and may be scarcer than is generally thought.

Emblems. Watermark of the stamps of G.B. introduced in the 6d. and 1s. values of 1856, and consisting of two conventional roses (for England), a thistle (for Scotland) and a shamrock (for Ireland), normally forming a square. There was an error in which three roses appeared—the 'bit' (q.v.) for the thistle having been accidentally replaced by a rose; that constitutes a 'major variety' in this series. See 'Watermarks', etc.

Embossed. Raised, or in low relief. A process allied to printing, whereby the whole or part of a design is raised up out of the surface of the paper by means of a pair of dies, or a die and a matrix, one die bearing the convex (male) design, and the other being concave (female). The process has been used for the production of stamps in both plain ('blind') or colour embossing, and in G.B. and U.S.A. especially for the stamping of postal stationery. Examples of embossed stamps are Germany's issues 1872–5; Heligoland 1867–75; Gambia 1869; Italy 1862; Portugal 1853–84; Sardinia 1851–5; and G.B. 1847–54. In the main it has been the fashion for the portrait head to be plain or colourless, but there have been exceptions. The embossed Portuguese colonial issues of Luis 1870 give the 'Embossed' title to this keytype.

Emission. Issue (of postage stamps)—a word more commonly used in America.

Emory. Virginia, U.S.A. A Confederate town with its own postmaster's hand-stamped provisional in 1861.

Emp. Ottoman. Turkish Empire.

'Empire'. The 1853–70 issues of France, released during the reign of Emperor Napoleon III, are referred to as the 'Empire' issues—distinguished by the inscription 'Empire Franc', or 'Français'. The 1882 and subsequent issues of India are sometimes similarly described as they followed the declaration of Queen Victoria as Empress of India.

Empire City Dispatch. 'Locals' issued by J. Bevan & Son in New York City, U.S.A., in 1881.

Encased Stamps. See: 'Money, Stamps as'.

Encomiendas. (Span.). Encomendas postais (Port.): Parcels post. Parcel.

En Epargne. (Fr.). 'Engraving by removing the background to leave in relief those parts which are to take the ink and to form the design' (*Larousse*). Often applied to line blocks used in letterpress printing.

Eng. Usually means 'Engraved', but also employed for 'England'.

'EMPIRE'   'EMBOSSED'   ERROR

Engine-turned. Mechanically engraved by a lathe rose-engine which cuts in a rhythmic pattern. A machine-produced repetitive pattern of great intricacy and impeccable symmetry, which has been used as a background, or part of the design, of many postage stamps, from the 1d. black 1840 G.B. onwards, to make forgery difficult; and been previously used for the engraving of plates for banknotes.

Engraved. Usually implies line engraved. See 'Line Engraving'.

Engraver's Proof. See 'Proofs'.

Entire. A complete folded letter-sheet with the communication on the inside and name and address on the outside. Sometimes the meaning is extended to include covers of other kinds.

Entrega Especial. (Span.). Special delivery. Entrega Inmediata: Express delivery.

Eono. (Hawaiian). Six.

'Epaulettes.' Name given to Belgium's first issue of 1849, so called from the epaulettes shown on the uniform of King Leopold I, in contrast to the succeeding 1850 issue known as the 'Medallions' from the resemblance of the design to a framed medal in relief.

Epirus. Former Turkish territory on the Adriatic, now divided between Greece and Albania. After the Balkan wars of 1912–13 north Epirus was assigned to Albania, but was proclaimed independent in 1914—in anticipation of union with Greece—by a provisional government which issued its own stamps. The area was subsequently occupied by Greece, and in 1916 by the French and Italians. In the French zone Albanian stamps were issued with the inscription Republika Korce Shqipetare (Republic of Korytza, Albania). In 1940–1 Greece again occupied north Epirus in the course of driving back the Italian invaders, and issued occupation stamps.

Épreuves de Luxe. (Fr.). First-class or special proofs. Introduced in France in 1933 by l'Administration des Postes. Usually consist of die proofs centred on sheets of paper approx. 11 × 8 cm. An issue of from 60 to 110 copies of new stamps is printed and copies distributed to high officials.

Equatorial Africa, French. See 'French Equatorial Africa'.

Eritrea. Former Italian colony in north-east Africa. Italian post offices were establshed at Assab and Massawa in 1885, using stamps of Italian

Post Offices Abroad. In 1890 all the Italian possessions on the Red Sea coast were united in the new colony of Eritrea, which issued its own stamps for the first time in 1893. Most subsequent issues until 1930 consisted of Italian stamps overprinted. In 1938 the colony was incorporated in Italian East Africa, and used the stamps of that territory until 1942. In that year, on the capitulation of the Italians, stamps of Great Britain overprinted M.E.F. came into use, to be replaced in 1948 by more British stamps overprinted B.M.A. (and subsequently B.A.) Eritrea. Since 1952 Eritrea has formed part of Ethiopia, and has used the stamps of that country. Area: 48,300 sq. m.; capital: Asmara; currency: as Italy; pop. (est. 1951): 1,000,000.

Error. Any major mistake in the design or production of a stamp. Examples are stamps printed in the wrong colour, on the wrong paper, or with the wrong watermark; stamps with the centre or frame inverted, or with part of the design missing altogether. Overprints, too, have been the subject of many errors. Errors of design are a fascinating subject, deserving a book to themselves. Fiji, for instance, has depicted a native canoe at sea with no-one aboard; Australia put the wrong portrait on a stamp commemorating an explorer; a Newfoundland stamp erroneously described Sir Francis Bacon as Lord Bacon. Among many others a surprising number of spelling mistakes are on record which escaped detection until after the stamp had been released. Minor variations in the actual printing are sometimes wrongly described as errors when they are in fact varieties.

Erste K.K. Pr. Donau Dampschiffahrt. Private issues of the Danube Steam-Packet Company, 1866–71.

Escudo. Unit of currency in Portugal and elsewhere.

Escuelas. (Span.). Schools. Stamps of Venezuela 1879–82 and 1887, which were primarily fiscals, or revenue issues to raise funds for the support of public schools, were used for postal purposes during a shortage of the regular stamps. The inscription was later altered to 'Instrucción' (Teaching), and the same general remarks apply to these issues also. The 1919 Brasil 'Instruccio' set had a similar history.

Esmeraldas. Province of Ecuador with a control mark as o/p on contemporary issues of 1902.

España, also Republica Española. Spain.

Essay. Literally, an attempt; in philately, a proposed stamp design submitted to the postal authorities but not accepted. Some essays exist only as artists' sketches; others as proofs of various kinds. America has an Essay-Proof Society, with its own journal, to promote this specialised branch of the hobby.

Essex Letter Express. Dubious 'locals' issued in New York, U.S.A., in 1856, were so inscribed.

Est Africain Allemand Occupation Belge. Belgian occupation of German East Africa.

ESPAÑA   ESCUELAS   ESTADO DA INDIA

Estado da India. (Port.). State of India. Portuguese India (q.v.).

Estados Unidos. (Spain.). United States.

Estensi. The ducal family of 'Este'. See 'Modena'.

Estero. (Ital.). Foreign. Stamps of Italian design were thus overprinted from 1874 to 1890 for use at Italian post offices abroad.

Estonia, also Esthonia (Eesti, Estland). Baltic province of Russia which became an independent republic in 1917 and issued its own stamps from 1918 until the country was reabsorbed by Russia in 1940. During the German occupation of 1941-2 stamps inscribed Estland were issued for use in Estonia; in the same period the German Ostland issues (q.v.), were also used there. At all other times Russian stamps have been employed. Area: 18,300 sq. m.; capital: Tallinn; currency: 1918, 100 kopecks = 1 rouble; 1919, 100 penni = 1 mark; 1928, 100 senti = 1 kroon; pop. (1940): 1,126,413.

Établissements Français dans l'Inde. (Fr.). French Indian Settlements. See 'French India'.

Établissements de l'Oceanie. (Fr.). Oceanic Settlements. Now known as French Polynesia (q.v.)

État Independant du Congo. Congo Free State. See under 'Congo'.

Ethiopia, Ethiopie, Etiopia (formerly known also as Abyssinia). Independent empire of north-east Africa. Stamps first issued, 1894. In 1935-6 the country was invaded and occupied by the Italians, and in 1936 an Italian Colonial series of stamps appeared. In 1938 Ethiopia was incorporated in Italian East Africa, and used the stamps of that territory until the liberation by British forces in 1941, when independence was restored. Since 1952 the country has included the former Italian colony of Eritrea. For a short time in 1941-2 British stamps were used at Addis Ababa. Area 458,000 sq. m.; capital: Addis Ababa; currency: 1894, 16 guerche = 1 menelik (or Maria Teresa dollar); 1905, 100 centimes = 1 franco; 1909, 16 guerche = 1 thaler; 1928, 16 mehalek = 1 thaler; 1936, and

ETHIOPIA ÉTAT INDEPENDANT ETIQUETTE
DU CONGO

again 1942, 100 centimes = 1 thaler; May 1936, as Italy; 1945, 100 cents = 1 Ethiopian dollar. The language of Ethiopia is Amharic, of which the numerals are illustrated below.

GUERCHE QUARTER HALF ONE TWO FOUR

EIGHT SIXTEEN

Etiquette. Label (French); especially an airmail label.

Eupen. District of Belgium, formerly part of Germany, ceded to Belgium under the Versailles Treaty 1919. Stamps of Belgium o/p 1920-1 'Eupen', 'Eupen and Malmédy', and 'Malmédy' (q.v.). See also 'Belgian occupation of German territory'.

Europa. Name given to issues produced by various European countries annually since 1956 on the theme of 'United Europe'. Many of the stamps of a particular year have shared a central design. Some Europa stamps have commemorated the European Postal and Telecommunications Conference, which meets annually; Great Britain's only Europa issues to date (which appeared in 1960 and 1961) were of this type.

Exchange Clubs. See 'Stamp Exchange Clubs.'

Exercito. (Port.). Army. In the war between Brasil and Paraguay 1865-70, stamps were issued free to the Brasilian troops bearing (in full) the following typeset inscription 'Exercito/en operacoes/contra/o Paraguay' (The army operating against Paraguay). They were issued in several colours. See also 'Army Post' and 'Soldiers' Stamps'.

Exhibitions. See 'Stamp Exhibitions'.

Expertising. A stamp or cover is said to have been expertised when a recognised expert, or expert committee, has examined it and given an opinion as to its genuineness or otherwise.

'Exploded'. A stamp booklet taken apart and displayed page by page is said to be 'exploded'.

Exposicion. (Span.) or **Exposition** (Fr.). Exhibition.

Express. Many countries issue stamps especially for prepayment of express, or expedited, postal services. Some are termed 'Express', others 'Special delivery'.

Extended Margins. See 'Wing Margins'.

Cyrillic

Й = Short 'E'.

E = E.

ЕРМАК = Ermak. Appears on the 1918 issues of the (Russian) Don Government.

Greek

The Epsilon (E) = the short 'e', and the H = the long form of the letter, thus:

ΕΛΛ. ΓΡΑΜΜ: Ellas Gramatosemon = Greek postage stamp.

ΕΛΛΑΣ: Ellas or Hellas = Greece. (See below.)

ΕΝΑΡΙΘΜΟΝ ΓΡΑΜΜΑΤΟΣΗΜΟΝ: Postage due. (Greece.)

ΗΠΕΙΡΟΣ: Epirus (N.W. Greece).

F

'F'. Abbreviation for fiscal or forgery. Overprinted on the SCADTA semi-official airmails of Colombia, the capital letter indicates that the stamp is a consular overprint sold in France. French stamps thus overprinted in 1939 (= Franco, free of charge) were supplied to Spanish refugees who were allowed free postage.

F.A. Fluorescent aniline. See 'Quartz Lamp.'

F.B.S. (Friend's Boarding School). A U.S.A. 'local' current 1877–84, used to frank letters to and from the Post Office at Barnesville, Ohio.

F.c. Fiscal cancellation, or fiscally cancelled.

F.D.C. First Day Cover.

F.I.P. Federation Internationale de Philatelie.

FIPEX. 5th International Philatelic Exhibition, New York, 1956.

F. J. Land. Inscribed on Franz Josef Land local issued in connection with the Fiala-Ziegler Polar Expedition of 1903–5. Designed by Mr. Russell Porter at Camp Abruzzi, 81°47′N.

F.M. (Fr.). Franchise Militaire. Special o/p for French soldiers' free letter stamps.

F.M.S. Federated Malay States.

F.N. These initials appear as a watermark, standing for Federation of Nigeria, on Nigerian issues since independence.

F.P.O. Field (or Forces) Post Office. A military marking.

F.R.P.S.,L. Fellow of the Royal Philatelic Society, London.

F.U. Fine used.

'Face', or Face Value. The value of a stamp as printed thereon, or its equivalent in English currency at the prevailing rate of exchange.

Faced Plate. A printing surface which has been coated with electrodeposited steel, nickel, copper, or chromium to resist wear.

Facsimile. A likeness or imitation of a genuine stamp, sometimes differing quite obviously from the original, openly described as such (unlike a forgery) and made with no intent to deceive or defraud.

Factaj. O/p (with surcharge) on 1919–22 stamps of Romania for parcels post use.

F.M.   'FAIDHERBE'   FARÖE IS.

Faded Stamp. The inks used in stamp printing are in most cases as fast to light as modern science will permit, but certain colours—usually red or blue or combinations of these primaries, the mauves and the purples—are liable to early fading if long exposed to light, especially sunlight and other illuminants rich in ultraviolet rays. Collectors should beware of specimens that have been subjected to long exposure in a dealer's window; and should protect their own collections. See 'Changeling' and 'Colour changes'.

'Faidherbe'. A French colonial keytype issued in 1906, featuring the portrait of General Faidherbe.

Fake. A genuine stamp which has been altered or repaired in some way to make it appear what it is not, for the purpose of deceiving collectors. Stamps may be faked either to hide a defect or to make a common item resemble a rare one. Great ingenuity has been used on fakes; stamps which were perforated have been made to appear imperforate, and vice versa; used stamps have had their postmarks removed and the backs regummed to make them appear mint; and so on.

Falkland Islands. British island group in the south Atlantic. Stamps first issued 1878. In the past the islands have been claimed by Argentina, who in 1936 issued a stamp with a map design showing the Falklands as part of Argentina. Area: 4,700 sq. m.; capital: Stanley; currency: sterling; pop. (1962): 2,140.

Falkland Islands Dependencies. Islands of the South Atlantic and Antarctic Oceans, and the British sector of Antarctica, all formerly dependencies of the Falkland Islands. On the comparatively few occasions when postal services were operated in these remote areas Falkland Island stamps were used until 1944, when the Dependencies, mainly for political reasons, received their own first stamp issue. These first stamps, overprinted on Falkland Island issues, comprised separate sets for each of the following: Graham Land; South Georgia; South Orkneys; and South Shetlands. The first definitives for all the Dependencies followed in 1946. In 1963 the southern Dependencies were reconstituted as the British Antarctic Territory, stamps thus inscribed superseding the Dependencies issues in February of that year. The latter continued to be current in South Georgia until July 1963, when that island too issued its own stamps for the first time.

III

Far Eastern Republic. Soviet republic of eastern Siberia, briefly independent from 1920 to 1922, when it produced its own stamp issues. In 1922 it was incorporated in Soviet Russia. There was a further surcharged issue in 1923.

Faridkot. One of the only two Indian states to issue stamps both as a native and as a convention state. It had its own stamps for internal use from 1879 until the end of 1886; it then gained convention status and used overprinted Indian stamps until March 1901. Since that date Indian stamps have been in use. Area: 643 sq. m.

'Farley's Follies'. The miniature sheets and imperf. reprints authorised 1934–7 by Postmaster General James A. Farley of the U.S.A. So named by the indignant philatelists in America who objected to these issues.

Faröe Islands. Danish possessions in the North Atlantic. Main islands are Strömö (with the town of Thorshavn, the capital), Ostero, Vaago, Sando, and Sudero. During 1914–18 bisected 4 öre stamps were authorised to make up increased postal charges, and (later) the 5 ö was surcharged 2 ö. During British occupation 1940 several values were surcharged, and on occasion main post offices met acute stamp shortages by franking with handstamps worded 'Faeroerne Franco Betalt', the amounts prepaid being written in ink, or by inserted figures, but general issues of Denmark are normally in use. Area: 540 sq. m.; pop. (1960): 34,596; capital: Thorshavn on Strömö, the largest of the 21 islands.

Fauconnière. See under 'Jethou'.

Faunce's Penny Post. An Atlantic City, U.S.A., local mail service operating from 1884 to 1887.

Feary & Co., Jabez. See 'Mustang Express'.

Federated Malay States. Stamps thus inscribed were issued from 1900 to 1935 for the federated states of Malaya, comprising Negri Sembilan, Pahang, Perak, and Selangor (q.v.). Throughout this period the low values were in the celebrated 'Tiger' design. Prior to 1900 and again from 1935 each of the four states had its own separate issues. Area: about 27,500 sq. m.; pop. (est. 1930): 1,723,000; currency: 100 cents = 1 Malayan dollar.

Federation of Malaya. See 'Malaya'.

Federation of South Arabia. See under 'South Arabian Federation'.

Feldpost. Field or army post. Appeared on stamps of Austria (Österreich) 1915–17, preceded by the initials K.U.K. 'Feldpost 2 Kg.', was o/p on the 48 pfg. 'Hitler Head' stamps of Germany late in World War II and was a frank-free parcel stamp valid for a weight of two kilogrammes, for the use of the troops in the field.

Fen. Chinese and Manchurian currency unit. 100 fen = 1 yen.

Fernando Poo. Spanish colony, an island in the Gulf of Guinea off the west African coast. A 20 ¢. stamp was issued for Fernando Poo in 1868,

FELDPOST   FIFI   FINLAND   FISCALS

but from 1867 to 1879 the issues of Spanish Cuba (inscribed 'Ultramar' —Overseas) were in use. Fernando Poo had its own stamps from 1879 until 1909, when they were replaced by those of Spanish Guinea (q.v.), with the exception of a set of overprints on Spain's Seville and Barcelona Exhibition issue of 1929. Distinctive stamps for Fernando Poo have again appeared since 1960. Area: 1,185 sq. m.; capital: Santa Isabel; currency: 1879, 100 centimos = 1 peseta; 1882, 100 centavos = 1 peso; 1901, 100 centavos = 1 peseta; pop. (1960): 61,197. Stamps of Great Britain (cancelled '247') were used on overseas mail from Fernando Poo from 1874 to 1878.

'Ferie-maerke'. Danish 'holiday' stamp, i.e. savings to pay for annual holidays. No postal validity.

Ferrary. Phillipp la Renotière von Ferrary (or Ferrari), a fabulous collector of postage stamps. A son of the wealthy Duchess of Galiera, born in 1848, he died in Switzerland in 1917, leaving the bulk of his huge collection in Paris, where it was sequestrated by the government and credited to the German reparations fund. It realised over £400,000.

Fezzan-Ghadames. Southern regions of the former Italian colony of Libya, occupied by Free French forces in 1942–3. The first issues of 1943 were Libyan stamps overprinted; pictorial definitives followed in 1946. Stamps for Fezzan only first appeared in 1948, and for Ghadames only in 1949. They were all superceded in 1951 when the territories became part of the new kingdom of Libya. Since then Libyan stamps have been in use. Currency: French.

'Figure'. The 1914 French Guinea postage dues—also issued to other colonies—bearing the value in a bold central panel, is sometimes known as the 'Figure' keytype of France. The 1894 King Carlos Portuguese colonials, with aslant corner figures of value panels, is also known as the 'Figures' keytype of Portugal.

Fiji. Group of Pacific islands, a native kingdom until 1874 when it became a British colony. The first stamps of 1860 were the locally typeset 'Times Express' series; these were followed in 1871 by stamps with the cipher of the native king Cakobau—later overprinted V.R. Fiji's 1½d. stamp issued in 1938 is a well-known design error, depicting a native sailing canoe at sea with no one aboard. The error was later corrected. Area: 7,036 sq. m.;

capital: Suva; currency: British notation, Fijian £ = 18s. sterling; pop. (1963): 428,000.

Filipinas. (Span.). Philippines (q.v.).

Fillér. Hungarian (Magyar) currency unit.

Finland. Former grand duchy of Imperial Russia, since 1917 an independent republic. Stamps first issued, 1856. Many of the issues from 1891 to 1917 bear a strong resemblance to contemporary Russian stamps, but can be readily distinguished by the different currency in which they are expressed. Area: 134,557 sq. m.; capital: Helsinki (Helsingfors); currency: 1856, 100 kopecks = 1 rouble; 1866, 100 penni = 1 mark; pop. (1963): 4,523,065.

First-day Cover. A cover bearing a stamp or stamps postmarked on the first day of issue.

First-flight Cover. A cover flown on the first flight of a new airmail service, usually bearing some endorsement of the circumstances and the route on which it was carried.

Fiscal. An adhesive or other stamp designed for revenue or taxation purposes only. Many postage stamps are also valid for revenue purposes and are thus inscribed; in used condition such stamps should be collected only with a postal cancellation. Copies fiscally cancelled are of little value. Many pen-cancellations indicate fiscal use, especially on such documents as receipts, but this is not invariably the case. In certain countries, for example, the Post Office cancelled the early stamps with pen-markings when postmarks were not available. A number of cases are on record in which fiscal stamps have been authorised for postal use; these are interesting items which should preferably be collected on complete cover to establish genuine use through the post. The outstanding example of fiscals used for postage occurred in November 1963 in Nyasaland, where on the achievement of independence a complete series of Revenue stamps was not merely authorised but specifically overprinted for postage.

Fiscal-Postal. It is a postage stamp fiscally used (see above). A postal-fiscal is a fiscal stamp postally used.

Fiske & Rice's Express. Stamps were issued for this New England, U.S.A., local mail service, 1851–4.

Fiume. Adriatic seaport and surrounding district, part of the Austro-Hungarian Empire until 1918, when it was occupied by Allied forces. The district was claimed by both Italy and Yugoslavia, but in 1919 the arguments were cut short when Gabriele d'Annunzio, the Italian poet and adventurer, occupied the place unofficially with his Italian Free Corps. In 1920 Fiume was recognised as a free state, but two years later it was occupied by Italian forces and in 1924 formally incorporated into Italy, with the exception of the suburb of Susak which went to Yugoslavia. The first stamps for Fiume, issued in December 1918, were Hungarian issues overprinted. Fiume continued to issue its own stamps until 1924. From that date Italian stamps were used until 1945, when Fiume was occupied by the Yugoslavs. In July of that year they issued a provisional set for Fiume, overprinted on Italian stamps. In the ensuing peace settlement the town became part of Yugoslavia. It is now known as Rijeka. In 1920 there were separate overprints for the Quarnero Islands (Reggenza Italiana del Carnaro), a group of islands off Fiume, and also for each of two individual islands of the group, Arbe and Veglia. Currency: 1918, 100 filler = 1 korona; 1919, 100 centesimi = 1 corona; 1920, as Italy: pop. (1961): 100,989.

Flag Postmarks. Have been used by U.S.A., Canada, and other postal administrations. U.S.A. flag cancellations were in use 1920–30, and consisted of the 'Stars and Stripes'; they are now coveted items.

'Flag' Sets. There have been several such, but the term has been principally used to denote the U.S.A. 1943–4 series, and the Korean United Nations flag set.

Flappers. See 'Wing Margins'.

Flat Plate. A printing plate for use in a flat-bed press, as opposed to the curved or cylindrical printing surface of a rotary.

Flaw. A minor variation from the normal stamp; in other words, a variety. The term is more often used to denote an inconstant variety occurring during the printing.

'Floating Off'. It is always advisable to see that used stamps are not totally immersed in water when it is desired to remove dirt and adherent paper or old hinges. This is because many stamps are printed in water-soluble inks, and others have been cancelled with ink of similar characteristics—usually one containing methyl-violet, an ink very susceptible to water. Stamps on paper should, therefore, be 'floated' off if there is any dubiety on the points mentioned, i.e. placed face upwards on the surface leaving the front surfaces as dry as possible. A preferable method is to lay the specimens on to dampened clean white blotting paper in a tray, or in a 'humidor' (q.v.). A piece of glass laid on top will ensure allover contact. Stamps on tinted papers may have to be steamed off to obviate staining of the specimens.

'Floating Safe' Stamps. The Netherlands, in 1921, issued a set of Marine Insurance Stamps, the unique feature of which was the provision of a floating safe for the safe-keeping of insured mail, which in the event of shipwreck would survive. The buoyant safe was carried on the deck of the mailboats. As no further issues appeared, the experiment was apparently not proceeded with.

Flong. See 'Moulds'.

Flown Cover. A cover bearing evidence that it has been carried by airmail.

Floyd's Penny Post. Operated as a local mail service in Chicago, U.S.A., in 1860. The stamps have been reprinted several times.

Flugpost. (Ger.); **Flygpost.** (Swed.). Flying post = airmail.

'Flyspeck Philately'. Term of disparagement applied to the collection of minor varieties, especially those only visible with the aid of a magnifier.

Fondul Aviatei. (Rom.). Aviation Fund. Roumanian charity issues.

Forcados River. One of the Royal Niger Company's posts, which in 1894 had its own rubber-stamp canceller for use on the stamps of G.B.

Forces Françaises Libres/Levant. Free French Forces, Levant, 1942–3, o/p on stamps of Syria.

Foreign. Though the general public may refer to all stamps except their own country's as 'Foreign', in philately the term applies (in Great Britain at least) only to stamps of countries outside the British Commonwealth. Stamps of certain countries often collected as part of the British Commonwealth group, such as Eire, Egypt, Burma, South Africa, etc., are also often excluded from the 'Foreign' definition.

Forerunner. Historical predecessor of a philatelic group or issue. For example the stamps of Palestine are the forerunners of those of Israel; stamps of Austrian Levant used in Palestine are forerunners of both groups. British stamps used in the West Indies may be described as forerunners of the islands' own stamps, the stamps of the Australian States as forerunners of issues for Australia as a whole, and so on.

Forgery. A fraudulent imitation of a genuine stamp. There are two principal types: the postal forgery, made to deceive the Post Office, and the philatelic forgery, made to deceive collectors. For postal forgeries, especially used on cover, there is a keen demand from specialists. A special type of postal forgery is the propaganda forgery, made to be smuggled into enemy territory and there used by secret agents or Resistance workers. Stamps of enemy or enemy-occupied countries were forged by the authorities in Britain in both the First and Second World Wars, though in the former case it seems unlikely that they were used for the purpose for which they were intended. Other items sometimes described as propaganda forgeries are imitations of enemy stamps never intended for postal use but in which the design is distorted for propaganda purposes; for example stamps in which Hitler's head appeared as a skull. These latter are better described as propaganda labels.

Philatelic forgeries of rare overprints or rare postmarks have sometimes been applied to perfectly genuine stamps; in such cases the complete item may be termed a fake (q.v.).

Format. A stamp's size, shape, and dimensional form. A stamp may be described as of square, rectangular (vertical or horizontal), diamond, triangular, etc., format.

Formosa (Taiwan). Large island off the coast of China. Formerly part of the Chinese Empire, it was ceded to Japan as a result of the Sino-Japanese War in 1894, and restored to China in May 1946. A local stamp appeared under Chinese auspices in 1887, and Lin, leader of the 'Black

FLUGPOST   FRAME   FORMOSA

Flag' movement, issued three more in 1895 during his resistance to the Japanese occupation. General issues of Japan were used until 1946, when overprinted Chinese stamps made their first appearance. Formosa continues to issue its own stamps, latterly as the independent republic of Nationalist China. These issues are usually catalogued under China. Area: 13,890 sq. m.; capital: Taipei; currency since 1949: 100 cents = 1 silver yuan; pop. (1962): 11,375,085.

Fractional Control. A marginal control (q.v.) in which the key letter is separated by a rule or bar from the year numerals, as found on modern photogravure printings of G.B. stamps, for example.

Frame. That part of a stamp design that encloses the central portrait, vignette, or other motif.

Franc. Unit of currency in France, Belgium, and elsewhere; also throughout the French territories overseas. There are several different francs currently in use, of widely differing values, all of which have a bearing on stamps. Collectors are well advised to gain some knowledge of them— and this applies equally to other currencies expressed on stamps. For example the Belgian franc is, at the time of writing, worth about 140 to the £ sterling—about 1¾d.—whereas the franc in metropolitan France is worth less than 14 to the £—about 1s. 5½d. The franc C.F.A. is the French African unit at 687 to the £ (not much more than a farthing) and the franc C.F.P. is the French Pacific unit at 251 to the £—just under a penny. The Djibouti franc, used in French Somali Coast, is different again— 603 to the £.

Franca, Franque, Franco, Franked. Free delivery. Usually by reason of the fact that postage has been paid in advance by the sender, although it may mean that the stamp so o/p has been provided free of charge (to a member of a state parliament, for instance) to enable the sender to despatch his letters free.

France. European country, a republic to 1852 and again since 1870; in the intervening period an empire under Napoleon III. Stamps first issued, 1849. Area: 217,736 sq. m.; capital: Paris; currency: 100 centimes = 1 franc (revalued in 1960); pop. (est. 1963): 47,600,000.

FRANCO BOLLO   FRANCE LIBRE   FRANQUEO

France Libre. Free France.

Franco Bollo. (Ital.). Prepaid postage stamp. The postage stamps of the Roman States were inscribed 'Franco Bollo Postale'; the newspaper stamps of Sardinia and Italy 'Franco Bollo Giornali Stampe'.

Franco de Porte. (Span.). Carried free of charge.

Franks. Signatures and postal markings (in Great Britain normally of the pre-adhesive period) indicating that a letter was to be carried free of postage. The British franking system was established in the middle of the seventeenth century, allowing the privilege of free postage to members of both Houses of Parliament, officers in the public service, and certain others. The privilege was much abused but persisted in various forms until the reforms of 1840. In some countries the system is still in use at the present time. Strictly speaking a frank is anything which permits a letter to be forwarded without payment of further postage; and stamps are therefore said to frank a letter.

Franqueo Deficiente. (Span.). Under-stamped = Postage due.

Franqueo Impressos. (Span.). Prepaid Journal, Newspaper, or Printed Matter stamps. Franqueo Oficial = Official prepaid.

Franquicia Postal. Private (exempted from payment) postage stamp of Spain. See 'Private Postage Stamps'.

Franz Josef Land. An unofficial stamp of the Fiala-Ziegler Polar Expedition, 1903–5, used for inter-camp dog-sleigh post, inscribed 'F. J. Land Postage/Two Cents/1905' and a drawing of a polar bear.

Frazer & Co.—City Despatch. A Cincinnati, U.S.A., local mail service of 1845–51 which issued several 'local' stamps.

Freak. An inconstant or once-occurring variety (q.v.).

Freedom from Hunger. In 1963 some 150 different countries issued special stamps to mark the U.N. Freedom from Hunger campaign.

Freedom Group. See under People's League.

Freie Stadt Danzig. Danzig (Free Town or City).

Freimarke. (Ger.). Frimarke (Swed.): Free (prepaid) stamp.

Freistaat Bayern. Bavaria.

French Colonies. General issues for use throughout all the French overseas possessions (except Algeria, which used French stamps at this period) were current from 1859 to about 1886, being gradually replaced by separate definitives for each of the territories. Postage Due stamps for the whole French colonial empire were in use until 1908. In 1943-4 the French provisional government in Algeria again issued a number of stamps for general use in French overseas territories, and in 1945 there was a general colonial issue of Postage Dues.

French Congo (Congo Français). Former French territory in central Africa, which issued its first stamps in 1891. In 1904 Gaboon, Oubangui-Chari, and Tchad, previously parts of French Congo, became separate territories; the remaining part was renamed Middle Congo in 1907, from which date the stamps of French Congo have been obsolete. The four territories were later reunited as French Equatorial Africa (q.v.).

French Equatorial Africa. Although Gaboon, Middle Congo, Oubangui-Chari, and Tchad were amalgamated to form French Equatorial Africa in 1910, the new name did not appear on stamps until 1924, when the issues of the four constituent territories were overprinted 'Afrique Equatoriale Française'. In the following year all four issues became valid for postage throughout the combined area. Despite this the four territories continued to issue separate stamps until 1936. Further overprints then appeared for the whole of French Equatorial Africa, followed by the first definitives in 1937. The final issues for the combined area appeared in 1958, when the four constituent territories became autonomous republics within the French Community. Since then each has again had its own stamps, Middle Congo being re-named Congo Republic, and Oubangui-Chari the Central African Republic. Area: 969,000 sq. m.; capital: Brazzaville; pop. (1956): 4,853,000 Africans, 25,221 Europeans.

French Guiana (Guyane). French territory on the north-east coast of South America, which had its own stamps from 1886 to 1946. Since the latter date the territory has been an overseas department of France, using French stamps. Inini (a region in the interior of French Guiana) had its own separate stamp issues from 1932 to 1946. Area: 34,750 sq. m.; capital: Cayenne; pop. (1961): 33,698 (including Inini with 2,980 inhabitants).

French Guinea (Guinée Française). Former French territory in West Africa; since 1958 the independent Republic of Guinea. Stamps were issued from 1892 until 1945, when Guinea was incorporated into French West Africa and used the stamps of the combined territory until separate issues for the new republic made their appearance early in 1959. Area: 95,000 sq. m.; capital: Conakry; pop. (1960): 2,726,868.

French India. Former French settlements on the coast of India, which had their own stamps from 1892 to 1954. Prior to 1892 the stamps of British India were in use there. The settlements comprised Chandernagore (ceded to India in 1952), Karikal, Mahé, Pondichéry and Yanaon, all of which were incorporated in India in 1954. Area: 196 sq. m.; capital: Pondichéry; currency: 1892, as France; 1923, 24 caches = 1 fanon, 8 fanons = 1 roupie (at par with Indian rupee); pop. (1948): 362,045.

French Levant. Stamps surcharged or inscribed for use in French post offices in the Ottoman Empire were issued from 1885 until the offices were closed in 1914. In 1921 the offices at Constantinople and Smyrna were reopened, and French stamps surcharged in Turkish currency were used there until they were finally closed in July 1923. There were also separate issues for the offices at Cavalle (1893-1914), Dedeagh or Dedeagatch (1893–1914), Port Lagos (1893–98), and Vathy (1893–1902). In 1942–3 there were further Levant issues for use by the Free French forces in the Middle East.

French Morocco. The first of the French post offices in Morocco was opened in 1863. Distinctive stamps for use at these offices were first issued in 1891. A French protectorate was established in 1912 and this lasted until 1956 when Morocco became an independent kingdom. See also under 'Morocco'. Currency: Spanish until 1912, then French until 1956.

French Oceania. See 'Oceanic Settlements'.

French Polynesia. Group of French islands in the Pacific, known as Oceanic Settlements (q.v.), until 1958 when stamps inscribed Polynésie Française were first issued. Area: 1,545 sq. m.; chief town: Papeete on Tahiti; pop. (1962): 84,550.

French Post Offices in China. Numerous o/p and surcharged French colonial keytypes and Indo-China issues were in use in the Treaty ports and French Post Offices up to the end of 1922, when they closed down. They are noted under separate headings.

French Post Offices in Crete. See 'Crete'.

French Post Offices in Egypt. The former French post offices at Alexandria and at Port Said each had their own stamps from 1899. Early issues were French stamps overprinted; afterwards there were French keytypes suitably inscribed. The offices were closed in 1931.

French Post Offices in Morocco. See 'French Morocco'.

French Post Offices in the Turkish Empire. See 'French Levant'.

French Post Office in Zanzibar. Stamps surcharged, overprinted, or inscribed for use at this office were issued from 1893 until the office closed in 1904.

French Somali Coast. French territory of north-east Africa. Stamps inscribed 'Côte Française des Somalis' were first issued in 1894, superseding those of Obock (q.v.). Area: 8,500 sq. m.; capital: Djibouti (q.v.); pop. (1961): 81,000.

French Soudan. Former French territory of west-central Africa. It issued its own stamps from 1894 to 1899, when it was abolished as a separate territory and divided among Senegal, French Guinea, Ivory Coast,

FRENCH ZONE   FUCHS   FUNCHAL

Dahomey, and the new territory of Senegambia and Niger, subsequently renamed Upper Senegal and Niger. In 1921 French Soudan was revived as the new name for Upper Senegal and Niger, and stamps overprinted and later inscribed Soudan Français were again issued from then until 1945, when the territory was incorporated into French West Africa. In 1959, after becoming an autonomous republic within the French Community, French Soudan joined Senegal to form the Mali Federation which then issued its own stamps. In the following year, however, Senegal seceded from the Federation, and since then the former French Soudan has had its own separate stamps as the Mali Republic (q.v.).

French Southern and Antarctic Territories. (Terres Australes et Antarctiques Française). French territories including Adelie Land in Antarctica, the islands of Nouvelle Amsterdam and St. Paul, and the Crozet and Kerguelen archipelagos. Stamps first issued, 1955. See also under 'Adelie Land'. Area: 118,888 sq. m.

French West Africa (Afrique Occidentale Française). Joint administration of the former French territories of Dahomey, French Guinea, French Soudan, Ivory Coast, Mauritania, Niger, Senegal, and Upper Volta. There was a charity stamp in 1944 for the whole of French West Africa, and in 1945 the first definitives superseded the separate issues of the constituent territories. In 1958 Guinea became an independent republic and the others autonomous republics within the French Community, each with its own separate stamps. These gradually replaced the issues of French West Africa, though the latter continued to be used until 1962. Area: 1,820,600 sq. m.; capital: Dakar; pop. (1957): 19,032,000.

French Zone of Germany. Area of south-west Germany occupied by French forces after the Second World War, including Baden, Rhineland-Palatinate, and Württemberg. There was a general issue of stamps for the whole zone in 1945–6, followed by separate issues for each of the three territories from 1947 until 1949, when they became part of West Germany. Saar (q.v.) was also part of the French zone in the immediate post-war years.

Fresh Entry. Process of substituting a new entry on an engraved printing plate for an unsatisfactory original one which has been erased. Sometimes residual traces of the first entry can result in part of the stamp design being doubly printed.

Friendly Islands. See 'Tonga'.

Front. The address side of a mailed cover, detached from the rest to facilitate filing or mounting, and to minimise bulk. A practice not greatly favoured by modern cover collectors. See 'Cover', 'Entire', etc.

Fuchs, Emil, R.A., M.V.O. Born Austria 1866. After study in Berlin came to London 1897. His etching of King Edward VII was the basis of many of the stamps of the short reign.

Fuerstentum Liechtenstein. Principality of Liechtenstein.

Fugitive Inks. These have been extensively used for stamp printing to deter forgery and to make re-use impossible. They present a problem to the collector, for stamps thus printed have to be treated and stored with great care. They are easily damaged by rubbing, and are also prone to fading; if allowed to become damp the colours run and ruin the stamp.

Fujeira. One of the Trucial States of Arabia. Stamps first issued, 1964. Currency: 100 naye paise = 1 rupee.

Fumigated Mail. See 'Disinfected Mail'.

Funchal. Capital and administrative district of Madeira (q.v.), a Portuguese island in the Atlantic off the west coast of Africa. Funchal had its own stamps from 1892 until 1905, when the stamps of the Azores were in use until 1931. Prior to 1892 (except from 1868 to 1880 when Madeira had its own stamps) and again since 1931 Funchal has used the normal Portuguese issues.

Futuna. See 'Wallis and Futuna Islands'.

Cyrillic and Greek

Ф: The pheta (Greek 'phi')—equivalent to the English 'F'. The Greek letter is used in Cyrillic, but normally only in words of foreign origin, thus:

ФИЛАТЕЛИСТИ: Philatelisti = philatelic.
ФРАНКЬ: Franc. (Bulgaria 1879). (See below.)

G

GABOON

GRAND LIBAN

G

'G'. Overprint on stamps of Cape of Good Hope for use in Griqualand West (q.v.).

G.B. Universal abbreviation for Great Britain. Overprinted on the SCADTA semi-official airmails of Colombia, the initials indicate that the stamp is a consular overprint sold in Great Britain.

G.C. Grande Consommation; i.e. Papier de Grande Consommation. See 'Consommation'. O/p or handstamped on Mexican revolutionary provisionals 1913–15 = Gobierno Constitucionalista (Constitutional Government).

GD-OT. Geschäfts Drucksache—Obchodni Tiskopis (German and Czech) = Commercial printed papers. O/p on Journals stamps of Bohemia and Moravia 1939.

G & D, or **G et D.** Guadeloupe (q.v.). O/p with surcharges 1903.

G.E.A. German East Africa. O/p on stamps of East Africa and Uganda 1917. See 'Tanganyika'.

G.N. On stamps of Venezuela (or punch-perforated) since 1915 means 'Gobierno National' (National Government). These stamps are therefore 'Officials'.

G.N.R. Guardia Nazional Repubblicana. Italian stamps with this overprint are the Republican National Guard issue, produced under the Mussolini regime in north Italy in 1943–4. They are regarded as locals and some catalogues do not recognise them.

G.P. De M. (Span.). Gobierno Provisionsal de Mexico. O/p on 1916–18 issues of Mexico.

GPE. Guadeloupe (q.v.).

G.P.U. General Postal Union (q.v.).

G.R. V., Geo. V., G. V. King George the Fifth.

G.R. VI., Geo. VI., G. VI. King George the Sixth.

G.R.I. Georgius Rex Imperator. British occupation overprint on stamps of German New Guinea, Samoa, and Marshall Islands in 1914.

G.R.-Post-Mafia.   See 'Mafia'.

G.W.   Overprint on stamps of Cape of Good Hope for use in Griqualand West (q.v.).

Gaboon, also Gabon, Gabun (Republique Gabonaise).   Former French territory of central Africa with a complicated stamp-issuing history. The first issue of 1886 consisted of a GAB overprint on French Colonial key-type stamps. In 1891 it was incorporated in French Congo, and used the stamps of that country until 1904 when it resumed issuing its own stamps. In 1936 these were superseded by stamps of French Equatorial Africa (q.v.). In 1958 Gaboon became an autonomous republic within the French Community, and since 1959 has had separate stamp issues once more. Area: 102,290 sq. m.; capital: Libreville; pop. (1961): about 450,000.

Galapagos Islands.   Group of islands in the Pacific, 600 miles west of Ecuador, of which they form part. A set of six stamps appeared in 1957. Though they were officially issued by Ecuador, there were no postal facilities of any kind on the islands; some of the stamps were reported to have been cancelled on board ships which called there. They are generally recognised to be no more than propaganda labels, since they have no postal validity on the mainland of Ecuador. The fact that the set includes three so-called 'airmails' also condemns them, since there are no landing facilities for aircraft. A triangular stamp which appeared on the market in 1959, purporting to be a United Nations commemorative of the Galapagos Islands, is bogus.

Gambia.   Former British colony and protectorate in West Africa, granted self-government in 1963 and independence in 1965. Stamps first issued, 1869. The early issues, up to 1898, were the famous 'Gambia Cameos', with the embossed head of Queen Victoria. Area: 4,132 sq. m.; capital: Bathurst, on St. Mary's Island; currency: sterling; pop. (1965): 300,000.

Gambiers.   A Pacific island group once under French protection, for which a certain Julian Copilon once o/p French colonial issues illegally and unofficially. An assortment of stamps have been found thus o/p and surcharged 10 ¢. They are spurious. Area; 6 sq. m.; pop. (1946): 1,569.

Gandon.   M. Pierre Gandon of Paris. Designer of many of the modern French and other stamps.

Garter Watermark.   Insignia of the Order of the Garter, used in three sizes on stamps of G.B. 1855–7: large, medium, and small.

Garzón.   Colombia, South America. Issued typeset provisionals in 1894.

Gauge.   A measure. See 'Stamp gauge', 'Perforation', etc.

Gdańsk.   (Pol.). Port Gdańsk. See 'Danzig'.

Gd. Liban.   Grand Liban. See 'Lebanon'.

Gebyr.   On stamps of Denmark. Indicates that a special late fee has been paid.

GEBYR   GEORGIAN   GERMAN OCC.   GERMANY:
              KEYTYPE   BOHEMIA & MORAVIA   ALLIED OCC.

General Collection. One that embraces stamps of many countries.

General Denikin's Volunteer Army. See 'South Russia'.

General Gouvernement. Inscription on stamps issued by the German occupying authorities for use in Poland, 1940–4. 'Gen.-Gouv. Warschau' in Gothic type appeared on the German occupation issues for Warsaw in the First World War.

General Issues. Synonym for definitives (q.v.).

General Post Office. Great Britain's G.P.O. has its headquarters at King Edward Street, St. Martin's le Grand, London, E.C.1.

General Postal Union. Early name for the Universal Postal Union, in use from 1874 to 1878.

General Wrangel. See 'South Russia'.

Geneva (Genève). Switzerland. City and Canton. The double cantonal administration stamp was issued 1 October 1843, followed by the single types of 1845–8; and the transitional issues of 1849–50. They were superseded on 5 April 1850, by the Swiss federal stamps. See also 'Basle', 'Switzerland', and 'Zürich'.

Georgia (La Georgie). Republic on the Black Sea, briefly independent from 1919 to 1923, when it issued its own stamps. In the latter year it joined the Trans-Caucasian Federation (q.v.). Now part of Soviet Russia. Area: 26,873 sq. m.; capital: Tiflis; currency: as Russia; pop. (est. 1956): 4,000,000.

Georgia, South. See South Georgia.

Georgian. Appertaining to the Georges: i.e. King George V and King George VI—principally the former.

Georgian Keytypes. The two King George V De La Rue dies for the standardised British colonial issues of 1912–28.

German 9th Army Post. Occupying forces which o/p German and Roumanian stamps 'Gültig 9 Armee' in 1918.

German Army of Occupation Issues, 1870–1. See 'Alsace and Lorraine'.

German Army of Occupation Issues, 1914–18. Include stamps for the 9th Army (see above), Belgium, Eastern Command, Poland, and Romania—all of which see below.

German Army of Occupation Issues, 1939–45. See under the various German Occupation entries below.

German Colonies. The territories held by Germany prior to 1914 were: Kamerun (Cameroons), Karolinen (Caroline Islands), Deutsch Ostafrika (German East Africa), Deutsch Neu-Guinea (German New Guinea), Deutsch Südwest-Afrika (German South-West Africa), Kiautschou—treaty port of China, Marianen (Marianne Islands), Marschall-Inseln (Marshall Islands), Samoa, and Togo; all of which see.

German Democratic Republic. Republic of East Germany, comprising the Russian zone of occupation, established in 1949. The inscription 'Deutsche Demokratische Republic' first appeared on East German stamps in 1950. Area: 41,535 sq. m.; capital: East Berlin; pop. (1962): 17,135,867. For earlier history, see under Germany.

German East Africa. Former German colony. Stamps first issued, 1893 (prior to which German stamps were used from 1890). During the First World War the country was occupied by British and Belgian forces, when occupation stamps were issued including those of East Africa and Uganda overprinted 'G.E.A.' A small part of the country on the west was mandated to Belgium under the name of Ruanda-Urundi (q.v.); the remainder to Britain as Tanganyika (q.v.) Area: 384,180 sq. m.; capital: Dar-es-Salaam; currency: 64 pesa = 1 rupee; 1905, 100 heller = 1 rupee; pop. (1913): 7,680,132.

German Federal Republic. Republic of West Germany, comprising the former British, American and French zones of occupation, established in 1949. The inscription 'Deutsche Bundespost' (the republic's title is Bundersrepublik Deutschland) first appeared on West German stamps in 1950. Area: 94,800 sq. m.; capital: Bonn; pop. (1962): 57,247,200. For earlier history, see under Germany. The republic has included West Berlin since 1951, and Saar since 1957.

German New Guinea. Former German protectorate comprising the north-eastern part of New Guinea and the Bismarck Archipelago. Stamps first issued, 1898 (prior to which German stamps were used from 1888). It was occupied by Australian forces during the First World War and mandated to Australia in 1920, afterwards issuing stamps as the Territory of New Guinea. It now forms part of the combined postal administration of Papua and New Guinea (q.v.). Area: About 93,000 sq. m.; capital: Herbertshohe; currency: as Germany; pop. (est. 1913): 600,000.

German Occupation of Belgium. German stamps were overprinted 'Belgien' for use during the occupation of Belgium in the First World War. In the Second World War occupation Belgium was allowed to continue its own stamp issues.

German Occupation of Estonia, Latvia, and Lithuania. German stamps were overprinted 'Postgebiet Ob. Ost' in 1916–18 and 'Ostland' in 1941–3 for use during the occupation of the Baltic States.

German Occupation of Luxemburg. German stamps were overprinted in 1940 for use during the occupation of Luxemburg. Earlier Luxemburg issues were also surcharged with new values in German currency. From 1942 to 1944 current German stamps were used in Luxemburg.

German Occupation of Poland. In 1915–17 German stamps were overprinted 'Russisch Polen' or 'Gen.-Gouv. Warschau' for use during the occupation of Poland. At the beginning of the Second World War German stamps were overprinted 'Deutsche Post Osten' for use in occupied Poland; these were succeeded by the 'General Gouvernement' issues of 1940–4.

German Occupation of Roumania. In 1917–18 German stamps were overprinted 'M.V.i.R.' or 'Rumanien' for use during the occupation of Roumania.

German Occupation of Ukraine. German stamps were overprinted in 1941–3 for use during the occupation of Ukraine.

German Post Offices in China. The first such office was that at Shanghai, opened in 1886. Until 1898 ordinary German stamps were used; thereafter German stamps overprinted 'China' were current until the offices were closed in 1917.

German Post Offices in Morocco. German stamps were overprinted 'Marocco' or 'Marokko' for use at these offices, the first issue appearing in 1899. The post offices in the French zone of Morocco closed in 1914, and in the Spanish zone in 1919, since when the stamps have been obsolete.

German Post Offices in Turkey. From 1870 tô 1872 these offices used stamps of the North German Confederation, thereafter those of Germany until 1884. From the latter date German issues were surcharged with new values in Turkish currency until the offices were closed in 1914.

German South-West Africa. Former German colony. Stamps first issued, 1897—prior to which German issues were in use from 1888. In the early part of the First World War the territory was occupied by South Africa, and South African stamps were introduced. In 1919 the country was mandated to South Africa, and since 1923, now known as South West Africa (q.v.), has again had its own stamps. Area: 317,725 sq. m.; capital: Windhoek; currency: As Germany; pop. (est. 1913): 95,000.

German States. Prior to the formation of the German Empire in 1871, Germany consisted of a large number of separate states of varying size. Those that issued their own stamps were Baden, Bavaria, Bergedorf, Bremen, Brunswick, Hamburg, Hanover, Lubeck, Mecklenburg-Schwerin, Mecklenburg-Strelitz, Oldenburg, Prussia, Saxony, Schleswig-Holstein, and Württemberg. Parts of Germany which did not have their own stamps used the issues of the Thurn and Taxis postal administration. Each state is mentioned separately in this book. Most of the states' issues were superseded either by those of the North German Confederation in 1868, or those of the German Empire in 1872, but Bavaria and Württemberg continued to issue their own stamps until shortly after the First World War. Following the Second World War Baden and Württemberg again became separate stamp-issuing entities for a time as part of the French zone of occupation.

'Germania'. Emblematic figure symbolical of the German Empire, pictured on the 1900–21 definitives, designed by Paul Waldraff from a portrait of Anna von Stratz-Führing, a Wagnerian operatic star.

Germany. State of north-central Europe; a monarchy until 1918, thereafter a republic. Prior to the formation of the German Empire in 1871, a number of the German states had their own separate issues; see 'German States' above. The first Empire issue appeared in 1872. The republican period is noted for the inflation issues of 1923, when face values rose to as high as 10,000 million marks, and for the stamps of the Hitler regime, 1933–45.

The Allied occupation at the close of the Second World War led to separate occupation stamps for the Anglo-American, French, and Russian zones. From 1946 to 1948 the same stamps were used throughout the British, American, and Russian Zones, until currency reform in West Germany resulted in the necessity for separate stamps once more for the Anglo-American zone. Since 1949 the country has been divided into West Germany (German Federal Republic) and East Germany (German Democratic Republic), each of which issues its own stamps. From 1948 there have also been separate stamps for West Berlin. See also under French and Russian zones of Germany, German Federal Republic, German Democratic Republic, and West Berlin. Area of German Empire: 208,000 sq. m.; capital: Berlin; currency: 1872, 30 groschen = 1 thaler (north) or 60 kreuzer = 1 gulden (south); 1875, 10 pfennig = 1 mark (1 reichsmark from 1924), total pop. (1962): 74,383,000.

Germany, Belgian Occupation of. See 'Belgian occupation of German territory'.

Gerusalemme. (Ital.). Jerusalem (q.v.).

Ghadames. See Fezzan-Ghadames.

Ghana. The former British West African colony of Gold Goast was renamed Ghana on achieving dominion status and independence in March 1957. The first stamps to carry the new name were the Independence issue of 1957. Area: 92,100 sq. m.: capital: Accra; currency: sterling; pop. (est. 1963): 7,100,000. Since 1960 Ghana has been a republic within the British Commonwealth. In July 1965 new decimal currency was introduced: 100 pesewa = 1 cedi (= 8s. 4d. sterling).

Gibbons, Stanley. Stanley Gibbons Ltd. of 391 Strand, London, are the leading British stamp dealers and philatelic publishers. The business is the only firm in the trade so far to have celebrated its centenary, which was reached in 1956. A century before, the youthful E. Stanley Gibbons had started dealing in stamps across the counter of his father's chemist's shop in Plymouth. The company is best known for the famous Gibbons' catalogues (see below), but also publishes philatelic books and albums.

Gibbons' Catalogues. First published as a 16-page booklet in 1865, the Gibbons' catalogue is a world-renowned work of reference. For many years the full catalogue was published in two volumes—British Empire, and Foreign. It was also obtainable as one large whole-world volume, the last edition to appear in this form being that of 1940. At the present time the catalogue is produced in three parts. Part I covers the British Commonwealth and appears annually; Part II covers Europe and Colonies, and Part III the rest of the world, each appearing in alternate years. There are also the self-descriptive Simplified—the only catalogue to list all the world's stamps in one volume, albeit on a simplified basis—and the Elizabethan, devoted to the stamps of Queen Elizabeth II only. Each of these is published annually. In 1965 it was announced that Part II would appear annually in future. In 1963 the first volume of a Specialised G.B. Catalogue appeared.

Gibbons' Stamp Monthly. House-magazine of Stanley Gibbons Ltd.

Gibraltar. British colony at the southern tip of Spain. From 1857 British stamps were used there with 'G' and 'A 26' cancellations until Gibraltar's first issue, a set of overprints on Bermuda, appeared in January 1886. The first definitives followed in December of the same year. From 1886 to 1897 Gibraltar stamps were also used by the British post offices in Morocco; see under Morocco Agencies. Area: 2½ sq. m.; currency: sterling; except 1889–98, 100 centimos = 1 peseta; pop. (1962): 24,151.

Gilbert and Ellice Islands. British protectorate in the Pacific, a colony since 1915. Stamps of New South Wales were used there from 1901 until the first Gilbert and Ellice issue, a set of overprints on Fiji, appeared in 1911. The first definitives followed in the same year. Area: 369 sq. m.; capital: Tarawa (Gilbert Is.); currency: as Australia; pop. (est. 1965): 34,000. See also under 'Christmas Island'.

Giornali. (Ital.). Journals or newspapers.

Giro. (Span.) = Draft. On stamps of Spain indicates fiscal use.

Glacé Paper. (Fr.). Glossy, glazed, enamelled (art) paper, infrequently used for stamp printing.

Gladstone Roulette. Experimental serpentine in temporary use 1853–4. Little is known or recorded, but it was done at the Treasury (hence sometimes referred to as the 'Treasury' roulette) when Gladstone was Chancellor of the Exchequer.

Glen Haven. Local 'carrier' stamps, typeset 'Glen Haven/Daily Mail/ One Cent' were in use 1854–8 in this one-time hamlet near Syracuse, N.Y., U.S.A., and are said to have had postal validity. These were three types and settings, printed black on green paper.

Goa. Capital of Portuguese India (q.v.).

Gobierno. (Span.). Government. O/p on general issues of Peru to authorise them as 'officials' for departmental use. See also 'Mexico'.

Goldbeater's Skin. A thin, tough, translucent, resin-impregnated paper, which was used for the 1886 parcels stamps of Prussia. These were printed upon a collodion surface on the reverse side, the gumming being done on top of the ink. They were not sold to the public, but were affixed to heavy parcels only, by the postal officials. See also 'Parcel post stamps'.

Gold Coast. Former British colony and protectorate in West Africa which achieved independence in 1957 and was then renamed Ghana (q.v.). Stamps first issued, 1875. Area: 91,843 sq. m.; capital: Accra; currency: Sterling; pop. (1953): 4,478,000.

Golfe. (Fr.). Gulf; i.e. Golfe de Bénin = the Benin Gulf.

Goliad and **Gonzales.** Texas, U.S.A., were two of the towns issuing Confederate 'Postmaster's' stamps during the Civil War.

'Gordon' Set. Commemoratives issued by the Sudan on 1 January 1935, the 50th anniversary of the death of General Gordon.

Gordon's City Express. A local mail service organised in 1848 by Samuel B. Gordon of New York, U.S.A.

Gorny Slask. (Pol.). Upper Silesia. Stamps bearing this inscription were issued by the Polish plebiscite official in 1920 without allied authority, and the Inter-Allied Commission prohibited their use, but copies used on mail with Poland are known.

Governatorato del Montenegro. Government of Montenegro. O/p on stamps of Yugoslavia by Italian occupation troops 1941.

Governo Militare Alleato. (Ital.). Allied Military Government.

Govt. Parcels. Government parcels. O/p on official stamps of G.B. 1883–1902.

Graffin's Baltimore Despatch. A Baltimore, U.S.A., local mail service, organised in 1856 by James Grafflin.

Graham Land. One of the Falkland Islands Dependencies in the Antarctic, the Dependencies' first issue of 1944 including a set specifically overprinted for Graham Land. Now part of the British Antarctic Territory (q.v.).

Granadine Confederation. Early name for the South American republic of Colombia. The inscription 'Confed. Granadina' appeared on the first issues of 1859–60. In 1861 the country was renamed the United States of New Granada, and in 1862 the United States of Colombia.

Grand Comoro. A French island of the Comoro group, off Madagascar, which had its own stamps from 1897 to 1914. Madagascar stamps were then used until the first issue for the Comoro Archipelago appeared in 1950. See under 'Comoro Islands'.

Grand Liban. See 'Lebanon'.

GREAT BRITAIN   GREECE   GREENLAND

Granite Paper. A paper with coloured fibres mixed with the pulp. Normally these are blue, the paper then being often known as 'Silurian'. Certain stamp issues of Switzerland, for instance, were printed on a granite paper with an admixture of chopped coloured fibres. It is a form of 'security' paper, used to deter forgery.

Graphite Line. Name given to the issue of Great Britain low values released in November 1957 with vertical lines of graphite printed in black on the backs of the stamps. They were introduced in connection with the experimental installation of the world's first electronic letter-facing machine at Southampton G.P.O., and were on sale only in the Southampton district. In November 1959 they were replaced by stamps with phosphor lines on the front. See also under Phosphor-Graphite and Phosphor Line.

Grease or Oil. Stamps can often be de-greased by the use of a moderately warm domestic iron and white, clean blotting paper. Benzine, petrol, or carbon-tetrachloride are also grease and oil solvents and can be used, but *not* on stamps printed by photogravure.

Great Britain. Geographically the term includes England, Scotland, Wales, and the various off shore islands, but in philately it invariably means the United Kingdom of Great Britain and Northern Ireland (all Ireland until 1922). Great Britain pioneered the use of adhesive stamps for the prepayment of postage, and the world's first stamps, the famous Penny Black and Twopence Blue, were issued on 1 May 1840, for use from 6 May. Alone of the major nations, Great Britain has never printed the name of the country on its stamps, the head of the sovereign being considered sufficient identification. The Channel Islands (q.v.) issued their own stamps during the German occupation of 1940–5. Since 1958 Regional stamps (q.v.), in certain values only, have been issued for Scotland, Wales, Northern Ireland, Jersey, Guernsey, and the Isle of Man. Lundy, Herm, and Jethou islands (q.v.) all have their own local stamps. Area of U.K.: 94,279 sq. m.; capital: London; currency: sterling; pop.: 51,402,623 in Great Britain proper (1961 census) plus 1,435,400 in Northern Ireland (est. 1962).

Great Lebanon. See 'Lebanon'.

Greece. Independent kingdom of southern Europe; a republic from 1924 to 1935, when the monarchy was restored. Stamps first issued, 1861. The early issues up to 1886, the famous 'Hermes Heads', are a popular specialist study. See also under 'Crete', 'Dodecanese Is.', and 'Epirus'. Area: 50,534 sq. m.; capital: Athens; currency: 100 lepta = 1 drachma; pop. (1961): 8,388,553.

Greek Post Offices in Turkey. Greece operated a number of post offices in the Ottoman Empire until 1881, and in Crete until 1882. Stamps used by these offices can be distinguished only by the cancellations.

'Green Gibbons'. Colloquial term in common use for *Stanley Gibbons' Catalogue*, Part II. Before the war it covered all Foreign countries; nowadays it includes Europe and Colonies only, formerly published every two years, now annually.

Green Label. Small, imperforate, white, oblong label printed in green with a diagonal cross (saltire), used as a priority identification on mail from G.B. to Malta, for service personnel, during the 1941–2 siege. Each man was issued with one per week, to enclose in letters, for use to identify replies from the United Kingdom. There was also one for civilian use. ('Phil. Adviser', July 1947.)

Greenland. Danish territory in the Arctic; a United States protectorate during the Second World War while Denmark was under German occupation. The earliest stamps were Parcel Post issues of the Royal Greenland Trading Company which first appeared in 1905. Thule, a colony in north-west Greenland outside the company's control, founded by the explorer Knud Rasmussen in 1910, issued its own stamps from 1935 but their postal use was extremely limited. Both the company's issues and the Thule stamps were superseded by the first government-issued definitives which appeared in 1938. Until that year all letters from Greenland were carried free; inland letters continued to be free of postage until 1958. Since 1953 Greenland has been regarded as an integral part of Denmark, but continues to issue its own stamps. Area: 840,000 sq. m.; capital: Godhavn; currency: as Denmark; pop. (1960): 33,140.

Greenville, Alabama; **Greenwood,** Virginia. Both of these U.S.A. towns had Confederate 'Postmasters'' stamps during the American Civil War.

Grenada. British colony, one of the Windward Islands in the West Indies. From 1858 to 1860 British stamps were in use with the 'A 15' cancellation. The colony's own first issue followed in 1861. Until 1883 all Grenada stamps featured the famous Chalon portrait. Area: 120 sq. m.; capital: St. George's; currency: 1861, sterling; 1949, 100 cents = 1 British West Indian dollar; pop. (1960): 88,677.

Grenville, or Greenville. Liberia. See 'Harper' and 'Liberia'.

Grill or **Grille.** A symmetrical pattern of cross lines forming rectangles, squares, or diamonds. The term has three philatelic applications and meanings: (*a*) the faint pattern of squares printed on to an album page or sheet, to assist symmetrical arrangement of the mounted specimens; (b) the 'security' embossing-cutting die employed by the United States Post Office on its issues of 1867–71, and of Peru in 1874–9; and (c) the diamond-shaped (and continuous) cancellations used on the stamps of France 1849–51, and known also as a 'grille' canceller. Quadrillé paper (q.v.) is sometimes known as 'grill' paper on account of its characteristic pattern.

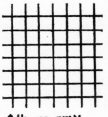

Album grill.

U.S.A. 1867–71. (greatly enlarged)

France 1849–51

Griqualand West. District of Cape Province, South Africa, annexed by Britain in 1871. From 1874 to 1880 it issued Cape of Good Hope stamps overprinted 'GW' or 'G'. Afterwards Cape stamps were used without overprint. The district now forms part of South Africa. Area: 15,197 sq. m.; chief town: Kimberley; currency: sterling; pop. (1891): 83,375.

Grønland. (Dan.). Greenland.

Grossdeutsches Reich. Greater Germany (literally, Great German State). The inscription appeared on certain issues of Germany, and of German-occupied Poland and Bohemia, in 1943–5.

Grove Hill. Alabama, U.S.A. Had its own Confederate 'Postmaster's' issue during the Civil War.

Guadalajara. Mexico. Revolutionary handstruck stamps were issued in this city in 1867.

Guadeloupe. Group of French islands in the West Indies, comprising the twin islands of Guadeloupe and various small dependencies. There were locally printed Postage Dues from 1876, but the first regular issue consisted of the French Colonial general series overprinted G.P.E. in 1884. Guadeloupe ceased to issue its own stamps in 1947. Since that date it has been regarded as an overseas department of France and has used French stamps. Area: 656 sq. m.; capital: Basse-Terre; pop. (1961): 283,223.

Guam. Largest and most southerly of the Ladrone group in the Pacific. Ceded to the U.S.A. by Spain in 1898. Contemporary stamps of the U.S.A. o/p 'Guam' were issued in 1899. It was occupied by Japan 1941–4. It now uses general issues of the U.S.A. Area: 206 sq. m.; pop. (1950): 67,044; capital: Agaña; American currency.

Guanacaste. Province of Costa Rica which had special overprints on Costa Rican stamps from 1885 to 1891. In this period Guanacaste was allowed nearly double the discount allowed to other provinces on purchases of stamps. The overprints were necessary to distinguish stamps thus sold at the lower rate. The concession was designed to encourage vendors to buy and stock large quantities of stamps in a remote province three days' travel from the capital. Area: 4,000 sq. m. approx.

Guatemala. Central American republic. A stamp purporting to have been issued by Guatemala appeared in 1867, but this proved to be a bogus production sponsored by Samuel Allan Taylor. Until its status was established it sold well enough for it actually to be forged! The first genuine issue appeared in 1871. Many of Guatemala's stamps feature the quetzal, a local bird which is the symbol of independence, and from which the present currency unit takes its name. Area: 42,042 sq. m.; capital: Guatemala City; currency: 1871, 100 centavos = 8 reales = 1 peso; 1927, 100 centavos = 1 quetzal; pop. (1962): 4,016,624.

Guayana. (Guiana). N.E. District of Venezuela with a series of typeset provisionals issued during the civil war in 1903.

Guayaquil Railway. See 'Quito'.

Guayas. Province of Ecuador with a script control o/p on 1899–1901 stamps of Ecuador in 1903.

Guerche. Ethiopian currency unit. Also used in Saudi-Arabia.

Guernsey. Channel Islands. Issued its own locals while under German occupation, valid from 1 April 1941 to 14 April 1946, and 'Regional' stamps since 1958. Area: 24½ sq. m.; pop. (1961): 45,150; capital: St. Peter Port; currency: British, but it has its own coinage. See also under 'Channel Islands', 'Herm', and 'Jethou'.

Guiana, British. See 'British Guiana'.

Guiana, Dutch. See 'Surinam'.

Guiana, French. See 'French Guiana'.

Guide Dot; Guide Line. Placed on a plate about to be engraved, or to which transfers are to be applied, to ensure correct alignment. Normally they are removed after the plate is finished, but on occasion have been forgotten, and as they pick up ink, they are clearly seen in subsequent printing, forming major or minor varieties. A modern variant takes the form of a letter 'T'.

Guillotine Perf. Single-line perforation, so-called from the supposed resemblance of the machine employed to a knife guillotine.

Guiné. Portuguese Guinea (q.v.).

Guinea, New. See 'New Guinea'.

Guinea, Portuguese. See 'Portuguese Guinea'.

Guinea, Republic of. Formerly French Guinea (q.v.), it became independent in 1958.

Guinea, Spanish. See 'Spanish Guinea'.

GUINÉ GUTTER GWALIOR

Guinée Française. French Guinea.

Gültig 9 Armee. German 9th Army Post--overprint on German stamps used during the occupation of Roumania, 1918.

Gum. Referred to in the early history of philately as 'cement', is the mucilage applied to the backs of adhesive postage stamps, and has as its basis crystalline gum arabic. The raw materials vary in colour from the finest 'water-white' to a deep orange, and these variations in colour are sometimes the only clue to the different printings of an issue which has been frequently reprinted. A perfect mint stamp is one with all its original gum (o.g.) as issued by the post office; an old stamp with full gum is referred to as 'o.g.' —original gum—one to which no addition of fresh mucilage has been made. In hot weather or under a strong light contraction of the gum can often cause mint stamps to curl. In extreme cases considerable damage can be done in this way. A temporary cure can be effected by breathing gently on the back of the stamp. Many modern stamp adhesives are dextrines, or of similar character, while some U.S.A. issues had an extract of cassava root (tapioca) as an adhesive. See paras. below.

'Gumpaps'. Early slang for 'labels' masquerading as postage stamps.

Gum Staining. Inter-action between an inferior gum, or one containing chemical and dye impurities, and the inherent substances in the paper base, or even in the ink used for printing, often give rise to unsightly stains, which adversely affect the appearance and intrinsic value of the affected specimens. Damp is a predisposing cause. The 6d. G.B. embossed stamps of 1847–54 had the gum tinted green to enable the operator to distinguish the right side of paper when embossing. See also 'Ivory Head'.

Gum Watermarks. The 1923 Republican Anniversary set of Czechoslovakia had its gum applied in a quadrillé pattern, each stamp showing the initials of the republic (C.S.P.) in gum design. This pseudo watermarking is unique and interesting.

Gutter. The space, usually blank, between the 'panes' (q.v.) of a sheet of stamps. See 'Millésime', 'Margins', etc.

Gutter Margin. See 'Wing Margin'.

Gutter Snipe. (U.S.A.). A single or pair of stamps with a full interpane or interplate blank gutter attached on any edge but bounded by a row of complete perfs. on both sides.

Guyane. French Guiana (q.v.).

Guy's City Despatch. A Philadelphia, U.S.A., local mail service operating in 1879.

Gwalior. Former Indian convention state which used overprinted Indian issues from 1885 to 1950. From the latter date ordinary Indian stamps have been in use. Area: 26,367 sq. m.; capital: Lashkar; pop. (1952): 4,006,159.

Cyrillic and Greek

Γ. The letter 'G' in both languages (the Greek 'Gamma').

ГОРОД: Gorod = 'town' in Russian.

H

'H'. On the SCADTA semi-official airmails of Colombia, the capital letter is a consular overprint, indicating that the stamp was sold in the Netherlands or in Curaçao.

HAPAG. (Ger.: Hamburg-Amerikanishce Paketfahrt-Aktien-Gesellschaft). The Hamburg American Line issued a 10 ¢. (black, green, and yellow) 'local' in 1875 to frank mail carried by their ships between the West Indian islands and ports of Central and South America. They were withdrawn in 1879, but reprints have been made in 1879, 1896, 1938, and a special centenary printing at Christmas, 1955. This latter is on watermarked paper and back-printed 'Nachdruck 1955'.

H. & B. Penny Post. An Atlantic City, U.S.A., local mail service organised in 1886 by Hackney & Bolte.

H.H. Nawab Shah Jahan Begam. Inscribed on stamps of Bhopal 1876–1901. The name and titles of the native ruler.

H. I. & U.S. Hawaiian Islands and United States (of America).

H.J.Z. (Hedjaz). Stamps of Palestine current in 1919 found so o/p are said to have been used by the Hedjaz Railway.

HM/OW. Her Majesty's Office of Works. See 'O.W./Official'.

H.P.N. Habilitado Por La Nación = Validated by authority. O/p on provisional stamps of Spain.

H.P.O. Highway Post Office (q.v.).

Habilitado. (Span.). Literally 'made good again'. Reauthorised. O/p on out-of-date issues to renew their validity.

Hadhramaut. Region of southern Arabia. Since 1955 the stamps of the Aden state of Qu'Aiti have been inscribed 'Qu'Aiti State in Hadhramaut'.

Hair Line. Diagonal white line across the 'check' letter tablet on the corner of some of the early G.B. surface-printed issues—the 1862 stamps in particular. The term is also applied to fine scratches on a plate or cylinder which print in the colour of the ink employed.

Haiti (Hayti). Negro republic in the West Indies, occupying the western third of the island of Hispaniola. Stamps first issued, 1881. Prior to this British stamps (cancelled 'C 59' at Jacmel from 1865 and 'E 53' at Port-au-Prince from 1869) were used on overseas mail, as were French stamps from about 1870 to 1881. As a consequence of internal chaos and mounting foreign debts, Haiti was occupied by United States forces from 1915 to 1934. In this period U.S. Marine post offices were established at Cap Haitien and Port-au-Prince, independent of the Haitian postal system and using American stamps. Area: 10,748 sq. m.; capital: Port-au-Prince; currency: 100 centimes = 1 gourde (also 1 piastre, 1906–16); pop. (1961): about 4,000,000.

Hale & Co. Organised a mail service from New York, U.S.A., to various towns and cities in 1884 and issued octagonal 'locals'.

Half-tone. Photo-mechanical printing process in which the tones of the original are represented by raised dots. Rarely used for stamp printing but instances are: Uruguay 1908 Declaration of Independence set (centres only), and Kishengarh, India, 1913.

Hall & Mills' Free Despatch Post. A local mail service between New York and Paterson, N.J., U.S.A., in 1847.

Hamburg. Former German state which issued its own stamps from 1859 until it joined the North German Confederation in 1868. Numerous ungummed remainders exist; also various reprints, some with forged postmarks. Area: 160 sq. m.; currency: 16 schilling = 1 mark; pop. (1880): 454,000. See also under 'Boten'.

Hamburg American Packet Company. Inscription on the local HAPAG stamp, see above.

Hamilton Counterfeit. (U.S.A.). Postal forgery of the 2 ¢ Washington stamp of 1894 which was discovered when large numbers were offered for sale in the U.S.A. at a discount by a Canadian firm who had bought them.

Hampton's City Despatch Post. A Philadelphia, U.S.A., local mail service run by T. A. Hampton in 1847.

Hand-chop. Overprint in Japanese characters applied by hand to stamps of countries occupied by Japan during the Second World War.

Hand-stamp. Postmark applied by hand. Such a marking is said to be 'hand-struck', see below.

Hand-struck Stamps. The term is usually applied to postal markings indicating that postage had been prepaid or was due, applied by hand in the pre-adhesive period. The phrase recalls that the original meaning of the word 'stamp' was an impression from a handstamp; it was extended to include the adhesive postage stamp because its purpose was similar—to indicate that postage had been paid.

Hanford's Pony Express. Local stamps with this inscription were issued in 1845 for John W. Hanford's Williamsburgh Express, a local mail and freight service operating between New York City and Brooklyn, U.S.A.

Hanover (Hannover). Former German state, an independent kingdom which issued its own stamps from 1850 until absorbed by Prussia in 1866. Area: 14,867 sq. m.; currency: 10 pfennig = 1 groschen; 24 gutegroschen = 1 thaler; 1858, 30 silbergroschen = 1 thaler.

HAMBURG   HAYTI   HANOVER

Harper. Seaport of Liberia. The 1893 registration issues of Liberia bore the letter 'R' and the names of the principal postal centres of issue—the towns of Harper, Buchanan, Grenville (or Greenville), Monrovia (the capital), and Robertsport.

Harrison & Sons Ltd. One of the leading firms of British stamp printers. Most of the low-value stamps of Great Britain since 1911 have been printed by Harrison's, who have also produced stamps in photogravure for 100 different stamp-issuing authorities overseas.

Harris's City Despatch Post. Local post operated by G. S. Harris at Philadelphia, U.S.A., for which local stamps were issued about 1847.

Harrow Perf. Both vertical and horizontal perforation done on a whole sheet of stamps in one pressure or operation, as opposed to the piecemeal methods of the 'guillotine' or line and 'comb'.

Hartford, Connecticut, U.S.A., had a local mail functioning to and from New York, Boston, Albany, and other points in 1847. Stamps depicted a top-hatted mailman—no inscription.

'Harvesters'. Name given to the reaper design stamps of Hungary introduced in 1916.

Hashemite Kingdom of the Jordan. See 'Jordan'.

Hatay (Alexandretta). Territory of northern Syria which became temporarily autonomous in 1938–9 before being returned to Turkey. In this period it issued its own stamps, including Syrian and Turkish issues overprinted 'Sandjak d'Alexandrette' or 'Hatay Devleti', definitives of 1939 with the latter inscription, and finally a set of overprints commemorating annexation to Turkey. Area: About 10,000 sq. m.; pop. (1939): 270,000; capital: Antioch.

Haut Senegal-Niger. See 'Senegambia and Niger'.

Haut Volta. See 'Upper Volta'.

Haute-Silesie. Upper Silesia (q.v.).

Hawaii. Group of islands in the Pacific, a former native kingdom which became a republic in 1894 and was annexed to the United States in 1898. The primitive early issues, of 1851–2, are known as the 'Missionaries', from the fact that many were used by missionaries writing home. In 1899

HAWAIIAN
ISLANDS

HEJAZ-NEJD

HELVETIA

a set of three Hawaiian stamps appeared under United States auspices, since when ordinary American issues have been used. In 1928 the current 2 ¢. and 5 ¢. stamps of the United States were overprinted 'HAWAII 1778–1928' to mark the 150th anniversary of the discovery of the islands by Captain James Cook; these were on sale only in Hawaii and at the Postal Agency in Washington, though valid for postage throughout the United States. Area: 6,423 sq. m.; capital: Honolulu; currency: as United States; pop. (est. 1963): 648,590.

Hawker. Stamps of Newfoundland o/p 'First Trans-Atlantic Air Post' were issued to frank the mail carried by H. G. Hawker on his abortive flight attempt in April 1919.

Hayti. Haiti (q.v.).

Head Plate. Alternative name for the keyplate (q.v.) of British Colonial designs; so called from the inclusion of the monarch's head.

Health Stamps. Charity stamps sold at more than their postal value, the surcharge being in aid of funds to promote health or combat disease, The best-known Health stamps are those of New Zealand, issued annually since 1929.

Heath, Charles. 1787–1848. Engraver to H.M. Queen Victoria. Engraver of the first die for the 1840 1d. black of G.B.

Heath, Frederick. Son of Charles Heath, whom he assisted. He engraved the 5s. 'coin' stamp for New South Wales, designed by E. H. Courbould (q.v.).

Heilungchang. See 'Kirin and Heilungchang'.

Hejaz, Hejaz-Nejd. See 'Saudi Arabia'.

Hela U-Boat stamp. Deutsche durch Feldpost U-boot—the German inscription reads. Was issued in 1945 to frank soldiers' letters to be sent from the isolated garrison on the Hela Peninsula in the Gulf of Danzig. The garrison capitulated soon after and there is little evidence of legitimate use over a period.

Helena. Texan, U.S.A., township which issued its own Confederate 'Postmasters'' typeset provisionals during the American Civil War.

Heligoland. Island in the North Sea, formerly a British possession. Stamps of Hamburg were in use from 1859 to 1867, when they were replaced by the first of Heligoland's own issues. These showed the embossed head of Queen Victoria, and are said to have been the inspiration for the famous 'Cameos' of Gambia. The island was ceded to Germany in 1890, whereupon Heligoland stamps were withdrawn and replaced by the ordinary issues of Germany. The existence of large quantities of reprints makes Heligoland a difficult subject for philatelic study. After the Second World War the fortifications constructed during the Hitler regime were destroyed, and the island used for bombing practice by the R.A.F. In 1952 it was returned to Germany, the occasion being marked by a West German commemorative. Area: $\frac{1}{4}$ sq. m.; currency: German and British; pop. (1900): 2,307.

Helio. Heliogravure. An early and alternative name for a type of photogravure, and still used for stamp production in Switzerland, etc.

Hellas. Greece.

Heller. Austrian unit of currency (100 heller = 1 krone) 1899–1925.

Helvetia. (Confederatio Helvetica). Switzerland.

Herm Island. One of the smaller Channel Islands, three miles east of Guernsey. Prior to the Second World War a sub-office of Guernsey functioned on the island but after the war the British Post Office declined to restore postal facilities. As a result the tenant of Herm has since 1949 issued local stamps to prepay postage on mail carried by his daily mailboat service to Guernsey. From May to September 1949 a pigeon post was also operated for urgent messages, and this too had its own local stamps; the service was discontinued on the installation of a radio-telephone, but the pigeon post stamps continued to be used on parcels until supplies were exhausted in 1953. No item of mail can be posted on Herm without a local stamp, but in addition ordinary British stamps are also required for onward transmission from Guernsey. The small permanent population is supplemented during the summer by large numbers of holidaymakers.

Hermes, or Mercury. The first issues of Greece bore the head of the 'Messenger' god, and are known to collectors as the 'Hermes' series. See also 'Mercuries'.

Herzegovina. See 'Bosnia and Herzegovina'.

Herzogth (or Herzogthum) Holstein. See 'Schleswig-Holstein'.

Hidalgos. Name given to the early issues of Mexico, so called from their portrait of Miguel Hidalgo y Castilla (1753–1811), a priest and social reformer who became the first leader of Mexico's independence movement and was executed by the Spanish.

HERMES   HELICOPTER   HOLSTEIN

Highway Post Offices of U.S.A. are motor vehicles using regular highway routes, picking up, sorting, and dropping mail *en route*. Originated in 1941. See 'Mobile Post Offices'.

Hilbre. Small island in the estuary of the River Dee, England. Stamp-like publicity labels were issued in 1961. They have no postal validity.

Hill, Pearson. Son of Sir Rowland Hill, is credited with the invention of the machine canceller or postmarker, in 1857. He introduced the 'duplex' dating stamp (q.v.).

Hill, Sir Rowland (1795–1879). Postal reformer who was responsible for introducing uniform penny postage to Britain, and with it the world's first adhesive postage stamps. His early experience in helping to colonise South Australia led him to feel the urgent need for simplifying and reducing the complex postage rates then in force. He expounded his views in a famous pamphlet, *Post Office Reform*, published in 1837.

In 1839 he was attached to the Treasury to put his reforms into practice, and on 10 January 1840 a uniform prepaid rate of one penny for all inland letters, irrespective of distance, came into force. The first stamps, the famous Penny Black and Twopence Blue, were introduced in the following May, at the same time as the first prepaid postal stationery, the 'Mulreadies', (q.v.) In 1842 he was dismissed from office, but in 1846 the sum of £13,000, raised by public subscription, was presented to him as a public benefactor. In the same year, following a change of government, he was appointed secretary to the Postmaster-General. He was Chief Secretary of the Post Office from 1854 until he resigned owing to ill health in 1864.

During this period Sir Rowland was responsible for a number of other measures to improve the postal service, including the founding of the Book Post. The effect of his reforms was to raise the number of inland letters from only some 77 million in 1838 to 642 million annually by the time of his retirement.

Hill's Post, Boston. Local post established by Oliver B. Hill, for which local stamps were issued in 1849.

Himriyya. In April 1965 the G.P.O. in London issued a statement that stamps purporting to have been issued by the Government of Himriyya might appear on the market. The statement added that Himriyya is not an independent state but is a village in Sharjah, and that Himriyya stamps are not recognised by the Sharjah postal administration.

Hind, Arthur. Amassed a wonderful collection in America. It contained the world's most valuable stamp—the one cent British Guiana—for which he paid over £7,000. The sale and dispersal of his collection after his death created some sensational new 'highs' in values of rarities and classics.

Hindustan. See 'India'.

Hinge. Stamp hinges are round-cornered oblong pieces of tough, thin paper, gummed on one side and designed for the neat mounting of stamps in the album. They were invented as long ago as the 1860s. The careful use of good-quality hinges, which peel easily when required, leaving little or no trace on either stamp or album leaf, cannot be too strongly recommended. Hinges are available in various sizes. Some are sold folded ready for use. Another type is partly gummed on either side for use unfolded, thus reducing bulk in the album. See also under 'Mounting'.

Hinkley's Express Co. A New York, U.S.A., city delivery service organised by Abraham M. Hinkley, and the Dixons, for which local stamps were issued in 1855.

Hirlapjegy (Magyar). Inscribed on 1900–22 newspaper or journal stamps of Hungary.

'Hlp'. (Magyar, Helyi lev. lap). 'Local Postcard' validity. O/p on Hungarian 1946 inflation issues. **'Hl'** (helyi levél) means 'local letter'.

Hochwasser. (Ger.). High water. Flood-relief o/p on stamps of Austria 1920.

'Hohenzollern'. The family name of the former rulers of Imperial Germany, and the name of the yacht of Kaiser Wilhelm depicted on the colonial stamps of Germany first issued in 1900, and known as the 'Yacht' or 'ship' keytypes.

Hoi-Hao (Hoihau). Chinese treaty port. Stamps of Indo-China were overprinted for use at the French post office there from 1901 to 1922.

Holkar. See 'Indore'.

Holland. See 'Netherlands'.

'Hollandshjalp'. (Ned.). Help for Holland. O/p on stamps of Iceland 1953 with surcharge in aid of flood victims.

Holstein. Former duchy, south of Denmark, under the Danish crown until 1864. Holstein and its neighbour-duchy of Schleswig were jointly occupied by Prussia and Austria following the war against Denmark, and the occupying powers issued separate stamps for Holstein in March 1864. In 1865 there was another issue by the Austrian administration. Following the defeat of Austria by Prussia in 1866, Prussia took over both duchies. The stamps of Holstein and of Schleswig, and of the combined issue for both, remained in use until the two duchies were incorporated in the North German Confederation from the beginning of 1868. See also under 'Schleswig-Holstein'.

Homan's Empire Express. A local mail service established by Richard S. Homan in New York City, U.S.A., for which local stamps were issued in 1852.

Honda. Town of Colombia which issued a provisional surcharge in 1896.

Honduras. Central American republic. Stamps first issued, 1866. Not to be confused with the colony of British Honduras. The early stamps are often found postally pen-cancelled, as few postmarks were available. Area: 43,227 sq. m.; capital: Tegucigalpa; currency: 1866, 8 reales = 1 peso; 1878, 100 centavos = 1 peso; 1933, 100 centavos = 1 lempira; pop. (1963): 2,007,990.

Honduras, British. See 'British Honduras'.

Hong Kong. British colony on the south China coast, comprising Victoria Island and the Kowloon peninsula, also the 'New Territories' on the mainland, leased from China for 99 years from 1898. Stamps first issued, 1862. The overprinted issue of 1891, marking the jubilee of the colony, is one of the earliest British Commonwealth commemorative stamps. The use of Hong Kong stamps at various treaty ports in China and Japan— distinguishable by the cancellations employed—has been intensively studied by specialists. From 1917 Hong Kong stamps were overprinted 'China' for use at these offices. With the exception of Wei Hai Wei, which remained open until 1930, these offices were closed in 1922. In 1941 the colony was occupied by the Japanese, and overprinted Japanese stamps were introduced for use there shortly before the liberation in 1945. Area: 398 sq. m.; capital: Victoria; currency: 1862, 96 cents = 1 Hong Kong dollar; 1880, 100 cents = 1 Hong Kong dollar (about 1s. 3d. sterling); pop. (1962): 3,526,500.

Hopedale Penny Post. A U.S.A. local of Milford, Mass., in use 1849–54.

Hópflug Italia/1933. O/p on stamps of Iceland. Commemorates Marshal Balbo's Transatlantic (Italian Air Force) Mass Formation Fight, 1933.

Horiz. Horizontal. (In reading the gauges of stamp perforations, the horizontal edges are given first.) As opposed to vert., the vertical or upright, when describing the format (q.v.) of a stamp.

Horta. Portuguese territory comprising the islands of Corvo, Fayal, Flores, and Pico in the Azores, which had its own stamps from 1892 until 1905. Prior to this period, and again from 1905 until 1931, stamps of the Azores were in use. Since then the group has used Portuguese stamps. Area: 294 sq. m.; capital: Horta, on Fayal; currency: as Portugal.

Hotel Stamps. Local stamps formerly issued by the managements of certain hotels at European health resorts to cover a fee charged for carrying guests' mail to and from the nearest post office, which was often some miles distant. There are three groups: the Swiss, the Hungarian-cum-Roumanian, and the Austrian.

The Swiss group is the largest. In the early 1860s there were a number of hotels situated high up in the mountains, remote from normal postal facilities. The first hotel to issue its own stamps was Rigi Kaltbad in 1864. The example was afterwards followed by Rigi Scheideck, Belalp, Kurort Stoos, Maderanerthal, and Rigi Kulm. Many of these stamps, especially on cover, are of great rarity. In 1883 their use was prohibited by the Swiss Government, and although further hotel stamps continued to appear until 1899, it seems probable that they were used only as advertising labels, and had no postal validity.

The Hungarian-cum-Roumanian group were issued by hotels at Carpathian resorts, originally part of Hungary but transferred to Roumania after the First World War. The group consists of Kurhaus auf der Hohen Rinne (1895–1926), Magura (during 1903 and again during 1911), and Bistra (1909–12).

The most modern group is the Austrian, comprising the issues of the Kesselfall-Alpenhaus and Moserboden (in use 1927–38), and Katschberghohe (winter months, 1933–8).

Hoyt's Letter Express. Operated at Rochester, N.Y., U.S.A. Local stamps issued, 1844.

Hrvatska. Croatia (q.v.).

Hrzgl. Post Frm. Inscription on first (1864) issues of Holstein (q.v.).

Huacho. Pacific port. Peruvian stamps o/p with a capital letter 'T' within a circle were authorised for temporary use in 1884.

Hulot, Anatole A. Assistant engraver to the Paris Mint, and (later) director of the stamp printing works responsible for the production of the stamps of France 1849–75.

'Hulp Nederland 1953'. (Ned.). Help for Holland, 1953. O/p on stamps of Dutch New Guinea. Surcharge in aid of Dutch flood victims.

Humboldt Express. Run in conjunction with Langton & Co.'s freight service, operated in Nevada Territory, U.S.A., in 1863.

Humidor. A humidifying box or cabinet; a 'sweat' box (U.S.A.). Consists essentially of an airtight container provided with a water-soaked pad over which is placed a perforated metal or other tray, upon which stamps to be bereft of unwanted paper, etc., are placed for treatment.

Humphrys, William: 1794–1865. Engraver to Perkins, Bacon & Co., engraved one of the U.S.A. 'Washingtons' while in America, and after his return about 1850 a number of G.B.'s classic designs, including a re-engraving of the first die for the penny (Die II).

Hungary. Former Magyar kingdom of central Europe, part of the Austro-Hungarian Empire until 1918. The first separate stamp issue for Hungary, which appeared in 1871, formed part of arrangements to give Hungary greater autonomy within the Empire; prior to this date Austrian stamps were in use. In 1918 a short-lived republic was set up, followed by an equally brief Soviet regime. Hungary was a regency from 1920 to 1945, when the present republic was established. All these political changes were reflected in the stamp issues of the time. A feature of the post-war

HYDERABAD   HUNGARY   HYPHENATED

period was the raging inflation of 1946, which led to the highest values ever to appear on stamps—up to the fantastic figure of 500,000 million million pengos! Area: 35,912 sq. m.; capital: Budapest; currency: 1871: 100 krajczar = 1 forint; 1900, 100 filler = 1 korona; 1926, 100 filler = 1 pengo; 1946, 100 filler = 1 forint; pop. (1960): 9,977,870.

Hussey's Post. A New York delivery service of 1854–80 which issued numerous local stamps.

Hwan. Korean currency unit, replacing woon or won in 1953.

Hyderabad (Deccan). Formerly the largest of the Indian native states, which had its own internal issues from 1869 until 1950, since when Indian stamps have been used. Area: 82,313 sq. m.; capital: Hyderabad.

Hydrogen Peroxide. A chemical bleaching and cleaning fluid, used diluted for the de-sulphurisation (or de-oxidisation) of used postage stamps and to restore whiteness to yellowed paper. Thorough after-washing is imperative. See 'Cleaning Stamps', 'De-sulphurisation', etc.

Hyphenated. With a hyphen connecting two parts of a compound word. In philately it applies particularly to the stamps of South Africa in which the Afrikaans name, Suidafrika, has appeared on certain issues both with and without hyphen.

Cyrillic

Н   = N in English.
И   = E in English.
НОВЧ = Novch, a Montenegro unit of currency 1874–1902.
Хелера = Helera (q.v.) a Montenegro unit of currency.

Greek: The Eta (H) = the long 'e', thus:

Η   = E in English
ΗΠΕΙΡΟΣ = Epirus.
ΗΡΑΚΛΕΙΟΥ = Heraklion.

I

'I' Overprinted on the SCADTA semi-official airmails of Colombia, the capital letter indicates that the stamp is a consular overprint sold in Italy.

I.E.F. Indian Expeditionary Force.

I.E.F. 'D'. See 'Mosul'.

I.G.Y. International Geophysical Year (1958).

I.R. Inland Revenue (Great Britain).

I.R.A. Irish Republican Army (q.v.).

Icaria or **Nicaria.** Formerly Turkish, this Aegean island was occupied and retained by the Greeks in 1912. A provisional government formed immediately before the occupation issued a set of stamps, which were superseded by an o/p issue of Greek stamps in 1913.

Iceland (Island). Island in the North Atlantic, formerly a Danish colony, an independent constitutional monarchy under the Danish crown from 1918, and a republic since 1944. Stamps first issued, 1873. Area: 39,758 sq. m.; capital: Reykjavik; currency: 1873, 96 skilling = 1 daler; 1876, 100 aurar = 1 krona; pop. (1962): 183,478.

Idar. Former Indian native state which had its own internal issues from 1939 to 1948. At other times it has used Indian stamps. Area: 1,668 sq. m.; capital: Himmatnagar; pop. (1941): 307,798.

Ifni. Spanish colony on the south-west coast of Morocco. The first definitive issue appeared in 1943. Prior to this, from 1941, various Spanish stamps appeared overprinted 'Territorio de Ifni', but their status is doubtful. Area: 579 sq. m.; capital: Sidi Ifni; currency: as Spain; pop. (1960): 49,889.

I Gildi. O/p on stamps of Iceland 1902–3 to validate the 'target' types being superseded by the King Christian IX portrait issues.

Île Rouad. Rouad Island. See 'Rouad, Île'.

Îles de Comoro. Comoro Islands (q.v.).

Îles Wallis et Futuna. Wallis and Futuna Islands (q.v.).

Ilmaposti. (Finnish). Air post.

Imper. reg. posta Austr. Inscription on 1883 'arms' types of Austria for use in the post offices in the Turkish Empire.

Imperf. Imperforate—see below.

Imperforate. Stamps printed in the sheet without aids to division or separation, i.e. without perforation or rouletting. The early issues of G.B. and many other pioneer countries were imperforate. They were separated with scissors or knife by the vendor. Imperforate stamps are always more valuable with clear margins.

Imperial Crown Watermark. Was introduced into the stamps of G.B. in 1880. It is wider and flatter in shape than the 'large' crown, and has a prominent circular orb under the surmounting cross. See illustration, p. 84, 'Watermarks', and 'Crown'.

Imperio Mexicano. The Mexican Empire. See 'Mexico'.

'Imperium' Proofs. Special prints of the Q.V. and K.E. VII British Colonial keytype designs made by De La Rue from small plates which were engraved 'Imperium' at the head of the duty plates. Are extant in various colours, imperf. and/or perforated, on paper with or without watermark.

Impressed Watermarks. See 'Watermarks'.

Impression. A copy taken by pressure from a plate, die, or block.

Imprimatur. (Lat. 'Let it be printed'). The first authorised sheets from a plate finally approved. 'Imprimatur' sheets are placed in the G.P.O. archives in Great Britain. See 'Abnormals'.

Imprimer. (Fr.). To imprint, print, stamp, or impress. Imprimerie: a printing office or works.

Imprimés. (Fr.). Printed papers or 'printed matter'.

Imprimés Sur Racord. (Fr.). Imprimaturs (q.v.).

Imprint Block. A block of four or more stamps to which is attached the margin bearing the printers' imprint.

Impuesto de Guerra. (Span.). War Tax—impost for war.

'Inclinados'. (Port.). The oblique numeral issues of Brasil of 1844–50.

Inde Française. French India.

Independence. Texas. One of the Confederate 'Postmasters' ' issues of the American Civil War.

India. Sub-continent of south Asia, under British rule until 1947. The first stamps issued in British India were the embossed seal types of 1852, known as the 'Scinde Dawks', authorised by Sir Bartle Frere, Commissioner for Scinde (Sind), a north-west province. They were followed by the first definitives in 1854. These and succeeding issues were produced under the auspices of the Honourable East India Company, and were inscribed 'East India Postage'—though intended for use throughout India. This practice continued until the 1882 issue, the first to appear after Queen Victoria had assumed the title of Empress of India in 1877. British rule came

INDIA   INDIA, BRITISH   INDIA, FRENCH

to an end in 1947, and the sub-continent was then divided into two new dominions, the predominantly Moslem areas forming the new state of Pakistan (q.v.), and the remainder continuing to be known as India. Since 1950 India has been an independent republic within the British commonwealth. For many years the stamps of British India were also widely used at various agencies in the Persian Gulf area; also at Aden prior to 1937. In recent years stamps of the Indian Republic have been overprinted for use by Indian forces serving with the United Nations in Korea, Indo-China, and the Congo. An extensive study in themselves are the often-primitive internal issues of many of the native princely states, and the overprinted issues (valid throughout India) of the convention states. Each of these is mentioned separately in this book; see also under Indian States below. Area of Indian Republic: 1,262,275 sq. m.; capital: New Delhi; currency: 12 pies = 1 anna; 16 annas = 1 rupee; since 1957 100 naye paise = 1 rupee (1s. 6d. sterling); pop. (1961): 439,235,082.

India, French. See 'French India'.

India Letter. See under 'Ship Letter'.

India Paper. A very thin, tough, but opaque paper, without any definite visible texture. The genuine variety is actually Chinese in origin, is made of bamboo fibre, averages ·002 in. to ·003 in. in thickness, and is of a white or creamy colour. Its principal use in stamp production is for proofing purposes, as its nature and texture are eminently suitable for obtaining clear impressions of fine and delicate engraving.

India, Portuguese. See 'Portuguese India'.

Indian Custodian Forces in Korea. Indian stamps overprinted for use by Indian forces serving in Korea were first issued in 1953.

Indian Expeditionary Forces. Indian stamps were overprinted I.E.F. for use by Indian forces serving during and after the First World War, 1914–22.

Indian Settlements. See 'French India'.

149

Indian States. The former semi-autonomous princely states of India are divided philatelically into two groups: the convention states and the feudatory native states. The former used Indian stamps with distinctive overprints with full national and international validity; many of the latter their own 'anchal' (or anchel) stamps, often in interesting and primitive designs, for use only within the borders of the state of issue. Each of the stamp-issuing states is mentioned separately in this book. The full list is as follows.

Convention states: Chamba, Faridkot, Gwalior, Jind (also Jeend, Jhind), Nabha, and Patiala (Puttiala).

Native states: Alwar, Bamra, Barwani, Bhopal, Bhor, Bundi, Bussahir, Charkhari, Cochin, Dhar, Duttia (also Datia), Faridkot, Hyderabad (Deccan), Idar, Indore (Holkar), Jaipur, Jammu and Kashmir, Jasdan, Jhalawar, Jind, Kishangarh, Morvi, Nandgaon, Nawanagar, Orchha, Poonch, Rajasthan, Rajpipla, Sirmoor, Soruth (also Sourashtra), Travancore, Travancore-Cochin, and Wadhwan.

The stamps of Travancore-Chochin were the last to go out of use, in 1951. Two further native states, Bahawalpur and Las Bela, are usually catalogued under Pakistan as they now form part of that country.

Indo-China. Former French territory in south-east Asia. It issued stamps from 1889 to 1950, when it was divided into Viet-Nam (North and South), Cambodia, and Laos (q.v.), each of which now has its own stamps. Area: 286,000 sq. m.; currency: 1889, 100 centimes = 1 franc; 1918, 100 cents = 1 piaster; pop. 27,030,000.

Indonesia. Formerly the Netherlands East Indies, this republic of southeast Asia was formed as the result of a revolutionary movement which ousted the Dutch administration in the years following the Second World War. The republicans started issuing stamps in 1945 for the areas under their control (central Java and most of Sumatra) while Netherlands Indies issues continued to circulate in the rest of the country. At this period numerous highly coloured pictorials, printed in Vienna and in the United States, appeared on the philatelic market; they are regarded as bogus, though at a later date token supplies were put on sale at Indonesian post offices. The Netherlands Indies were officially renamed Indonesia in 1948, and in 1949 the name first appeared on stamps for use throughout the country. Indonesia was recognised as an independent republic in 1950. West New Guinea, however, remained under Netherlands control until 1963; see under Netherlands New Guinea. Area: 575,450 sq. m.; capital: Djakarta; currency: 100 sen = 1 rupiah; pop. (1962): about 98,000,000.

Indore (Holkar). Former Indian native state which had its own internal issues from 1886 to 1950; from the latter date Indian stamps have been used. Area: 9,934 sq. m.; pop. (1952): 1,513,966.

Ingermanland, North. (Pohjois Inkeri). Russian territory (Ingria) adjoining Finland, which issued two series of stamps in 1920 during a period of temporary independence. Currency: Finnish.

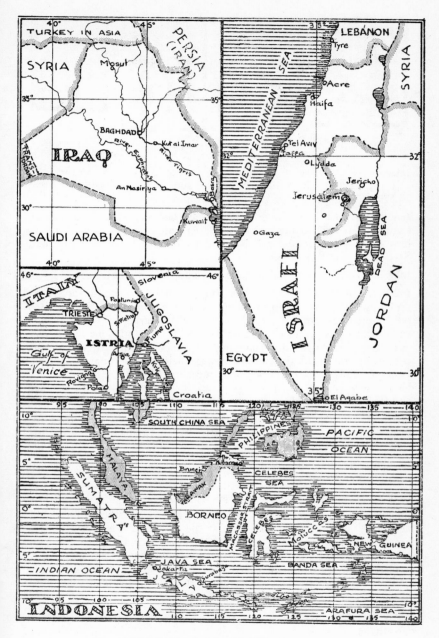

INDONESIA. IRAQ. ISRAEL. ISTRIA.

151

INDORE INGERMANLAND IMHAMBANE IRAN

Inhambane. District of Moçambique, Portuguese East Africa, with its own o/p keytypes 1895–1918. Now uses stamps of Moçambique. Area: 25,579 sq. m.; pop. (1950): 570,044; Portuguese currency.

Inini. Territory in the interior of French Guiana, which had its own stamps from 1932 to 1946; since the latter date ordinary French stamps have been in use. See under 'French Guiana'. Area: 30,310 sq. m.; capital: St. Elie; pop. (1961): 2,980.

Inkeri. (Pohjois Inkeri). See 'Ingermanland, North' above.

Inland Revenue. The headquarters of G.B.'s Inland Revenue are at Somerset House, Strand, London, and a number of the stamp issues were printed on the premises, notably the embossed 1847–54 series, and the sixpenny value which was produced here until 1934. This stamp value had a very large revenue use for the 'stamping' of minor documents, and it was considered convenient to print them where their greatest use was involved. Issues of 1882–1904 of G.B. are found o/p 'I.R./Official' the practice having now ceased. It is customary to inscribe the stamps of G.B. 'Postage and Revenue', as they have this dual validity. See 'Fiscals', etc.

Inselpost. (Ger.). Island post. German stamps so o/p were used for franked airmail service to occupying troops in Crete, Rhodes, and the Aegean Islands during World War II.

Instanta. Trade-name of a well-known perforation gauge, published by Stanley Gibbons Ltd.

Insurance Stamps. See 'Life Insurance Stamps'.

Intaglio. (Ital.). In recess. Strictly speaking all recess methods of printing, i.e. hand or machine engraving, and the photogravure processes, are 'intaglio', a word originally applied to the art of recess engraving on precious stones, and for the production of seals. In philately, it can be correctly applied to all processes where the inked image is *below* the surface of the plate, 'cliché', or cylinder. See 'Printing' and allied subjects. Pronounced 'in*tal*yo'.

Integrals. See 'Precancels'.

Interisland. Interinsular posts are postal services linking up a group of islands. See 'Bahamas'.

Internal Postage. See under 'Cheque Stamp'.

'International' Cancelling Machines. Postmarks from these may be identified on U.S.A. mail as the circle (dial) has the year date at the bottom. In 'Universal' machine markings the name of the state appears there.

International Commission in Indo-China. Indian stamps overprinted for use by Indian forces serving with the Commission were first issued in 1954. There are separate overprints for Cambodia, Laos, and Viet-Nam.

International Geophysical Year, 1958. Many of the nations co-operating in the I.G.Y. programme issued commemorative stamps to mark the occasion.

International Labour Office. Bureau International du Travail, one of the international agencies with headquarters in Switzerland. From 1923 various Swiss issues have been overprinted for B.I.T. use, and in 1956 the Office's first set of definitives appeared.

Interprovincial. A stamp issued by one province of South Africa but used in another. On the formation of the Union of South Africa on 31 May 1910, the stamps of the individual colonies of Cape of Good Hope, Natal, Transvaal, and Orange River Colony became valid for postage throughout the Union. To qualify as a true interprovincial, a stamp should be postmarked in a province other than that of issue on a date prior to the issue of the first Union definitives on 1 September 1913, although the colonies' stamps were not actually demonetised until 1938.

Interrupted Perf. Designed to give added strength to 'coil' stamps for use in stamp-vending machines. One or more of the transverse punches are removed, giving a broken line of perforation between each stamp, and thus leaving one or more 'bridges' of unbroken paper to take the strain of operating the mechanism. Thus in the Netherlands 1924–6 series the perforation has one punch missing at either end and two in the centre, leaving two groups of four holes. Interrupted perfs. are also found in the experimental coils of the U.S.A. The 1862 stamps of Peru were printed 'on the reel' on a Lecocq machine and were often rouletted with an interrupted series of cuts—sometimes known as 'syncopated' perfs.

Interverted. Wrong way round or a pair of stamps cut the wrong way or transposed in wrong sequence. Example, a dominical label on the top of a Belgian stamp instead of below.

Invalidated. No longer valid for prepayment of postage.

Inverted. Turned upside-down. In stamp printing there have been inverted centres, inverted frames, inverted surcharges and overprints and inverted watermarks, all of which are minor or major varieties, with more or less importance to the philatelist.

Ionian Islands. Group of islands off the west coast of Greece, a British protectorate until 1864 when they were ceded to Greece. A set of three stamps with Queen Victoria's portrait appeared during the British regime in 1859; the design included no indication of the face value, which could

ISLAND   IRELAND   ITALIAN P.O.S
ABROAD

be distinguished only by the colour. They were replaced by Greek stamps in 1864. In 1923 the chief island of Corfu was briefly occupied by the Italians, who issued overprinted Italian stamps for use there. During the Second World War the group was occupied by Italy, there being separate occupation issues (Greek stamps overprinted) for Corfu and Paxo, and for Cephalonia and Ithaca, followed by a general issue in 1941 for the whole group consisting of Italian stamps overprinted 'Isole Jonie'. In 1943 there was a further overprint applied during the German occupation of the island of Zante.

Iran. Independent kingdom of Asia, otherwise known as Persia. Stamps first issued, 1868. From 1867 to 1923 there were also a number of Indian post offices in Iran, using Indian stamps. Area: 627,000 sq. m.; capital: Teheran; currency: 1868, 20 chahis (or shahis) = 1 kran; 10 krans = 1 toman (also 100 centimes = 1 franc, 1881–4); 1933, 100 dinars = 1 rial; pop. (1960): about 21,000,000.

Iraq. Asian country formerly known as Mesopotamia, part of the Ottoman Empire prior to the First World War. Placed under British mandate in 1920, it became a kingdom in 1921 (though not fully independent until 1930); since 1958 it has been a republic. Indian stamps were used in the early stages of the British occupation in 1917–18. In 1918 Turkish stamps were overprinted 'Iraq in British Occupation'. The first definitives followed in 1923. Area: 169,240 sq. m.; capital: Baghdad; currency: As India until 1932, thereafter 1,000 fils = 1 dinar; pop. (1962): 6,803, 153.

Ireland (Republic of), Irish Free State. See 'Eire'.

Irish Republican Army. In July 1922 the I.R.A. issued three values for use in Cork during the disturbances prior to the formation of the Irish Free State (Eire). There is reason to believe that some of these were legitimately used for postal purposes, but they are normally classified as 'prepared for use but not issued'.

Irregular Perf. Where the holes vary in their relation one to another on any side of a stamp.

Island. Iceland (q.v.).

Islas de Juan Fernandez. Juan Fernandez Islands (q.v.).

Isole Italiane dell'Egeo. Italian Aegean Islands; see under 'Dodecanese.'

154

ISRAEL   ITALY (WITH   ITALY
                   PROPAGANDA LABEL)

Isole Jonie. Overprint applied to Italian stamps for use in the occupation of the Ionian Islands, (q.v.), during the Second World War.

Israel. Jewish republic on the western Mediterranean, formed in 1948 from part of the former British mandate of Palestine. Stamps first issued, 1948. Area: 7,993 sq. m.; currency: 1948, 1,000 mils = 1 Israeli pound; 1949, 1,000 pruta = 1 pound; 1960, 100 agorot = 1 pound; pop. (1963): 2,330,300.

Istria. Former Italian province occupied by Yugoslavia at the close of the Second World War. Occupation stamps were issued 1945–7. Now part of Yugoslavia.

Ita Karjala. Eastern Karelia (q.v.).

Italia. Italy.

Italia Repubblicana Fascista Base Atlantica or 'Repubblica Sociale Italiana Base Atlantica' o/p on stamps of Italy authorised for use in Bordeaux, France, by personnel manning submarines based there from June 1940 to 1944.

Italian Colonies. Several sets of commemorative stamps, issued between 1932 and 1934, were inscribed 'Colonie Italiane' or 'Poste Coloniali Italiane' for general use in all the Italian colonies.

Italian East Africa (Africa Orientale Italiana). Former joint Italian administration of Eritrea, Ethiopia, and Italian Somaliland. Stamps of Italian East Africa were in use from 1938 to 1942, replacing the issues of the three separate territories. With the British occupation in 1942, Ethiopia was restored to independence and resumed issuing its own stamps; British stamps were overprinted for use in Eritrea and Italian Somaliland (q.v.). Area: 666,000 sq. m.; capital: Addis Ababa; pop.: about 12,000,000; currency: as Italy.

Italian Occupation of Austria. Austrian stamps were overprinted for use in Trentino, and Austrian and Italian stamps for use in Venezia Giulia, during the Italian occupation of parts of Austria in 1918–19. In 1919–20 Italian stamps were surcharged for use throughout these areas, which were later incorporated into Italy. In 1921–2 there were further surcharges for use in the Zara region of Dalmatia, which became an Italian enclave in Yugoslavia until the Second World War.

Italian Post Offices in Albania. See 'Albania'.

Italian Post Offices Abroad. From 1874 to 1889 various Italian stamps were overprinted 'ESTERO' (Foreign) for use at Italian post offices in Egypt, Eritrea, Tripolitania, Tunisia, Argentina, and Uruguay.

Italian Post Offices in China. These started in 1901 as military offices for use by legation protection troops stationed in north China after the Boxer Rebellion. Ordinary Italian stamps were used until 1910. From 1917 to 1919 Italian stamps were overprinted for use at Italian post offices at Peking (Pechino) and Tientsin. Thereafter ordinary Italian stamps were used until the offices were closed in 1922.

Italian Post Offices in Turkey (Italian Levant). A number of Italian post offices were operated in various parts of the Ottoman Empire up to 1914, and again from 1921 to 1923. For use at these offices, at various times from 1901 onwards, Italian stamps were overprinted 'Bengasi' (see Benghazi), 'Albania', 'Constantinopoli' (Constantinople), 'Durazzo', 'Janina', 'Gerusalemme' (Jerusalem), 'Salonicco' (Salonika), 'Soutari di Albania', 'Smirne' (Smyrna), 'Valona', 'Tripoli de Barberia' (see Tripolitania), and 'Levante'.

Italian Somaliland (Somalia Italiana). Former Italian territory in East Africa, originally known as Benadir. The first stamps of 1903 was thus inscribed, and were issued by the Benadir Company. Many of the succeeding issues were Italian stamps suitably overprinted up to 1932, when Italian Somaliland received its first distinctive definitives. From 1938 its stamps were replaced by those of Italian East Africa (q.v.). For later history, see Somalia.

Italian States. Prior to the unification of Italy the country consisted of a number of separate states which issued their own stamps. These states were Modena, Naples (succeeded by Neapolitan Provinces), Roman States (Papal States), Parma, Romagna, Sardinia, Sicily, and Tuscany. In the north Lombardy and Venetia were Austrian territory (Lombardy until 1859, Venetia until 1866) and issued their own stamps as Austrian Italy (q.v.). Each of the Italian states is separately mentioned in this book. Rome itself, formerly part of the Roman States under the rule of the Pope, was not incorporated into Italy until 1870.

Italy (Italia). Former kingdom of southern Europe, a republic since 1946. Up to 1861 Italy consisted of a number of separate states which issued their own stamps. The campaign for Italian unification, brought to a successful conclusion by Garibaldi, centred around the kingdom of Sardinia, whose King Victor Emmanuel II became the first king of united Italy. The first stamps for all Italy, which appeared in 1862, were similar to the preceding issues of Sardinia and Neapolitan Provinces. In 1917 Italy produced the world's first government-issued airmail stamp. The Mussolini regime was marked by the inclusion of the fasces (symbol of authority in ancient Rome which became the Fascist emblem) in many stamp designs from 1923. In 1943 Mussolini was deposed and arrested, but subsequently rescued by the Germans and set up as head of a puppet republican government in German-occupied north Italy, which issued its own stamps as the Italian Social Republic (Repubblica Sociale Italiana) in 1944–5. See also under 'Italian States' and 'Austrian Italy'. Within the borders of Italy are Vatican City and the tiny republic of San Marino (q.v.). Area: 116,370 sq. m.; capital: Rome; currency: 100 centisimi = 1 lira; pop. (1961): 50,463,762.

Ithaca. Ionian island for which Italian occupying forces o/p Greek stamps in 1941. See 'Cephalonia.'

Ivory Coast (Côte d'Ivoire). Former French territory in West Africa, since 1958 an autonomous republic within the French Community. Stamps first issued, 1892. Between 1945 and 1959 Ivory Coast used the stamps of French West Africa (q.v.). Area: 127,520 sq. m.; capital: Abidjan; pop. (1960): about 3,200,000.

Ivory Head. A variety of the G.B. 1d. red and the 2d. blue of 1841–57. Electro-chemical action between the constituents of the ink used and the paper content caused eventual and variable blueing of the paper. Owing to the comparatively little ink upon the portrait of the Queen, the local staining was practically non-existent and (viewed from the back) the head often appears almost white upon a blued ground.

Cyrillic

Sometimes as in English, but the character И is a near equivalent to the 'I', thus:

ИРЛАНДИЯ = Irlandia = Ireland.

Greek

The Iota (I), thus:

ΙΚΑΡΙΑΣ: Icarias = Icaria (q.v.).

IVORY HEAD

JAIPUR   JAPAN   JAMAICA

J

J.P.S. Junior Philatelic Society (q.v.).

Jaffa. Palestine (now Israel). Russian stamps were o/p for use in the post office 1904–10.

Jaipur. Former feudatory native state of Rajputana, British India, which issued its own internal stamps from 1904 to 1949. From then to April 1950 it used those of the Indian Union of Rajasthan, and since, stamps of the Republic of India. Area: 15,610 sq. m.; pop.: 3,040,876; capital: Jaipur; Indian currency.

Jamaica. Island of the British West Indies, since 1962 an independent member of the British Commonwealth. British stamps cancelled 'A O1' and 'A 27' to 'A 78' were used in Jamaica from 1858 to 1860, when the island's own first stamps appeared. Area: 4,411 sq. m.; capital: Kingston; currency: sterling; pop. (est. 1962): 1,663,000.

Jamhuri. Swahili for Republic; overprint applied to Zanzibar stamps following the revolution of January 1964.

Jammu and Kashmir (Cashmere). Former Indian native state which had its own internal issues from 1866 to 1894, since when Indian stamps have been used. Many of these primitive stamps were printed in water colours, the design being liable to disappear altogether in excessive heat or damp! On the partition of India in 1947 Jammu and Kashmir were incorporated into India, though claimed by Pakistan. In 1960 Pakistan issued map stamps drawing attention to the disputed territory. Area: 82,260 sq. m.; capital: Srinagar (summer) or Jammu (winter); pop. (est. 1950): 4,370,000.

Janina. Greece, formerly a Turkish Albanian town, later known as Yannina, now Ioannina. Stamps of Italy o/p and surcharged were in use in the Italian post office from 1909 to the Greek occupation in 1913. See 'Albania'.

ELEMENTS OF THE JAPANESE NOTATION.

158

Japan. (Nippon, Nihon, or Dai Nippon). Empire of Eastern Asia, a constitutional monarchy since 1947. On 20 April 1871, it issued its first postage stamps, of imperf. square format, in a typically native design. Area: 142,747 sq. m.; capital: Tokyo; currency: 10 mon = 1 rin; 10 rin = 1 sen; 100 sen = 1 yen or en; pop. (est. 1956): 90,017,000. See also under 'B.C.O.F.'.

Japanese 'Chops'. These characteristic obliterations and o/ps were in use upon the stamps of the various occupied territories in and around the Pacific 1942–5.

Japanese Naval Control 1942-3. From 15 July 1942 all Netherlands Indies stamps in the area under naval control were o/p with 'Dai Nippon' (in Japanese) and an anchor. There are types associated with the following places: Bandjermasin, Pontienak, and Samarinda in Borneo; Macassar and Menado in the Celebes; Amboina in the Moluccas; and Bali, Lombok, and Timor in the lesser Sunda Is. A set of letterpress-printed definitives appeared in 1943.

Japanese Post Offices in China. Contemporary stamps o/p in Chinese were in use from 1900 to the closing of the offices in 1922.

Japanese Post Offices in Korea. (Chosen). General issues of Japan were in use in 1900 o/p, but after annexation were issued without o/p.

Japanese Occupation Issues. At the furthest point of the Japanese conquests in 1942, Japan controlled a vast empire covering most of southeast Asia. In some Japanese-occupied countries, for example Indo-China, stamp issues continued very much as before; in certain others, for example the British Solomon Islands, the Japanese occupation was too brief to have any philatelic effect. Elsewhere, however, the stamps of the occupied countries were variously overprinted with 'Dai Nippon' and/or 'chops' in Japanese characters; for yet other countries, for example Burma, entirely new stamps were prepared. Japanese occupation stamps are mentioned in the separate entries in this book for the following: Brunei (whose occupation stamps were also used in North Borneo, Sarawak, and Labuan), Burma, Hong Kong, Malaya (Straits Settlements and Malayan States), Netherlands East Indies, North Borneo, Philippines, and Sarawak (whose occupation stamps were also valid in Brunei, North Borneo, and Labuan).

Jasdan. Former Indian native state which had its own internal issue from 1942 to 1950. At other times Indian stamps have been used. Area: 296 sq. m.

Java. Malay Archipelago. Stamps of the Netherlands East Indies were o/p 'Java' in 1908. During the Japanese occupation the invaders prepared special occupation issues. The Indonesian fighting, and consequent formation of the new Republic, produced other stamps, some of very doubtful postal status. See 'Netherlands East Indies' and 'Indonesia'.

Jeend. See 'Jind' (below).

Jeens, Charles Henry. 1827–79. Engraver to Perkins, Bacon & Co. Engraved Chile's 'Christopher Columbus' first issue; 1860 'cents' issues for Canada; designs for Newfoundland; and for the 1860 set of the U.S.A.

Jefferson Market Post Office. A local delivery service organised by Godfrey Schmidt, in New York, U.S.A., in 1850.

Jenkins' Camden Dispatch. Was established in Camden, New Jersey, U.S.A., in 1853. Its stamps have been reprinted in various unoriginal colours.

Jersey. See 'Channel Islands'.

Jerusalem. Both Italian and Russian post offices in Turkey were provided with stamps bearing special o/ps.

Jetersville. Virginian town with a hand-struck 'Postmasters'' issue during the American Civil War.

Jethou. The Isle of Jethou is one of the smaller Channel Islands, close to Herm. There are no official postal facilities and since 1960 local stamps have been issued to prepay fees charged by the tenant for carrying mail by the daily mailboat service to Guernsey, which operates during the summer months. The status of these locals is similar to the issues of Herm (q.v.). Two stamps of the first 1960 issue were inscribed not with the name of Jethou but with those of Fauconnière and Crevichon, two islets belonging to Jethou.

Jhalawar. Former Indian native state which had its own internal issues between 1887 and 1900; at other times Indian stamps have been in use. Area: 824 sq. m.; pop. (1941): 123,000.

Jibuti. Djibuti (q.v.).

Jind (Jeend or Jhind). One of the only two former Indian states to issue stamps both as a native and a convention state. It had its own internal issues from 1874 to 1885; then acquired convention status and issued overprinted Indian stamps until 1950. Since then ordinary Indian issues have been in use. Area: 1,229 sq. m.; capital: Sangrur; pop. (1941): 361,812.

Johnson & Co.'s City Despatch Post. Mail service operated by Ezekiel C. Johnson at Baltimore, U.S.A., for which local stamps were issued in 1848.

Johore (Johor). Malayan state (sultanate). Stamps first issued, 1876. The early issues consisted of overprints on Straits Settlements up to 1891, when Johore's first definitives appeared. For overseas postage Johore continued to use Straits Settlements stamps up to 1916. During the Second World War Postage Due stamps of Johore were overprinted by the Japanese authorities; ordinary postage issues so overprinted were intended for revenue purposes only. Area: 7,321 sq. m.; capital: Johore Bahru; currency: 100 cents = 1 Malayan dollar (2s. 4d. sterling); pop. (1962): 1,126,038.

Jones' City Express. A mail service established by George C. Jones at Brooklyn, N.Y., U.S.A., for which local stamps were issued in 1845.

Jordan (Jordania). Independent kingdom of western Asia, formerly known as Transjordan. Part of the Ottoman Empire until the First World War, it then came under British mandate as part of Palestine. In 1920 it became an autonomous emirate, and in 1946 an independent kingdom on the ending of the British mandate. In 1948 Transjordan joined other Arab

JORNAES   JUGOSLAVIA   JOURNAL STAMP
                                                        (AUSTRIA)

nations in a war against Israel. In the resulting partition of Palestine much new territory was acquired and Transjordan was officially renamed the Hashemite Kingdom of Jordan. Stamps were first issued in 1920, the early issues being stamps of Palestine overprinted. The first definitives portraying the Emir Abdullah (afterwards first king of Jordan) appeared in 1927. Area: 36,715 sq. m.; capital: Amman; currency: 1920, 10 milliemes = 1 piastre; 1930, 1,000 milliemes = 1 Palestine pound; 1951, 1,000 fils = 1 dinar; pop. (1962): 1,824,614. In the 1948–50 period Transjordan stamps were overprinted for use in the occupied parts of Palestine.

Jornaes. (Port.). Journals. See below.

Journal Stamp. Low-value stamps have been specially designed and produced to prepay postage on newspapers, periodicals, magazines, journals, and general printed matter by many countries, and are often classified under this generic name. The one and two centesimi stamps of Italy of 1863 are typical examples. The term is applied also to the taxation stamps levied upon the publication of certain newspapers in the past, and which, in the case of the 1868 issues of France, incorporated the postal charges also.

Journaux-Dagbladen. (Fr. and Flem.). Journals or newspapers. O/p on parcel post stamps of Belgium 1928–32.

Juan Fernandez Islands. Group of small islands in the Pacific, forming part of Chile. Mas-a-Tierra, the largest, is known as Robinson Crusoe's island, as it was here that Alexander Selkirk, whose experiences inspired Defoe's story, was wrecked and lived from 1704 to 1708. In 1910 Chile overprinted four stamps 'Islas de Juan Fernandez'. They were intended for use on the islands but were in fact used throughout Chile.

Jubaland (Trans-Juba). Former Italian territory in East Africa, part of Kenya until 1925 when it was ceded to Italy. Jubaland had its own stamps (overprinted or inscribed 'Oltre Guiba') in 1925–6, after which it was incorporated in Italian Somaliland. Area: 36,000 sq. m.; capital: Kismayu; currency: as Italy; pop.: about 130,000.

Jubilee. Strictly, a fiftieth anniversary. In philately the term usually refers to the 1935 Silver Jubilee of King George V, marked by an omnibus series of stamps for all the territories of the British Commonwealth. The silver (25th anniversary), golden (50th) and diamond (60th) jubilees of a ruler's reign or a country's independence are favourite subjects for commemorative stamps. The 1887 issue of Great Britain is sometimes described as the Jubilee series, because its appearance coincided with Queen Victoria's golden jubilee; it was not a commemorative issue, however, remaining in use until 1902.

Jubilee Line. The inked printer's rule, frame, or line surround, enclosing a pane of stamps. It was first introduced into sheets of stamps of G.B. in 1887—Queen Victoria's Jubilee year—hence the name. It is due to the inking of a framework of brass 'rule' placed around the plates to more evenly distribute the weight and impact of the inking rollers, and thus to prevent the undue wear formerly occasioned by the rollers 'kicking' the edges of the marginal 'clichés' or plates, on making and breaking contact. An unbroken 'Jubilee' is known as 'Continuous'; if broken, it is 'Co-extensive', terms used in connection with the study of 'controls' (q.v.).

Judenpost (Ger. Jewish Post). Ghetto stamps issued for the use of Jews only were in use in the concentration centres of Lodz (or Litzmannstadt) in 1944. There were three sets of three values, but their true philatelic status is in some doubt.

Jugoslavia (Jugoslavija). See 'Yugoslavia'.

Julen (Scand.). Christmas. Inscription on Scandinavian Christmas seals. These have no postal validity.

'Jump' pair (U.S.A.). Misaligned coil stamps; i.e. one stamp higher or lower than the next one in the coil or strip, due to slight progressive deviation of the transfer roll.

Junagadh (Junagarh). See 'Saurashtra'.

Junior Philatelic Society. One of the leading British philatelic organisations, founded in London in 1899. The society publishes its own magazine *The Stamp Lover* (every two months). The term 'junior' in the title has nothing to do with the age of the members; it indicates merely that it was established later than the Royal Philatelic Society of London. Hon. secretary: 44 Fleet Street, London, E.C 4. In September 1965 the name was changed to National Philatelic Society.

Cyrillic

(Absent in Russian).

ЈУГОСЛАВИЈА =

Jugoslavija or Jugo-Slavia.

(See below.)

K

K.E. VII. King Edward the Seventh of Great Britain, who reigned from 22 January 1901 to 6 May 1910.

K.E. VIII. King Edward the Eighth of Great Britain, who reigned from 20 January 1936 to 11 December 1936, but was not crowned. Is now Duke of Windsor.

K.G. V. King George the Fifth of Great Britain, who reigned from 6 May 1910 to 20 January 1936.

K.G. VI. King George the Sixth of Great Britain, who reigned from 11 December 1936 to 6 February 1952. The Silver Wedding Anniversary of his marriage to Queen Elizabeth was celebrated by an omnibus series of stamps in May 1948, et seq.

K.G.C.A. Karen Government Commission (Zone A). See 'Carinthia'.

KGL/POST/FRM. (Danish). Konglilgt Post Frimerke = Royal (King's) Post Prepaid Stamp. Inscribed on the early issues of Denmark.

K.K. (or **K.u.K.**). (Ger.) Kaiserliche und Königliche = Imperial and Royal.

Kr. Kreuzer, a unit of coinage of the German States: Baden, Bavaria, etc., and Austro-Hungary.

K.R.N. Krajowa Rada Narodowa (Polish). National Federal Council.

K.u.K. See 'K.K.' (above).

K. Württ. Post. Konigliche Württemberg Post.

Kaiserliche und Königliche. (Ger.). Imperial and Royal.

Kalayan Nan Pilipinas. Inscribed on Japanese-inspired 'Independence' issues of the Philippines 1943.

Kamerun. (Ger.). Cameroons (q.v.).

'Kangaroos'. The name given to the 1913 map and kangaroo design of the Commonwealth of Australia. Often shortened to 'Roos'.

Kap. Kaplika, a former Latvian currency unit, the equivalent of the Russian kopec or copeek.

Karelia (Carelia). Autonomous north-western republic of the U.S.S.R., which during its short independence in 1922 issued its own stamps. Area: 55,198 sq. m.; est. pop. (1956): 600,000; capital: Petrozavodsk. See also 'Eastern Karelia'.

Karjala. Karelia.

Karki. Carchi; see under 'Dodecanese Islands'.

Karlfonds. Inscribed on Austrian war charity issues 1918 (Emperor Karl's Fund).

Karnten. (Ger.). Carinthia.

Karolinen. (Ger.). See Caroline Islands.

Kashmir. See 'Jammu & Kashmir'.

Kata Kana. The Japanese syllabic alphabet, part of which was used for identifying the various plates used in printing the 1874 issues. See 'Syllabics'.

Katanga. Breakaway province of the former Belgian Congo, which started issuing its own stamps in September 1960. It was reunited with the Congo early in 1963. Area: about 200,000 sq. m.; capital: Elisabethville; pop. about 1,700,000.

Kathiri State of Seiyun. Sultanate of the Aden protectorate in Arabia. Its stamps, first issued in 1942, are usually catalogued under Aden (Kathiri). See under 'Aden States'.

Kavala. Cavalle (q.v.).

Kedah. Malayan state, a sultanate which was part of Siam until 1909, when it was transferred to British protection. Stamps of Straits Settlements and Federated Malay States were then used until Kedah's first issue appeared in 1912. Under the Japanese occupation Kedah stamps were overprinted 'Dai Nippon' in 1942; from 1943 to 1945 the state was returned to Siam, but after the war was restored to Malaya. Thereupon the B.M.A. Malaya issue was in use until 1950. Since then Kedah has again issued its own stamps. Area: 3,600 sq. m.; capital: Allor Star; currency: 100 cents = 1 Malayan dollar; pop. (1962): 817,119.

Kelantan. Malayan state, a sultanate with a very similar history to Kedah, see above. Part of Siam until 1909, it issued its first stamps in 1911. Kelantan stamps were variously overprinted and surcharged during the Japanese occupation 1942–3; the state was then returned to Siam until 1945. The B.M.A. Malaya issue was in use from 1945 to 1951, since when Kelantan has had its own stamps once more. Area: 5,746 sq. m.; capital: Kota Baru; currency: 100 cents = 1 Malayan dollar; pop. (1962): 596,293.

Kellogg's Penny Post. A private mail service at Cleveland, Ohio, U.S.A., for which local stamps were issued in 1853.

Kemahkotaan. O/p on 1896 stamps of Johore, to mark accession of Sultan Ibrahim.

Keneta. (Hawaiian). Cent or cents.

Kenttäpostia. Inscribed on Military Post stamps of Finland 1941–4.

Kenya. Former British colony in East Africa, since December 1963 an independent member of the British Commonwealth. The Uhuru (Independence) issue of 1963 was the first to be inscribed with the name of

KEDAH KENYA KEY PLATE

Kenya alone; for earlier issues, see under 'British East Africa'; 'East Africa and Uganda'; 'Kenya and Uganda'; and 'Kenya, Uganda, and Tanganyika'. Area: 224,960 sq. m.; capital: Nairobi; currency: 100 cents = 1 E. African shilling; pop. (1962): 8,626,000.

Kenya and Uganda. Stamps thus inscribed, for use in the two territories named, were first issued in 1922, replacing the earlier issues inscribed East Africa and Uganda. They were in turn replaced in 1935 by stamps inscribed for use in Kenya, Uganda, and Tanganyika, see below.

Kenya, Uganda, and Tanganyika. These three British Commonwealth territories were linked in a joint East African Postal Administration in 1930. Stamps inscribed with the names of all three were first issued in 1935, replacing the earlier separate issues for Kenya and Uganda, and for Tanganyika. Such issues continued to be valid throughout the three territories even after Uganda and Tanganyika secured independence and issued their own stamps again in 1961 and 1962 respectively, and they remained the only stamps available for use in Kenya. They were finally withdrawn when Kenya too became independent in December 1963. See also the separate entries for the three territories.

Kérassunde, Kerason, Gireson, or Kerasos. The traditional home of the cherry. Turkish town in Asia Minor, on the Black Sea. The Russians issued o/p stamps for use in their postal agency 1909–10. Pop. about 10,000.

Kessler's Catalogue of Aerograms. See under 'Aerogramme'.

Khor Fakkan. Dependency of Sharjah on the Gulf of Oman. Sharjah stamps thus overprinted first appeared in 1965.

Key Plate. Carries the unaltered portion of the design common to two or more values or colonies in bi-coloured stamps. When this bears the portrait of the monarch, it is alternatively known as the 'Head' plate. The second plate is the 'Duty' plate (q.v.).

Keytypes. A basic design used for two or more colonies, the names of which are included either by type inserted in a name-panel, or (in two-colour) by means of a 'Duty' plate; or by over-printing across the design.

Such keytypes have been widely used by Great Britain, France, Portugal, and Spain for their smaller dependencies and colonies.

Kiautschou (Kiauchau). Chinese treaty port and territory, leased to Germany in 1897. Stamps of German post offices in China were used until separate stamps for Kiautschou in the German colonial 'Yacht' keytypes were issued in 1900. The territory was captured by Anglo-Japanese forces in 1914, and stamps of Japan were used, without overprint, during the Japanese occupation. In 1922 it was returned to China. Area: 200 sq. m.; chief town: Tsingtau; currency: 1897, 100 pfennig = 1 mark; 1905, 100 cents = 1 dollar; pop. (1914): about 190,000.

'Kicking Mule' Cancellation. A fancy U.S.A. cancellation which depicts the animal with flying heels, and which is much sought by collectors. It dates from the period prior to about 1880, when postmasters were allowed to purchase or improvise their own obliterators. See 'Cork Cancellers'.

Kidder's City Express Post. Inscription on a U.S.A. 'local' issued in 1847.

'Killer'. Colloquialism for any cancellation sufficiently heavy to disfigure most of the design; especially the barred oval part of a Duplex postmark.

Kiloware. Post Office parcel-card, 'Hospital' or 'Missionary' stamps collected by or on behalf of charitable institutions, for sale to stamp dealers, and sold on paper as received, by weight, and listed by Continental dealers at so much per kilo (about $2\frac{1}{3}$ lb.). It is therefore a mass of mixed stamps torn from miscellaneous correspondence, or parcel cards, unsorted, unclassified, on pieces of paper, and sold by the kilo or pound.

King Edward VII Land. Part of the Antarctic, on the Ross Sea. 1901 stamps of New Zealand so o/p were issued to the members of the 1908 Shackleton Antarctic Expedition. A similar issue was made for Victoria Land, for the 1911 Scott Expedition.

Kionga. Former region of German East Africa (Tanganyika) occupied by the Portuguese in the First World War, a set of four overprints on Lourenço Marques appearing in 1916. After the war Kionga was incorporated into Mozambique, and now uses the stamps of that territory. Area: 400 sq. m.

Kirin and Heilungchang, or Heilungkiang. Manchurian provices for which China o/p stamps in 1927, for use in her postal agencies. Combined area is about 330,000 sq. m.; and approx. pop. 23 million.

Kishangarh. Former Indian native state which had its own internal issues from 1899 to 1949. It then used stamps of Rajasthan, but since 1950 has used Indian stamps. Area: 837 sq. m.; pop. (1952): 104,127.

Klaipeda. See 'Memel'.

Knoxville. Town of Tennessee, and one of the Confederate 'Postmasters' Provisionals' of the American Civil War.

Kocher. A. Kocher et Fils of La Chaux de Fonds and Vevey took advantage of the right to have private postal stationery franked with

'KILLER'   KUBAN   КИТАЙ   КРНТН

impressions of current postage stamps by having, in 1909, gummed advertising labels officially printed with the 'Son of Tell' design then in use, within a frame provided. After some 16,000 had thus been supplied the Swiss authorities withdrew the privilege, and these 'stamp-on-a-sticker' varieties became obsolete.

Kohl Briefmarken-Handbuch. Created and edited by Dr. Herbert Munk who died in April 1953, although incomplete (only countries from A to K being then listed) is still one of the outstanding works of philatelic reference of the century.

Kookaburra Bird. There have been two Australian 6d. stamps depicting the 'Laughing Jackass'—the Kookaburra—one in 1913 (S.G. 19) and the other in 1932 (S.G. 146).

Kopec, Kopeck or copeek. Russian unit of currency. 100 = 1 ruble or rouble.

Korce. Korytza (q.v.).

Korea (Corea, Chosen). Former empire of eastern Asia under nominal Chinese suzerainty but subject to increasing Japanese influence from the 1880s and annexed by Japan 1910–45. Now divided into North Korea and South Korea, see below. The introduction of the first stamps by the Japanese in 1884 was the occasion for an uprising by Korean nationalists, who burned down the post office building and scattered sheets of the new stamps through the streets. On the pretext of restoring law and order Japanese troops moved in and occupied the country. In 1905 Korean stamps were replaced by Japanese issues, which continued in use until the end of the Second World War. The northern part of the country was then occupied by Russia, and the southern part by the Americans, and separate stamps for each of the two occupation zones were first issued in 1946. From these zones have arisen the present communist administration in North Korea and the independent republic of South Korea. Area of all Korea: 85,225 sq. m.; capital: Seoul; currency: 1884, 100 mon = 1 tempo; 1895, 5 poon = 1 cheun; 1900, 1,000 re = 100 cheun = 1 weun.

Korea, North. The Russian zone of occupation in Korea after the Second World War, formed into a communist people's republic in 1948. Stamps first issued, 1946. Area: 46,814 sq. m.; capital: Pyongyang; currency:

100 chon = 1 won; pop. (est. 1963): 11,040,000. Most of the stamps of North Korea have been issued without gum.

Korea, South. The American zone of occupation in Korea after the Second World War, since 1948 an independent republic. Stamps first issued, 1946. In the Korean war of 1950–1 the North Koreans invaded South Korea, applying certain occupation overprints to South Korean stamps. United Nations forces landed to repel the attack, and gradually drove the invaders back, restoring the border on the 38th parallel. Area: 38,452 sq. m.; capital: Seoul; currency: 1946, 100 cheun = 1 weun (or won); 1953, 100 weun = 1 hwan; 1962, 10 (old) hwan = 1 won. Pop. (1960): 24,994,117. Indian troops with the Armistice Commission in South Korea use Indian stamps with special overprint; see under Indian Custodian Forces in Korea.

Korytza (also Korce, Korca, Koritsa, or Coritsa). Town of Albania, centre of a short-lived Eastern Albanian republic under French protection, for which stamps were issued in 1917–18. Earlier, in the unsettled conditions of 1914, two stamps issued by the provisional government for Epirus were overprinted for use in Korytza. In the same year there were two local Military Post stamps.

Kotor, or Boka Kotorska (q.v.).

Kouang-Tchéou (also Kouang-Tchéou-Wan). Territory in southern China formerly leased by France, for which stamps were issued (mostly overprints on Indo-China) from 1906 until the territory was returned to China after the Second World War. Area: 190 sq. m.; chief town: Fort Bayard; pop. about 250,000; currency: as Indo-China.

Köztársaság. (Magyar). Republic.

Kraljestvo or **Kraljevina.** Kingdom (of Yugoslavia).

Kuban. The anti-Bolshevik provisional government surcharged Russian monarchical 'arms' types at Ekaterinodar 1919. See 'South Russia'.

Kume or **Kume-Shima.** A two-colour hectographed 7-sen provisional stated to have been sponsored by the U.S. Navy and issued by the postmaster of Kume Island in the Ryukyu Group in 1945.

Kurtz Union despatch post. A U.S.A. 'local' in use in New York, 1851–3.

Kurland. (Ger.). Courland part of Latvia. O/p on contemporary German stamps for provisional use in April 1945.

Kuruman. Town in Bechuanaland. A Boer War siege o/p on stamps of Cape of Good Hope was stated to have been prepared for issue in November 1899, but not officially issued. There are, however, a few souvenir copies in used condition extant.

Küstendje. Constanza or Constanta. Black Sea port. The Danube and Black Sea Railway Company in conjunction with the Küstendje Harbour Company, issued local stamps in 1867, for use between that port and Czernawoda (Cernavodä). These labels have been reprinted on various coloured papers over a period of years, and have been dropped from most catalogues as discredited issues.

Kuwait. Arab skeikhdom, seaport, and oil-producing centre on the Persian Gulf, under British protection from 1899 to 1961 when it became independent. The postal service was operated by India from 1914, the ordinary Indian stamps being used until 1923, and Indian stamps overprinted for Kuwait thereafter. In 1948 the postal agency was transferred to Britain, using British stamps overprinted until 1959. In 1958 the local government issued its own stamps for internal use, and in the following year took over the postal service entirely. Since then Kuwait has had its own distinctive issues. Area: about 5,800 sq. m.; currency: as India until 1961, thereafter 1,000 fils = 1 dinar; pop. (1961): 321,621.

Kwang-Chau-Wan. See 'Kouang-Tchéou', above.

Cyrillic

КРАЛЕВСТВО or
  КРАЛЕВИНА: (Kralyevstvo or Kralevina). See 'Yugoslavia'
КОП: Kop. Abbreviation for kopec (q.v.).
КОПЬЙКА: Kopeeca = one kopec.
КИТАЙ: Kitai = Cathay the ancient name for China. (See illustration on
  page 167.)

Greek

The Kappa (K) or hard 'c':
  The Chi (X) = 'Kh' in English, thus:
КРНТН: Krete = Crete.
КОРῩΤΣΑ: Korytza.
ΔΡΑΧΜΗ: Drakhmi (Drachma), the Greek currency unit.

L

'L'.   Lansa. O/p on airmail stamps of Colombia 1948. An air transport company authorised to use these stamps to prepay additional air charges.

L.c.   Large crown (watermark).

LKT/C/C/P.   Labels bearing these initials are stated to be 'local' stamps prepaying mail carried by courier between Wei-hai-wei and Chefoo in the Chinese province of Shantung. 'LKT,' it is said, represents 'Liu Kung Tao' (British Office), and 'C.C.P' for 'Chefoo Courier Post'. There were two values—2 ¢. and 5 ¢., and were only in use from January to April 1891.

L.Mc.L.   The *Lady McLeod* steamship (q.v.).

L.O.F.   And airplane. London-Orient-Flight. O/p on 1928 air issues of the Philippine Islands.

L. & S. Post.   (Land and Sea). Sideways o/p on Newfoundland 1931 Air stamp, converting its use for ordinary postage.

La Agüera.   District of Spanish West Africa near Cape Blanco. Stamps issued 1920-4. Now part of Spanish Western Sahara.

La Canea.   Italian stamps thus overprinted were for use at the Italian post office in Crete, 1900-14.

La Georgie.   Georgia, Europe (q.v.).

La Guayra.   (La Guaira), Venezuela, issued interesting 'locals' 1864-8, used on private steamer service to St. Thomas, Danish West Indies.

'La Maja Desnuda'.   Francisco Goya's famous painting of Maria del Pilar Teresa Cayetana, 13th Duchess of Alva (or Alba), reproduced on Spain's 1930 commemoratives.

Label.   In philately, usually any adhesive item not valid for postage, for example a charity or propaganda label; also a term of disparagement often applied to a bogus stamp. It is worth noting, however, that 'label' was originally the official term for a stamp, and it appears in the inscription on the sheet margin of the Penny Black. Even today the British Post Office refers to Postage Due stamps as labels.

Labuan.   Former British colony, an island off North Borneo. Stamps of India were used until 1867, then those of Hong Kong or Straits Settlements until 1879, when Labuan's own first stamps appeared. The British North Borneo Company administered the island from 1890 to 1906, over-printing North Borneo stamps for use there from 1894 until 1906, when

L.MC.L.   LABUAN   LAGOS

Labuan was incorporated in the Straits Settlements. Stamps of the latter colony were then current until 1942; then the stamps of Japanese-occupied North Borneo until 1945 when the island was incorporated into North Borneo. Area: 35 sq. m. Capital: Victoria. Currency: 100 cents = 1 Malayan dollar; pop. (1951): 8,784.

'Lady McLeod'. The steam packet depicted on a local stamp of Trinidad, a 5 ¢. value issued by David Bryce, the owner and captain, in April 1847, to prepay the carriage on letters carried by the vessel between Port of Spain and San Fernando. The 'Lady McLeod' stamp is recognised and listed by Gibbons, and thus ranks as the first catalogued Colonial issue, preceding the Mauritius Post Office stamps by six months. The latter were, however, the first officially issued colonial stamps.

Lagerlöf, Col. Hans. Swedish-American collector. Died in U.S.A., aged 72, in 1952. Donated over six thousand album pages to the Swedish Postal Museum, Stockholm, a few years before his death. The rest of his vast collection was auctioned in the U.S.A. in 1953.

Lagos. British town and colony on the south coast of Nigeria. It had its own issues from 1874 to 1906, when it was absorbed into Southern Nigeria, whose stamps were then used. Now part of Nigeria (q.v.). Area: 3,460 sq. m.; pop. (1901): about 1½ million (Lagos town: 75,000).

Laibach. See 'Yugoslavia'.

Laid. One of the two principal types of paper used for stamp printing, the other being wove. Close examination of laid paper shows a texture of closely parallel lines, either horizontal or vertical, due to the impress of the wires of the dandy-roll of the paper-making machine. Many stamps have been printed on laid paper in the past, but it is now much less frequently used. It is not to be confused with Repp or ribbed paper, in which the parallel lines are seen in relief on the surface.

Laid Bâtonné. (Fr. vergé bâtonné). A bâtonné (q.v.) paper which has the spaces between the watermarked 'rules' filled with the characteristic laid pattern detailed above.

Land-Post. 'Land-post/Porto-marke'. Rural post stamps of Baden 1862. Three values printed black on yellow, perf. 10, were affixed by postal officials on mail on which extra charges were payable in respect of rates, outstanding accounts, etc., on behalf of local authorities. The charge for this service was one kreuzer per florin collected and was denoted by these stamps, which are therefore not strictly postage 'dues' as usually described and listed. (See illustration on page 32).

Landstormen. O/p on 1916–18 issues of Sweden. A surcharge levied to provide uniforms for men on the army reserve.

Langton & Co. See 'Humboldt Express'.

Laos. Formerly part of Indo-China, since 1949 an independent kingdom within the French Union. Area: 88,780 sq. m.; pop. (est. 1962): 2,200,000. First issues appeared in November 1951, replacing issues of Indo-China.

Las Bela. Former feudatory native state on the south-east of Baluchistan, British India, which issued its own series of local stamps 1897–1907. It then used stamps of British India. Area: 7,043 sq. m.; pop.: 76,000; capital of same name; Indian currency. It is now in Pakistan, and is often catalogued under that country.

Latakia. (Fr. Lattaquié). Territory of Syria formerly known as Alaouites (q.v.). Under French mandate until Syria became independent, it was issued with Syrian contemporary stamps o/p from 1931 to 1937. Area: 2,433 sq. m.; pop. (1952): 471,673; capital: Latakia; currency: 100 centimes = 1 piastre.

Late Fee Stamps. Are issued by a number of postal administrations to prepay extra charges for mail posted after normal hours.

Latvia. (Latvija). Former independent republic on the Baltic which achieved independence from Russia in 1918 and in December of that year issued its first stamps, printed on the backs of abandoned German war maps. Latvia was occupied by Soviet Russia in 1939, and after a series of stamps inscribed 'Latvijas PSR', marking the incorporation of Latvia into the Soviet Union, Latvian stamps were replaced by the ordinary Russian issues. During the subsequent German occupation of 1941–4 Russian stamps were overprinted 'Latvija' and afterwards the German Ostland issues were in use. Since 1944 Latvia has again formed part of Soviet Russia. Area: 25,390 sq. m.; Capital: Riga. Currency: 1918, 100 kapeikas = 1 rublis; 1923, 100 santims = 1 lat; pop. (1954): 2,100,000.

'Latvijas Aizsargi'. (Lettish). Latvian Militia. O/p on 1931 Latvian stamps as surcharge to raise funds for the rearming of this force.

'Laureated'. Crowned or wreathed with laurel. Applied to the 1850–63 Queen Victoria issues of New South Wales; the 1862–70 Napoleon III issues of France, and others, to distinguish monarchical and other portraits from 'crowned' heads.

Lawinenopfer 1954. (Ger.). Avalanche Relief. O/p on Austrian 'landscape' stamp issued February 1954 with surcharge in aid of avalanche victims in the Austrian Tyrol.

League of Nations. Swiss current issues were o/p 'Société des Nations', 'Service de la Société des Nations', and 'Courrier De La Société Des Nations', 1923–44, for the use of the League at its Geneva headquarters.

LATVIA   'LEOPARDS'   'LAUREATED'

Lebanon. (Liban). Otherwise known as Great Lebanon (Grand Liban), this Syrian territory, formerly part of the Ottoman Empire, came under French mandate in 1918. It became autonomous in 1920, and its first stamps were French issues overprinted 'Grand Liban' which appeared in 1924. A republic was established in 1926, achieving full independence in 1942 on the ending of the French mandate. Area: 3,475 sq. m.; capital: Beirût (Beyrouth); currency: 100 centimes = 1 piastre; 100 piastres = 1 Lebanese pound.; pop. (1963): 1,750,000.

Lecocq Machine. This ingenious French machine printed the embossed and other issues of Peru in a continuous strip or ribbon, the stamps being either cut up or issued in lengths after being rouletted or pierced by three cuts between each pair of stamps. See also 'Interrupted perfs'.

Ledger Dispatch, The. A Brooklyn, U.S.A., local delivery service established in New York by Edwin Pidgeon, in 1882.

Leeward Islands. British colony in the West Indies, comprising the presidencies of Antigua; St. Christopher, Nevis, and Anguilla; Montserrat; and the Virgin Islands. Dominica was also part of the group until 1940, when it was transferred to the Windward Islands. Stamps inscribed Leeward Islands, for use throughout the group, were first issued in 1890, replacing the earlier issues for individual islands. They were the only stamps available in the Virgin islands until 1899 and in the other islands until 1903; thereafter the individual islands again had their own stamp issues. Leeward Islands stamps, however, continued in use concurrently until they were finally withdrawn in 1956. Area: 422 sq. m.; capital: St. John's, Antigua; currency: sterling until 1951, then 100 cents = 1 British West Indian dollar; pop. (1952): 120,145.

Lemnos. Aegean Island. Formerly Turkish, was occupied by the Greeks in 1912, and stamps of Greece were o/p in 1912–13. Now uses stamps of Greece. Area: 186 sq. m.; pop. (1952): 23,842.

Lenoir. North Carolina, from which came a hand-struck Confederate 'Postmasters'' stamp during the Civil War.

Leon. (De Leon). Province of Ecuador. A control overprint was applied there to local stocks in 1902 following the theft of large quantities of stamps during a fire at Guayaquil. Leon is also the name of a Mexican province with revolutionary provisional overprints 'Gob–Const.' in 1914.

'Leopards'. The 1934 and 1938 Nyasaland Protectorate designs are thus known to collectors.

Lepta. Greek unit of currency.

Leros. (Lero). See under 'Dodecanese Is.'

Lesbos, or Mytilene, Mitilini, or Metelin (q.v.). Aegean island.

Letadlem. (Czech.). By air, Airborne mails.

Letter Dispatch. See: 'Prince's Letter Dispatch'.

Letter Express. Inscribed on the 'locals' issued by Henry Wells to frank mail carried between Western New York, Chicago, Detroit, and Duluth in 1844.

Letterpress. Alternative and preferable name for typography or 'surface' printing. In stamp production it implies that normal typesetting methods of printing and machinery are employed. Line and, more rarely, halftone blocks, are thus printed on ordinary letterpress platens or rotaries, and many thousands of stamps are still turned out by these methods. The typeset (q.v.) early stamps of many nations are letterpress productions. See also: 'Printing', 'Surface Printing', 'Typography', and Frontispiece, etc.

Lettland. Latvia (q.v.).

Leu. A Romanian currency unit = 100 bani. Plural is lei.

Leva. Bulgarian currency unit = 100 stotinki.

Levant. (Fr.). Towards the rising sun = the East. Name applied to the Eastern Mediterranean in general, and the coastal areas of the former Ottoman (Turkish) Empire in particular. Austria, France, Germany, Great Britain, Italy, Poland, Roumania, and Russia have all issued stamps o/p or inscribed for use in the many postal agencies in the area and both Egypt and Greece had offices, the stamps used being identifiable by postmarks only. Under the Treaty of Lausanne all foreign post offices were closed down *circa* 1923; but there was a further Free French 'Levant' series for use in Syria in 1942. See 'British Levant', and under Levantine post office headings for the countries cited above.

Liban. Lebanon (q.v.).

Libau. (Ger.). Latvia. O/p on German occupation stamps 1919.

Liberia. Negro republic of West Africa, founded by the American Colonisation Society in 1816 as a home for emancipated slaves. Stamps first issued, 1860. Area: 43,000 sq. m.; capital: Monrovia.; currency: 100 cents = 1 dollar; pop. (1953): 1,500,000.

Libya. (Libia, Libye). North African territory formerly part of the Ottoman Empire, an Italian colony from 1911 until the British occupation during the Second World War, and an independent kingdom since December 1951. Stamps first issued, 1912. From 1943 to 1951 British stamps overprinted M.E.F. were in use. Libya comprises the three regions of Tripolitania, Cirenaica, and Fezzan, all of which have had their own stamps in the past and which are mentioned separately in this book. Area: 679,340 sq. m.; capital: Tripoli; currency: 1912, as Italy; 1951, 480 military authority lire (M.A.L.) = 1 Libyan pound in Tripolitania, Egyptian currency in Cirenaica; 1952, 1,000 milliemes = 1 pound.; pop. (1954): 1,092,000.

Liechtenstein. Independent principality of Central Europe. Stamps first issued, 1912. The postal service was operated by Austria until the end of the First World War. Afterwards Liechtenstein became associated with Switzerland, and joined the Swiss customs union in 1924; since the latter date Liechtenstein stamps have been printed in Switzerland. Area: 61 sq. m.; capital: Vaduz; currency: Austrian until 1921, thereafter Swiss; pop. (1960): 16,628.

Lietuva. Lithuania (q.v.).

Life Insurance Stamps. In philately, the Official stamps issued for the postal use of the New Zealand Government's Life Insurance Department; often referred to as the 'Lighthouses', from their designs.

Lightly Cancelled. Copies of used stamps lightly but legibly cancelled are the collector's ideal; but where there is a disparity in values between a mint specimen as compared with a used—with the advantage in favour of the latter—the postmark must be unmistakably there, and genuine. A legible mark showing date and place of origin is sometimes of more importance than a light cancellation; but normally a heavily cancelled or 'killed' stamp is at a heavy discount. See 'Condition' and allied subjects.

Lignes Aeriennes F.A.F.L. Air Lines, Free French Forces in the Levant.

Lima. Capital and department of Peru. The name appears on the 1871 issue of Peru—often described as the world's first commemorative— which paid postage on mail carried by rail between Lima, Callao, and Chorrillos. In 1873 another stamp inscribed Lima was issued to cover the local letter rate within the city. The name appeared again on various locally overprinted issues of 1881–9, during and after the war against Chile.

Limbagan. Lit. Printing Press. 'Limbagan 1593–1943' o/p on stamps of the Philippine Islands (under Japanese occupation) commemorating the 350th Anniversary of the introduction of the printing press.

Line Block. An unscreened photo-mechanical printing block, normally of zinc (zinco), which is used as a 'master' for the requisite number of 'electros' or 'stereos' from which stamps are printed by the letterpress, typographic, or 'surface' method. For short runs the original zinco may be used, and both the original block, and the copies, may be steel, chromium, or nickel faced to resist wear. See also 'Half-tone', and 'Printing', etc. It is also used (in U.S.A. especially) to describe a block of stamps with either a vertical or horizontal line gap (see 'Line-gap pair' below) running between rows of stamps or an inserted guide line for colour registration, perforating, or slitting.

Line Engraving. The early line-engraved stamps were produced by the process invented by Jacob Perkins of the British firm of Perkins, Bacon & Petch, and consisted of hand engraving with a steel tool known as a burin, on softened steel. The 'mother' or original die was then hardened, and a softened steel roller passed over it under very great pressure to produce the 'matrix' or secondary die. After hardening, this roller was used to produce multiple-impressioned plates from which the actual printing was done—the 'tertiary' dies. The final plate bore the design in intaglio (recess). Printing was done by inking the plate, wiping off the surplus surface ink, and applying pressure to an imposed sheet of dampened paper, the paper picking out the ink from the incised design in the plate. Modern 'recess' printing is done from a plate mechanically inked and wiped, and on specially designed high-speed rotary presses. See 'Printing', 'Line block', 'Litho', 'Photogravure', and allied subjects.

Line-gap pair. A coloured line between a pair of U.S.A., Canadian, or other 'coils' (q.v.) caused by the join in the printing plate. A variety much sought after by specialists and precancel collectors.

Line Perf. A single row of perforating punches, doing one line of perforations at one stroke. Sometimes called 'guillotine' perforating (q.v.). See 'Harrow', 'Comb', and 'Perforation', etc.

Lipso (Lisso). See under 'Dodecanese Islands'.

Litho., Lithography. Plane surface printing method based upon the antipathy of oil (or grease) and water. A specially prepared limestone or soapstone was formerly used. Upon this the design was drawn in reverse direct, with a greasy ink; or transferred thereon by means of special transfers. In printing, the stone is kept damp, and only the greasy ink image, with its affinity for the special inks used, transfers the design the right-way round on to the paper. In offset lithography, the image is first picked up by a rubber blanket, which in its turn transfers the design to the paper. In modern photo-lithography the image is printed photographically on to an etched or grained zinc or aluminium foil or plate, which can then be attached to the cylinder of a rotary press. It will be seen therefore that the process is radically different from the recess (or intaglio) methods, and the relief (or typographic or surface) processes. See 'Printing', 'Recess', 'Line engraving', 'Surface', and other relevant headings.

Lithuania (Lietuva). Former independent republic on the Baltic, which achieved independence from Russia in 1918 and in the same year issued its first stamps—typeset provisionals. The first definitives followed in 1919. Lithuania was occupied by Soviet Russia in 1939, and after a set of LTSR overprints marking the incorporation of the country into the Soviet Union, Lithuanian stamps were replaced by the ordinary Russian issues. During the German occupation of 1941–4 Russian stamps were overprinted Lietuva for use in Lithuania, and afterwards the German Ostland issues were in use. Since 1944 Lithuania has again formed part of Soviet Russia. Area: 31,200 sq. m.; capital: Kaunas 1920–39, thereafter Vilnius

LOCALS:

SHUNA (G.B.)　　　　NEW HEBRIDES　　　　CHEFOO, CHINA

(Vilna); currency: 1918, 100 skatiku = 1 auksinas; 1922, 100 centu = 1 litas; pop. (1906): 2,700,000.

Litwa. Srodkowa Litwa. Central Lithuania (q.v.).

Livingston. Alabama. One of the Confederate 'Postmasters'' stamps issued during the American Civil War.

Livonia. See 'Wenden'.

Ljubljana (Laibach). See under 'Yugoslavia'.

Locals. Local stamps are those, whether issued privately or officially, whose postal validity is restricted to a particular district, route, or service, and are not available for general national or international use. Stamps valid only within the borders of the state of issue (for example Indian native states) are occasionally referred to as locals, but this much wider definition (by which even the Penny Black would be a local) is not generally accepted. Stamps of this kind are better described as internal issues. Locals have not been catalogued by Gibbons since the turn of the century, and for many years they were not favoured by collectors. They are, however, an interesting study and in recent years they have enjoyed a revival.

Lockport. New York, U.S.A. One of the rarer 'Postmasters'' of the American Civil War.

Locomotive Express Post. A U.S.A. local stamp of 1854 bears this inscription.

Loftleiois. (Icelandic). By air.

Loja. A province of Ecuador, with the authorised control o/p 'Loja Franca', in 1902.

Lokalbref. (Swed.). Local letter. A Stockholm 'local' 1856–85.

Lokoja. One of the Niger Coast and River post offices with a dated canceller in use on stamps of G.B. from 1899–1900 by the Royal Niger Company (q.v.).

Lombardy-Venetia. See 'Austrian Italy'.

Long Island. Turkish island of Uzun, in the Izmir Körfesi Gulf in the Aegean Sea, dominating the outer harbour of Smyrna (now Izmir), so temporarily named and occupied by the British 7 to 26 May 1916. They o/p Turkish fiscals 'G.R.I./Postage' and, later, typewritten provisionals, using various coloured ribbons and carbons.

Loomis Letter Express. See 'Carne's City Letter Express'.

Loose-Leaf Album. See 'Album'.

Loose Letter. Mail arriving at an office of delivery or for forwarding, without cancel or mark of origin, and usually from an incoming ship, was formerly marked in this manner.

Lord Howe Island. Dependency of N.S.W. in the South Pacific administered by a Board of Control from Sydney, and uses Australian stamps. During a shortage of 2d. values the postmaster issued some 1½d. red K.G. V issues, and 1930 Sturt commems. with a manuscript o/p and surcharge '2d' Paid/P.M.L.H.I.' (Postmaster Lord Howe Island). These were not recognized as valid by the Australian postal authorities. Area: 5 sq. m.; pop. (1958): 270.

Lorraine. (Ger. Lothringen). See 'Alsace and Lorraine'.

Lösen. Postage due, Sweden.

Los Ríos. (Span. The Rivers). Province of Ecuador with an authorised control o/p in 1902.

Lothringen. Lorraine.

Lotnicza. (Polish). Airborne (post).

'Lotus' Watermark. See 'Rosace Watermark'.

Louisville. Kentucky, U.S.A., with two 'Carriers'' issues 1857-8 (Wharton's, and Brown & McGill's Posts).

Lourenço Marques. Portuguese East African city and settlement north of Delagoa Bay, and capital of Moçambique (q.v.). Inscribed keytypes were issued from 1894 to 1925, when it became part of Moçambique, whose stamps are now used. 1950 Commune pop.: 93,516.

Lozenge (or diamond) **Roulette.** See 'Percé en Lozanges'.

L'press. Letterpress.

Lübeck. Former German Hanseatic port on the Baltic. A stamp-issuing free state from 1859 to 1867. Present pop. about 238,000; stamp currency: 16 schilling = 1 mark.

Luchtpost. (Dutch) ⎫
Luftpost. (Ger.) ⎬ Air(borne) Post.
Lugpos. (Afrik.) ⎭

Luftfeldpost. (Ger.). Airborne military mail. A blue stamp so inscribed, picturing an aeroplane in flight, was issued as a forces priority stamp to German troops in 1941-2, especially for use by personnel cut off from their bases, and for isolated garrisons.

LUCHTPOST   LUXEMBOURG   ΛΕΠΤΑ

Lundy. Privately owned island in the Bristol Channel, England. Since the closing of a British sub-post office on the island, the owner has issued local stamps which prepay postage on mail conveyed by sea or by air to the mainland. The first locals appeared in 1929; the Lundy issues therefore have the longest history of all the British island locals. Their status is similar to those of Herm (q.v.). Lundy stamps are valued in 'puffins', a puffin being equal to a penny.

Luxemburg (Luxembourg). Independent European grand duchy, in personal union with the Netherlands from 1815 to 1890. The first stamps of 1852 showed William III of the Netherlands who was also Grand Duke of Luxemburg. During the German occupation of 1940–4 German stamps were overprinted for use in Luxemburg and Luxemburg stamps were surcharged with values in German currency. Area: 999 sq. m.; capital: Luxembourg; currency: 100 centimes = 1 Luxemburg franc; pop. (1962): 323,971.

Lydenburg. South African Republic (Transvaal) 1895 penny red stamp was o/p 'V.R.I.' and surcharged in this former Boer township in September–October 1900, and other Transvaal issues were similarly treated.

Lynchburg. Virginia. Had a Confederate 'Postmasters' ' issue at the time of the Civil War.

Luzons, The. Luzon, the main island of the Philippines, provides this alternative name for the group.

Russian and Cyrillic

Л = The letter 'L' in English. Thus ЛЕНИН = Lenin.

Greek

The Lamda (Λ).

Λ   = The letter 'L' in English.
ΛΕΠΤΑ   = Lepta. 100 lepta (ΛΕΠΤΟΝ) = 1 drachma.
ΛΕΡΟΣ   = Leros.
ΛΗΜΝΟΣ   = Lemnos.

M.E.F. M.V.İ.R. MAGYAR

M

M. Mint.

M.A. Ministry of Agriculture. O/p on officials of Argentina.

M.A.L. Military Authority Lire. O/p surcharge on stamps of G.B. for Tripolitania, 1948.

M.B. Movable Box. See 'Boîte mobile'.

M.B.D. (Maharajah). Machant Balram Das. The initials of the ruler of Nandgaon (India) State, 1894.

M.C. Maltese Cross (cancel).

M.E.F. Middle East Forces.

M.G. Ministry of War, and

M.H. Ministry of Finance, and

M.I. Ministry of the Interior, and

M.J.I. Ministry of Justice and Instruction, and

M.M. Ministry of Marine, and

MM., M.M., or **M/M.** Millimètres (q.v.).

M.O.P. Ministry of Public Works, and

M.P.O. Military Post Office.

MQE. Martinique.

M.R.C. Ministry of Foreign Affairs and Cultural Relations, are all departmental overprints on the 'officials' of Argentina, 1913–39, now replaced by the present 'Servicio Official' o/p.

M.V.i.R. (Ger.). Militar Verwaltung in Rumanien = Military Administration in Roumania.

Macao. (Port.: Macau). Portuguese colony at the mouth of the Canton River, China. Stamps first issued, March 1884. Area: 6 sq. m.; pop. (1960):

169,299; currency: 1884, 1,000 reis = 1 milreis; 1894, 100 avos = 1 pataca (dollar) = 5·50 escudos.

Macedonia. Puppet state set up by the German occupation authorities on 8 September 1944. Stamps of Bulgaria were o/p in Cyrillic, and surcharged with new values. They were in use until 13 November of the same year. Now divided between Bulgaria, Greece, and Yugoslavia.

Macon. Georgia, from which emanated a set of five typeset values in the Confederate 'Postmasters' ' during the American Civil War.

Madagascar. Large island in the Indian Ocean, off the south-east coast of Africa, formerly French territory but an autonomous republic in the French Community since 1958 under the style of Malagasy Republic (Republique Malgache). In the early 1880s France revived claims to a protectorate over Madagascar. In 1889 French post offices were opened there, the first Madagascar stamps of the same year being surcharges on the general issues for the French Colonies. After a native revolt France annexed the island in 1896. Prior to this date, British consular agents arranged an inland mail service for British subjects, stamps being issued 1884–7; a similar service, for which stamps were again issued, operated during 1895. See under 'British Consular Mail' and 'British Inland Mail'. In addition, the Norwegian Missionary Society operated a parcel post service from 1875 to the end of 1899. It started as a private service, but from 1888 the general public, as well as the British Consulate and the native government, were able to use it for letters and parcels. From 1894 the service had its own stamps. In 1898 Diego Suarez, Nossi Bé, and Ste. Marie (q.v.), all of which formerly had their own stamps under French administration, were attached to Madagascar. Area: 229,975 sq. m.; capital: Antananarivo (Tananarive); currency: French (C.F.A.); pop. (1962): 5,657,601.

Madeira. Island group off the north-east coast of Africa, forming part of Portugal. Madeira had its own stamps from 1868 to 1880, when they were succeeded by those of Funchal (q.v.). From 1905 to 1931 stamps of the Azores were in use. Prior to 1868 and again since 1931 Madeira has used Portuguese stamps. An exception was the series of tax stamps issued for Madeira in 1929 for obligatory use on certain dates in aid of the Funchal Museum Fund. Area: 302 sq. m.; capital: Funchal; currency: as Portugal.

Madison. Wisconsin, U.S.A. One of the Confederate 'Postmasters' ' issues of the American Civil War came from this city.

Madrid. Capital of Spain. There were two local stamps bearing the city arms issued in 1853. In 1907 there was a set published for the Industrial Exhibition, bearing the portraits of the King and Queen, which had no legitimate postal use, and is not normally recognised by catalogue publishers and collectors.

Mafeking. Town in Bechuanaland, South Africa, which was besieged in 1900 during the Boer War, and which issued its own stamps by authority of Major-General Baden-Powell. There were two types: the 'Baden-Powell portrait', and the 'Goodyear cycle'. They were unique in that they were printed on ferro-prussiate plan-copying paper, and were thus in the typically blue colour of architects' and engineers' plans. There were also stamps of Bechuanaland Protectorate, and the Cape of Good Hope o/p 'Mafeking Besieged' and surcharged.

Mafia. Small island on the East African coast at the mouth of the Rufiji river, south of Zanzibar. Formerly part of German East Africa, it was occupied by British forces in December 1914, mainly to prevent the German cruiser *Koenigsberg* from using the island as a base for raids on Allied shipping. In the early stages of the occupation captured stocks of German East African postage and revenue stamps were overprinted 'Mafia' or 'G.R.I.—Mafia' and used for postage. Later, stocks of Indian I.E.F. stamps were introduced with a similar overprint, and these were used until the island was incorporated into the new mandated territory of Tanganyika. Area: 200 sq. m.; pop. (1914): about 40,000.

Magdalena. Province of Colombia. Typeset provisionals for the town of Rio Hacha were issued in 1901. Each stamp bore the autographed initials of the authorising agent.

Magic Letter Express. A Richmond, Virginia, U.S.A., local mail service organised in 1865 by Evans, Porter & Co. which used a typeset stamp.

Magnifier. A reasonably good magnifying glass is an essential adjunct to the serious collector's outfit, as it enables the critical examination of the fine detail of a design, or the quality of a specimen. The intricate detail and beauty of some of the designs thus brought to light are one of the pleasures of the hobby. Magnifiers are obtainable ranging from the modern all-plastic models cheap enough for the slimmest purse, to the electrically lit super-magnifiers now available. See 'Accessories'.

Magyar. Hungarian. Magyarorszag: State of Hungary. Magyar (Kir) Posta: Hungarian (Royal) Post. Magyar Tanácsköztársaság = Hungarian Soviet Republic, was o/p on 1919 stamps during the Bolshevik regime.

Mailcoach. Horse-drawn coaches were being used for the transport of mail by the Thurn and Taxis post in Europe by the middle of the seventeenth century. In England they were not introduced until 1784, the first run being between London and Bristol. Before this time the mail was carried by dilatory postboys on horseback; they were often accused of being in league with highwaymen! Mailcoaches proved to be a vast improvement, but in Britain their heyday was brief, being soon superseded by the railways. In the remoter districts mailcoaches continued to operate for a number of years even after many of the trunk railways had been constructed. The last one, in the north of Scotland, survived until 1874.

Mailometer Perforations. U.S.A. vending machine, large hole, perforation on coil stamps in use from 1909 to about 1918. See 'Attleboro',' 'Schermack', etc.

'Major' Varieties. Are variations of importance, either in type, colour, design, or format, from the basic design, and which the serious collector would feel he must include in his collection. See 'Minor Varieties', etc.

Majunga. Province and seaport of Madagascar. Stamps of France with handwritten and hand-struck surcharges were used in February 1895.

Malacca. Component state of the Federation of Malaya, formerly part of Straits Settlements (q.v.). In 1948 a K.G. VI Silver Wedding stamp was issued, and first definitives appeared 1 March 1949. Area: 649 sq. m.; pop. (1962): 355,279; capital: Malacca; currency: 100 cents = 1 Malayan dollar.

Malagasy Republic (Republique Malgache). See 'Madagascar'.

Malaku Selatan. South Moluccas (q.v.).

Malaria Eradication. See under 'Anti-Malaria'.

Malawi. Name adopted by the former British protectorate of Nyasaland (q.v.) on achieving independence as a member of the Commonwealth in 1964. The new name first appeared on stamps with the 'Ufulu' (Independence) commemoratives and a definitive series issued in July 1964.

Malaya. Peninsula of south-east Asia. Since August 1957 the Malayan Federation has been an independent member of the British Commonwealth. In addition to the Federation issues which have appeared since then, the various Malayan states continue to issue their own stamps—in many cases in uniform designs but with their own local rulers' portraits. The states' issues, however, are all valid throughout the Federation. The states in question are eleven in number, Johore, Kedah, Kelantan, Malacca, Negri Sembilan, Pahang, Penang, Perak, Perlis, Selangor, and Trengganu, all of which are separately mentioned in this book. Another Malayan state which formerly had its own stamps was Sungei Ujong (q.v.), incorporated in Negri Sembilan in 1895. The name 'Malaya' first appeared on stamps in 1935-6, on the issues of Straits Settlements, Negri Sembilan, Pahang, Perak, and Selangor. This reflected the formation of the Malayan Postal Union, for the whole of which Postage Due stamps were first issued in 1936. The practice of including the 'Malaya' inscription was extended after the war to the other Malayan states as the result of the establishment in 1946 of the Malayan Union, predecessor of the Malayan Federation. See also under 'Federated Malay States', and 'Singapore'. Area: 50,600 sq. m.; capital: Kuala Lumpur; currency: 100 cents (or sen) = 1 Malayan dollar; pop. (1962): 7,491,325.

Malayan Postal Union. Stamps thus inscribed are Postage Dues first issued in 1936 for use in Straits Settlements, Negri Sembilan, Pahang, Perak, and Selangor. After the war similar stamps were used throughout the Malayan Federation and in Singapore, and at the time of writing are still current.

Malaysia. Federation formed in 1963 comprising the Malayan Federation, Singapore, Sarawak, and North Borneo (Sabah). The first stamps for use throughout Malaysia were the Federation commemoratives of September 1963. The constituent states of the new Federation are continuing to issue their own stamps. Singapore seceded from the Federation in 1965.

MANCHURIA   MALTA   'MANOEL'

Maldives. The Maldive Islands, a sultanate in the Indian Ocean, west of Ceylon, have issued their own stamps since 1909. From 1 January 1953, a republic under British protection, with an elected President as ruler, it reverted to a Sultanate early in 1954. Area: 115 sq. m.; pop. (1956): 81,950; capital: Malé; currency (1953): 100 larees = 1 rupee—formerly Sinhalese.

Mali. The Mali Federation was formed in 1959, when its first stamps were issued, and consisted of the former French Soudan and Senegal. In August 1960 Senegal seceded from the Federation and resumed its own stamp issues. Since then the former French Soudan has had separate stamps under the title of Mali Republic. Area of Mali Republic: 464,744 sq. m.; capital: Bamako; pop. (1959): 4,330,000.

Malmédy. A Prussian Rhine province since 1815, became Belgian by plebiscite in 1919. See 'Eupen'.

Malta. British island colony in the central Mediterranean. Malta's first stamp was a ½d. value for internal use issued in 1860, but the first definitive series did not appear until 1882. British stamps, cancelled 'M' or 'A 25', were used on overseas mail from 1857 to 1885. Area: 122 sq. m.; capital: Valletta; currency: sterling; pop. (1962): 329,326.

'Malta' Keytype. The design of the K.G. V 1914 series of Malta was used for several of the Crown Colonies, and is thus referenced as a keytype.

Malta 'Ticks'. The 1885 2½d. blue of Malta was surcharged 'One Penny' in 1902. Once on each pane, the error 'One Pnney' appeared, and to counter forgery, the Postmaster at Valletta ticked all the remaining unsurcharged sheets in the upper left-hand corner in red ink.

Maltese Cross. Obliterators made to Maltese Cross design were used on the G.B. 1840 1d. blacks, and were the first cancellers used on British stamps. They vary in detail as they were hand-cut. They were in use from 1840 to 1844. The London stamps bore central numbers, from 1 to 12, and a red ink was at first used, but was changed to black when the penny red stamp was introduced; there are, however, records of blue, magenta, and yellow inks having been employed, but they are rare. The maltese cross as a watermark was introduced on the 5s. value of G.B. 1867–83. It not unnaturally forms the motif of many of the stamps of Malta, the 1886 5s.

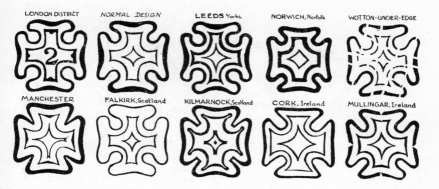

LONDON DISTRICT   NORMAL DESIGN   LEEDS Yorks.   NORWICH, Norfolk   WOTTON-UNDER-EDGE

MANCHESTER   FALKIRK, Scotland   KILMARNOCK, Scotland   CORK, Ireland   MULLINGAR, Ireland

value having no less than seven in its design. The Victory issue of Malta, 1946, bore both the Maltese and the George Crosses, the latter having been awarded the island for its war services and courage. The device was also used as a fiscal cancel on issues of Hawaii in the early eighties.

Manchukuo. Manchuria.

Manchuria (Manchukuo). Chinese province, a nominally independent state under Japanese control from 1932 to 1945—from 1934 as an empire under the last Manchu emperor of China. During this period Manchuria had its own stamps. After a short Russian occupation Manchuria was returned to China in 1946. From that date Chinese North Eastern Provinces issues have been in use. Area: 585,000 sq. m.; capital: Hsinking (Changchun); currency: 100 fen = 1 yuan; pop. (1940): 43,234,000.

Manizales. Colombian city which issued its own typeset locals in 1909.

'Manoel' Keytype. The 1910 portrait stamp of King Manoel (February 1908 to October 1910) of Portugal, with republican o/p was in use as a colonial keytype for some time after his abdication.

Manuscript Cancellation. Pen-cancelled (q.v.).

'Map Backs'. Stamps of Latvia (Latvija) issued 18 December 1918, were printed on the backs of German ordnance-survey war maps.

Map Stamps. Maps have a very wide use as designs for stamps, and can form a most interesting 'subject' collection. Canada's 1898 Xmas British Empire map stamp is a popular item; while the controversial map stamps that were used as 'ammunition' in the 1948 Antarctic 'war' deserve special attention. The South American republics have produced numbers of such map designs, and they have always a popular appeal to the average collector.

Mapka. (Cyr.). Marka. A stamp.

Marca da bollo. Italian revenue stamp.

Margin. The word has two philatelic meanings. In one it refers to the blank bordering paper of a sheet of stamps and in the other to the borders

MAPKA   'MARIANNE'   MAROKKO   MAURITIUS

of individual stamps. The margins of a sheet often carry the imprint and authority of the printer or Government printing establishment; instructions and notes for separation or division into specified values and amounts; arrows and other marks for a similar purpose; control letters and/or figures; cylinder numbers; perforating alignment holes, and details that help in identifying the form of perforator used, and other interesting details which to the philatelist tell quite a story. There are marginal watermarks that normally appear there only, the stamps themselves being without mark. These margins—known to the general public as 'stamp edging'—have many uses, and the first stamp hinges or mounts were undoubtedly made from them. See also 'Gutter', 'Wing Margins', 'Millésime', etc. The stamp margins in an imperforate specimen are most important, and should not under any circumstances be re-cut, for the wider the margin, within reason, the more obvious is the authenticity of the specimen and the more value to the collector. All four margins should be good and clear of the design, and it should be quite obvious that it is not a perforated copy which has had its perfs. removed. See 'Fakes', 'Wing Margins', etc.

'Marianne'. Figure symbolising France, featured on certain post-war French issues.

Marianne Islands, also Marianas Españolas (Sp.) and Marianen (Ger.). Group of islands in the Pacific, Spanish until 1899 when they were sold to Germany (except for Guam which was ceded to the United States). They were under Japanese mandate between the wars, and since 1945 have been under United States trusteeship. The islands' first stamps were a short-lived set of overprints on a Spanish Philippines issue which appeared in 1899 shortly before the German take-over; thereafter the Mariannes used German stamps overprinted or German Colonial keytypes until the Japanese occupation in 1914, when Japanese stamps were introduced. Since the end of the Second World War the issues of the United States have been in use. Area: about 250 sq. m.; capital: Garapan on Saipan island; pop. (1963): 10,062.

Marienwerder. Town and district of West Prussia, where a plebiscite was held in 1920, and special stamps appeared—German contemporary issues o/p 'Commission Interallée Marienwerder'. It voted to remain German.

186

Marino. District of Venezuela for which typeset provisionals were issued in 1903.

Marion (Virginia). One of the towns of the Confederate States where two 'Postmasters' provisionals' were issued in the early part of the Civil War.

Marion and Prince Edward Islands. Twin Antarctic islands occupied by South Africa as weather-report stations January 1948. A temporary postal agency was established on Marion Island in March 1958.

Maritime Mail. Although this term is often used in philately to denote all types of seaborne mail, the postal marking with this wording is used exclusively on mail received from ships and overseas shore stations of the Royal Navy. It was introduced in 1939, and as a security measure gives neither the port of landing nor even the date.

Maroc. French Morocco.

Marocco, Marokko. Morocco. See 'German Post Offices in Morocco'.

'Married' pairs. Phrase applied to G.B. 1840 penny blacks matched with subsequent penny reds printed from the same plates, thus bearing identical check letters. See also 'Black Plates'.

Marruecos. (Span.). Morocco.

Marshall Islands. (Marschall Inseln). Former German protectorate in the Pacific. German stamps were in use 1889–97, then German stamps overprinted and from 1900 German Colonial keytypes until 1914 when the islands were occupied by the Japanese. Subsequent history similar to Marianne Islands. Area: about 150 sq. m.; capital: Jaluit; pop.: 15,000 (1913); 12,231 (1957).

Martinique. French island in the West Indies, one of the Windward group. Stamps first issued, 1886. Since 1947 the normal French stamps have been used. Area: 380 sq. m.; capital: Fort-de-France; currency: French; pop. (1961): 292,062.

Mason's New Orleans City Express. Locals issued in New Orleans, Louisiana, 1850–7.

Matrix. Intermediate die or mould used in duplicating an original die, line-block, or other engraving.

Maturin. (Span. Estado Maturin). Maturin state, Venezuela, had its own typeset provisionals in 1903.

Mauritania (Mauritanie). Former French protectorate in north-west Africa, an autonomous Islamic republic within the French Community since 1958 and independent since 1960. Stamps first issued, 1906. From 1945 to 1959 Mauritania used the stamps of French West Africa; since 1960 it has again had its own issues. Area: 418,120 sq. m.; currency: French; pop. (1960): 727,000.

Mauritius. Island in the Indian Ocean, east of Madagascar, named after Maurice of Nassau when colonised originally by the Dutch. Has been British since 1810. The first British colony to issue postage stamps, the first of which appeared on 21 September 1847—the now famous 'Post Office' locally engraved on a copper plate by J. Barnard. A centenary reproduction was issued in 1948. It used the stamps of G.B. 1874–7 concurrently, and was issued with canceller 'B 53'. Area: 720 sq. m.; pop. (est. 1956): 579,123; capital: Port Louis; currency: British to 1878, then decimal: 100 cents = 1 rupee = 1s. 6d. British sterling.

Maximum Cards. Are pictorial postal cards bearing (a) a relevant picture or design, (b) a stamp related to the subject on the card, and (c) a postmark relevant to both postage stamp, postal card, and event, personage, place, or other subject thereon. The Maximum Card Society of America is active from: 420 W. 121st St., New York 27, N.Y., U.S.A.

'Mayfair' Find. Stanley Phillips records that 'in the fifties a London youth wrote to Colonial postmasters enclosing £5 for a supply of stamps' then current. These duly arrived, but either through waning interest or absence they were put away, to be unearthed some sixty or seventy years later to realise several thousands of pounds. See also 'Buccleuch'.

Mayflower Mail. In 1957 a replica of the Pilgrim Fathers' vessel *Mayflower* was sailed across the Atlantic to the original landfall of 1610 at Plymouth, Massachusetts. The ship's mail consisted of souvenir envelopes, which were postmarked on board with a special cancellation and backstamped on arrival by the American Post Office, who forwarded them to their destinations.

Mayotte. A French island of the Comoro group, off Madagascar, which had its own stamps from 1892 to 1914. Madagascar stamps were then used until the first issue for the Comoro Archipelago appeared in 1950. See under 'Comoro Islands'.

Mbledhja Kushtetuëse. O/p on 1939 Albanian stamps during Italian occupation.

Mbretnija Shqiptare. (Kingdom of Albania). O/p on Albania's stamps in 1928 on accession of King Zog, also inscribed on issues during 1939–43 Italian occupation.

McGreely's Express. A river motor-boat mail service run by S. C. Marcuse between Dyea and Skagway, Alaska, during the 1898 gold rush used 'locals' so inscribed. They depicted a dog sleigh.

McIntire's City Express Post. A New York mail service for which locals were issued in 1859.

McKennal, K.C.V.O., Sir Bertram. Australian sculptor, whose profile portrait of K.G. V was the basis of most of the stamp designs of the reign.

McMillan's City Despatch Post. A Chicago mail service for which locals were issued in 1855.

Mearis' City Despatch Post. Various 'locals' were issued in Baltimore, U.S.A., in connection with a mail service organised by Malcolm W. Mearis in 1864.

MAYOTTE   'MERSON'   MEXICO

Mecklenburg-Schwerin. Former grand duchy of Germany, which issued its own stamps from 1856 to 1867. In 1868 stamps of the North German Confederation were introduced, and since 1871 those of Germany have been used. Area: 5,100 sq. m.; capital: Schwerin; currency: 48 schilling = 1 thaler.

Mecklenburg-Strelitz. Former grand duchy of Germany, which issued its own stamps from 1864 to 1867. Subsequent history similar to Mecklenburg-Schwerin. Area: 1,130 sq. m.; capital: Neu-Strelitz; currency: 48 schilling = 30 silbergroschen = 1 thaler.

'Medallions'. Name given to the 1850–65 issues of Belgium (so called from their medallion-style portrait of Leopold I) in contrast to the 1849 issue known as the 'Epaulettes'.

Medellin. Town of Colombia which issued its own local stamps 1888, 1903–4, 1909–14. It has an altitude of 4,900 feet and a pop. of about 120,000.

Media or **Medio.** (Span.). Half. Values found on Spanish 'officials' 1854–5 and on early stamps of Mexico, etc.

Mehalek. Ethiopian currency unit 1894–1907.

Méjico. Mexico.

Melville, Fred J. Prolific philatelic author and writer, founder of the Junior Philatelic Society. He died in January 1940.

Melville Memorial Awards. The Philatelic Congress of Great Britain holds an annual competition open to junior collectors in any part of the world up to the age of 17 as a permanent memorial to the late F. J. Melville. There are three age-group classes, for each of which a silver cup (to be held for one year), cash, and other awards are given.

Memel or **Klaipéda.** Lithuanian seaport and district on the Baltic, formerly a part of Germany. Under Allied control after World War I, and occupied by French forces until February 1923. Both France and Germany o/p stamps during this French occupation. In 1923 it became a part of Lithuania, was renamed Klaipéda, and was issued with o/p provisionals. It was restored to Germany 1939 but is now part of the Soviet Union. Area: 1,099 sq. m.; pop.: 151,960.

Memphis. City and port of Tennessee. One of the Confederate 'Postmasters'' Provisionals of the Civil War.

Menant & Co.'s Express Post. New Orleans, U.S.A., mail service for which local stamps were issued in 1853–5.

Mercantile Library. A U.S.A. local book delivery service of New York operating 1869–75.

'Mercuries'. The god Mercury (or Hermes)—the messenger—has been a favourite subject for stamp design, but when philatelists refer to 'Mercuries' they usually mean the Austrian 1851 journal or newspaper stamps, although the head of the god adorned many special issues right up to 1918. See 'Hermes'.

'Merkur'. (Ger.). Mercury. Inscription on local stamps of Aachen (Aix-la-Chapelle), 1895.

'Merson'. Luc-Olivier Merson designed the large 1900–6 high-value stamps of France. These were suitably inscribed for a number of colonies, becoming the keytype, known by his name.

Mesopotamia. (Iraq). See 'Mosul'.

Messenkope's Union Square Post Office. The inscription on a New York, U.S.A., 'local' in use in 1849.

Metallic Inks have been employed on occasion to produce distinctive effects upon stamps. The 'Darius' and other issues of Persia (Iran), some Greek issues, and o/ps on stamps of Palestine and Arabia have been embellished with gold and silver inks. A British Commonwealth instance was the South African Silver Wedding (1948) issue.

Métélin, Mitilini, or Mytilene. City on Lesbos (Lesvos), a former Turkish island off the coast of Asia Minor in the Aegean Sea, where Russia maintained a postal agency and for which she o/p stamps in 1910. In 1912 it was occupied by Greece, and Turkish stamps were o/p for use in the island; Italy occupied it in World War II, and it is now back in Greek hands. Area: (Lesbos) 632 sq. m.; pop. (1951): 25,518.

Metered Mail. The use of the automatic-machine meter frank was authorised internationally by the Universal Postal Union in 1920, and they are now in use by large mailing organisations throughout the world. The franking has to be done in red and must bear the name of the country of origin. A parcel-franking machine was introduced experimentally in a few G.B. post offices in 1947 and many are now in regular use. The first machine was invented in 1905 by Mr. Moss of New Zealand. The collection of meter postmarks is an interesting branch of philately. The Meter Postage Stamp Catalogue by Barfoot & Simon was published in 1953 by Universal Postal Frankers Limited, of 90 Regent St., London. In the U.S.A. a collector is known as a philometrist.

Metropolitan Errand & Carrier Express Company. Was a New York, U.S.A., local delivery service of 1855–9 which used engraved stamps so inscribed.

Mexico. (Méjico). Central American republic, temporarily an empire 1821–4 and 1864–7. First postage stamps were the 1856 imperforates.

During the civil war of 1913–16 numerous provisionals were made. A general o/p 'Gobierno Constitucionalista' was applied by the Constitutionalists under General Carranza. Stamps were also o/p with the monograms of both Generals Carranza and Villa; and numerous local 'controls' o/p for various districts and towns. Area: 760,375 sq. m.; pop. (est. 1957): 31,454,190; capital: México City; currency: 8 reales = 100 centavos = 1 peso. See also 'Porte de Mar', 'Sonora', and 'Oaxaca'.

Mezzo. (Ital.). Half.

Michel. Leading German-language catalogue, published in Munich.

Middle Congo (Moyen Congo). Former French territory in Central Africa which had its own stamps from 1907 to 1936, when they were replaced by those of French Equatorial Africa (q.v.). The territory is now known as Congo Republic (q.v.).

Middle East Forces. Stamps of G.B. were o/p 'M.E.F.' in 1942–3 for the use of British forces stationed in Eritrea (1942), Italian Somaliland (1942), Cyrenaica (1943), Tripolitania (1943), N. Africa; and in the Dodecanese (1945).

Militarpost Eilmarke. (Ger.). Army Post, Express Newspapers. Journal stamps of Bosnia. Also found surcharged in Italian currency for the Austrian occupation of Italy 1918.

Millbury. Town of Massachusetts, U.S.A., where one of the rarest 'Postmasters'' Provisionals was issued in 1846.

Millésime. Name given to the figures denoting the year or date of manufacture printed in the gutters of sheets of certain French general and colonial stamps, and the margins of sheets of the 'Medallion' (q.v.) issues of Belgium.

Millimètres, or Millimeters. One thousandth of a metre (39.37 in.). Twenty millimètres have been adopted as the international standard of measurement to gauge stamp perforations, i.e. the number of perfs. to 20 mm. being quoted as the perf. number. All-over measurements of a stamp, the height, length, and spacing of an o/p, and all other vital philatelic measurements are usually given in millimètres (mm.).

Mills' Free Despatch Post. A New York, U.S.A., 'local' of 1847 issued by Gustavus A. Mills.

Miniature sheet. A sheet of stamps much smaller than the normal sheet size; sometimes containing only one stamp! Many, but by no means all, have exaggerated margins with special inscriptions, and are designed as souvenirs rather than for postal purposes, though they are valid for postage. In recent years the annual Health stamps of New Zealand have been produced in miniature sheets of six or eight, as convenient units for sale by the charitable organisations which benefit from the surcharge, as well as in normal sheets of 120 for post office use. Miniature sheets are widely collected, particularly on the continent of Europe.

Minkus. One of the two leading general catalogues published in the United States. Its full title is the *New World-Wide Postage Stamp Catalog*, produced annually by Minkus Publications Inc. of New York. The same firm publishes a specialised catalogue of the United States and United Nations.

Minor Varieties. As the name implies, slight variations from the normal stamp, of interest to specialists but not usually of sufficient importance to be listed in general catalogues.

Mint. A stamp in pristine condition, exactly as issued by the post office—unused, unfaded, undamaged, and with original gum.

Mission Mixture. Unsorted accumulation of stamps, usually with much duplication, sold as received from the country of origin. So called from the fact that missionary organisations collect large quantities of common used stamps and sell them to the stamp trade as a means of raising funds.

'Missionaries'. Name applied to the early typeset issues of Hawaii. They are so called from the fact that most surviving copies were used on letters sent home by missionaries in the islands.

Mixed Perfs. Sheets of stamps badly perforated in one gauge have been known to be backed with narrow strips of gummed paper and re-perforated to another gauge, thus producing stamps with two opposed sides in differing perforations. This happened with certain New Zealand issues in 1901. See 'Perforation', 'Compound Perfs.', etc.

Mixed Postage. Covers franked with stamps of two or more postal administrations, or countries; or different regimes of the same country; or with originating country's postage stamps and with country of destination's postage 'dues'. See also 'Combination cover'.

Mobile. City and seaport of Alabama, where two Confederate 'Postmasters'' Provisionals were issued in the Civil War.

Mobile Post Offices. Are in use in many countries, including Great Britain. The term is normally applied to a mechanically-propelled vehicle fitted out to serve as a temporary post office to deal with emergency mail, or to visit isolated places regularly, or for some special occasion or event. Both Switzerland and China have depicted them on stamps, and America had tramcars fitted out as mobiles to travel certain cities at stated times to collect and sort mail. The Highway Post Office service was inaugurated in 1941—the first was from Washington, D.C., to Harrisonburg, Virginia. Many mobile offices use distinctive postmarks which are eagerly sought by specialist collectors. See also 'Travelling Post Offices', and 'Highway Post Offices'.

Moçambique. Mozambique (q.v.).

Modena. Formerly a Duchy in Upper Italy, publishing its own stamps. The first issues in 1852 bore the Este arms (are inscribed 'Poste Estensi'), the family name of its ducal rulers. The provisional government set up in 1859, on the exile of Duke Francis V, issued stamps bearing the arms of the House of Savoy, and inscribed 'Provincie Modonesi'. It used the stamps of Sardinia from 1860 to 1862, after which it was absorbed into the kingdom of Italy.

MONACO   MOBILE P.O.S.   MONEY

Moheli. A French island of the Comoro group, off Madagascar, which had its own stamps from 1906 to 1914. Madagascar stamps were then used until the first issue for the Comoro Archipelago appeared in 1950. See under 'Comoro Islands'.

Moiré. A pattern reminiscent of 'watered' silk, and used as a security device on certain of the world's stamps. There was a moiré pattern printed in blue on the backs of the 1872 issues of Mexico; as a burelé band on the backs of Queensland's postal fiscals; and on the Russian controls of 1921.

Moldavia. Former Turkish province of eastern Europe which secured autonomy in 1856 and is now part of Roumania. Its primitive stamps, issued in 1858-9, are known as the 'Moldavian Bulls', from the bull's head which is the central feature of the design. There were two types: Porto Scrisori (letter stamp) and Porto Gazetti (newspaper stamp). Moldavia then merged with the neighbouring province of Wallachia to become known as Moldo-Wallachia. On the unification of the two governments in 1861 the name of Roumania was adopted for the new principality. Stamps for the combined provinces were first issued in 1862, but the new name (Posta Romana) did not appear on stamps until 1865. Capital of Moldavia: Jassy; currency: 40 parale = 1 piastre.

Moldo-Wallachia. See 'Moldavia' above.

Monaco. Small principality in the south of France, near the Italian frontier and comprising the towns of Monte Carlo, La Condamine, and Monaco. Its present ruler is Prince Rainier III. It first issued stamps in 1885; prior to this it used stamps of Sardinia (1851–60) and French general issues (1860–85). Area: 368 acres; pop. (1961): 20,441; French currency.

Money, Stamps as. The back-printed card stamps of Russia 1915–17 are, strictly speaking, money vouchers or paper currency, although many were used as postage stamps. Stamps of G.B. (and on the European continent) were in use as small change during the 1914–18 War. In the American Civil War, and later on the Continent of Europe, stamps were often provided with small circular transparent cases, known as 'Jetons', which often bore advertising. The stamps of Rhodesia were also authorised to be used as cash during an emergency, 1898–1900, and were stuck on cards and circulated as money.

193

MONTENEGRO   MONGOLIA   'MOUCHON'

Mongolia. Formerly known as Outer Mongolia, this vast region of Asia was a dependency of the Chinese Manchu Empire for 200 years until independence was proclaimed in 1911. A Soviet republic was set up in 1924, when the first Mongolian stamps were issued. Prior to this both the Russians and the Chinese operated post offices in Mongolia, using their own stamps. Area: 604,095 sq. m.; capital: Ulan Bator; currency: 1924, 100 cents = 1 dollar; 1926, 100 mung = 1 tuhrik; pop. (1963): 1,018,000.

Mong-Tseu. Mongseu or Mongtzé (now Mengtzé). French concession post office in China, using o/p stamps of Indo-China 1903–22.

Monster. Dutch and Afrikaans word, found on stamps of the Netherlands and Transvaal, indicating 'Specimen'. See under 'Specimens'.

Mont Athos. See 'Mount Athos'.

Monte Bello Islands. British atomic experimental station off N.W. coast of Western Australia. A crude litho set of three stamps, said to have been printed in Perth, W.A., sponsored by a naval officer, appeared in 1951–2. Few copies seemingly exist and are of doubtful status and validity.

Montenegrin Government in Exile. A set of stamps was prepared in Rome in 1920–1 in anticipation of a revival of the monarchy, but the death of King Nicholas (whose laureated head they bear) rendered them abortive. They were never officially issued or used, but may be found in mint condition perf. 11 × 11¼ or imperf., with or without overprint in red or in blue 'Slobodna Sherna Gora' (A Free Montenegro), in Cyrillic. They have no status except as curios.

Montenegro. Formerly a separate Adriatic kingdom; since 1918 a part of Yugoslavia. Its first stamps were issued in May 1874. Austrian stamps were o/p during the 1917 occupation. Germany and Italy revived the postal administration and issued new 'liberation' stamps: first in 1941 with Yugoslav stamps o/p and then in 1943 Italian-printed definitives in centesimi and lire values. Area: approx. 5,603 sq. m.; pop. (1953): 419,873; capital: Cettinje (now known as Titograd); currency: 1874, 100 novcic = 1 florin; 1902, 100 helera = 1 kruna; 1907, 100 paras = 1 krona; 1910, 100 paras = 1 perper.

Montevideo. Capital of Uruguay. Many of the early issues of this country, between 1859 and 1866, were inscribed 'Montevideo', but were for use throughout Uruguay and are usually listed under that country. British stamps with the 'C 28' postmark were used at Montevideo from 1862 to 1872.

Montserrat. British colony in the Caribbean, one of the Leeward Islands. In 1858–60 British stamps with the 'A 09' postmark were used there on overseas mail, but the island's own first issue did not appear until 1876. Montserrat stamps were temporarily superseded by general issues for the Leeward Islands in 1890, but were again issued from 1903, the Leeward Islands issues remaining in use concurrently until 1956. Area: 32 sq. m.; capital: Plymouth; currency: sterling until 1951, thereafter 100 cents = 1 B.W.I. dollar; pop. (1960): 12,157.

Moody Penny Dispatch. A Chicago, U.S.A., 'local' of 1856.

Moquegua. Peru. 'Arequipa' (q.v.) issues were o/p 1881–5.

Morocco. Kingdom of north-west Africa. In the absence of any official postal service the first facilities were provided in the latter part of the nineteenth century by post offices set up in Morocco by rival European powers. France, Spain, Britain, and also (up to 1914) Germany all overprinted their stamps for use at their respective post offices in Morocco. In the 1890s a number of private posts were established between the principal towns with their own local stamps; there was also the semi-official Sherifian (Cheriffien) Post, again with its own stamps. In 1912 the country was divided into three zones: the independent zone of Tangier (where the rival European post offices continued to function); a Spanish protectorate in the north; and a French protectorate over the remainder. In 1956 the two protectorates were ended and Morocco's independence was recognised. Until 1958, however, separate stamps were issued for the northern and southern zones, with values in Spanish and French currency respectively. Stamps in Spanish currency were then withdrawn and since then those in French currency have been used throughout the country. See also under 'French Morocco', 'Spanish Morocco', 'German Post Offices in Morocco', and 'Morocco Agencies'. Area: about 171,000 sq. m.; capital: Rabat; pop. (1961): 11,598,070; currency since 1959: 100 francs = 1 dirham.

Morocco Agencies. British post offices formerly operated in Morocco and Tangier. The normal British stamps were used between 1872 and 1886. Gibraltar stamps were then introduced, and from 1898 the colony's stamps were overprinted for use in Morocco. The Morocco Agencies were controlled from Gibraltar until 1907. From the latter date overprinted British stamps were used, some surcharged with new values in Spanish or French currency. From 1927, there were also special overprints for Tangier. Stamps surcharged in French currency were withdrawn in January 1938 when by agreement with the French Government the offices in French Morocco were closed. Those in Spanish Morocco continued to function until the end of 1956, when they were closed following the recognition of Moroccan independence. The office at Tangier, the first to open, was also the last to close—on 30 April 1957, after just over a hundred years of existence. The centenary was marked by a series of commemorative overprints.

Morocco, French. See 'French Morocco'.

Morocco, Spanish. See 'Spanish Morocco'.

Morvi. Former feudatory native state in the Bombay Presidency in British India, which issued its own internal stamps from 1 April 1931 to 1950. Now uses Indian stamps. Area: 822 sq. m.; pop.: 141,761; Indian currency.

Mosul. Vilayet and town of Iraq. Fiscal stamps of Turkey were o/p 'I.E.F. "D" ' during the British occupation of 1919 for the use of the Indian troops of the Mesopotamia Force. The vilayet covered 36,211 sq. m.; and the town's pop. (1952): 203,273.

'Mother' Die. The name sometimes applied to the original engraved die in line engraving, and—erroneously—to the secondary die.

Motive Collecting. (Ger.: Motiv). Thematic, subject, or topical collecting. IMOSA (Die Erste Internationale Motivbrief-marken-Austellung) held by the Saar Philatelic Federation in March–April 1952, was the first exhibition devoted to this phase of the hobby. IMA, the second of such shows, was held in Berne, Switzerland, in May 1953. See 'Subject Collecting', 'Thematics', and 'Topicals'.

Mouchon, Eugéne Louis. Born 1843. Designed the 'Peace and Commerce', 'Tablet', and other keytypes of France, also engraved the 'Sower' (La Semeuse) general issues, and the first stamps for Ethiopia. See below.

'Mouchon' Type. A stamp design of France with a seated female figure displaying a tablet engraved 'Droits de l'homme' (The Rights of Man), which has been named after the artist who designed and engraved it in 1900; it was re-drawn in 1902. See above.

Mount Athos. (Áyion Óros). A mountain on the Athos arm of the Chalcidice Peninsula, famous for its monasteries, formerly in European Turkey, and now an autonomous monastic district in Greece. Russia maintained a post office 1909–10 and o/p general issues for use there.

Mount Brown Stamp Catalogue. Issued in 1863, was one of the first in Great Britain.

Mount Currie Express. Local stamps, value 1d., issued by Messrs. Ballance & Goodliffe for use in franking letters carried by native runners in Griqualand East and Natal, South Africa, 1874–7.

Mount Everest Expedition. Issues so inscribed are poster stamps (with no validity) designed to raise funds for the 1924 attempt to conquer this Himalayan mountain. It is stated that some copies were used to frank mail between the expeditionary camps and the official British Indian post office, and thus had some claim to 'local' status.

Mounting. To preserve the condition and value of a collection it is important that stamps should be correctly mounted in the album. Only good-quality stamp hinges (sometimes called stamp mounts) should be used, as these can afterwards, if necessary, be peeled from stamp and album leaf, leaving little or no mark on either. To mount a stamp, fold over the top

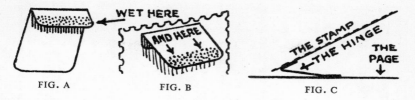

FIG. A   FIG. B   FIG. C

quarter of the hinge, lightly moisten and affix it to the top of the stamp (Fig. A). Next, lightly moisten the other end of the hinge (Fig. B). Then, holding the foot of the stamp away from the album leaf by means of tweezers, press the hinge (not the stamp) firmly to the page (Fig. C). By this method the backs as well as the fronts of stamps can be easily examined in the album; it should be used whether mounting stamps directly to the album leaf or to a mat. An alternative (though more expensive) method of

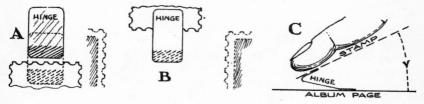

AN ALTERNATIVE METHOD

mounting is to place stamps in pochettes (q.v.), which are then themselves mounted on the album page. Covers are best mounted by the use of ready-gummed 'corners', of the kind sold for mounting snapshots.

Mourning Stamps. There have been a number of stamps paying sad tribute to deceased heads of states, etc., and which have been edged or printed in black. The following may be noted: Austria 1934 (Dolfuss); Belgium and Belgian Congo 1934 (King Albert); Belgium 1935 (Queen Astrid); Germany 1934 (Hindenburg); Greece 1936 (King Constantine) and 1945 (King George II): Yugoslavia 1934 (King Alexander); Liechtenstein 1947 (Princess Elsa); Lithuania 1927 (Dr. Basanavicus); Poland 1935 (Marshal Pilsudski); Russia 1924 (Lenin); Bulgaria 1944 (King Boris III); and quite a number from various countries, in memory of Presidents Roosevelt and Kennedy of the U.S.A.

Moveable Box. For many years moveable posting-boxes were placed on board various cross-Channel steamers plying between England and the Continent. They were first used as early as the 1840s and their use was regularised under the Anglo-French Postal Convention of 1856. Letters posted in these boxes received special postmarks inscribed variously 'Moveable Box', 'Boîte Mobile', or the initials 'M.B.' or 'B.M.' Moveable Box facilities were discontinued shortly before the Second World War.

Moyen Congo. Middle Congo (q.v.).

MOZAMBIQUE   MOURNING   MOZAMBIQUE
                 STAMPS   COMPANY

Mozambique. Moçambique. Portuguese East Africa. The first issues were made in 1877. Area: 302,250 sq. m.; pop. (1960): 6,592,994; capital: Lourenço Marques (q.v.); currency Portuguese. It embraces the former stamp-issuing territories of: Lourenço Marques, Inhambane, Téte, Zambezia, and the Mozambique and Nyassa Companies, all of which see.

Mozambique Company. (Port. Companhia de Moçambique). Was responsible for the exploitation of the territories of Manica and Sofala up to 1946. It issued its own stamps under authority from 1892 to 1946. The company's territory is now included in Mozambique.

Mestra. (Span.). Specimen or pattern. See 'Specimens'.

Mukalla. See 'Aden States'.

'Mulreadies'. Name given to the prepaid envelopes and letter-sheets, probably the best known items of postal stationery, issued on 6 May 1840 in conjunction with the Penny Black. So called after their designer, William Mulready, R.A. The Mulreadies were widely caricatured (the caricatures are themselves keenly collected by specialists) and were so ridiculed that they were withdrawn after a short life.

Mult. Multiple. See 'Multiple Watermarks' below.

Multa. (Port.). Mulct, or fine, e.g. Postage Due.

Multada. (Span.). Postage dues of Chile, 1895.

Multiple, also Multiple Piece. A group of stamps unseparated, of any size more than two but less than a complete sheet.

Multiple Watermarks. Those where the watermark device is duplicated all over the sheet without regard to the size of the actual stamp, so that each stamp normally shows the whole or parts of more than one device. The term is used in contrast to the single watermark where each device is planned to fall neatly into the area of one stamp only. Multiple or 'all-over' watermarks are nowadays in much more frequent use than the single type. The first multiple watermark in British Empire stamps—the Mult. Crown CA—was introduced in 1904, replacing the single Crown CA.

Muscat. Independent sultanate of Arabia, on the Gulf of Oman, in special treaty relationship with Great Britain. For many years the postal service was provided by the Indian Post Office, and Indian stamps were used there from 1856. Special overprints for use in Muscat were first applied in 1944. In 1948 the post office was taken over by Great Britain, and since that date British stamps, surcharged with new values in Indian currency, have been in use. At various times Muscat stamps have also been employed at other Indian (later British) post offices in the Persian Gulf area, notably at Qatar until 1957 and at Dubai until 1961.

Mustang Express. A local mail service run by Jabez Fearey at Newark, N.J., U.S.A., in 1870.

Muster. (Ger.). Specimen.

Mytilene. See 'Métélin'.

Cyrillic

MAPKA = Marka—a stamp.
MOCKBA = Moskva—Moscow.

The letter 'M' in both Cyrillic and Greek (the Mu) is identical with English usage.

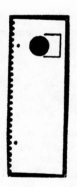

MARGINAL PERFORATION ALIGNMENT HOLES AND GUIDE ON STAMPS OF GREAT BRITAIN. SEE 'MARGIN'

N

N-C.E. (Fr. Nouvelle-Caledonie). New Caledonia.

N.E.I. Netherlands East Indies.

N.F. Nyasa-Rhodesian Force. O/p on stamps of Nyasaland Protectorate for the temporary occupation of German East Africa in 1916.

NFF. Natal Field Force. Hand-stamped on stamps of G.B. used in South Africa during 1899–1902 Boer War.

NGR. Punch-perforated on stamps of Natal. Natal Government Railways.

N.H. In an auction catalogue indicates 'never hinged'.

N.L. Netherlands. O/p with a plus sign and surcharge on 1953 stamps of Denmark. Surcharge as aid for flood victims of Holland.

N.M.S. Post. Parcel post stamps of the Norwegian Missionary Society in Madagascar 1894–9, intended for local and internal parcels, were extended to include local letters.

n.P. Naya Paise. New Indian coinage unit introduced 1957. 100 = 1 rupee.

N.P.B. News Paper Branch. A London cancel found on many early G.B. stamps.

NSB. Nossi-Bé (q.v.).

N.S.D.A.P. National Socialist Workers' Party. Special issues of German stamps issued 1938 and 1942 for use by officials of the Nazi Party.

N.S.W. New South Wales.

N.W. Pacific Islands. Australian stamps with this overprint were first prepared on the outbreak of the First World War in readiness for an Australian occupation of the German island possessions in the northwest Pacific. Japan, however, forestalled this plan and occupied the islands first, securing a mandate over them after the war. As a result the N.W. Pacific Islands stamps were pressed into service in the Australian-occupied former German colony of New Guinea, remaining in use, with variations, until 1925. They were also issued in Nauru for a short period in 1915–16. See also under 'Nauru' and 'New Guinea'.

Nabha. Former Indian Convention State which used Indian stamps overprinted from 1885 to 1950. Normal Indian stamps are now current. Area: 966 sq. m.; capital: Nabha; pop. (1941): 340,044.

Nandgaon (Rajnandgaon). Former Indian Native State which issued its own internal stamps 1892–5. Area: 871 sq. m.; capital: Nandgaon; pop. (1941): 190,000.

Nanking. The southern capital of China, the seat of the Japanese-sponsored 'Puppet' government prior to and during World War II. It issued many series of postage stamps. Pop. (est. 1950): 1,020,000.

Naphthadag. Great Britain's Graphite Line issue was at first known by this name, which is in fact a description of the substance used for the graphite lines (Naphtha plus the initials of Defloculated Acheson's Graphite—though the final formula used was varied). See under 'Graphite Line'.

'Napier' Perforating Machines constructed on Archer's principles at a cost of £400 each were used at Somerset House. First 1d. stamps, perf. 16, coming from these machines, were issued 28 January 1854. (A detailed check list appears on p. 100 of Todd's *History of British Postage Stamps*.) They were made by David Napier & Son of Vine St., Lambeth.

Naples. Napoli. Former Italian kingdom which issued stamps from 1 January 1858. King Ferdinand II was driven out by Garibaldi and his volunteers in 1860, and union with Sardinia was followed by an issue for the Neapolitan Provinces (q.v.) bearing the head of the King of Sardinia. There have been numerous forgeries. Pemberton says that the genuine stamps have a tiny letter engraved under the value. Pop. (1951): 1,024,543. Stamp currency: 3 tornese = 1 grano. See also 'Secret Marks'.

Napoletana. (Italian). Neapolitan. Naples, or the Two Sicilies.

Nashville. Town of Tennessee where Confederate 'Postmasters' Provisionals' were issued during the Civil War.

Na Slask. (Polish: Upper Silesia). O/p on 1920 issues of Central Lithuania, with surcharge to provide funds to enable Poles to vote in the Upper Silesian plebiscite.

Natal. Former British colony, now part of the Republic of South Africa. Its first issue, of 1857–8, was unique among British Colonial stamps in being embossed in plain relief on coloured papers. Stamps of Natal were superseded in 1913 by those of South Africa. Area: 35,284 sq. m.; capital: Pietermaritzburg; currency: sterling; pop. (1951): 2,408,433.

Nationalist China. See under 'Formosa'.

National Philatelic Society. New name for the Junior Philatelic Society (q.v.).

Nations Unies Office Européen. O/p on modern stamps of Switzerland indicates use by the Office of the United Nations in Europe.

'Natives'. French Colonial keytype design for Postage Dues, showing two native heads, one either side of the value panel.

Nauru. Equatorial West Pacific phosphate island, a former German possession placed under Australian mandate after World War I. Its first

NAURU NEDERLAND NEW CALEDONIA

stamps were the German Marshall Islands issues. The current 'Yacht' key-types were o/p and surcharged by Australian occupying forces in 1914—'G.R.I.' and new values—with issues of the N.W. Pacific Islands validated from March to October 1915. In 1916 came contemporary K.G. V stamps of G.B. o/p, superseded in 1924 by the 'Steamship' definitives. Nauru was occupied by the Japanese during World War II, but is now back again in British hands and administered by Australia. Area: 8 sq. m.; pop. (1962): 4,849; Australian currency.

Nawanagar (Nowanuggar). Former Indian Native State which issued its own internal stamps 1875–95. Area: 3,791 sq. m.; capital: Nawanagar; pop. (1941): 504,000.

Naya Paisa (n.P.). Indian currency unit, introduced in 1957. Plural form: Naye Paise. 100 n.P. = 1 rupee (1s. 6d. sterling).

Neapolitan Provinces. A transitory administration, absorbing Naples (q.v.), and being later (1862) incorporated into the kingdom of Italy. Stamps were issued, bearing the embossed head of Victor Emmanuel II, from February 1861 to March 1862. Currency: 3 tornese = 1 grano.

Ned. Antillen. Nederlandse-Antillen. The Netherlands Antilles (q.v.). The group of islands listed under Curaçao (q.v.) up to 1948.

Ned. Indie. Netherlands (or Dutch) East Indies (q.v.).

Nederland. The Netherlands (q.v.). Holland.

Negri Sembilan. One of the Malayan States, a sultanate, since 1895 in-corporating Sungei Ujong (q.v.). Stamps first issued, 1891. From 1900 to 1935 Negri Sembilan used the stamps of Federated Malay States, but since the latter date has again had its own stamps. During the Japanese occupa-tion, 1942–5, stamps of Negri Sembilan were overprinted by the occupying power. Area: 2,565 sq. m.; capital: Seremban; pop. (1962): 446,217.

Nejd. See 'Saudi-Arabia'.

Nepal. Independent kingdom in the Himalayas, between India and Tibet. Stamps first issued, 1881. Until 1959, when Nepal joined the U.P.U., Nepalese stamps were valid only for internal use, and on mail to India. Indian stamps, however, were in use at the Indian post office in Kathmandu from as early as 1854. Area: 54,600 sq. m.; capital: Kathmandu; currency:

4 pice = 1 anna; 100 pice = 25 annas = 1 Nepalese rupee; pop. (est. 1959): 9,000,000.

Ne Pas Livrer le Dimanche. (Fr.). Do not deliver on Sunday. See 'Dominical label'.

Netherlands. Nederland. Holland. Independent kingdom of Western Europe. Its first issues were on 1 January 1852. Area: 12,868 sq. m.; pop. (est. 1962): 11,889,962; administrative capital: The Hague ('S Gravenhage, or Den Haag); commercial capital: Amsterdam; currency: 100 cents = 1 guilder.

Netherlands Antilles. Netherlands West Indies, formerly known as Curaçao (q.v.). The new name first appeared on stamps as Nederlandse Antillen in 1949.

Netherlands East Indies (Nederlandsch Indie). Large group of islands off south-east Asia, formerly a Dutch colony and now forming the independent republic of Indonesia. Stamps first issued, 1864. During the Japanese occupation 1942–5 the occupying authorities applied various overprints to stamps of the Netherlands East Indies, and also produced their own issues for Java, for Sumatra, and for the 'Japanese Naval Control Area', the latter including Borneo, Celebes, the Moluccas, and the Lesser Sunda Islands. The last stamps to be inscribed 'NED. INDIE' were issued in 1948. For subsequent history, see under 'Indonesia'. Area: 725,000 sq. m.; capital: Batavia on Java; pop.: about 67,000,000.

Netherlands New Guinea (Nederlands Nieuw Guinea). The western part of the island of New Guinea, formerly part of the Netherlands East Indies, which remained under Dutch control for a time after the establishment of Indonesia, and issued its own first stamps in 1950. It was finally ceded to Indonesia in 1963, and renamed West Irian (q.v.). It now uses Indonesian stamps overprinted. Area: 160,618 sq. m.; capital: Hollandia; pop. (1958): 730,000.

Nevis. One of the Leeward Islands group in the British West Indies. It had its own stamps from 1861 to 1890, when they were replaced by general issues for the Leeward Islands. Earlier, from 1858 to 1860, British stamps with the 'A 09' cancellation were used on overseas mail. From 1903 stamps inscribed St. Kitts-Nevis were issued for use in both St. Christopher and Nevis. Since 1952 stamps inscribed St. Christopher, Nevis, and Anguilla have been in use. Area: 50 sq. m.; chief town: Charlestown; currency: sterling; pop. (1960): 12,761.

New Britain. Large Pacific island near Papua-New Guinea, whose stamps it uses. Once Neu-Pommern, a German possession. Area: 14,600 sq. m.; pop. (est. 1956): 96,822; capital: Rabaul. See 'New Guinea'.

New Brunswick. Eastern province of Canada. Its first diamond-square series of 1851 are classics. The 1860 set contained the famous suppressed portrait of the Hon. Charles Connell (q.v.). In 1868 the stamps of Canada superseded. Area: 27,985 sq. m.; pop. (1956): 554,616; capital: Fredericton; currency: 1851, 12 pence = 1 shilling; 20 shillings = one pound (£1); 1860, 100 cents = 1 dollar (Canadian).

New Caledonia. (Fr. Nouvelle-Calédonie). South-West Pacific island group, and a French penal settlement 1864–95. Its first issue was a 10 centime value bearing the head of Napoleon III, and drawn by a Sgt. Triquerat. It was superseded in 1862 by French general colonials which were o/p and surcharged in 1881. 'Tablet' keytypes followed in 1892. First distinctive definitives appeared in 1905. Area: 7,218 sq. m.; pop. (1962): 82,500; capital: Nouméa; French (C.F.P.) currency.

New Constitution. To signify the granting of wider political freedom and responsibility various British Colonials have been so inscribed or overprinted, e.g. Jamaica 1945–6; Windward Islands (Dominica, Grenada, St. Lucia, and St. Vincent, etc.) 1951.

Newfoundland. British island Dominion off the eastern coast of Canada, and including Labrador on the mainland in its administration. Its first set was issued on 1 January 1857, and contains some of the rarer classics. Area: 156,185 sq m.; pop. (1956): 415,074; capital: St. John's; currency: 1857, British; 1866, Canadian. Since 30 March 1949, included in, and using the stamps of, the Canadian Commonwealth. Known as the land of 'Fogs, dogs, and cod'—an apt description.

New Granada, United States of. Former name of the country now known as Colombia (q.v.). The 1861 issue was inscribed 'Estados Unidas de Nueva Granada'.

New Guinea. This large Pacific island north of Australia is divided into three parts, each of which has at different times had its own stamps. The western half was Netherlands New Guinea (q.v.), formerly part of the Netherlands East Indies and now part of Indonesia. The south-eastern part is Papua (q.v.), formerly known as British New Guinea; and the north-eastern part is the Territory of New Guinea, a former German colony which came under Australian mandate after the First World War. The two latter have since 1952 been combined in the joint Australian administration of Papua–New Guinea, for which many attractive pictorial stamps have been issued.

In philatelic parlance 'New Guinea' usually refers to the Territory of New Guinea. When Australian forces occupied this territory in 1914, stamps of the German Colonial period were overprinted 'G.R.I.' with new values. In 1915 Australian stamps overprinted 'N.W. Pacific Islands' (q.v) were introduced. New Guinea had its own issues from 1925 to 1942, when the civil administration was suspended as the result of the Japanese invasion, which was afterwards repulsed. Australian stamps were then used until the appearance of the first issue for Papua–New Guinea. Area: 93,000 sq. m.; capital: Lae; currency: Australian; pop. (1962): about 1,500,000.

New Haven. Connecticut. Issued one of the U.S.A. 'Postmasters' ' stamps n 1845.

New Hebrides (Nouvelles Hebrides). Group of Polynesian islands in the Pacific; since 1906 a condominium under joint British and French administration. Prior to the condominium, stamps of New Caledonia were used on mails dispatched via Noumea, and those of New South Wales on mails dispatched via Sydney. In 1897 the Australasian New Hebrides Co. issued local stamps for use on inter-island mails carried by their vessels; they were in use until 1899. In 1903 a French company produced some short-lived locals, inscribed 'Nouvelles Hebrides—Syndicat Français—Poste Locale', which had a similar purpose. The first stamps to be officially issued under the condominium appeared in 1908 and consisted of stamps of New Caledonia and of Fiji with an appropriate overprint. The first definitives of 1911 were produced in two versions, one with French inscriptions, the other with English. The same system of parallel sets in French and English was continued with subsequent issues and is still in use today. Area: 5,790 sq. m.; capital: Vila; currency: 1908, British and French; 1958, 100 centimes = 1 gold franc (2s. 4d. sterling); pop. (est. 1962): 62,000.

New Issue Service. Probably the best way of keeping a collection up-to-date with new issues at a minimum of trouble and expense is to subscribe to a reliable New Issue Service. Under this system the dealer agrees to supply, and the collector agrees to accept and pay for, all new issues of the chosen country or countries, up to a pre-selected limit of face value, at a given percentage over face or cost. New issue services are available for stamps of British Commonwealth and Foreign countries, for mint or used, and in at least one case even for stamp booklets and aerogrammes. In many cases the subscriber can choose from a wide range of facilities; he can include or exclude varieties, Officials, Postage Dues, commemoratives, etc. By joining such a service the collector makes sure of receiving all the new issues he requires, automatically, on the most favourable terms and at regular intervals. It must be emphasised, however, that in return he is obliged to take and pay for all the stamps sent, and in this important respect a New Issue Service is, of course, quite different from receiving new issues on approval.

New Orleans. City of Louisiana where Confederate 'Postmasters' Provisionals' were issued during the American Civil War.

New Republic (Nieuwe Republiek). Former Boer republic in South Africa which had its own primitive stamps during a short-lived period of independence 1886–8. In the latter year it was incorporated in the Transvaal; since 1903 it has formed part of Natal, which is now a province of South Africa. The New Republic was situated in the Zulu territory; its area was never specifically defined and was much restricted after the British annexation of Zululand in 1887. Capital: Vryheid; currency: sterling. The stamps were rubber-stamped impressions on ready-gummed and perforated paper sent out from Europe.

New Smyrna. Town of Florida where Confederate 'Postmasters' Provisionals' were issued during the American Civil War.

New South Wales. Former British colony, now the south-eastern state of Australia, which had its own stamps from January 1850 until 1913, when they were replaced by those of Australia. The first issues were the famous 'Sydney Views', much studied by specialists. The embossed stamped

NEW GUINEA

NEWSPAPER STAMPS
(NEW ZEALAND)

NEW SOUTH WALES

envelopes issued in Sydney in November 1838, for use in the local penny post, are claimed to be the world's first prepaid postal stationery, antedating the Mulreadies by eighteen months. Stamps of New South Wales were used in Victoria until 1851, and in Queensland until 1860. Area: 310,000 sq. m.; capital: Sydney; pop. (1911): 1,646,734; (1963): 4,048,598.

'Newspaper' Keytype. Gibbons' identification for a Portuguese Colonial design, used for postage on journals and newspapers.

Newspaper Stamps. Special issues to prepay postage on newspapers, journals, periodicals, and all printed matter, have been made by many countries. Some of them combine news tax with postage, and thus serve as both revenue and postage stamps.

New York, U.S.A. In this American city the famous 'Post Office' post-masters' stamps appeared in 1845, preceding the first United States general issue by two years. Here, too, in the 1842–50 period, stamps inscribed 'City Despatch Post' were issued for the official local delivery service. Numerous privately operated postal services of various types formerly operated in the city and state of New York, and many of these issued their own local stamps. The first of these appeared in 1844 and some were still in use in the early 1880s. These services are all noted under their respective headings in this book.

New Zealand. Former British colony in Australasia, now an independent member of the British Commonwealth. Its first stamps, in the famous 'Chalon Head' design, were issued on 18 July 1855. The country is well known for the annual Health stamps, the first of which appeared in 1929, and which raise large sums each year for children's health camps. Area: 103,736 sq. m.; capital: Wellington (on North Island); currency: sterling; pop. (est. 1963): 2,533,000.

Nezavisna Drzava Hrvatska. Inscribed on stamps of Croatia (q.v.) 1941–4 during German occupation. It is now part of Yugoslavia.

Nicaragua. Central American republic. For three centuries a Spanish possession, it became independent in 1821. It first issued stamps in 1862. Area: 57,143 sq. m.; pop. (1959): 1,399,000; capital: Managua; currency: 1862, 100 centavos = 1 peso; 1913, 100 centavos = 1 cordoba. See 'Seebeck'.

NICARAGUA   NIGER COAST   NIGER TERRITORY

Nicaria. Icaria (q.v.).

Nieuw Guinea. (Ned.). See 'Netherlands New Guinea'.

Nieuwe Republiek. (Afrik.). New Republic, South Africa (q.v.).

Niger Coast Protectorate. Former British protectorate in West Africa, originally known as the Oil Rivers Protectorate and now part of Nigeria. It had its own stamps from 1893 until they were superseded by those of Southern Nigeria in 1901.

Niger. Former French territory in West Africa, since 1958 an autonomous republic within the French Community. It was part of Upper Senegal and Niger (q.v.) until 1919. Stamps first issued, 1921. From 1945 to 1959 Niger used the stamps of French West Africa, but since 1959 has again had its own issues. Area: 490,000 sq. m.; capital: Niamey; pop.: about 2,800,000.

Nigeria. Former British colony and protectorate of West Africa, since 1960 an independent member of the British Commonwealth. It was formed in 1914 from the amalgamation of Southern Nigeria and Northern Nigeria (q.v.), and in the same year the first stamps were issued. Area: 356,669 sq. m.; capital: Lagos; currency: sterling; pop. (1963): 55,653,821.

Nippon. Japan.

Nisiros. See under 'Dodecanese Islands'.

Niuafoou Island. One of the Tonga group. See under 'Tincan Mail'.

Niue. One of the Cook Islands group in the South Pacific, a dependency of New Zealand since 1901. Stamps of Cook Islands were used in Niue from 1892 until New Zealand stamps overprinted for Niue were introduced in 1902. The first definitives followed in 1920. Area: 100 sq. m.; chief town: Alofi; currency: sterling; pop. (1962): 4,935.

Niwin. Initials of 'National Inspanning Welzijnszorg in Netherlandsch Indie'. O/p and surcharge on stamps of Netherlands Antilles in 1947 in aid of the Social Welfare Fund.

No Hay Estampillas. (Span.). Having no stamps. O/p on typeset emergency issues of Barbacaos, Colombia, 1903.

Norddeutscher. North German (Confederation).

Norfolk Island. Pacific Ocean, about 400 miles north-west of North Island, New Zealand, administered by Australia, whose stamps were in use until 10 June 1947, when the 'Whispering Pines' pictorials appeared as first definitives. Romantically named 'The Madeira of the Pacific' it is actually one of a group, the others being Nepean and Phillip Islands. Area: $13\frac{1}{4}$ sq. m.; pop. (1961): 844. Australian currency.

Norge. Norway. **Noreg** (Neo-Norwegian). Norway.

North Borneo. Also known as British North Borneo, a former British protectorate in the island of Borneo in the East Indies, formerly under the administration of the British North Borneo Company who issued stamps for the territory from 1883 until the Japanese occupation in December 1941. Various overprints were applied to North Borneo stamps by the Japanese authorities, who also produced their own stamps for the territory. Specially overprinted Japanese stamps were introduced in 1945. By the end of that year the Japanese had surrendered and British forces were in control, leading to the appearance of B.M.A. overprints on the pre-war issue in December 1945. In the following year, with Labuan, North Borneo was reconstituted as a Crown Colony, leading to yet another overprint, this time the crown and Royal Cipher. In 1963 North Borneo was incorporated into the Federation of Malaysia, but has continued to issue its own stamps. In 1964 it was renamed Sabah (q.v.). Area: 29,388 sq. m.; capital: Jesselton; currency: 100 cents = 1 Malayan dollar; pop. (1960): 454,421.

North China Government. A temporary stamp-issuing authority as a Japanese 'puppet' state prior to, and during, 1941–5.

North German Confederation. Combined in its postal union and political federation the former stamp-issuing authorities of Bremen, Hamburg, Hanover, Mecklenburg-Schwerin and Strelitz, Oldenburg, Prussia, Saxony, Schleswig, and Holstein. In 1868 it made its own stamp issues, and in 1871 it was merged into the German Empire. Currency: 30 groschen = 1 thaler, 60 kreuzer = 1 gulden or thaler.

North Ingermanland. See 'Ingermanland'.

North Korea. See under 'Korea, North'.

North Mongolia. See under 'Touva'.

Northern (Russian) Army. The O.K.C.A. (Special Corps, Northern Army) commanded by General Rodzinko, issued an imperf. set of somewhat dubious stamps in 1919, of which there are many forgeries extant.

Northern Nigeria. Former British protectorate of West Africa, now part of Nigeria, set up on the revocation of the charter of the Royal Niger Company in 1900. The protectorate had its own stamps from 1900 to 1914, when it was incorporated into Nigeria. Area: 281,703 sq. m.; capital: Zungeru.

Northern Rhodesia. Former British protectorate of Central Africa, under the administration of the British South Africa Company until 1924. Its first stamps appeared in 1925, prior to which the issues of Rhodesia were in use.

NORTHERN
RHODESIA

NORTH BORNEO

NORTH GERMAN
CONFEDERATION

In 1953 Northern Rhodesia was incorporated into the Central African Federation of Rhodesia and Nyasaland, and used Federation issues from 1954. On the dissolution of the Federation, stamps for Northern Rhodesia alone were again issued in December 1963. In the following year the country became independent and was renamed Zambia (q.v.). Area: 290,323 sq. m.; capital: Lusaka; currency: sterling; pop. (1963): about 3,500,000.

North-West Pacific Islands. See under 'N.W. Pacific Islands' and 'New Guinea'.

North Western (Russian) Army. Russian 'arms' types were o/p at Pskov by General Yudenitch's 1919 provisional government. They are stated to have been available for two days only.

Norway (Norge, also Noreg). Scandinavian kingdom, formerly an autonomous state under the Swedish crown but independent since 1905, with its own royal house. Stamps first issued, 1885. Stamp issues continued under the German occupation of 1940–5, but in 1943 the exiled Norwegian government in London issued its own stamps for use of the Free Norwegian forces and on board Norwegian ships. These stamps were subsequently placed on sale in Norway after the liberation. Area: 125,064 sq. m.; capital: Oslo (formerly known as Christiania); currency: 1855, 120 skilling = 1 daler; 1877, 100 ore = 1 krone; pop. (1963): 3,654,030.

Norwegian Missionary Society. See under 'Madagascar'.

Nossi-Bé, or Noss Be. Island in Passandava Bay, Madagascar, for which French keytypes were o/p and surcharged or inscribed from 1889–96. Area: 115 sq. m.; pop. (1948): 16,900; chief town: Hellville; French currency.

'Not For Use'. About 1910, a Natal 1d. King's Head multiple CA watermark, S.G. 147, appeared printed over in black with the words 'NOT FOR USE' in three boxes within a design covering nearly the whole stamp. It is from the last pane of Natal's booklet, issued in 1909 or 1910. The booklet contained, because of the cancellation of this one stamp, 2s. 5d. in postage. It sold for 2s. 6d.; the additional penny paid for the booklet. The entire booklet pane, showing this blacked-out stamp, is a choice piece.

NYASALAND   NORWAY   NYASSA

Notopfer/2 Berlin/Steuermarke. Inscription of German compulsory tax stamp on internal mail, without post-validity, in use in Western Germany since 1948, to raise funds for the rebuilding of Berlin.

Nouvelle-Calédonie. New Caledonia (q.v.).

Nouvelle-Hébrides. New Hebrides (q.v.).

Nova Scotia. Former British colony on the eastern coast of North America, now part of Canada. Its first issue of 1851 consisted of beautiful Perkins, Bacon engravings in square and diamond formats. Nova Scotia joined the Canadian Confederation in 1867, and in the following year its stamps were replaced by those of Canada. At a later date numerous remainders were sold to the stamp trade. Area: 21,068 sq. m.; capital: Halifax; currency: 1851, 12 pence = 1 shilling; 1860, 100 cents = 1 dollar; pop. (est. 1963): 758,000.

Novocherkassk. See 'South Russia'.

Nowanuggar. Nawanagar (q.v.).

Nyasaland. Former British protectorate, originally known as British Central Africa, and now an independent member of the British Commonwealth under the name of Malawi (q.v.). Stamps for British Central Africa were first issued in 1891, the name of Nyasaland first appearing on the 1908 issue. In 1953 it was incorporated in the Central African Federation of Rhodesia and Nyasaland, using Federation issues from 1954 until November 1963. Then, on the approaching dissolution of the Federation, Nyasaland again issued its own stamps, the first set being a series of provisionals overprinted on Revenue stamps. The name of Malawi first appeared on the country's stamps in July 1964. Area: 36,870 sq. m.; capital: Zomba; chief town: Blantyre; currency: sterling; pop. (1962): about 3,000,000.

'Nyasaland' Keytype. Name given to the King Edward VII design first adopted for Nyasaland in 1908, and afterwards used for other colonies. Later, with change of portrait, it was used during the reign of King George V.

Nyassa. Portuguese East Africa, formerly administered by the Nyassa Company. First issues in 1897 were colonial keytypes of Mozambique o/p. In 1901 the Company issued a striking set designed by Sir Robert Edgcumbe for Waterlow's, depicting camels, giraffes, and zebras, accompanied by elaborate triangular postage dues—an obvious speculative issue to attract collectors. In 1929 it was absorbed into Mozambique, whose stamps are now used. Area: 73,292 sq. m.; pop.: about 3,000,000; Portuguese currency.

Nyomtatv. (Magyar). O/p on inflated pengo issues of Hungary 1946 indicated 'Printed Matter'.

Cyrillic

N in Cyrillic is represented by the character 'H', thus:

НА ВАРРИКАДЕ = (Na barricade). On the Barricade (Russia S.G. 577).

Greek
The Nu.

N as in English, thus: ΝΑΥΑΡΙΝΟΝ = Navarinon—Navarino.

Endorsed on the Grecian Navarino Centenary issue of 1927–8, one stamp of which portrays Sir Edward Codrington (see below).

THE 'SIR CODRINGTON' ERROR. (SEE PAGE 278.)

O.B.   O.M.F.   O.S.

O

O. An accepted abbreviation in philately signifying 'ordinary' as opposed to 'chalky' (q.v.) or other unusual paper or finish of a printed stamp.

O.A.S. On Active Service.

O.A.T. Onward air transmission.

O.B. Official Business. 'Official' issues of the Philippines (U.S.A. occupation).

O.D.E.C.A. (Span.). Organiscion de Estados Centro Americanos = Central American States Organisation.

O.F. Castelloriso. Occupation Française, Castelrosso. See 'B.N.F.'

O.g. Original gum. Denoting that the mucilage as originally applied is still intact. P.g. = part gum.

O.H.B.M.S. On His Britannic Majesty's Service. O/p on German East African fiscals 1915. See 'Mafia'.

O.H.E.M.S. On His Exalted Majesty's Service. On Egypt's 1922 'Officials'.

O.H.H.S. On His Highness's Service. On the Khedive's 'Officials' of Egypt 1907–22—preceding the above.

O.H.M.S. On His (or Her) Majesty's Service. Frank for official correspondence G.B.

O.K.C.A. (Rus.) Special Corps, Northern Army. See 'Northern (Russian) Army'.

O.L. (Fr.). Origine locale. O/p on stamps of Monaco as a control on mail posted in Monte Carlo Supérior (French territory) up to 1904.

O.M.F. Occupation Militaire Française. O/p on stamps of France 1920–2, for Cilicia and for Syria.

O.N.F. Castellorizo. Occupation navale Française. See 'B.N.F.'

O/p, also **opt., optd.** Overprint, or overprinted. Abbreviation used throughout this work.

O.P.A.L.　Oriental Philatelic Association (of) London.

O.P.D.A.　Ottoman Public Debts Administration. O/p on low values first issues of Palestine under British Mandate 1920–21. Although primarily fiscal issues, some were postally used.

O.P.S.O.　On Public Service Only. Diagonal o/p on New Zealand's 1892–1901 'Officials'.

OR.　(Fr.). Origine Rurale—rural cancel on stamps of France.

O.S.　On Service. Public or official service inferred. Found notably overprinted or punch-perforated on stamps of Australia and Australian States. On Official stamps of Norway the letters stand for Offentlig (or Offentleg) Sak (q.v.).

O.S.G.S.　On Sudan Government Service. O/p on Sudanese 'Officials' 1902–36.

O.T.　(Czech). Obchodni Tiskovina = commercial printed matter. O/p on newspaper stamps of 1934. Three values.

O.U.S.　Oxford Union Society. O/p or back-printed in red on 1858–79 issues of G.B. The privilege of o/p was withdrawn in 1870.

O.W./Official.　Office of Works/Official. Stamps punch-perforated HM/OW appeared in August 1895; changed to crown over OW in October; and overprinted OW/Official from March 1896 to 1902. G.B. 'Official' issues now obsolete.

'OXO'　Postmark. The 'Star between Ciphers' obliteration used on the Crimean War 'used abroad' stamps of G.B. 1854–7. The companion mark was the 'Crown between Stars'.

Oaxaca.　State of Mexico with Civil War issues of its own, 1914.

Ober Schelsien.　(Ger.). Upper Silesia.

Obliteration.　Has two distinct philatelic meanings. (1) As a synonym for cancellation, often incorrectly; and (2) to define an o/p designed to render illegible, or to deface, any inscription, monarchial emblem, obsolete value, or other unwanted arts of a stamp's design. In regard to (1) the official definition is 'a special postmark employed for defacing stamps is . . . properly termed an obliterating mark'. It is, therefore, also a canceller; but a dating stamp, or other postmark, is not necessarily an 'obliteration', this latter term implying an actual and physical defacement, and colloquially known to collectors as a 'Killer' (q.v.). See 'Cancellation'.

Obock.　Seaport of French Somaliland. Colonial 'Commerce' keytypes first appeared in 1892. Striking triangular and large oblong stamps were issued the next year. Since 1901 has used stamps of the French Somali Coast.

Obsolescent.　About to become obsolete—to remain in use until existing stocks are exhausted or withdrawn. Example: the death or abdication of a king renders all existing stamps bearing his portrait obsolescent immediately. They normally become obsolete when the new issues appear.

OBLITERATION OCEANIC SETTLEMENTS OBOCK

Obsolete. Philatelically—no longer in use; or, that issue has ceased, i.e. stamps that have been discarded or replaced by a new issue, value, colour, or other variant. No longer available to the public at post offices in the country of origin, but not necessarily invalid for prepayment. See 'Demonetised'.

Occupation Azirbayedjan. See 'Azerbaijan' (Iran) Persia.

Oceanic Settlements (Établissements de l'Oceanie). French islands in the eastern Pacific, including Tahiti, the Society Islands, the Marquesas, etc. Stamps first issued, 1892—though a few of the general French Colonial issues were overprinted for Tahiti from 1882. The islands were renamed French Polynesia (q.v.) in 1958. Area: 1,544 sq. m.; capital: Papeete on Tahiti; pop.: about 73,000.

Oceanie. Oceanic Settlements (q.v.).

Odontomètre. (Fr.). Tooth measure. The Continental name for perforation gauge. Invented 1886 by Dr. Legrand of Paris.

Öesterr. or Öesterreich. Austria.

Off-Centre. A stamp not centrally printed within the limits of the paper, i.e. with margins of uneven width, as opposed to a 'well-centred' copy. Stamps off-centre are generally regarded as less valuable or desirable than those perfectly centred.

Offentlig Sak, Offentleg Sak. Inscription of certain Official issues of Norway, now abbreviated to O.S.

Officials. Stamps issued for the use of Government departments, public servants, members of parliament or senate, etc. Such stamps may, or may not, be supplied free, but are a check upon usage and expenditure. In some countries, for example India, they are known as Service stamps.

Official 'Paid' Stamps. Are 'Franks' (q.v.) in the strict sense of that word in that they indicate that the letter or package so impressed is not liable for payment, either in advance or upon receipt. They were in use as hand-struck stamps since the seventeenth century, and are still so used in all parts of the world. Normally they 'franked' official government correspondence, but the G.P.O. frank bulk prepaid mail, circulars, etc., in G.B. with the well-known triangular frank postmark, usually in red, up to the present day.

OFFICIALS:

NEW ZEALAND   SALVADOR   GREAT BRITAIN   INDIA

Official Reprints. Are stamps reprinted by the original stamp-issuing authority for a special purpose, person, or body, or as a commemorative; either in the original colours, on the same type of paper, or otherwise. See also 'Royal reprint'.

Officially Sealed. See 'Post Office Seals'.

Offisieel (Afrik.). Official.

Off Paper. Stamps soaked free from superfluous paper.

Offset, or Set-Off. A printing term for an accidental impression of a design or o/p from a wet-inked sheet transferred to the back of a succeeding sheet, which, in its turn, may again set-off to a third. It can occur also if a sheet of paper misses in the machine, and the impression is taken off by the underlay instead. The next sheet is then liable to pick up the wet impression. The term also applies philatelically to actual set-off from stamps lying a long time in a album under pressure. They have been known to transfer their design to the back of the opposing page. Interleaving and storing albums on their edges in an upright position will obviate.

Offset Litho. See 'Lithography' and 'Printing'.

Oil Rivers Protectorate. Former British protectorate in West Africa, afterwards known as the Niger Coast Protectorate (q.v.). In July 1892 a set of British stamps were overprinted for use in the protectorate, and this was the only issue to carry the name 'Oil Rivers'. A set of definitives was prepared, but before issue in 1893 the old name was obliterated and 'Niger Coast' substituted.

Okca. (Rus.). Special Corps Northern Army. Inscribed on stamps issued for General Rodzinko's troops in North Russia 1919.

Old Calabar. A Niger Coast Protectorate post with dating canceller used on stamps of G.B.

Oldenburg. Former grand duchy and city of North Germany, with its own issues 1852–67. Area: 2,482 sq. m.; pop. (1910): 483,042; currency: 30 groschen = 1 thaler.

Olonetz. See 'Aunus'.

Olsztyn Allenstein. See 'Allenstein'.

Oltre Giuba. (Ital.). Jubaland (q.v.).

Omaha. Name given to the set of pictorials issued by the United States in June 1898 to commemorate the Trans-Mississippi Exposition of that year, held at Omaha, Nebraska.

Omnibus Issues. Any group of stamps, frequently sharing a common design, issued by a number of stamp-issuing authorities to mark the same occasion. The first such issue in the British Commonwealth was the extensive Silver Jubilee series of 1935. By extension the term is often also applied to world-wide issues on the same theme but in differing designs, for example Anti-Malaria, World Refugee Year, etc.

On C.G.S. On Cochin Government Service.

On Cover. A stamp *in situ*, on the envelope or wrapper as received. See also 'Entire', 'Tied', etc.

On/H.M.S. On His or Her Majesty's Service.

On/KDS. On Kishengarh Durbar Service. O/p on stamps of Kishengarh, India, 1918.

On paper. Stamps still adhering to parts of the covers on which they were used.

On Piece. A stamp on sufficient of the original envelope or wrapper to show complete postmark, or other philatelic evidence of importance to prove authenticity—as in a bisect, for instance. See 'Bisects', 'Tied', etc.

One Cent Despatch. A Baltimore, U.S.A., 'local' of 1856.

'One Pound Jimmy'. The aboriginal pictured on the 1950 8½d. value of Australia (S.G. 238) and the 1952 2s. 6d. (S.G. 253).

Onza. (Span.). 16 onzas = 1 libra. Currency units of Spain 1854–5.

'Opera Glass' cancel. Twin circular date stamp devised by Pearson Hill and used for a short while in G.B. about 1848.

Oradea. (Nagyvárad) Eastern Hungary. A special set of surcharged stamps of Hungary was issued by the Russians in 1945 to commemorate its being handed back to Roumania.

Orange Free State (Oranje Vrij Staat). Former independent Boer Republic in South Africa. Stamps first issued, 1868. In the Anglo-Boer War the British occupation led to the appearance of 'V.R.I.' overprints on Orange Free State stamps, well known for their orange-tree design. The country was then renamed Orange River Colony, see below. Area: 49,647 sq. m.; capital: Bloemfontein; currency: sterling; pop.: about 629,000.

| OLYMPIC
GAMES | ON C.G.S. | ORANGE RIVER
COLONY | OSTEN |

Orange River Colony. Former British colony in South Africa, previously known as Orange Free State, see above. The first stamps thus inscribed were overprints on Cape of Good Hope issues, 1900–2. Definitives followed in 1903. In 1910 the territory became a province of South Africa, and since 1913 South African stamps have been used.

Orangeburg Coil. (Scott's No. 389). Is the rarest known U.S.A. pre-cancel, as only one 500-coil was made for the Bell Chemical Co. of that town.

Orb. The ball, cross-surmounted, and emblem of British royalty, which was the basis of the watermark design used in the stamps of G.B. of 1873.

Orchha. Former Indian native state which issued its own internal stamps, 1913–50. Indian stamps are now used. Area: 1,999 sq. m.; capital: Tehri (Tikamgarh); pop. (1941): 363,405.

Orchid. The emblem on stamps of Manchuria (see page 184).

'Ordinaries'. (U.S.A.). Definitives; regular and general issues.

Öre. Or Øre. Scandinavian monetary unit. Denmark and Greenland since 1875; Norway since 1876, and Sweden since 1858.

Organisation Internationale pour Les Refugies. Or Organisation Mondiale de la Santé, o/p on 1948–50 stamps of Switzerland, indicates use by the Internation Office for Refugees, and for the World Health Organisation, respectively.

Orlof. O/p on stamps of Iceland indicates use for holiday or vacation savings—a government-sponsored scheme of social welfare. They are therefore not postage stamps but fiscals.

Oro Pastas. (Lithuanian). Air-post. Airmails of Lithuania.

Orts Post. (Ger.). Local Post. Inscription on 1850 Swiss Federal issue. See 'Rayon'.

Osmanie. Turkish.

217

Osten. (Ger.). Eastern. German stamps were o/p 'Deutsche Post Osten' in 1939 for use in occupied Poland.

Österreich. (Ger.). Austria.

Ostland. (Ger.). Eastland. Comprised the northern part of Russian-occupied Poland, the former Baltic republics of Estonia, Latvia and Lithuania, and part of White Russia occupied by the Germans 1941–2. Captured Russian stamps, o/p for the various cities and chief towns, were locally employed pending arrival of German ('Hitler head') issues o/p 'Ostland'.

Ottoman Empire. Turkish Empire.

Oubangui-Chari (Ubangi-Chari). Former French territory of Central Africa, at one time part of French Congo. Stamps of Middle Congo were overprinted 'Oubangui-Chari-Tchad' in 1916, afterwards 'Oubangui-Chari' only. The first definitives followed in 1930. From 1937 to 1960 Oubangui-Chari used the stamps of French Equatorial Africa. Since 1958 it has been known as the Central African Republic (q.v.), and now issues its own stamps once more.

Overland Mail. A privately run mail service between England and India, established by Thomas Waghorn via the 'Overland Route', i.e. by land across Egypt from Alexandria to Suez. An experimental service started in 1829 met with only a small measure of success, mainly due to the unreliability of the early steamers. But in the 1835–40 period Waghorn provided the finest service seen up to that time, often taking personal charge of the mails himself. Letters were accepted at a fee of 5s. each, and were often conveyed to India in about two months, compared with the usual four or five months' voyage by slow sailing ship via the Cape of Good Hope. By the early 1840s the P. & O. Line were conveying the Indian mails via Egypt under Post Office contract, but Waghorn continued to operate a travel agency for passengers on the Overland Route until his death in January 1850 at the age of forty-nine. Covers carried by the Waghorn service were stamped 'Care of Mr. Waghorn', and are today keenly collected by postal historians.

The term Overland Mail is also applied to the American transcontinental stage-coach mails of the 1860s. In addition it is found as an endorsement on mail carried across the desert between Baghdad and Haifa in 1923 by the motor transport of Nairn Transport Ltd.

Overprint. Commonly abbreviated to o/p or opt. Any printing on top of and in addition to the original design. Where the face value of a stamp is altered (or in rare cases confirmed) by an overprint, it is more correctly described as a surcharge.

Overton & Co. Letter Express. A local U.S.A. mail operating from New York in 1844 which issued its own stamps.

Oxidation. See 'De-sulphurisation'.

Greek Omikron (O) = the short 'O'; the Omega

(Ω) = the long form of the letter:

ОСВОБОДИТЕЛНА ⎫
ОСВОБ. ВОЙИА ⎬ = War of Liberation. Bulgaria 1913 and 1921.

ΟΛΥΜΠΙΑΚΟΙ ΑΓΩΝΕΣ = Olympic Games. Greece 1906.

ORCHID EMBLEM
OF MANCHURIA

P

'**P**'. Overprinted on the SCADTA semi-official airmails of Colombia, the capital letter indicates that the stamp is a consular overprint sold in Panama. Overprinted with star and crescent in oval on the 1878 2 ¢. brown stamp of Straits Settlements it stands for Perak. Occasionally the letter is also used as an abbreviation for pen-cancelled.

Pa. Para. Turkish and Eastern European unit of currency.

P.C.C.P. Russian Socialist Soviet Republic.

P.C.G.B. Philatelic Congress of Great Britain.

P.c.p. Progressive colour proofs.

PD. (Fr. Paye á Destination). Paid to destination.

PE. Overprinted on the SCADTA semi-official airmails of Colombia, these letters indicate that the stamp is a consular overprint sold in Peru.

P.g. In some stamp auction catalogues, means 'part gum'.

P.G.S. Perak Government Service.

Pi. Piastre. N. African, Turkish and Eastern European unit of currency.

P.I. Perforated initials. A U.S.A. auction catalogue annotation in occasional use, used also to indicate 'poorly inked'.

'**P.J. of G.B.**'. *Philatelic Journal of Great Britain.*

P.K.W.N. Polskie Komitet Wolnosci Narodowej (Polish). Polish National Liberation Committee.

P.M. Posta Militaire. O/p on stamps of Italy used to frank mail from armed forces in 1939–45 War.

PLL. (Ger.: Polizei). Punch-perforated on German stamps used as Prussian Police 'officials'.

P.S.I. Philatelic Society of India.

P.S.N.C. Pacific Steam Navigation Company (q.v.).

P.T.M. These initials appear as a watermark on Malayan issues. It was introduced in November 1961.

P.T.S. Philatelic Traders' Society (q.v.). Or (U.S.A.) Postal Transport Service, formerly the Railroad Mail Service (R.M.S.).

Pacchi Postali. (Ital.). Postal Package. Parcel Post.

Pacific Steam Navigation Company. This old-established British shipping company, trading to the west coast of South America, produced its own stamps in 1847 to prepay charges on mail carried by its steamers. Supplies of two values, each showing an old-time paddle-steamer of the period, were duly printed, but were apparently never used owing to the objections of the Peruvian Government. In the 1850's, however, the government began to consider the introduction of postage stamps. The company thereupon presented the government with a supply of its stamps, and it was decided to try these out pending the arrival of Peru's first regular issue. The P.S.N.C. stamps—the initials appearing in the four corners of the designs—were used in very small quantities, probably fewer than 100 all told. Genuine examples are now great rarities, though they have been extensively forged. They were introduced on 1 December 1857, and were current for only about three months until the appearance of Peru's first definitives in March 1858. The company's stamps therefore rank as the first issue of Peru, and are unique in having been prepared as locals but eventually issued with government authority.

Packet Letter. A letter brought in by a packet, that is a ship either maintained by the government or carrying mail under Post Office contract; as distinct from a ship letter (q.v.) brought in by a private ship. Packet letter postmarks were introduced at a number of British ports in the 1840s, and continued in use into the early part of the twentieth century. Separate markings were required since at this period the postal rates on packet letters were considerably higher than on ship letters.

Packhoi. Pakhei or Pak-Hoi. Chinese treaty port in Kwantung province. France o/p and surcharged issues of Indo-China 1903–22. Pop. (est. 1952): 36,000.

Pahang. One of the Malayan States; a sultanate. The first stamps of 1890 were overprints on Straits Settlements, followed by definitives in the following year. From 1900 to 1935 stamps of the Federated Malay States were in use, but since the latter date Pahang has again had its own issues. Some were overprinted by the Japanese authorities during the occupation of 1942–5. Area: 13,873 sq. m.; capital: Kuala Lipis; pop. (1962): 371,552.

Pair. Two unsevered stamps, joined horizontally or vertically—the former being normally preferred by collectors.

Paisa. Unit of currency in Pakistan and India (100 paise = 1 rupee); also formerly in Afghanistan.

Paita. Peruvian city and province with a control o/p on 1876–84 stamps of Peru, April 1884.

Pakistan. Independent member of the British Commonwealth, formed by the partition of the Indian Empire in 1947; a republic since 1956. The first stamps were Indian issues overprinted in 1947; the first definitives followed in 1948. Area: 365,929 sq. m.; capital: Rawalpindi; currency:

1947, 16 annas = 1 rupee; 1961, 100 paise = 1 rupee; pop. (1961): 93,720,613.

Pakke-Porto. Inscription on the Parcel Post stamps of the Royal Greenland Trading Company, 1905–38. See under 'Greenland'.

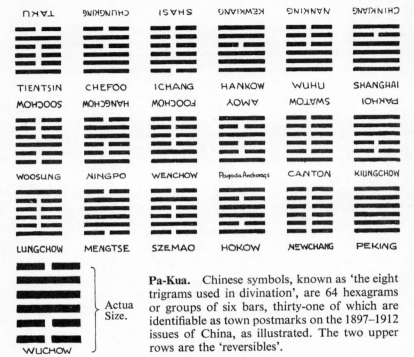

TAKU	CHUNGKING	SHASI	KEWKIANG	NANKING	CHINKIANG
TIENTSIN	CHEFOO	ICHANG	HANKOW	WUHU	SHANGHAI
SOOCHOW	HANGCHOW	FOOCHOW	AMOY	SWATOW	PAKHOI
WOOSUNG	NINGPO	WENCHOW	Pagoda Anchorage	CANTON	KIUNGCHOW
LUNGCHOW	MENGTSE	SZEMAO	HOKOW	NEWCHANG	PEKING

Actua Size.

WUCHOW

Pa-Kua. Chinese symbols, known as 'the eight trigrams used in divination', are 64 hexagrams or groups of six bars, thirty-one of which are identifiable as town postmarks on the 1897–1912 issues of China, as illustrated. The two upper rows are the 'reversibles'.

Palatinate. Former French zone now incorporated into West Germany. Provisional 'Arms' type (three antlers within a shield) issued 1945. Part of the Rhineland (Rheinland Pfalz) (q.v.).

Palestine. Country of Western Asia, formerly part of the Ottoman Empire and placed under British mandate after the First World War. First stamps were issues of the Egyptian Expeditionary Force (E.E.F.) in 1918; from 1920 these were overprinted 'Palestine' in Arabic, English, and Hebrew. The first definitives appeared in 1927. In May 1948 Palestine stamps were withdrawn on the termination of the British mandate, and in the Jewish parts of the country were succeeded by the first stamps of Israel (q.v.). Parts of central Palestine were incorporated into Jordan, and Egypt occupied the Gaza region in the south. Since 1948 numerous Egyptian stamps have been overprinted 'Palestine' (or latterly produced with an additional inscription) for use in the Egyptian-occupied area. Area: 10,429 sq. m.; capital: Jerusalem; currency: 10 milliemes = 1 piastre; 1,000 milliemes = £1 Palestinian; pop. (1947): 1,933,673.

PAKISTAN   'PALMS'   PALESTINE

'Palms'. 1941 set of Sudan, designed by Miss H. M. Herbert, depicting the palm trees on Tuti Island at the junction of the Blue and White Niles at Khartoum. A popular modern set.

Paludismo. (Span.). Paludism, malaria. Mexico's 1947 special Mosquito Tax 1 ¢. stamp, which had to be compulsorily affixed to all letters in addition to the usual postage.

Panamá. Independent republic of Central America; until 1903 a department of Colombia. Stamps first issued, 1878. Colombian issues were in use from 1859 to 1903, concurrently with those of Panamá after 1878. Following independence the new republic granted to the United States the right of perpetual administration over a zone on either side of the Panamá Canal, then under construction. The Canal Zone (q.v.), has had its own separate stamps since 1904. British stamps were used on overseas mail from Panamá City, 1863–84, with the 'C 35' cancellation, and at Colón, 1870–81, with the 'E 88' cancellation. Area: 28,576 sq. m.; capital: Panamá City; currency: 1878, 100 centavos = 1 peso; 1906, 100 centesimos = 1 balboa; pop. (1960): 1,075,541.

Panamá Canal Zone. See 'Canal Zone'.

Pane. Sheets of stamps are sometimes subdivided into sections by 'gutters' (q.v.). Such subdivisions are known as 'panes' owing to their similarity to the panes of a window. A pane is usually a fourth or half of a sheet. A booklet pane is one complete leaf—usually six stamps.

Pantograph. A draughting, designing, or engraving instrument or device to reproduce or re-duplicate an enlarged, reduced, or exact-sized copy of a plane figure, used extensively in stamp production.

Papal States. See 'Roman States' and 'Vatican City'.

Paper. The paper upon which stamps are printed forms an interesting philatelic study, and the many varieties are dealt with in detail under their separate headings in this work: art; bâtonné; bond; chalky; coated; deckle-edged; 'Dickinson'; double; glacé; goldbeaters' skin; granite; grill; India; laid; pelure; quadrillé; repp; safety or security; surface-coloured; white-back; wove, etc. The quality normally used is a good machine-made white wove paper, with a surface suited to the printing process employed.

PAQUEBOT
PARAGUAY
'PEACE & COMMERCE'

Papillon de Metz. Message carried by balloon from the beleaguered city of Metz during the Franco-Prussian War, August–October 1870. Thirty-one such balloons were dispatched. So called after Dr. Papillon, a medical officer serving with the garrison, who suggested the scheme.

Papua. The south-eastern part of the island of New Guinea, a British territory under Australian administration since 1901 and originally known as British New Guinea. Stamps of Queensland were used from 1898 until the first British New Guinea issue appeared in 1901. The new name of Papua first appeared as an overprint in 1906, and on definitives in 1907. All the stamps of Papua until 1932 were in the well-known native canoe ('Lakatoi') type. On the Japanese invasion of New Guinea in 1942, Papua stamps were withdrawn. With the repulse of the invaders Australian stamps were introduced and remained in use until stamps for the combined postal administration of Papua and New Guinea were first issued in 1952. Area: 90,516 sq. m.; capital: Port Moresby; currency: Australian; pop. (1962): about 539,000.

Papua & New Guinea. Stamps thus inscribed were first issued in 1952 for use in the combined Australian administration of Papua and the Territory of New Guinea. See under 'Papua' and under 'New Guinea'.

Paquebot. French term (= Packet (mail) boat) used internationally since 1894 on postmarks applied to mail posted on board ship. Paquebot markings are a popular and interesting study.

Paraguay. South American republic. The dictator Francisco Lopez ordered stamps from Paris in 1862; various essays and proofs have survived, but no further action was taken. In 1868 a completely bogus 5 ¢. stamp was put on the market by Samuel Allan Taylor. The first stamps genuinely used within the borders of Paraguay were Argentine issues used by the Argentine forces occupying Hamaita in the south during the Paraguayan War of 1865–70. Paraguay's own first stamps appeared in 1870, shortly after the war had ended. Area: 157,046 sq. m.; capital: Asunción; currency: 1870, 8 reales = 1 peso; 1878, 100 centavos = 1 peso; 1944, 100 centimos = 1 guarani; pop. (1962): 1,816,890.

Paraph. A flourish, or a contraction of a signature, or initials. The o/p on the stamps of Cuba used in Porto Rico 1873–6 is an example, and the Arabic motif in the centre of early Turkish issues is another.

Par Avion. (Fr.). By air (plane), or airborne.

Par L'Etat (or État). (Fr.) By the State. O/p on 1912 issues of Belgium are Railway Parcels validation on issues used to frank parcels traffic transferred at Huy from a private line (Le Compagnie du Nord Belge) to the State-owned network.

Parcel Post Stamps. Many countries have special stamps for this service, the U.S.A. 1912–13 set being particularly interesting. The *pacchi postali* issues of Italy and San Marino are in two parts, one half being retained by the sender as a receipt, the other (left hand) is therefore the only portion postally used and postmarked. Uruguay, in addition to a general parcels issue, produced in 1929 a special triangular 'Agricultural' or farmers' parcels or produce stamp (Encomiendas de Granja).

Park, Bertram. London portrait photographer, whose profile of King George VI was used for many G.B. Crown Colony issues.

Parma. Former duchy of northern Italy. Issued its own imperforate stamps from June 1852 to 1860, when it was annexed by Sardinia and subsequently absorbed into the new Italian kingdom. Area: 2,750 sq. m.; pop. (1860): about 500,000; currency: 100 centesimi = 1 lira.

Pasco. Peruvian district with a control o/p 1884.

Patiala. Former native Convention state of Punjab, which used the stamps of British India o/p from 1884. Area: 5,942 sq. m.; capital of the same name; Indian currency; pop. (1952): 1,936,259. Since 1 April 1950, uses stamps of the Republic of India.

Patmos. See under 'Dodecanese Islands'.

'Peace and Commerce'. French keytype designed by J. A. Sage, and engraved by E. L. Mouchon. It was also the general issue for France 1876–1900. Sometimes known as the 'Sage' type.

'Peace and Navigation'. Also known as the 'Tablet' keytype, and used for the French oversea possessions from 1892 onwards. Another Mouchon engraving.

Peace Issues. No less than 165 stamps were issued by countries of the British Commonweath to commemorate the victorious end of the 1939–45 war.

'Peacocks'. This royal emblem of Burma was o/p on current stamps by the Japanese invader in 1942, and such issues are known to collectors by that name.

'Pearls'. A circle, with or without a semi-circular dash or shading, thus ◑. Is a favourite motif with artists and they appear on many of the stamps of the world. Outstanding examples are the 1913–19, and 1923–6 issues of China; and the 1870 and 1863 one cent values of the U.S.A.—one engraving has the pearls unshaded, the other a tiny dash that distinguishes one set from the other.

Pears' Soap. See 'Advertisements on Stamps'.

Pechino. (Ital.). Peking—otherwise known as Pei-Ching—China.

Peking. (Pei-Ching). Italian stamps o/p 'Pechino' and surcharged for the Italian Military Mission post in China 1918–19.

Pelita. Overprint on Netherlands Indies stamp of 1948, with surcharge in aid of 'Victims of the Terror'.

Pelure Paper. (Fr. Pelure—a skin). A strong, thin, translucent paper with a barely perceptible wove or laid pattern. The imprinted design shows clearly from the back.

Pemberton, Edward Loines (1844–78). Famous pioneer philatelist and stamp-dealer, one of the founders of the Royal Philatelic Society of London and one of the earliest philatelic authors. One of his best-known works is *The Stamp Collector's Handbook*, first published in 1874.

Pembina Twins. Name given to a pair of Canadian 7½d. stamps of 1857 (S.G.22) pmkd. at Pembina, North Dakota, U.S.A., in November 1858. Off cover and separated, were re-united by consent of the owning Canadian collectors. Now a unique philatelic treasure.

Pen or **Penni.** Finnish monetary unit since 1866. 100 penni = 1 mark.

Penang. The oldest British settlement in Malaya; since 1957 part of the Malayan Federation. Indian stamps were used there from 1854 to 1867, thereafter those of Straits Settlements, and after the Second World War B.M.A. Malaya issues until 1949, when Penang's first definitives appeared. Shortly before this, in December 1948, there were two Royal Silver Wedding stamps for Penang. Like the other Malayan States, Penang continues to issue its own stamps though those of the Malayan Federation are used concurrently. Area: 400 sq. m.; capital: George Town; pop. (1962): 671,262.

Pen-cancelled. Cancellation of a stamp with pen or pencil usually indicates fiscal use. There are, however, a considerable number of cases where postage stamps have been pen-cancelled, either in emergency or otherwise. In a few countries stamps were introduced before suitable postmarks were available to cancel them; an example is Nicaragua, all of whose stamps were pen-cancelled for some seven years after the first issue appeared in 1862. Except in circumstances such as these, pen-cancelled stamps should be collected on cover or large piece to demonstrate genuine postal use.

'Pence' Issues. British currency was at first in use in both Canada and Ceylon, but both changed to decimal notation—Canada in 1859 and Ceylon in 1872. Stamps in use before those dates are therefore known as the 'pence' issues to distinguish them. The 12d. stamp of Canada is a great rarity.

Penrhyn Island. Coral atoll, one of the Cook Islands (q.v.) in the Pacific Ocean, administered by New Zealand, whose stamps o/p in 1902 were its first issues. The 1920 definitives were replaced on 15 March 1932 by stamps of the Cook Islands. The lagoon has a land area of 90 sq. m.; pop. (1956): 619; British notation.

Penny Black. The world-renowned first issue of Great Britain, introduced on 6 May 1840. It shows the head of Queen Victoria, taken from the medal engraved by William Wyon to mark the Queen's first visit to the City of London after her accession in 1837. The choice of the Sovereign's head—which has continued to influence stamp design to the present day—appears to have been adopted first because it was difficult to forge with accuracy, and secondly because the authorities regarded the new stamp in the light of a paper coin, and from pre-Roman times the coinage had always shown the head of the monarch. With its companion, the Twopence Blue, which was issued on the same day, the Penny Black shares the distinction of having been the first adhesive postage stamp in the world.

Penny Blue. Trial sheets (in blue) of G.B.'s 1d. stamp Plate 8, printed 15 December 1840, for Rowland Hill, who wished to make a decision on the shade of the 2d. A used specimen was found in the post in March 1857, and is now in the Royal collection.

Penny Express Company. Subsidiary of the U.S.A. Holladay Overland Mail & Express Company which issued the stamp so inscribed in 1866.

Penny Lilac. Name given to the 1d. stamp of Great Britain printed in various shades of lilac and purple, in use from 1881 to 1902.

Penny Post. The term was introduced by William Dockwra, who set up a London Penny Post as a private venture in 1680, delivering letters and packets within a prescribed area of London for a penny each. It had its own triangular 'Penny Post Paid' markings. With its flat rate of prepaid postage and its frequent deliveries, Dockwra's post was a remarkable precursor of modern postal systems. It was so successful that in November 1682 it was suppressed as an infringement of the State postal monopoly, and subsequently reopened as a government service. Later on there were Twopenny and Threepenny Posts covering the outlying districts of London.

Penny posts were introduced in Edinburgh and Dublin in 1773, and afterwards in many other towns. The postal markings of these are widely studied and collected. The introduction of a national Penny Post, replacing the previous system under which charges had varied according to the distance a letter was carried, was the central feature of Sir Rowland Hill's great postal reform of 1840. It came into operation on 10 January of that year, preceding the issue of the first postage stamps by nearly four months.

Penny Red. Name given to the 1d. stamps of Great Britain, successors of the Penny Black, printed in many shades between red and brown, which lasted with a number of variations from 1841 until 1880.

People's League. The People's League for the Defence of Freedom, led by Edward Martell, organised an emergency mail service during the work-to-rule of British Post Office employees in January 1962. A letter delivery service was suppressed by the Postmaster-General within a few hours of it being started, but a parcel delivery service, for which the League issued its own typeset stamps, lasted for three weeks until the work-to-rule came to an end. In July 1964 a similar parcel service was operated for a short time by the Freedom Group (of which the People's League forms part), during a one-day strike and subsequent overtime ban by postal workers. Special stamps were used which had been prepared in anticipation of a similar stoppage which failed to materialise in the previous April.

Per Luchpost. (Dutch). By airpost, or airborne.

Per Lugpos. (Afrik.). By airpost, or airborne.

Perak. One of the Malayan States; a sultanate. Stamps of Straits Settlements were used prior to 1878—and on overseas mail until 1895. The first Perak stamp was a 2 ¢. value of Straits Settlements locally hand-stamped with a crescent and star above the letter P in a circle. Further overprints on Straits Settlements followed from 1880 until the first definitives appeared in 1891. From 1900 to 1935 stamps of the Federated Malay States were in use, but from the latter date Perak has again had its own stamps. Perak stamps were overprinted by the Japanese during the occupation of 1942–5. Area: 7,980 sq. m.; capital: Taiping (formerly Kuala Kangsar); pop. (1962): 1,449,224.

ARC	∩∩∩∩∩∩∩∩∩∩∩∩
LIGNES (colourless)	— — — — — — — —
LIGNES de couleur	— — — — — — — —
LIGNES OBLIQUES	//
LOSANGES	XXXXXXXXXXXXXXXXXXXXX
POINTS	. . . .
POINTES	∧∧∧∧∧∧∧∧∧∧∧
SCIE	⌃⌃⌃⌃⌃⌃⌃⌃⌃⌃⌃⌃
SERPENTINE	∿∿∿∿∿∿∿∿

Percé en Arc. (Fr.). Arc-pierced.

Percé en Lignes. (Fr.). Line-pierced.

Percé en Lignes de Couleur. (Fr.). Line-pierced in colour.

Percé en Lignes Obliques. (Fr.). Pierced in oblique lines.

Percé en Losanges. (Fr.). Lozenge-pierced.

Percé en Points. (Fr.). Pin-pierced or perforated.

Percé en Pointes. (Fr.). Zig-zag pierced.

Percé en Scie. (Fr.). Saw-tooth pierced.

Percé en Serpentine. (Fr.). Serpentine-pierced—in wavy lines.

Percevoir. See 'À Percevoir'.

Perçue. (Fr.). Tax collected, e.g. postage prepaid.

Percussion à Froid. (Fr.). Cold pressing. An early process used by Albert Barré at the Paris Mint for making the plates (clichés) used for printing the stamps of France and Greece.

Perf. Perforation or perforated.

Perfins. Punch-perforated or 'branded' stamps (q.v.).

Perforation. Denotes, in philately, a series or row of round or other shaped holes, punched out between the rows of stamps in a sheet (or coil)

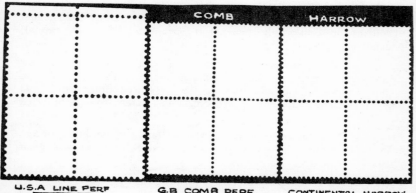

U.S.A LINE PERF
NOTE CONFUSION
WHERE LINES CROSS

G.B COMB PERF.
NOTE SLIGHT LACK OF
ALIGNMENT AT CENTRE

CONTINENTAL HARROW.
NOTE PERFECTION AT
CENTRE.

of stamps to facilitate partition, separation, or division. Henry Archer (q.v.) is credited with the invention of the first perforating machine. There are three basic methods of perforating employed today: (1) Line or guillotine, where one straight row of punches perforates a line at a time; (2) Comb, where three sides of each of a row are done at one stroke; and (3) Harrow, where a whole block, pane or sheet is perforated at one operation, the punches being arranged in transverse rows. In line perforation there is little co-ordination at the corners where the lines cross, and irregularities can be detected at these points. It is often difficult to detect the difference between 'comb' and 'harrow'. Initials or devices perforated through the stamp to obviate pilfering are dealt with under 'Punch perforating' (q.v.). See 'Percé en arc, etc.', 'Rouletting', and other related headings.

Perforation Gauge. (Fr. Odontomètre). Perforations are measured by the number of holes (perfs.) or teeth to 20 mm., or 2 centimetres—this figure is known as the perf. number, and may be expressed in whole numbers or with a fraction, although anything below a half perf. may be varied by paper shrinkage. Measurement is done by means of a gauge, which may be a simple printed scale on card or paper, or engraved on transparent plastic.

Perkins, Bacon & Co. Known as Perkins, Bacon & Petch until 1852, this British firm printed the first line-engraved stamps of Great Britain and of a number of the colonies.

Perkins Paper. An azure safety paper invented by Dr. Perkins (a partner of Barclay, Perkins & Co. the famous brewers), and used on the 1855-6 and other G.B. issues.

Perlis. Princely State of Malaya, formerly attached to Thailand (Siam), using Siamese stamps until 1909. Thereafter stamps of the Federated Malay States were used until 1912, then stamps of Kedah until 1943, when under the Japanese occupation it was for a short time returned to Thailand. In 1945 B.M.A. Malaya issues were introduced. The first stamps inscribed specifically for use in Perlis were a pair of Royal Silver Wedding commemoratives in December 1948; there was a U.P.U. set in 1949. The first definitives for Perlis finally appeared in 1951. Area: 310 sq. m.; capital: Kangar; pop. (1962): 105,526.

Permit. A postage prepayment system in use in the U.S.A., Canada, New Zealand, etc., whereby the licensee prints his registered 'permit' number on all postal packages, hands the mail over the post office counter in bulk, and makes immediate cash payment. Is distinct and different from the 'metered mail' (q.v.) system.

Perot. W. B. Perot, one-time postmaster of Hamilton, Bermuda, who in 1848 produced and issued unauthorised postage stamps, now great philatelic rarities. See 'Bermuda'.

Persanes. Persian. (Or Iranian.)

Persia. See 'Iran'.

Persian Gulf Agencies. Group of past and present British (formerly Indian) postal agencies on the shores of the Persian Gulf and Gulf of Oman. The term applies particularly to the Indian and British stamps used (often with special overprint) in these places, including Bahrain, Kuwait, Muscat, Qatar, etc.

Personal Delivery Stamps. Stamps ensuring that only the actual addressee receives a postal package were issued in Czechoslovakia 1937, and Bohemia 1939.

Peru. South American republic. The first stamps were those of the Pacific Steam Navigation Co. (q.v.), introduced in December 1857, but the first regular definitives followed in March 1858. Area: 496,093 sq. m.; capital: Lima; currency: 1857, 8 reales = 1 peso; 1858, 100 centavos = 10 dineros = 5 pesetas = 1 peso; 1874, 100 centavos = 1 sol; pop. (est. 1961): 10,500,000. See also under 'Arequipa' and 'Chilean Occupation of Peru'.

Pesa. East African monetary unit. 64 pesas = 1 rupee. Found surcharged on German issues for German East Africa 1893–1905.

Peseta. Spanish monetary unit since 1872. 100 centimos = 1 peseta.

Peso. South American monetary unit. 100 centavos = 1 peso.

PERSANES   PHILIPPINES   PLAGIARISM

Petersburg. Virginia. One of the Confederate 'Postmasters' ' towns of the American Civil War.

Pfennig. German monetary unit. 100 pfennig = 1 mark.

Phantasy. A bogus stamp, *timbre de fantasie*.

Phantom philately. The study and collection of bogus stamps (q.v.); so called after a famous book on the subject by Fred J. Melville.

Philadelphia. Pennsylvania, U.S.A., issued a series of 'Carriers' ' stamps in 1849, all in 1 ¢. values and inscribed 'U.S.P.O.' (United States Post Office).

Phila. Despatch Post. Inscribed on the U.S.A. 'locals' issued by D. O. Blood & Co., in Philadelphia, 1841-3.

'Philarule'. Gauge designed for measurement of postmarks, overprints, etc.

'Philatector'. A watermark detector utilising electrically lit colour filters.

Philatelic. Phila-*tel*-ic. Adjective of philately (phil-*at*-ely). Appertaining to the study of adhesive postage stamps.

Philatelic Agencies. See under 'Agencies'.

Philatelic Congress of Great Britain. Was instituted in 1909 at Manchester as an affiliation of philatelic societies. It normally holds an annual congress with a change of venue each year.

'Philatelic Journal of Great Britain'. The oldest continuously-published British stamp periodical. It has an advanced outlook and serious style and is now published quarterly by Robson Lowe Ltd., 50 Pall Mall, London, W.1.

'Philatelic Magazine'. A popular fortnightly periodical. Published by Harris Publications Ltd., 27 Maiden Lane, Strand, London, W.C.2, England. They publish also the *Philatelic Trader*, and *The Stamp Collector's Annual*.

Philatelic Traders' Society. Established 1930 to encourage, promote, protect, and advance the interests of all persons trading in postage or other stamps, in co-operation with bodies in other countries having similar objects. Offices: 27 John Adam Street, London, W.C.2. It is a company limited by guarantee with a large membership of dealers (whether whole or part time), auctioneers, publishers, and insurance brokers. Its organ is the *P.T.S. Journal*.

Philately. Phil-*at*-ely. (Gr. *Philo*—lover, or fond of; *ateleia*—free of payment—or tax.) The intelligent study of postage stamps and their production. Name coined by M. G. Herpin, a French collector. A philatelist is a student of philately. The Greeks name it 'phil*o*tely'—the more correct rendering.

'Philately'. The official organ of the British Philatelic Association (q.v.), and published alternate months from 446 Strand, London, W.C.2, England.

Philippines. The Philippine Islands, in the Malay Archipelago, formerly Spanish, but ceded to the U.S.A. in 1899. Its first issues were the Queen Isabella II imperfs. of Spain issued February 1854, inscribed 'Correos Y 55'. First American issues were contemporary stamps of U.S.A. o/p diagonally. First Japanese occupation stamps were an o/p on current issues 4 March 1942, with a definitive set 1943; last Japanese set was released 12 January 1945, and on 3 February 1945, American forces liberated the islands. On 4 July 1946, an issue to commemorate the complete independence of the new republic made its appearance. Total area of the group of over 7,000 islands and islets is 114,830 sq. m.; pop. (1960): 27,087,685; capital: Manila, on Luzon; the native language is Tagalog; currency since 1906: 100 centavos = 1 peso. (There have been nine changes of currency since 1854.)

Philometrist. (U.S.A.). Collector of metered mail (q.v.) markings.

Phono-Postal Stamps. (Span. Correos Fonopostal). See 'Recorded Message Stamps'.

Phosphor-Graphite. Stamps of Great Britain issued in 1959 with graphite lines on the back and phosphor lines on the front.

Phosphor Line. Since 1959 certain stamps of Great Britain have been issued with phosphor lines on the front for use in connection with electronic letter-facing machines, superseding the earlier Graphite Line issue (q.v.). These machines react to the phosphor on the stamps and 'face' the letters: i.e. turn them the right way up and the right way round in readiness for cancellation. The stamp covering the current printed paper rate has only one phosphor line whereas the other values have two. This enables the machine to separate printed papers from the rest of the mail. Since 1962 British commemoratives have appeared in both phosphor-lined and non-phosphor versions. Phosphor-lined stamps are sold only in those districts where letter-facing machines are installed. On mint stamps the lines can be easily seen by holding horizontally to a strong light.

Canada issued its first phosphor-lined stamps in 1962 in readiness for the installation of a British-made letter-facing machine at Winnipeg. Similar machines are in use in West Germany, Denmark, and the Netherlands, but in these cases stamps have been printed on phosphorescent paper, instead of overprinted with phosphor lines. In 1963 the United States started to treat certain stamps with phosphor for a similar purpose. In Canada and the United States phosphor-treated stamps are described as 'tagged'.

Photo-Engraving. Is the photo-mechanical process of producing line and half-tone blocks, used for what the philatelist calls the 'surface' or 'typographic' methods of print production (neither of which definitions are exact or descriptive of the means employed). Briefly, the process consists of photographing the artist's drawing, printing down on to sensitised zinc or copper, etching in acids leaving the printing surface in relief, and finally mounting the block type-high. This master block can be re-duplicated the requisite number of times to produce the set required to print a whole sheet of stamps. See 'Printing', 'Stereos', 'Electros', 'Surface printing', 'Typography', etc.

Photogravure. This modern stamp-printing process consists of photographing the artist's finished drawing on to process film and printing down on to sensitised carbon tissue which is transferred to a copper plate (or cylinder for rotogravure), and etched. It is distinct from photo-mechanical engraving (see above) in that the final image is in intaglio, or recess. Ink is forced into the design hollows, the surface wiped clean (see under 'Doctor Blade Flaws'), and picked up by the paper being pressed into contact with the recessed design, in very similar manner to the early line-engraved (q.v.) processes. High-speed rotary presses are now usually employed, and the process is known as 'Rotogravure'. See 'Printing', etc.

Photo-Litho or Photo-lithography. A true 'surface' or planographic printing process, a method intermediate to the two preceding processes. Again the original drawing is photographed and printed down on to sensitised zinc or aluminium plates or foil, and, by the 'step and repeat' camera or printing frame, printed down as many times as are required to print a sheet of stamps. The images are developed up, hardened, and inked up, the resultant design having now an affinity for the greasy ink used. The grained surface of the plate is kept damp and thus the clear parts repel ink. It is a process especially suited for multi-coloured printing. See also 'Lithography', 'Printing', and allied subjects.

Philmark. (U.S.A.). A coded system of designating centering of the design within a stamp's perforations—'a' being perfect, and 'd' where perfs. cut into it, (1) vertically, and (2) horizontally.

Piacenza. Town and province of Northern Italy. In 1944 the local 'partisans' are said to have o/p general issues of Italy. Four wordings are reported: 'C.L.N. Piacenza', 'Comitato Liberazione Nazionale Piacenza', '13 Zone Partigiana Piacenza', and a charity issue 'Pro Patrioti Piacenza'; apparently purely local.

Piaster. (Ger.). Piastre.

Piastre. Turkish monetary unit. 40 paras = 1 piastre. Also used in Egypt (q.v.) and Cyprus (to 1955).

Pichincha. Ecuadorean province with a control o/p 1902.

Pictorials. Stamps with a 'picture' design—for example landscapes, buildings, flowers, animals, etc.—as opposed to those of more traditional motif such as portrait or coat-of-arms.

Pies. Former Indian currency, 12 to one anna.

Piece. See 'On Piece'.

Pietersburg. Town of the Transvaal where, during the South African War, President Kruger authorised typeset locally-printed provisionals in March 1901. Used copies are pen-cancelled with the Controller's initials.

Pigeon Posts. The use of pigeons for carrying messages goes back to ancient times. Perhaps the most famous example in the philatelic era occurred during the Siege of Paris in 1870, when pigeons were flown out of the beleaguered city by balloon to Tours. There microfilmed messages were attached to the birds before they were released for their return flights to Paris. Messages thus carried are today rare and valuable collectors' items. Several cases are on record where local stamps have been issued for privately operated pigeon posts. The best-known of these is the New Zealand Great Barrier Island Pigeongram Service, which had its own locally typeset stamps. There were also stamps for Herm Island's pigeon post which operated during the summer of 1949, prior to the installation of a radio-telephone; afterwards the pigeon post stamps were used up on parcel post until the supply was exhausted.

Pillar Boxes. The first four hexagonal pillar boxes for the collection of mail were erected in Great Britain on 23 October 1852 in Jersey; and three in Guernsey, as an experiment devised by Anthony Trollope the novelist, then a G.P.O. surveyor in the S.W. district of which the Channel Islands formed a part. They had, however, been in use in France several years previously. There are now about 900,000 boxes of all types in use in the British Isles.

Pillars, or **Pillar Blocks.** Type-set or engraved 'filling' on wide stamp margins to prevent the use of blanks by counterfeiters.

Pinkney's Express Post. A New York, U.S.A., local mail service of 1851.

Pin-perforated (Fr. Percé en points). Form of perforation (perhaps more strictly described as rouletting) in which the paper is pierced by a series of pin-points but no paper is removed. The best-known examples are the 1859 issue of Trinidad and the 1860 issue of Barbados, both of which were pin-perf. by Perkins, Bacon & Co. before that firm acquired their first efficient perforating machine.

Pinsin. (Erse). Penny, or pence. On stamps of the Republic of Ireland (Eire).

Pisco. Peru. It had a control o/p in April 1884.

Piscopi. See under 'Dodecanese Islands'.

Pitcairn Island. In the eastern Pacific, peopled by the descendants of the mutineers of the *Bounty*, incidents from which are pictured on the first definitive stamps of 1940. It is situated on the Tropic of Capricorn in longitude 130° 8′ W., is the most southerly of the islands of the Low Archipelago, and was annexed by Britain in 1839. Administration transferred to Governor of Fiji as from the summer of 1952. Area: 2 sq. m.; pop. (1962): 128.

Pittsylvania. Virginia. One of the Confederate 'Postmasters' ' towns of the American Civil War.

Piura. Department of Peru with a control o/p April 1884.

Plagiarism. Literary and artistic theft. Corrientes, Argentina, made a flagrant copy of the 1849 'Cres' design of France when they issued their first stamp in 1856; Uruguay appropriated the essentials of the 1890 Newfoundland 3 ¢ for their 1898 'Liberty' stamp; while the Griazovetz (Vologda) locals of Russia of 1899 were amusing copies of most of the outstanding stamp designs of the day. There have been many 'near' thefts, but not many quite so flagrant.

Plata. (Span.). Silver. O/p on stamps of Peru 1880–1 to indicate that these issues could only be purchased with silver coin, as the paper money was so depreciated as to be almost worthless.

Plate. (Fr. Cliché). The base from which stamps are printed.

Plate Numbers. In the early British and British colonial stamps these were indicated on the sheet margins, and showed the serial order of plate manufacture. In the 1858–80 Penny Reds of G.B. and in certain other issues they are also shown in addition in minute figures on individual stamps.

Plate Number Block. Four or more stamps to which are attached the marginal paper bearing the printing plate or cylinder number. Also known as a Plate Block.

Plate Varieties. See 'Varieties'.

Plating. Term used to describe the collecting of stamps according to their position on the sheet; in many issues, particularly the older ones, this can be determined by close study of the design. In the case of early British stamps with differing check-letters in the corners it is, of course, a much easier process. When stamps representing a complete sheet have thus been assembled, it is said to be a 'reconstructed sheet'.

Plauen. Town of Saxony which had a set of local stamps in 1945.

Pleasant Shade. Virginia. Contributed a typeset issue to the Confederate 'Postmasters' ' during the American Civil War.

Plebiscite Issues. After the First World War plebiscites were held in certain localities of Europe to allow the people to decide under which country or government they wished to live. In certain cases, for example Schleswig, Carinthia, and Allenstein, special stamps were issued for use during the plebiscite period.

Pleskau. (Ger.) Pskov. Russian district and town S.S.W. of Leningrad. German occupying troops issued o/p and special stamps in 1941–2.

Pmk. Recognised abbreviation for postmark.

Pneumatic Post. A form of air-tubed letter distribution in use in some large towns of France and Italy—the latter country issues special stamps (Posta Pneumatica) for the service.

PLEBISCITE   PNEUMATIC POST   'POACHED EGG'

'Poached Egg' Labels.   Popular name given to the 'dummy' stamps used by British post office engineers to test the mechanisms of stamp-vending machines. Coils of these dummy stamps were prepared, perforated, and printed with a graduated solid green oval (from which the sobriquet derives), so that mechanically they compared in every way with actual stamps. Specimens came into the possession of the public, and there are even authenticated instances of postal use without detection or surcharge.

Pochette.   Literally, 'little pocket'; small wrapper of plastic material, transparent at the front with dark-coloured backing, designed to hold and effectively protect and display a single stamp. The pochette can then itself be mounted on to the album leaf. Pochettes are available in a wide range of sizes, for covers as well as stamps. They are an expensive means of mounting a collection, but have the advantage of displaying mint stamps without the necessity of mounting the actual stamps and so risking a disturbance of the original gum.

Poczta Polska.   Polish Post. See 'Poland'.

Pohjois Inkeri.   Ingermanland (q.v.).

Poland.   One-time kingdom of Central Europe, partitioned between Austria, Prussia, and Russia in the eighteenth century. The eastern part became nominally a kingdom in personal union with Russia, and for this region the first stamps were issued in January 1860. They were a special version of the Arms type then current in Russia. Following an unsuccessful rebellion against Russian rule, the last vestiges of Polish independence disappeared and the stamps were withdrawn in 1865. After the First World War Poland reappeared as an independent republic; provisional stamps (overprinted on German and Austrian issues and on unissued local stamps of Warsaw) appeared in 1918, to be succeeded by the first definitives in the following year. During the German occupation of 1939–44 stamps of German type inscribed 'General Gouvernement' were in use. The Polish Government-in-exile in London produced its own issues 1941–6 for use by Polish forces and seamen serving with the Allies, but these stamps were never placed on sale in Poland itself. Area: 120,733 sq. m.; capital: Warsaw; currency: 1860, 100 kopecks = 1 rouble (Russian); 1915, 100 fenigi = 1 marka (in South Poland, 100 halerzy = 1 korona until 1920) 1924, 100 groszy = 1 zloty (revalued in 1950); pop. (1960): 29,731,000.

Polish Levant.   See 'Polish Post Offices Abroad' below.

236

POLAND   'POPE AND KING'   PORTEADO

Polish Post Offices Abroad. Polish stamps overprinted 'Levant' were used in 1919 to frank mail handed in to the Polish Consulate at Constantinople. Polish stamps were also overprinted 'Port Gdansk' for use by the Polish post in Danzig from 1925 to 1937, followed by a set for the twentieth anniversary of Polish independence in 1938.

Polska. Poland, or Polish. See 'Poland' above.

Polynesia, Polynésie Française. See 'French Polynesia' and 'Oceanic Settlements'.

Pomeroy's Letter Express. Private mail service of New York State, U.S.A., established in 1844, which had its own local stamps.

Ponta Delgada. Portuguese territory comprising the islands of São Miguel and Santa Maria in the Azores. Ponta Delgada had its own stamps in Portuguese keytypes from 1892 to 1905, when they were replaced by those of the Azores. Stamps of Portugal have been used since 1931. Area: 340 sq. m.; capital: Ponta Delgada on São Miguel; pop.: 130,000.

Pony Express. A famous American mail service operated by pony riders over 2,000 miles of hazardous country between St. Joseph, Missouri, and Sacramento, California. The service started in April 1860, when William H. Russell, one of the proprietors, won a $200,000 wager by proving that the mail could be carried over this route in ten days. In 1861 stamps inscribed 'Pony Express' were issued by Wells, Fargo and Co., who were the San Francisco agents for the Pony Express. Genuine used examples are now rare, and the stamps have been extensively forged. Despite its great achievements in speeding up the California mails—which previously had been taken by sea via Panama—the Pony Express was not a financial success and after eighteen months it was discontinued on the completion of the transcontinental telegraph. In that time about 35,000 letters were carried. A second Pony Express was operated by Wells, Fargo and Co. in 1862–4 between San Francisco and Virginia City, Nevada, at the time of the great Comstock Lode operations, and stamps similar to the earlier issue were used. This became known as the 'Little Pony' in contrast to the 'Big Pony' original service.

Poonch. Former Indian native state which issued its own primitive internal stamps (all printed in water-colours!) from 1876 to 1894, after which Indian stamps were used. Area: 1,627 sq. m.; pop. (1941): 290,000.

237

'Pope and King'. Two Spanish sets issued 23 December 1928, to raise funds for catacomb excavation, bore the head of the Pope (by special dispensation) and the portrait of King Alfonso XIII. One set was issued at Santiago, the other at Toledo, each set differing from the other in colour combinations. Typical speculative issues for which Spain won an unenviable reputation.

Popper, Julius. See under 'Tierra del Fuego'.

Port Arthur and Dairen. By a Sino-Soviet Treaty arrangement of 1945, these Manchurian ports were placed under Chinese administration. The first stamps were Manchurian and Japanese issues overprinted in Chinese characters 'Liaoning Posts' in 1946. Further issues followed until superseded by Chinese stamps about 1950.

Port Cantonal. (Lit. Prepaid within the Canton). Local stamps of Geneva, Switzerland, issued 1843–50 bore this inscription. Valid only within the Canton (Genève) they are now rare. See 'Geneva'.

Port Fouad. O/p on Egyptian pictorials 1926 to commemorate the inauguration of the new port. A restricted speculative issue now commanding high prices.

Port Gdansk. The port of Danzig. O/p on stamps used by the Polish post office 1925–38.

Port Hood Provisionals. Q.V. 3 ¢. 1897–8 issues of Canada were 'split' and unofficially surcharged one and two cents during a temporary shortage of these values by the Assistant Postmaster of Port Hood. Acceptable only on genuinely cancelled cover or piece.

Port Lagos. See under 'French Levant'.

'Portmanteaux' issues. Alternative name occasionally applied to Omnibus issues (q.v.).

Port Said. Mediterranean seaport of Egypt for which stamps of France were o/p for use in French post offices 1899–1937. Gibbons says: 'Stamps (G.B.) issued after 1877 can be found with cancellation "Port Said", but these are on letters posted on British ships'. See also 'Suez Canal Company', and 'Levant'.

Porteado (Port.). Extra postage to receive. Postage due.

Porte de Conducción. Inscribed on Peruvian parcels post stamps of 1898.

Porte de Mar. (Span.). Carried by sea, or seaborne (mails). Mexico prepared stamps 1875–9 for use on seaborne European mail, to collect the added charges then required, but owing to her becoming a signatory to the U.P.U. pact few were used or issued.

Porte Franco. (Port.). Carried free. Postage prepaid. On early stamps of Peru.

Porto. Inscribed on postage due stamps of Austria 1894–1921.

Porto Rico. See 'Puerto Rico'.

Portugal. Country of south-west Europe; a kingdom until 1910, thereafter a republic. Stamps first issued, 1853. Area: 35,598 sq. m.; capital: Lisbon; currency: 1853, 10 reis = 1 centimo, 1,000 reis = 1 milreis; 1912, 100 centavos = 1 escudo; pop. (1960): 8,889,392.

Portuguese Africa. In 1898, on the fourth centenary of Vasco da Gama's discovery of the Cape route to India, a series of stamps similar to the corresponding issue of Portugal but inscribed simply 'Africa—Correios' was issued for use throughout all the Portuguese territories in Africa. Other stamps used throughout Portuguese Africa were a War Tax overprint on a fiscal stamp in 1918, and a set of Postage Dues in 1945. Apart from these the various territories have always had their own stamps.

Portuguese Congo. On the west coast of Africa, immediately north and south of the Congo River, and now a province of Angola. Portuguese keytypes were in use 1893–1920. Stamps of Angola (q.v.) replaced them. Capital: Cabinda; Portuguese currency.

Portuguese East Africa. See 'Moçambique' and 'Nyassa'.

Portuguese Guinea (Guine). Portuguese territory on west coast of Africa. The first stamps were overprints on Cape Verde in 1881; the first of a succession of definitive issues in Portuguese Colonial keytypes followed in 1886. Area: 13,948 sq. m.; capital: Bissau; currency: as Portugal; pop. (1960): 544,184.

Portuguese India. Former Portuguese settlements on the west coast of India, comprising Goa, Damao, and Diu. Stamps first issued, 1871. In 1962 Indian forces occupied the settlements which were incorporated into India. Since then Indian stamps have been in use. Area: 1,620 sq. m.; capital: Goa; currency: 1871, 1,000 reis = 1 milreis; 1881, 12 reis = 1 tanga, 16 tangas = 1 rupee; 1959, 100 centavos = 1 escudo; pop. (1958): 648,000.

Portuguese West Africa. See 'Angola'.

Post. (Lat. Posta, meaning originally a place where relays of messengers and horses were kept). In its relation to philately derives from the stagecoach which carried the early mails—'post haste', and infers travelling with speed.

Post Boxes. See 'Pillar Boxes'.

'Post Office', Mauritius. Name given to the first issue of Mauritius—also the first official issue of any British colony—which appeared on 21 September 1847. They are so called from the words 'Post Office' at the left-hand side of the stamp, as distinct from the 'Post Paid' of later issues. There were two values, 1d. and 2d., in a Queen's head design engraved by J. Barnard, a local watchmaker. Only 500 of each value were printed, most of which were used by Lady Gomm, wife of the island's governor, on invitations to a ball at Government House. Surviving examples are now among the world's greatest rarities.

Posta Ajrore (or **Aerore**). Inscribed on Albanian air stamps.

Postage Dues. Or 'Unpaid letter' stamps, are labels affixed to under-stamped postal packets at the office of delivery. It is the obligation of the postman to collect the amount indicated. The office of collection normally assesses the charge (in G.B.), weighs the packet, and indicates by hand-stamp the amount to be collected (double the deficiency). Most countries use this or a similar system, but where stamps are not used, the wrapper is often marked with the letter 'T' (Fr. Taxe), the internationally accepted symbol, or normal issues so o/p or hand-stamped affixed. Some authorities use parcel post dues also, as instance the 1912 set of five values of the U.S.A. The following are a few of the many foreign inscriptions to assist recognition of these important stamps:

À payer	French (Belgium, etc.).
À percevoir . . .	French (Belgium, Egypt, France).
Bajar Porto . . .	Indonesian Republic.
Déficit	Spanish (Peru, etc.).
Doplata	Polish and Cyrillic.
Doplatit or Doplatné .	Czech.
Efterporto . . .	Danish (West Indies).
Franqueo deficiente .	Spanish.
Land-post/porto-marke .	German (Baden).
Lösen	Swedish (Sweden).
Multa	Portuguese.
Multada	Spanish (Chile, etc.).
Porteado . . .	Portuguese.
Porto	Danish, Magyar (Hungary) etc.
Portomarke . . .	German.
Portzegel . . .	Dutch (Netherlands).
Postas le ńioc . . .	Irish (Erse). See illustration above.
Recouvrement . . .	French (Monaco).
Segnatasse . . .	Italian.
Sobreporte . . .	Spanish.
Sobretassa . . .	Spanish.
T = Taxe . . .	French (U.P.U. acceptance).
Takca	Bulgarian.
Taksë	Albanian.
Tasa por cobrar . .	Spanish.
Taxa de plata . . .	Latin (Roumania).
Taxa devida . . .	Portuguese (Brasil).
Te betaal . . .	Afrikaans.
Te betalen . . .	Dutch and Flemish.
Vom Empfänger Einzuziehen	German (Danzig.).

Postal-Fiscal. Fiscal or revenue stamp used postally.

Postal Centenary Issues. To celebrate the 100th anniversary of the intro-duction of the penny post, or of adhesive postage stamps, many countries issued special commemoratives, some of which pictured early issues, including G.B.'s Penny Black, and others portrayed Sir Rowland Hill.

POSTAL-FISCAL   POSTAL CENTENARY   POSTAS LE ŃIOC

Postal Charges. Overprint or inscription on stamps of Papua and New Guinea: equivalent to 'Postage Due'.

Postal Commission. O/p with 3 ¢. surcharge on stamps of Ceylon 1872–80 series, was for payment of fines on overdue postal orders, but were, for a short while, permitted to prepay postage.

Postal Surcharge. O/p on various early issues of Cyprus indicated internal accounting usage within the postal service. Stamps so o/p have therefore not prepaid postage, but are, nevertheless, eagerly sought by collectors, as they can be classified as 'dues', which strictly speaking they were.

Postal Union. See 'Universal Postal Union'.

Postal Union Colours. See 'Colours, Postal Union'.

Postally used implies that a stamp bears irrefutable evidence of having been genuinely and legitimately used to prepay postage, as opposed to being cancelled to order, used for revenue or fiscal purposes; or that (though not catalogued or officially issued) copies exist thus.

Poste Estensi. Modena (q.v.).

Postes Egyptiennes. Egyptian Posts or Postal Services.

Poste Khedevie Egiziane. The Khedive's Egyptian Post. Inscribed on 1872–9 stamps of Egypt.

Postal History. An extension of the hobby of philately, including the study not only of stamps but of postal markings and covers, postage rates and postal routes, in fact of anything pertaining to the history and development of the postal services.

Postal Stationery. Various types of stationery including envelopes, letter-sheets, letter-cards, postcards, and wrappers, usually but not necessarily of the kind sold by post offices, and officially imprinted with a non-adhesive stamp. Postal stationery was much more widely collected in the latter part of the nineteenth century than in recent years, but there are now signs of a revival of interest. Airletter sheets are a modern form of postal stationery which has a considerable following.

Poste Locale. French inscription on a Turkish local stamp of 1865 intended for use in Constantinople and its suburbs (Istanbul). Found both perf. 14 or 16, and imperforate; also hand-stamped for use as newspaper stamps. Have been frequently reprinted. Philatelic status dubious.

Postfaerge. (Danish). Ferry post (between Esbjerg in Jutland and the island of Fanö).

Postgebiet Ob. Ost. (Ger.). Postal area of the Eastern Command (Estonia, Latvia, Lithuania). Gothic type o/p on contemporary stamps of Germany 1916–18.

Postmark. Any form of marking, with a postal meaning, applied to any kind of postal matter by a competent authority. In practice, the term is most often applied to the impression which gives the date of posting and the office of origin. Postmarks designed to cancel stamps so that they cannot be used again for postage are usually referred to as cancellations.

Postmasters' Stamps. Also known as Postmasters' Provisionals, these are stamps produced and issued locally by the postmaster of a particular town, with or without official sanction from Post Office headquarters. A number of well-known Postmasters' stamps were issued in the United States from 1845 until the appearance of the first general issue in 1847. A similar state of affairs existed in the Confederate States in the early stages of the American Civil War, and Postmasters' stamps were used as a temporary measure until a regular issue could be prepared. The famous Perot issue of Bermuda also ranks as Postmasters' stamps.

Post Office Seals. The adhesive labels used to re-seal damaged or opened postal packages, or (in U.S.A.) to secure registered letters from being tampered with. Many consider them to be collectable items.

Postzegel. (Ned. and Afrik.). Postage stamp.

Pos Udara. (Indonesian). Airpost.

Poznan. (Posen). Stamps of Germany were o/p 'Poczta Polska' in 1919 when this former German province was occupied by the Poles, to whom it was allocated by the Treaty of Versailles.

Prayer on Stamps. The outstanding example is the Latin prayer on the backs of the 1895 St. Anthony of Padua stamps of Portugal (q.v.).

Pre-adhesive. Any item dating from prior to the introduction of adhesive postage stamps in the country concerned (not necessarily prior to 1840).

Precancels. Are machine-printed cancellations applied by authority to save time in handling large blocks of mail, as stamps so treated normally do not require or receive further cancellation. In the U.S.A. large mailing organisations use them as a matter of routine, such mail being handed over to the post office in bulk. If a U.S.A. precancel is applied by a town or city office it is known as a local; if by Washington as a 'bureau' cancellation. It is possible to collect a named stamp from every important town and city in that country, and there has grown up a specialised type of collection devoted to precancels, with its own catalogues and literature. Precancels have been used by Algeria, Austria, Belgium, Canada, France, Hungary, Luxembourg, Monaco, Netherlands (1912–29 in the form of a roll-cancel with the town name in small double circles connected by short rules or lines), Panamá Canal Zone, and Tunis; but Hungary and Luxembourg have ceased the practice. 'Dateds', or dated-initialled copies, conform to a July 1938 postal ruling applicable to certain authorised large users of precancels. Where these details are printed (instead of being hand-stamped) with the precancelling, they are known as 'Integrals'. They form interesting sideline collections. The numeral type of precancel has been in use in Canada since 1931. The numerals of the cities correspond with the accounting number assigned to the individual Post and Money Order office.

Numeral	City	Numeral	City
X 275	Halifax, N.S.	3893	Oshawa, Ont.
X 030	Charlottetown, P.E.I.	3900	Ottawa, Ont.
X 809	Moncton, N.B.	3975	Owen Sound, Ont.
X 910	St. John, N.B.	4004	Paris, Ont.
X 945	Sackville, N.B.	4035	Peterborough, Ont.
0592	Lennoxville, P.Q.	4260	St. Thomas, Ont.
0700	Montreal, P.Q.	4530	Toronto, Ont.
1050	Quebec, P.Q.	4900	Weston, Ont.
1142	Rock Island, P.Q.	4940	Windsor, Ont.
1470	St. Hyacinthe, P.Q.	4970	Woodstock, Ont.
1810	Sherbrooke, P.Q.	5099	Brandon, Man.
2186	Beamsville, Ont.	5850	Winnipeg, Man.
2310	Brantford, Ont.	7120	Moose Jaw, Sask.
2342	Brockville, Ont.	7420	Regina, Sask.
2450	Carleton Place, Ont.	7550	Saskatoon, Sask.
2575	Coburg, Ont.	7977	Yorkton, Sask.
2980	Galt, Ont.	8160	Calgary, Alta.
3080	Guelph, Ont.	8360	Edmonton, Alta.
3100	Hamilton, Ont.	8605	Lethbridge, Alta.
3340	Kingston, Ont.	8802	Red Deer, Alta.
3366	Kitchener, Ont.	9500	New Westminster, B.C.
3445	Lindsay, Ont.	9780	Vancouver, B.C.
3470	London, Ont.	9890	Victoria, B.C.
3800	Niagara Falls, Ont.		

Key to abbreviations:—

Alta. Alberta; B.C. British Columbia; Man. Manitoba; N.B. New Brunswick; Ont. Ontario; P.E.I. Prince Edward Island; P.Q. Province Quebec; Sask. Saskatchewan. See: 'F.E.C.T.P.'.

Premières Gravures. (Fr.). First engravings. Term applied to the U.S.A. issues of 17 August 1861, engraved and printed by the National Bank Note Company of New York. In September of the same year the stamps were re-issued from plates to which certain slight and subtle alterations had been made, and in slightly varying colours. As the life of the primary set was short, and it is doubtful if some of them were actually postally used, they are among the rarities. With the possible exception of the 10 ¢, recent opinion is that these specimens were printers' samples or essays, and Gibbons (in particular) now omits them from the catalogue.

PRECANCELS   'PREFIXES'   PRINCIPAUTÉ   PRIVATE POSTAGE
                          DE MONACO   STAMP

Pre-stamp Covers. Envelopes, wrappers, and letter-sheets bearing evidence of postal use before the introduction of adhesive postage stamps or of pre-stamped staionery. Their collection is primarily a branch of postal history.

Preussen. (Ger.). Prussia (q.v.).

'Prexies'. American nickname for the 1938–9 U.S.A. Presidential series.

Price's City Express Post. Operated in New York, U.S.A., in 1857–8, and —

Price's 8th Ave. Post Office was another local mail service of 1854. Both issued 'local' stamps.

Priest's Despatch. Was a Philadelphia local post originated by Solomon Priest in 1851.

'Primitives'. The so-called primitives were the early successors to G.B.'s Penny Black: 1847–59 Mauritius, 1850–1 New South Wales, 1850–2 Victoria, 1853 Tasmania, and 1854 India.

Prince's Letter Dispatch. A night steamer mail service run by J. H. Prince from Portland, Maine, to Boston, Mass., U.S.A., in 1861.

Prince Edward Island. Off the east coast of the Commonwealth of Canada. It had its own issues January 1861–July 1873. A bogus 10 ¢ stamp, attributed to Samuel Allan Taylor (q.v.), was produced and foisted off as genuine to an unsuspecting dealer in 1872—there was no official stamp of that value. Remainders of the official stamps were sold when they became obsolete, and the final (1872) set is still available at low prices. Area: 2,184 sq. m.; pop. (1956): 99,285; capital: Charlottetown; currency: 1861, British; 1872, Canadian decimal. (Not to be confused with the island of the same name in the Antarctic. See 'Marion and Prince Edward Island'.)

Principauté de Monaco. Principality of Monaco. See under 'Monaco'.

Printers' Waste. Term used to describe badly printed or otherwise faulty stamps which are or ought to be destroyed by the printers—as distinct from genuinely unnoticed errors or varieties sold over the post office counter.

Printing. The four printing methods most commonly used for the production of postage stamps are: Line-engraving (widely referred to as recess-printing); Typography (letterpress); Photogravure; and Lithography (nowadays more usually offset-litho). Since some issues have been printed by more than one process, it is useful for the collector to learn to distinguish them. In a line-engraved stamp the ink 'stands up' on the paper; the merest touch with the fingertips is usually enough to detect it. A photogravure stamp is also easy to distinguish; apart from the general impression it gives of a reproduction of a photograph, the fine screen of dots of which the design is composed can be clearly seen with the aid of a magnifier. A typographed stamp and a lithographed are less easy to tell apart, but in general the ink of a lithographed stamp lies extremely flat on the surface and lacks the 'bite' of typography. The latter is often evidenced by the impression of parts of the design, the lettering in particular, showing through on the back of the stamp.

Printing Varieties. See 'Varieties'.

Private Postage Stamps. There are a number of early German locals inscribed 'Privat'. These had a restricted validity. The 1867–77 Swiss hotel stamps were private emissions; as are the Lundy 'Puffins' of G.B. Spain authorised two unusual private stamps: the first in 1869 was a right granted to Señor Diego Castell Fernandez, to frank his pamphlet 'Cartilla Postal de España' (Postcards of Spain), which was thus sent free to 25,000 Spanish primary schools. The other was for Señor A. F. Duro for the franking of a similar work in 1881. A private stamp for Portugal's civilian rifle clubs is illustrated on a previous page. See also under 'Locals'.

'Private Post Office'. The inscription on U.S.A. 'locals' issued 1864 in San Francisco used to frank a city mail service.

Pro Desocupados. (Span.). For the unemployed. O/p on stamps of Peru 1931–6.

Pro Juventute. (Lat.). For Youth. Inscribed on the charity stamps of Switzerland.

Proof Paper. A white, or yellowish, soft rice paper with a laid screen watermark, and from 0.003 to 0.005 in thickness, used to take progress and final impressions from engravings and dies. See also 'India paper'.

Proofs. Trial impressions, or 'progress' prints, classified as follows:
    (a) Engraver's progress and final prints.
    (b) Die proofs taken from an engraved die just completed, before duplicating it on to a plate or stone.
    (c) Plate impressions taken before the actual printing is proceeded with.
    (d) Colour proofs in the officially-approved ink before the 'run' is commenced.

Their collection is an expert and specialised branch of philately, and in America there is an Essay-Proof Society devoted to the study, and which publishes a quarterly journal. See also 'Colour trials', 'Essays', etc.

Providence. Rhode Island, U.S.A. Had two stamps in the 'Postmasters'' series issued in 1846, in advance of the U.S.P.O. general issues. Also a 'local' inscribed 'Providence Despatch' issued in 1849.

Provincie Modonesi. Provisional government stamps of Modena (q.v.).

Provinz Laibach. Laibach province (Ljubljana), Yugoslavia (q.v.).

Provisionals. Stamps with a temporary life and purpose. An issue pending a new or revised definitive or general issue.

Provisorio. (Span.). Provisional.

Prussia. Former kingdom of central and eastern Germany, issuing its own stamps 1850–67. Its king became Emperor of the new Germany 1871. Prussia used the stamps of the North German Confederation in the interim (1868–71). Area: 113,883 sq. m.; capital: Berlin; currency: 1850, 12 pfennige = 1 silbergroschen; 1867, 60 kreuzer = 1 gulden.

'Pubs'. (Fr.: Timbres de Publicité). Applied to both Belgian and French stamps from booklets in which advertising labels are *se tenant*. In France also referred to as 'Timbres avec bandelette-publicité'. They are an interesting sideline study, and are listed in Belgium by Prinet, and specially catalogued in Paris.

Puerto Principe. Now Camaguëy. City of Cuba and capital of the province of that name. Stamps of Cuba were surcharged with new values during the U.S. occupation 1899, during the Spanish-American War.

Puerto Rico (Porto Rico). Island of the West Indies, a Spanish colony until 1898 when it was ceded to the United States. Puerto Rico used the same stamps as Cuba until 1873, when the first stamps for Puerto Rico alone were issued to prevent currency manipulation. Early issues consisted of Cuban stamps overprinted with a paraph (script monogram), and were followed by Spanish Colonial keytypes from 1877. Following the Spanish-American War, certain United States stamps were overprinted for use in Puerto Rico in 1898–1900, since when American stamps have been in use without overprint. Area: 3,434 sq. m.; capital: San Juan; currency: 1873, 100 centimos = 1 peseta; 1881, 1,000 milesimas = 100 centavos = 1 peso; 1898, 100 cents = 1 U.S. dollar; pop. (1960): 2,349,000. British stamps were used at the former British post offices in Puerto Rico; the 'C 61' cancellation was in use there 1865–77, also 'F 83' at Arroyo (1872–7), 'F 34' at Aguadilla (1873–7), 'F 85' at Mayaguez (1873–7), 'F 88' at Ponce (1873–7), and '582' at Naguabo (1875–7).

'Puffins'. See 'Lundy'.

Punch-Perforated Stamps, or Spifs: Stamps Punched with the Initials of Firms, etc. Are specimens into the face of which perforating of initials or a

private device has been done with a series of punches arranged into the required pattern. This practice had official approval in G.B. in 1869, and was primarily designed to prevent petty pilferage, and illegitimate use of the firm's stamps by its employees, and as a precaution against theft. An ingenious machine to perform the operation was invented by Joseph Sloper, founder of J. Sloper & Co., Ltd., which has been extensively used by large mailing organisations. From a philatelic point of view, stamps so perforated lose about 50 per cent of their catalogue value, but there are collectors, on the other hand, who make their collection and the tracing of their origins a fascinating speciality. See 'O.S.'. Known to U.S.A. collectors as 'Branded' stamps or 'Perfins'.

Punctuated Stamps. Stamps of Spain (used for the prepayment of telegrams), 'Officials' of Australasia, Sudan, etc., are found punch-cancelled, or punctured with small round or oval holes. Many early G.B. stamps were pinholed through their having been pinned to envelopes owing to inferior gumming, and many of the early specimens were mutilated by being strung on cotton—an early form of 'collecting'! See also 'Punch-perforated stamps' above.

Puno. Capital of the department of Puno in Peru. Supported the Arequipa government (q.v.) during the war with Chile and in the civil war which followed. Stamps o/p 1881–5 with the canceller normally used to obliterate the morning mail. (See note in Gibbons Part III.)

Puttialla. See 'Patiala'.

Cyrillic and Greek

P. both in Cyrillic and in Greek (The Rho) is the equivalent of the English 'R', thus:

РУБ	= Roub.—ruble or rouble, curtailed. (See below.)
РУБЛЯ	= Roublya or rublea, the plural of ruble.
Р.С.Ф.С.Р.	= Russian Socialist Federated Soviet Republic.
РОССІЯ	= Russia (phonetically: Roosiyah).

The Cyrillic and Greek 'P' is represented by the character Π in Cyrillic, and Π in Greek (The Pi).

ПОЧТОВАЯ	= Poschtavayah	= Postal.
ПОЧТА МАРКА	= Poschta marka	= Postage stamp.

QUADRILLÉ   QU'AITI   QUEENSLAND   QUETZAL

Q

'Q' for 'O' variety. This variety appears in the value tablet of G.B.'s S.G. No. 357*a*—'ONE' reads 'QNE'. It is the ninth stamp in the fifteenth row, on sheets of a particular printing, and is a much sought-after stamp.

Q.E. II. Queen Elizabeth the Second.

Q.V. Queen Victoria.

q.v. (Lat. Quod vide). Which see.

Qatar. Independent Arab sheikdom, a peninsula on the Persian Gulf, which had a British postal administration until 1963. Stamps surcharged for use in Muscat were used until 1957, when British stamps first appeared overprinted for Qatar and surcharged with values in Indian currency. The first distinctive designs for Qatar followed in 1961. Qatar took over its own postal services on 23 May 1963. Area: 4,000 sq. m.; capital: Doha; currency: as India; pop.: about 50,000.

Qint. Quind or Qindar. Unit of currency, Albania. 100 = 1 franc.

Quadrillé. Term used to describe album-leaf printed with a faint network of squares as a guide for the neat arrangement of stamps thereon.

Quadrillé Paper. Watermarked with cross lines forming rectangles. The 1892 15 ¢. issues of France bear a pseudo-watermark (quadrillé) of oil or transparent varnish.

Qu'aiti State of Shihr and Mukalla: See under 'Aden States'

'Quaker' Postmark. (U.S.A.). One in which the month is designated by a number and not by name. The Society of Friends—the Quakers—is opposed to the pagan naming of the months.

Quarnero (Carnaro) Islands. See under 'Fiume'.

Quartz Lamp. An electric lamp consisting of a filament or other light source encased in transparent fused quartz, emitting and passing the maximum of ultra-violet rays, which on striking certain substances cause fluorescence—each substance having its own degree of fluorescence. It is used for the expert examination of postage stamps to determine whether specimens under test have been tampered with, or are as genuine as alleged. Any added alien ink or paper will be inevitably revealed, and 'aniline' inks are readily detected and identified.

Quatrefoil Watermark. See 'Rosace Watermark'.

'Queen Enthroned'. See 'Victoria'.

Queensland. North-eastern state of the Commonwealth of Australia. From 26 January to 1 November 1860, the stamps of New South Wales were in temporary use, but on the latter date the new 'Chalon Head' stamps by Humphrys appeared, one of the classic definitives. Stamps of the Commonwealth have been used since 1913. Area: approx. 670,500 sq. m.; pop. (est. 1957): 1,383,535; capital: Brisbane; British currency.

Quelimane. River port of Moçambique, Portuguese East Africa (q.v.), formerly administered by the Zambezia Company, and capital of Zambezia (q.v.). Used Portuguese colonial o/p and surcharged keytypes 1914–22, when the stamps of Moçambique superseded. Pop. (1940): 4,451; Portuguese currency.

Quetzal. The beautiful and rare sacred bird of Guatemala which has been so often pictured on their stamps, and after which the 1919 new unit of currency was named.

Quinta de Goya. Centenary of (the death of) Goya, the painter. Inscribed on the peseta values of the 1930 issues.

Quito. Capital of Ecuador, reputed to be the highest in the world—9,350 feet above sea level. The Quito to Guayaquil Railway Company used a five-pointed star control o/p in 1902.

R
(See overleaf)

AN EARLY STAMP OF JIND,
AN INDIAN NATIVE STATE

R

R., RR., RRR. (Rare). Used in some stamp catalogues to indicate varying degrees of rarity.

R. Initial of (former) Rajah, Raghbir Singh, the only English in the inscription of the stamps of Jhind (or Jind), British India.

R. With surcharge, on the stamps of French colonies denotes 'Réunion'.

R. (Span. Registro). Registered.

R. O/p in black on modern issues of Northern Rhodesia indicates 'Revenue', and converts the postage stamp to a fiscal.

R. de C. (Span. Recargo de Construcción). O/p stamps of Nicaragua carrying a 'compulsory tax for the rebuilding of Managua General Post Office.

R.D.P. Roll of Distinguished Philatelists (q.v.).

R.F. République Française (French Republic).

R.F.D. (U.S.A.). Rural free delivery.

R.H. République d'Haïti.

R.H./Official. Royal Household/Official. O/p on ½d. and 1d. stamps of G.B. K.E. VII, 1902, for the use of the staff at the royal residences. In use for a few months only, and now rarities.

R.I.S. Republik Indonesia Serikat.

R.M.S. (U.S.A.). Railway Mail Service. Now replaced by P.T.S. (Postal Transport Service).

R.O. Roumelie Orientale. See 'Eastern Roumelia'.

R.P.O. (G.B. & U.S.A.). Railway Post Office.

R.P.R. Republica Populara Romina (or Romana): See under 'Roumania'.

R.P.S.L. Royal Philatelic Society, London.

R.R. Poste Coloniali Italiane. Royal Italian colonial posts.

R.S.M. Repubblica di San Marino.

R.T.R.P. Initials of Polish inscription meaning: Provisional Government, Polish Republic.

Rabaul. Capital of New Britain, Bismarck Archipelago. Air registration labels o/p 'G.R.I.' and used as postage stamps, British occupation of German New Guinea, 1914.

Railway Air Stamps. The Great Western Railway issued an air label in 1933, each serially numbered, value 3d. for use on G.B. internal airlines. As the issue was unauthorised it was withdrawn at the request of the G.P.O. A similar label was issued by Provincial Airlines for their Westcountry service—London, Southampton, Plymouth—which suffered the same fate. Gibbons does not list them but they find a place in some airmail catalogues.

Railway Cancellations. Are in use in G.B. and U.S.A. to indicate handling on postal mail vans or travelling post offices (T.P.O.s). In France and Belgium the marking is usually 'Poste Ambulante'; in Germany and Egypt the names of terminal points are normally postmarked—sometimes accompanied by the train number. See also 'Mobile post offices'.

Railway Letter Stamps. Introduced in 1891, these were formerly issued by all the main-line railway companies in Great Britain to pay charges on letters handed in at stations for conveyance by passenger train. They were mostly of 2d. face value, but have been obsolete for many years. In recent years their use has been revived by the Talyllyn Railway, the privately operated narrow-gauge line in North Wales, who have issued several attractive stamps for the purpose.

Rainbow Proofs. Were officially made for experimenting with coloured inks, cancellations, papers, etc., and were printed from plates of three or twelve impressions of the G.B. 1840 penny black design, with top right-hand corner void, May–Dec. 1840.

Rajasthan. Union of certain Indian native states in Rajputana, including Bundi, Jaipur, and Kishangarh, whose internal issues were thus overprinted in 1949. The posts of each state continued to function separately, however, until they were closed by the Indian Government in April 1950.

Rajnandgaon. See 'Nandgaon'.

Rajpipla. Former Indian native state which had its own internal stamp issue 1880–6.

Raj. Service. O/p on early stamps of British India. Control applied by officials of an Indian Rajah's household to obviate misuse and theft.

Rand. South African unit of currency introduced in 1961, equal to 10s. sterling. 100 cents = 1 rand.

Rarotonga. Largest of the Cook Islands in the Pacific. New Zealand stamps overprinted for Rarotonga in 1919 were succeeded by definitives in 1920. Though inscribed 'Rarotonga', they were for use throughout the Cook Islands group. They were replaced by stamps inscribed 'Cook Islands' in 1932. See under 'Cook Islands'.

Ras Al Khaima. One of the Trucial States of Arabia. Stamps first issued, December 1964. Currency: 100 naye paise = 1 rupee.

Rayon. (Fr.). Radius or zone. 1850–2 federal issues of Switzerland were inscribed for Rayons I, II, and III—postal circuits with a circumscribed validity and postal service. There were originally four 'rayons': 1st was up to 10 hrs.; 2nd 10–25 hrs.; 3rd 25–40 hrs.; and 4th over 40 hrs. The 'road-hour' was 4·8 km. Rayon IV was abolished in 1851 and no stamps were issued for it.

Real Plata Fuerta. (Span.). The silver real (or 'royal') currency in Cuba and Puerto Rico during 1871–7 and used as payment for stamps, as opposed to the 'accounting' currency, e.g. for cash, as against entered credit.

Recapito Autorizzato. (Ital.). Stamps so inscribed do not prepay postage.

Recargo. (Span. Additional tax.). Inscribed on 1898–9 war-tax stamps of Alphonso XIII of Spain.

Recess Printing. Strictly speaking, any process where the inked image is below the plane surface of the plate, cliché, block, or cylinder; but in modern philatelic parlance refers to the present-day machine-printed, photo-mechanically engraved plate method of reproduction, which in its essentials is similar to the line-engraving by which most of the first and early stamps were printed. A 'recess' printed stamp has a distinct raised image which can be felt by passing a fingernail gently over the surface. See 'Printing' and allied subjects.

Reconstructed sheet. See under 'Plating'.

Recorded Message Stamps. Argentina issued three stamps in 1939 to frank 'letters' recorded verbatim on to specially prepared flexible gramophone records. (Span. Correos-Fonopostal.) The first recorded-speech letters were sent to scientists in the Antarctic in 1937. The scheme seems to have fallen into disuse.

Recouvrements Valeurs Impayees. (Fr.). Recovery of unpaid dues. Postage dues, but with restricted use for returned C.O.D. packages. In use in France since 1908 and Monaco 1910 on.

Re-cut. When a die or plate has been extensively retouched (q.v.) it is normally termed as re-cut, or re-engraved.

Red Cross Stamps. Many countries have issued charity stamps with surcharge in aid of Red Cross funds, notably on the occasion of the centenary of the movement in 1963.

Re-drawn. A stamp design that has been repeated in most of its main essentials, and still retains all the salient characteristics of its 'type', but betrays its having been re-drawn by minor variations from the original. The 1936 1 peso of Argentina is a case in point. In 1937 it was re-drawn with country boundaries omitted.

'Red' error. The 5 ¢ red error of U.S.A. In 1917 plate number 7492 of the 2 ¢. carmine value, bearing Washington's portrait (S.G. 722), was inadvertently re-entered in three positions from the 5 ¢. transfer roll, the mistake passing undetected prior to distribution of some forty thousand

RE-DRAWN

RED CROSS STAMPS

sheets—a large number of which were recalled and destroyed. S.G. 734 is catalogued in mint condition at £18.

'Red Gibbons'. Colloquial term in common use for Stanley Gibbons' Catalogue Part I, covering stamps of the British Commonwealth, published annually.

Reed's City Despatch Post. Pioneer private mail service of San Francisco, U.S.A., for which local stamps were issued in 1853–4.

Re-entry. Duplication of part of a stamp design due to a first impression having been inadequately erased, and thus enabling traces of its 'entry' to appear in conjunction with the new impression, causing a doubling of a part of the image. The famous 'Union Jack' (q.v.) re-entry is an example of the former; the double lettering on the 1929 Centenary of Western Australia is a recess re-entry; and there are many instances of the litho variety, more correctly named 'double transfer'.

Regatul Romaniei. O/p on stamps of Hungary by Roumanian occupying forces in Transylvania 1919.

Regionals. The so-called Regional stamps of Great Britain were first issued in 1958. Certain of the most widely used values are produced in special versions for Scotland, Wales, Northern Ireland, Jersey, Guernsey, and the Isle of Man. Regional stamps are normally on sale only in the particular region to which they apply, but they are valid for postage throughout the U.K.

Registration Labels. The numbered, blue adhesive labels to U.P.U. specification employed upon registered packages and mail by member countries are an interesting sideline, and attract the attention of many collectors.

Regno d'Italia. Kingdom of Italy.

Regno d'Italia Venezia Giulia. Stamps of Austria o/p by the Italians for the 1918 occupation of Trieste. See also 'Venezia Giulia', and 'Trieste'. 'Regno d'Italia' was also o/p on 1924 issues of Fiume.

Reichspost. (Ger.). State post. Stamps of Germany 1889–1901 (in particular) bore this inscription.

Remainders. Stocks of an obsolete stamp issue, thrown on to the market by the issuing authority, often at a price below face value. See also 'Barred', 'Seebeck', etc.

Repaired Stamps. As the older 'classics' age and become brittle and easily damaged, the number of repaired specimens will inevitably increase, and it may well be that in course of time they will be in the majority. In the meantime there are many faked and patched stamps extant upon which much misplaced skill has been expended, and which the unwary collector is warned to guard against. The Federation Internationale de Philatelie in 1947 passed a resolution calling upon its members to mark such repaired stamps on the back in indelible ink 'Réparé', and decreed that even when this is done, such an endorsement should not be signed by a recognised philatelic expert. They further suggested that if repaired stamps are found in an open exhibit, not marked 'Réparé', the whole entry should be removed.

Replicas. In the early days of stamp collecting, printed sheets of stamp reproductions were obtainable as 'space fillers' (q.v.) to enable a collector to show at least a replica of those specimens not yet obtained, or—often—unobtainable. These 'stamps' were all printed in one colour (blue was usual), were approximately of correct dimensions, and in many instances were very close copies of the original stamps, and are thus often wrongly denounced as forgeries. They still turn up from time to time in old collections.

Repp Paper. A ribbed paper, very similar in appearance to a 'laid' (q.v.), but the fine ribbing is actually on the surface, and is not due to 'watermarking'.

Reprints. Stamps printed from plates after official issues have ceased, for official files, as philatelic curiosities, as official souvenirs, or for sale to meet a collector demand. When done officially, such reprints are often in new colours, or are imperf. or have some other distinction so that the initiate is not deceived, but there have been many reprints done with an ulterior motive. There is a confusing modern tendency to apply the name to fresh printings of current stamps from existing plates to renew stocks.

Republica, Repubblica, Republik, or République. Republic.

Republica Oriental. Uruguay (q.v.).

République Autonome du Togo. Former French African colony, which became an independent republic within the French Union in October 1956. See 'Togo'.

République Centrafricaine. See 'Central African Republic'.

Resellada. (Span.). Re-sealed, or re-authorised. O/p on stamps of Venezulea 1900 to validate an obsolete issue.

Resmi. With crescent and star o/p on stamps of Turkey denotes official use.

Retardo. (Span.). Delayed. Inscribed on the 'Too Late' stamps of Colombia, Panamá, etc.

Rethymo (now Rethimnon or Rethymne). Department and town of northern Crete which was in the Russian sphere of administration during the 1899 allied occupation, and for which the Russians issued special hand-struck and lithoed stamps in May and June 1899.

Retouch. Minor handwork made to a cliché, plate, or die to repair accidental damage or wear. See also 'Re-cut' above.

Retourbrief. (Ger.). Returned letter. Labels, typeset, bearing the words 'Retourbrief/Kgl. Oberamt'. together with a town name printed in black, are (in the words of Gibbons) 'not postage stamps in any sense'! But are none the less listed in Yvert and some other stamp catalogues, under 'Bavaria'.

Retta. A canceller consisting of an elongated diamond or lozenge, of dots, applied in Egypt and the Sudan to casual mail collected from remote and rural districts.

Returned Letter Stamps. Were in use in Norway. The issue was made in 1872. See 'Retourbrief' above.

Reversed Watermark. Due to the paper having been inserted into the machine upside-down (wrong way up), the paper being thus printed on the wrong side thus reversing the already-impressed watermark. A watermark should read correctly when viewed from the *front* of a stamp. See also 'Inverted watermarks', 'Watermarks', etc.

Rheatown. Tennessee. One of the typeset issues of the American Civil War, Confederate 'Postmasters'' series.

Rheinland Pfalz. Rhine province of Germany, part of the French Zone of occupation after the Second World War, which had its own stamps 1947–9. Now part of the German Federal Republic.

Rhodes (Rodi). See under 'Dodecanese Islands'.

Rhodesia. Large region of Central Africa, formerly administered by the British South Africa Company who first issued stamps for the territory in 1890. The name of Rhodesia, however, did not appear until 1909 as an overprint, and until 1910 as an inscription on definitives. In 1924 the region was divided into the British colony of Southern Rhodesia and the protectorate of Northern Rhodesia, each with its own stamps. In 1953 they were again combined in the Central African Federation; see under Rhodesia and Nyasaland below. Ten years later the Federation was dissolved. The name of Rhodesia is now applied to Southern Rhodesia only, Northern Rhodesia having become the republic of Zambia (q.v.).

Rhodesia and Nyasaland. Stamps thus inscribed were first issued in 1954 by the Central African Federation, which was formed in 1953 and consisted

REVENUES   RIALTAR   'RIVADAVIAS'

of Southern Rhodesia, Northern Rhodesia and Nyasaland. The Federation was dissolved in 1963, whereupon Northern Rhodesia and Nyasaland each issued their own stamps once more. Federation stamps continued in use in Southern Rhodesia until February 1964 when that territory too produced a new series of definitives. Area: 487,513 sq. m.; capital: Salisbury; currency: sterling; pop. (1959): 7,990,000.

Rialtar Sealadač na héireann. (Erse) Provisional Irish Government. O/p on stamps of G.B. 1922. See also 'Eire', 'Saorstát', etc.

Ricketts & Hall. A private mail service of Baltimore, U.S.A., for which local stamps were issued in 1857.

Rigsbank skilling. State Bank shilling (Danish). The first issue of Denmark (1851) was in this currency. Also abbreviated to R.B.S.

Rin. Obsolete currency unit of Japan (q.v.).

Rio de Oro. Spanish territory in north-west Africa. Stamps first issued, 1905. It now forms part of Spanish Sahara, whose stamps have been used since 1924.

Rio Hacha. See 'Magdalena'.

Rio Muni. Spanish territory of west Africa, formerly known as Spanish Guinea (q.v.). The first stamps to show the new name were definitives issued in 1960.

Riouw Islands. Known also as the Riau-Lingga, or Rhio-Linga Archipelago, S.E. of Singapore, formerly part of Netherlands East Indies. A surcharged issue in Straits currency on stamps of Indonesia was announced in 1954.

'Rivadavias'. Bernardino Rivadavia's portrait on the 1864–90 issues of Argentina display so many variations that their study and collection has been a speciality of many collectors.

Rizeh, Rise, or Curoh. Turkish Black Sea port between Trebizond and Batum, where Russian stamps o/p were in use 1909–10.

'Robes' set. Name commonly applied to the Australian high values first issued in 1937, showing King George VI and Queen Elizabeth in their coronation robes.

Robison & Co. Private mail service of Brooklyn, New York, for which local stamps were issued in 1855–6.

Roche's City Dispatch. Private mail service of Wilmington in Delaware, U.S.A., for which local stamps (and a postal stationery envelope) were issued in 1850.

Rocket Mail. Despite the rapid development of rocket propulsion in the last few years in connection with space research, very little use of rockets has been made so far for carrying mail. Various experimental flights were made in pre-war years but most were over very short distances—in some cases only a few yards—and were of little or no practical use. All were private ventures, some of whose sponsors produced labels to be affixed to the mail carried, often in defiance of postal regulations. These labels were manufactured for sale to collectors as a means of raising funds. They may be regarded as interesting curios, but hardly as postage stamps, even of a local character. After the flights most of the mail was posted in the ordinary way.

The first mail-carrying rocket on record was dispatched by Friedrich Schmiedl in Austria in February 1931. This was the forerunner of a series of Austrian experiments. The first in Great Britain was Gerhard Zucker's trial on the Sussex Downs in 1934. The first American flight took place in the following year. In post-war years the Rocket Research Institute of America has conducted a series of more successful trials.

America was also responsible for the first official experiment in 1959. This was described as a 'missile mail'. Afterwards the American Postmaster-General forecast that even before man reached the moon, mail would be delivered within hours between America, Britain, India or Australia by guided missile. Whether such hopes are ever fulfilled, and whether rockets will eventually become a regular means of mail transport, are matters for the problematic future.

Rocking-in. The action whereby the image of the transfer roller is transferred to the printing plate in the Perkins line-engraving process. See 'Line Engraving', 'Printing', etc.

Rodi. (Ital.). The Isle of Rhodes. See under 'Dodecanese Islands'.

Roll-cancel. Roll-type cancellers have been used by many nations. See 'Precancels'. One easily identified type is found on the stamps of Belgium and indicates post office savings bank use. Such stamps are not postally used. It was also used on certain 2 f. and 5 f. issues sold as remainders to the stamp trade.

Roll of Distinguished Philatelists. (R.D.P.). Was established at the Philatelic Congress of Great Britain (q.v.) in 1921. H.M. King George V gave it royal assent, and his signature is first on the Roll. There is a similar Roll of Honour in connection with the Collector's Club of New York, and in the 'Hall of Fame' of the American Philatelic Society.

Rolls of Stamps. See 'Coils'.

Romagna (Romagne). North-east region of the former Roman or Papal States, briefly independent in 1859–60, when the provisional government issued its own stamps for a short time before the area became part first of

ROMANIA   ROMANOV-RUSSIA   RUSSIAN ZONE

Sardinia and then of the new kingdom of Italy. After a life of only five months, stamps of Romagna were replaced in February 1860 by those of Sardinia. They have been extensively forged. Forged postmarks have been widely applied to unused remainders, and the stamps were also unofficially reprinted in 1892 and 1897. Area: 5,626 sq. m.; capital: Ravenna; currency: 100 bajocchi = 1 scudo; pop. (1853): 1,341,091.

Roman States. Those regions of central Italy, otherwise known as the Papal States, over which the Pope was formerly temporal ruler. After several insurrections, Romagna (q.v.) broke away in 1859 to join Sardinia. In the remainder the occupation of Rome by French troops maintained the Papal power until 1870, when the temporal rule of the Pope came to an end and the Roman States were incorporated into the new kingdom of Italy. From 1852 to 1870 the Roman States issued their own stamps, all of which bore the insignia of the crossed keys of St. Peter surmounted by the Papal crown. The modern successor of the Roman States is Vatican City (q.v.). Capital: Rome; currency: 1852, 100 bajocchi = 1 scudo; 1867, 100 centesimi = 1 lira.

Roman type. An upright letter with thick and thin strokes, and with serifs; as distinct from sanserif type (without serifs) or italic (sloping letter).

Romania. Roumania (q.v.).

Romanov (Romanoff). The 1913 issue of Czarist Russia is often so described from the portraits of the Romanov dynasty, the former royal family, which appear on the stamps.

Romina. Roumania. New spelling on stamps issued since 1954.

Roode Kruis. (Dutch). Red Cross.

'Roos. Abbreviation commonly used for the Kangaroo stamps of Australia, the first issue of 1913, so called from the design which shows a kangaroo on a map of the country.

Roosevelt. Franklin Delano Roosevelt, former President of the U.S.A., had many world-wide commemorative stamps dedicated to his memory. He was a renowned collector and philatelist.

Rosace Watermark. A British Colonial type used in stamps of Zanzibar 1896; Sudan 1898; and Johore, Malaya, 1896–9. Also known as the 'Lotus' (or Ball flower); Maltese Cross, Quatrefoil, or Rosette.

Rosbach. The 'Rosbach' perforating machine was tested by the U.S.P.O. Bureau of Engraving and Printing in Washington, on the 1919 one-cent grey-green 'Washington' offset stamps, perf. 12½. About 2½ million were issued before it was finally rejected.

Ross Dependency. New Zealand dependency in Antarctica. Stamps first issued, 1957.

Rossyeny (Rossieny or Raseinai). Lithuanian town for which a local provisional was issued January 1919 during a Bolshevik incursion.

Rotary. The Golden Jubilee of World Rotary was commemorated in 1955 by stamps issued by several countries including Australia, Brasil, Belgium, the Saar, France, and the U.S.A.

Rotogravure. Photogravure (q.v.) printing on a modern rotary press, a copper cylinder replacing the flat plate of the early slow process.

Rouad, Ile. (Fr.). The Isle of Ruad (or Arwad) off the coast of Syria, between Latakia and Tripoli. Stamps of French Levant were o/p in 1916.

Rouletting. A method of piercing the paper between stamps, usually in the form of a series of slits, to facilitate separation. An alternative to perforation, it was originally performed by a toothed wheel cutter; hence the name. An important difference between rouletting and perforation proper is that in rouletting no paper is actually removed.

Roumania (also Romania, Rumania, Romina). Country of south-east Europe, formerly Moldo-Wallachia (q.v.), a principality until 1881 when Carol I assumed the title of king, and a republic since December 1947. Stamps first issued, 1865. Both Germany and Austria issued optd. occupation stamps for use in the parts of Roumania occupied by them during the First World War. In the Second World War Roumania was occupied by Germany but continued to issue her own stamps. Area: 91,671 sq. m.; capital: Bucharest; currency: 1858, 40 paras = 1 piastre; 1868, 100 bani = 1 leu (revalued in 1947 and again in 1952); pop. (1962): 18,680,721.

Roumanian Occupation of Hungary, 1919. Hungarian stamps were overprinted by the Roumanians during their occupation of Banat Bacska, Debreczin, Temesvar, and Transylvania.

Roumanian Post Offices in Constantinople, etc. In 1896 general issues were surcharged for use in Roumanian post offices in the Turkish Empire, but Turkey refused to allow their use, so the agency was opened on 15 March 1896, on a Roumanian Steamship Co.'s vessel moored alongside one of the quays, but was closed down by Turkish police on 25 May. In 1919 a special circular o/p was applied on current issues, for use in the office in Constantinople.

Roumélie Orientale. 'Eastern Roumelia' (q.v.).

Rowland Hill, Sir. See 'Hill, Rowland'.

Royal Cypher. The sovereign's initials in script, with or without the accompanying roman number, thus: 'G. v R.' = King George the Fifth (Georgius V Rex). Used to designate certain watermarks.

Royal Mail Steam Packet Company. Established postal agencies at Curaçao, Surinam, San Domingo, Porto Plata, and Porto Cabello in 1875 after losing part of the Royal Mail contract. By arrangement with the P.M.G. of Great Britain, a 10 ¢. stamp printed by De La Rue was issued and used until 1880. Normally pen-cancelled, it has been forged, is p. 11 (instead of p. 12½), on thicker paper, poorly printed. Classed as a 'local'.

Royal Niger Company. Obtained its charter 1886 and administered the Niger and Benue Rivers and the delta between the Forcados and Brass Rivers. The charter was revoked on 21 December 1899, and the territory included in Southern Nigeria. The Company used British stamps, cancelled by office rubber dating stamps at offices at: Akassa, Abutshi, Burutu, and Lokoja. See 'Niger Coast Protectorate'.

'Royal Philatelic Collection, The'. This book published in November 1952, is of 568 pages, 14½" × 10", contains sixty-four pages of monochrome, twelve pages of colour and two of collotype (Royal portraits) illustrations; a 30,000 word monograph by Sir John Wilson (q.v.); a detailed descriptive catalogue; and was published at sixty guineas. Bound in leather, stamped with the royal arms in gold (a whole Nigerian goatskin is used for each volume), it was edited by Mr. Clarence Winchester, and was fully approved by His late Majesty K.G. VI.

Royal Philatelic Society, London. Formerly the Philatelic Society, London, founded in 1869. In 1893 King George V, then Prince of Wales, became Hon. Vice-President, and in 1896 its President. It was granted the privileged prefix 'Royal' by command of King Edward VII in 1906. The Headquarters are at 41 Devonshire Place, London, W.1.

Royal Philatelic Society (Exhibition) Medal. Instituted in 1948, was specially designed by Mr. Cecil Thomas, and was shown at the Royal Academy's Summer Exhibition in 1949. It is struck in bronze, and is offered for competition at recognised International Exhibitions, it being left to the Jury of such Exhibitions to adjudicate the winner. It was first awarded at the Paris International Exhibition of 1949.

'Royal' Reprint. A special printing of the G.B. 1854–7 penny red, Plate 66, Die II, on paper wmkd. large crown inverted and imperf., but made *in black* in 1864 for the amusement and edification of the royal children at the request of Queen Victoria. A few sheets were also printed in both carmine and rose, wmk. normal.

Royaume d'Egypte. Kingdom of Egypt.

Royaume de l'Arabie Soudite. Kingdom of Saudi-Arabia.

Ruanda-Urundi. Former Belgian mandated territory in central Africa. Previously part of German East Africa, it was occupied by Belgian forces during the First World War. The early issues of 1916 were in the nature of Belgian occupation stamps; subsequent issues were overprints on the stamps of Belgian Congo until 1931 when the first distinctive definitives appeared. Stamps of Ruanda-Urandi were withdrawn in 1962 when the territory was divided into the kingdom of Burundi and the republic of Rwanda (q.v.). Area: 20,916 sq. m.; capital: Usumbura; currency: Belgian; pop.: about 5,000,000.

Ruled Feint. Paper ruled in pale blue horizontal lines as writing guides. Used for the printing of the 1887 Mexican issues, and 1919 Latvian emergency stamps.

Rumania. See under 'Roumania'.

Rumanien. Overprint applied by the German authorities to stamps of Germany and Roumania during the German occupation of Roumania in 1917.

Rupee. Currency unit in use in India, Pakistan, Ceylon, etc. Worth about 1s. 6d. in British currency.

Russell 8th Ave. Post Office. Successor to Price's (q.v.) used stamps of similar design for a New York local delivery in 1854–8.

Russia. Country covering a huge area of eastern Europe and northern Asia, the Czarist Empire until 1917 when the Russian Revolution led to the establishment of the present Soviet Union (U.S.S.R.). Stamps first issued, 1858. The early issues, showing the armorial bearings of the Romanov dynasty, are known as the Arms types. As a result of the revolution the Ukraine and the Trans-Caucasus region became independent for a time, and for several years issued their own stamps. During the civil war period there were also a number of dubious counter-revolutionary issues attributed to the Northern (OCKA), North-western, Western, Siberian, Kuban, General Denikin's and the Novocherkask armies, and also to White Russia. In the Second World War Germany overprinted stamps for use in the German-occupied regions of Eastern Europe (Ostland (q.v.)) and the Ukraine. In the immediate post-war years Russia issued stamps for the Russian-occupied provinces of East Germany, see below. In philately Soviet Russia is known as a pioneer in the production of large numbers of large and gaudy multicoloured pictorials. Area: 8,649,798 sq. m.; capital: St. Petersburg (the modern Leningrad) until 1918, thereafter Moscow; currency: 100 kopecs = 1 rouble; pop. (1959): 208,800,000.

Russian Post Offices Abroad. Include o/p issues for China (Cathay) 1899–1920; the Levant (Turkish Empire) 1863–1914; and for places occupied before, during, and after the World Wars.

Russian Refugee's Post. See 'South Russia'.

Russian Zone of Germany. The Russian zone of occupation after the Second World War comprised the eastern provinces of Berlin (Brandenburg), Mecklenburg-Vorpommern, Saxony, and Thuringia. Each of these areas had its own stamps for a short time in the immediate post-war period.

Russisch-Polen. (Ger.). Gothic type o/p on stamps of Germany used in occupied Russian Poland, 1915.

Rust. A brown mould infection that disfigures and depreciates postage stamps in humid climates, and under other unsatisfactory storage conditions. The following preventive and curative methods have been recommended: *The South African Philatelist* advises thymol crystals melted into clean, white blotting paper by the use of a hot iron, interleaving the album with the impregnated paper, and leaving it under a weight for several days so as to thoroughly sterilise the book and its contents. Used stamps (but not mint) can be brush-treated with Chloramine T, 2 grammes to 1,000 ccs. of distilled water, then thoroughly wash and dry the stamps—two or more applications may be necessary in very obstinate cases. Chalky (q.v.) papers must be floated on to the liquid. Dr. A. O. Crane, in H. & A. Wallace's *Bulletin*, says that modern antiseptic washing and cleansing fluids applied undiluted with the tip of a matchstick to the actual visible spots, bleaches the stains out with no visible effect on fast-coloured inks. Blot off immediately, and thoroughly wash and dry the treated specimens—again applicable only to 'used' copies. He also advises the occasional 'airing' of albums. See also 'Cleaning stamps', 'Boiling', and other headings.

Rustenburg. Transvaal stamps were o/p 'V.R.' in violet in 1900 during the South African War. It was then a town of some 3,000 inhabitants.

Rwanda. Independent republic of central Africa, established in 1962 when the first stamps were issued. Formerly part of the Belgian mandated territory of Ruanda-Urundi (q.v.). Area: 10,166 sq. m.; capital: Kigali; pop.: about 3,000,000.

Ryukyu Islands. Group of islands in the Pacific, between Japan and Formosa; part of Japan until 1945 and now mandated to the United States. In the early days of the American administration provisional overprints were applied to stocks of Japanese stamps; for a time no stamps were available and postage was prepaid in cash. The first regular issue of Ryukyu stamps appeared in July 1948. Area: 848 sq. m.; capital: Naha on Okinawa; currency: 1948, 100 sen = 1 Japanese military yen; 1958, 100 cents = 1 U.S. dollar; pop. (est. 1963): 908,000.

Cyrillic and Greek

R in both Cyrillic and Greek is represented by the letter 'P'. In Russian the letter reversed, thus: Я is the 'Yah' and so pronounced—it is terminative of many proper and common nouns; thus:

РОССІЯ = Russia (phonetically: Roociyah).

S

'S'. Overprinted on the SCADTA semi-official airmails of Colombia, the capital letter indicates that the stamp is a consular overprint sold in Switzerland. In other contexts 'S' can be an abbreviation for Specimen, Surcharge, or Selangor.

$. The international sign for dollar, but also used by Portugal on contemporary stamps to denote 'Escudo'.

S.a.e. Stamped addressed envelope (please!).

S.A.I.D.E. (Fr. Service Aerien Internationale d'Egypte). O/p on stamps of Egypt 23 August 1948, for airmail use.

S.A.R. South African Railways.

'S.C.'. 'Stamp Collecting' (q.v.).

S.c. Small crown (watermark).

SCADTA. Initials of Sociedad Colombo-Alemana de Transportes Aereos, Colombian airline which operated that country's internal airmail services from October 1920, until it was succeeded by AVIANCA in 1939. During this period the company was authorised to issue semi-official airmail stamps for use in conjunction with ordinary Colombian adhesives. The earlier SCADTA issues were the subject of the Consular overprints (q.v.).

S.D. or S.O. Stamp Duty, or Stamp Office. Fiscal o/ps on 1891 stamps of Hong Kong. Copies are known postally used.

S.D.D. (Gr. Stratioki Dyikisis Dodekanison). O/p (as $\Sigma\Delta\Delta$) on Greek stamps for Rhodes and the Dodecanese, upon restoration after the evacuation of the British garrison on 31 March 1947.

S. de N. or S.D.N. (Fr.). Société des Nations. See 'League of Nations'.

S.E. Straight edge. An American auction catalogue annotation to denote stamps with one imperf. edge.

S.F. (Swed. Soldater Frimarke). O/p on stamps issued to the armed forces of Sweden. Soldiers' stamps.

S.G. Universally recognised abbreviation for Stanley Gibbons. The initials followed by a number indicate the number of the stamp in Stanley Gibbons' catalogue. For example the British 1937 Coronation stamp may be identified as S.G. 461 of Great Britain. As a watermark or overprint on stamps of Sudan, the same initials stand for Sudan Government.

S.O.   SAAR   ST. LUCIA

S.H.S. Srba (Serbia), Hrvata (Croatia), Slovenaca (Slovenia) = Yugo-slavia.

S.O. Punch-perforated (with crown) on stamps of G.B. = Stationery Office. See also 'S.D. or S.O.' above.

S.O. 1920. (Fr. Silesie Orientale 1920). O/p on stamps of Czechoslovakia and Poland for the plebiscite in East Silesia (q.v.) in 1920.

S.P. O/p on 1881–99 issues of Luxembourg indicate 'Service Public', i.e. official usage.

S.P.A. Society of Philatelic Americans (U.S.A.).

S.P.I.F.S., or **SPIFS.** The colloquial name for the collection of Stamps Perforated (with the) Initials (of) Firms, Societies (etc.). Also known as 'Perfins'.

S.P.M. St. Pierre and Michelon (Miquelon). O/p on stamps of France 1885–92

STT-VUJA. Inscription or overprint on stamps issued by Yugoslavia for use in their zone of Trieste 1948–54.

S.U. Sungei Ujong (q.v.), one of the Malayan states.

S.W.A. South West Africa (q.v.).

Saar. Industrial region lying between France and Germany, administered by France under the League of Nations from 1920 to 1935, when after a plebiscite it was returned to Germany. In this period the Saar had its own stamps, the first issues consisting of stamps of Germany and Bavaria over-printed 'Sarre' (French) or 'Saargebiet'. The first definitives followed in 1921. German stamps were in use from 1935 until 1945, when the Saar became part of the French zone of occupation. From 1947 the region again issued its own stamps. Following a referendum in 1955, it became part of the German Federal Republic in 1957 under the name of Saarland, con-tinuing to issue stamps until 1959. Since then German stamps have again been in use. Area: 991 sq. m.; chief town: Saarbrucken; currency: 1920, German; 1921–35, French; 1947, German and French; 1948–59, French; pop. (1962): 1,096,600.

Sabah. The new name for North Borneo (q.v.), introduced in 1964. In July of that year the name first appeared on stamps in the form of an overprint on the current issue of North Borneo.

Sachsen. (Ger.). Saxony (q.v.).

Safad Issue of Israel. A provisional issue of 2,200 10 mil. stamps authorised by Dov Geiger, Commissioner for Postal Services in Safad in April 1942. Printed letterpress on blue envelope linings.

'Sage' Keytype. See 'Peace and Commerce'.

Saggio. (Ital.). Specimen or pattern. See 'Specimens'.

Sahara Español. (Spanish Sahara). See 'La Aguera' and 'Spanish Western Sahara'.

Sahara Occidental. Western Sahara (Spanish).

St. Andrew's Cross Labels. A blank rectangle in a sheet or book of stamps is conventionally filled in by printing a St. Andrew's cross. The 1850 issues of Austria and of Austrian Italy, and the 1906 K.E. VII stamp booklet panes of G.B. are examples. They should, of course, be collected *se tenant* with the adjoining stamp.

'St. Andrew's Cross' Postmark. A much-prized penny black (G.B.) cancellation from Edinburgh, Scotland, consisting of two lines or rows of crosses with the office number (131) in between.

St. Christopher. Island of the British West Indies, now more popularly known as St. Kitts. Stamps first issued, 1870. In addition British stamps were used at the capital of Basseterre with the 'A 12' cancellation on overseas mail, 1856–60. In 1890 St. Christopher stamps were superseded by those of the Leeward Islands (q.v.). From 1903 St. Christopher used the stamps of St. Kitts-Nevis, and since 1952 has used those of St. Christopher, Nevis and Anguilla. Currency, sterling.

St. Christopher, Nevis and Anguilla. Islands of the British West Indies. Stamps thus inscribed, first issued in 1952, replaced those inscribed St. Kitts-Nevis. Area: 155 sq. m.; chief town: Basseterre; currency: 100 cents = 1 British West Indian dollar; pop. (1960): 56,644.

St. Edward's Crown. A watermark design introduced to British stamps in 1955, replacing the Tudor Crown previously in use. In the following year it was announced that a corresponding watermark with the St. Edward's Crown accompanied by the initials CA in block capitals would appear on all new issues of British Colonial stamps. During 1964 the new watermark also began to make its appearance on issues already current in 1956, and it is now practically universal on all Colonial stamps released through the Crown Agents.

St. Edward's Crown variety. A watermark error found on certain British Colonials (mainly postage dues) in 1954. A substituted 'bit' bore a crude and incorrect crown.

St. Helena. Napoleon's exile isle in the South Atlantic, which has been a British stamp-issuing colony since 1856. Its first issue was a sixpenny stamp which was reprinted in various colours and surcharged to make the other values. Ascension and Tristan da Cunha are dependencies. Area:

47 sq. m.; pop (1962): 4,614; chief town: Jamestown; British sterling currency.

St. Kilda 'Mail-boat'. Mail from this isolated island—about 100 miles from the Scottish mainland—was often sealed in a tin canister placed in a hollow block of wood roughly shaped as a toy boat. It was decked over by a flat piece of wood inscribed 'ST KILDA—Please open', and launched. Wind and tide cast these singular post carriers ashore or they were picked up by passing vessels. The island was evacuated on 28 August 1930.

In 1957 the island was reoccupied by the armed forces, and since then mail has occasionally been dispatched by 'tin-can mail', the covers so transmitted bearing an appropriate cachet.

St. Kitts-Nevis. The neighbouring islands of St. Christopher and Nevis in the British West Indies. Each formerly had its own stamps but these were replaced by those of the Leeward Islands in 1890. In 1903 the first combined issue for St. Kitts-Nevis appeared, the design showing the now well-known anachronism of Columbus seen examining one of the islands through a telescope—an instrument which in Columbus's day had not been invented! This design was taken from the official seal of the colony. Leeward Islands stamps continued in use concurrently with those of St. Kitts-Nevis until the former were withdrawn in July 1956. St. Kitts-Nevis stamps were replaced in 1952 by those inscribed St. Christopher, Nevis, Anguilla. Area: 152 sq. m.; chief town: Basseterre; currency: sterling until 1951; thereafter 100 cents = 1 B.W.I. dollar; pop. (1956): 55,335.

St. Louis. Missouri. The 'St. Louis Bears'—the supporters of the town's arms—published in 1845, are amongst the most sought-after of the U.S.A. 'Postmasters' ', which preceded the general issues of the U.S.P.O. See illustration on page 36. The St. Louis City Delivery issued a stamp to frank local deliveries in 1883.

St. Lucia. Island of the British West Indies. Stamps first issued, 1860. From 1858 to 1860 British stamps were used at Castries with the 'A 11' cancellation on overseas mail. Area: 238 sq. m.; capital: Castries; currency: sterling to 1949; thereafter 100 cents = 1 B.W.I. dollar.; pop. (1960): 94,718.

Ste. Marie de Madagascar. French island off the Madagascar coast. A series of appropriately inscribed French Colonial keytypes, first issued in 1894, was replaced two years later by Madagascar stamps.

St. Martin, or S. Maarten. An island of the Lesser Antilles (Leeward Is.), West Indies, 180 miles east of Porto Rico. The north part is French (attached to Guadeloupe), and the south is Dutch administered by the Netherlands Antilles. Area about 32·8 sq. m.; total pop. about 8,000.

St. Pierre et Miquelon. Islands off the coast of Newfoundland, the only remaining French colony in North America. First issues in 1885 were 'Peace and Commerce' keytypes o/p and surcharged '25/SPM.'. Area: 93 sq. m.; pop. (1962): 4,312; chief town: St. Pierre; French (C.F.A.) currency; principal trade: cod and other fish.

St. Thomas and Prince Islands (São Tomé e Príncipe). Portuguese territory in the Gulf of Guinea, West Africa. Stamps first issued, 1870. For many years the islands used a succession of Portuguese Colonial keytypes until the first distinctive definitives appeared in 1948. Total area: 373 sq. m.; chief town: São Tomé (St. Thomas); currency: Portuguese; pop. (1960): 63,676.

St. Thomas-Porto Rico. A bogus set of nine values appeared in the Danish West Indies in 1869. Design showed the S.S. *Clara Rothe* surmounted by Danish royal insignia.

St. Vincent. Island of the British West Indies. Stamps first issued, 1861. In the 1858-60 period British stamps were used at Kingston with the 'A 10' cancellation on overseas mail. Area: 150 sq. m.; capital: Kingston; currency: sterling to 1949; thereafter 100 cents = 1 B.W.I. dollar; pop. (1960): 80,042.

Salem. Virginia, U.S.A. One of the Confederate 'Postmasters'' towns of the American Civil War.

Salonica, Salonika, Salonique, or (Ital.) Salonicco. Formerly known as Thessalonica, now the Greek port of Thessaloniki. Stamps of Italy were o/p and in use 1909; and Russia o/p 'Salonique' on its 'Arms' types in 1909, while in 1916 stamps of G.B. o/p 'Levant' were in use during World War I. Pop. about 240,000.

Salvador (El Salvador). Central American republic. Stamps first issued, 1867. Area: 8,236 sq. m.; capital: San Salvador; currency: 1867, 8 reales = 1 peso; 1879, 100 centavos = 1 peso; 1911, 100 centavos = 1 colon. Pop. (1961): 2,510,984.

Samoa. Group of Islands in the Pacific, formerly a native kingdom under British influence. The first stamps were the 'Samoa Express' series first issued in 1877 for a postal service set up by a local newspaper proprietor. This service was closed in 1881, and the stamps were afterwards extensively reprinted. The first definitives followed in 1887. In 1900, by an Anglo-German-American agreement, the islands were divided between Germany and the United States. The eastern group have been under American administration ever since and use United States stamps. The larger western group used first German stamps overprinted and then German Colonial keytypes until 1914, when the islands were occupied by New Zealand forces, who overprinted the German Colonial stamps 'G.R.I.' and surcharged them with values in sterling. New Zealand stamps were overprinted for use in Samoa from 1914 until 1921, when distinctive definitives appeared. Meanwhile the group had been placed under New Zealand mandate, and this continued until 1962 when the islands became independent. Although the 1921 series were inscribed 'Samoa', subsequent issues from 1935 onwards were inscribed 'Western Samoa', the higher values (and the 1946 Peace set) continuing to be provided by means of an overprint on New Zealand stamps. Since 1958, with the opening of the Western Samoan Parliament, the inscription has changed to 'Samoa i

SALVADOR   SAN MARINO   SAN MARTIN

Sisifo'. Area of Western Samoa: 1,130 sq. m.; capital: Apia; currency: sterling (except 1900–14, German currency); pop. (1961): 114,427.

Samos. Aegean island, formerly Turkish and now part of Greece. The inhabitants proclaimed union with Greece on the outbreak of the Balkan War in 1912, and set up a provisional government which issued its own stamps. Greek stamps have been used there since 1915. Area: about 180 sq. m.; capital: Limen Vatheos; currency: Greek.

Sample. Written, or printed, upon a stamp shows it to be an approved specimen sent to a contractor or printer, to enable him to quote for its reprinting and re-issue. A practice of the U.S.P.O.

Sanabria Airmail Catalogue is published by Nicolas Sanabria Co. Inc., 421 Fifth Avenue, New York, 17.

Sanda. Small island off the Argyllshire coast, Scotland. Local stamps which have appeared in the last few years have apparently been produced mainly for the philatelic market, and have seen very little if any genuine postal use. They have been condemned as worthless by the B.P.A. and P.T.S.

Sandjak d'Alexandrette. Alexandretta, N.W. Syria. See 'Hatay'. A sandjak is a minor (Turkish) province.

Sandwich Islands. Former name for the Hawaiian Islands.

San Marino. Tiny European republic, surrounded by Italian territory, and an independent and prolific stamp-issuing authority. Its first finely-engraved stamps appeared in 1877. Area: 23 sq. m.; pop. (est. 1964): 17,000; capital: San Marino; Italian currency.

San Martin. General San Martin, military hero whose portrait appears on many of Argentina's stamps.

San Paulo. (São Paulo). Province of Brasil in which a revolutionary government was established for three months in 1932, and which issued stamps in September of that year.

Sans Serif. (Fr.). Without caps or serifs. Applied to a printer's type without cross finials—a plain 'block' or similar type. Also written as Sanserif.

SAUDI ARABIA   SARKARI-SAURASHTRA

Santander. Department of Colombia, which issued its own stamps, 1884–1907.

Saorstat Eireaan, 1922. (Erse). Irish Free State, 1922. O/p on stamps of G.B. December 1922, and again in 1925–7. See also 'Eire', 'Rialtar', 'I.R.A.', etc.

São Tomé e Príncipe. St. Thomas and Prince Islands (q.v.).

Sarawak. Country on the north coast of Borneo, ruled up to the Second World War by the famous 'White Rajahs' of the Brooke family. A British protectorate from 1888. Stamps first issued, 1869. Sarawak stamps have portrayed all three of the White Rajahs, ending with Sir Charles Vyner Brooke whose portrait first appeared in 1918. Stamps of the 1934 issue were overprinted by the Japanese during their occupation of Sarawak from December 1941 until 1945. Australian stamps were in use for a short time towards the close of 1945 but on 17 December of that year the pre-war Sarawak stamps reappeared with a B.M.A. overprint (British Military Administration). The commemoratives for the centenary of the Brooke dynasty, planned for 1941, were belatedly issued in May 1946, but in July of that year Sir Charles Vyner Brooke handed over control to the British Government, and Sarawak became a Crown Colony—a change reflected in the Royal Cipher overprints of 1947. New definitives followed in 1950. Though now part of the Malaysian Federation, Sarawak continues to issue its own stamps. Area: 48,250 sq. m.; capital: Kuching; currency: 100 cents = 1 Malayan dollar; pop. (1962): 776,990.

Sardinia. Former kingdom comprising the Mediterranean island of that name and part of the Italian mainland, which became the nucleus of the kingdom of Italy. Stamps first issued, 1851. From 1859 Sardinian stamps were also used in those parts of Italy which became united to Sardinia until they were finally superseded by the first issue for the new kingdom of Italy in 1862. The 1855 issue of Sardinia is in fact identical to the first issue of Italy except that the former is imperforate and the latter per-forated.

Sarkari. 'Service'. O/p on stamps of Saurashtra (q.v. below).

Sarre. Saar (q.v.).

Saseno. Albanian island controlling the port of Valona, occupied by Italy in 1923 when Italian stamps were overprinted for use there. The island, now known as Sazan, was returned to Albania by peace treaty of 1947.

Saudi Arabia. Arabian kingdom comprising the former kingdom of Hejaz and sultanate of Nejd. Hejaz first issued stamps in 1916 and Nejd in 1925. Following the successful invasion of Hejaz by Nejd forces, the stamps of the two territories were succeeded in 1926 by the first issue for the combined administration of Hejaz-Nejd. The kingdom of Saudi Arabia (Royaume de l'Arabie Soudite) was proclaimed in 1934, and the new name appeared on stamps in the same year. Area: 617,600 sq. m.; capital: Riyah (with a legislature at Mecca); currency: 1916, 40 paras = 1 piastre or guerche; 1934, 110 guerches = 1 sovereign (gold), shortly afterwards revalued to 880 guerches = 1 sovereign; 1960, 800 piastres = 1 sovereign; pop.: over 6,000,000.

Saurashtra. Stamps thus inscribed (first issued in 1929), and also those inscribed Sourashtra (from 1923), were in fact issued by Junagadh, one of the Indian native states. They are usually catalogued under the alternative name of Soruth. Saurashtra was in fact the name given to an area containing a group of small states of which Junagadh was the only one to issue its own internal stamps. In 1948 the Union of Saurashtra was formed, including the former stamp-issuing states of Soruth, Jasdan, Morvi, Nawanagar, and Wadhwan. Several stamps were issued by this Union before they were replaced by Indian issues in 1950.

Saxony. Former central German kingdom, and its own stamp-issuing authority 1850–68, when it joined the North German Confederation (q.v.). Area: 5,786 sq. m.; pop. about 5 million; capital: Dresden; currency: 10 pfenninge = 1 neugroschen. As part of the Russian zone of occupation after the Second World War, Saxony again had its own stamps for a short time in 1945–6. There were also separate short-lived issues for North-West Saxony (Leipzig) and South-East Saxony (Dresden).

Scandinavia. Comprises Norway, Sweden, and Denmark, although Iceland, the Faröes, and Greenland can be bracketed philatelically to form a Scandinavian group for collection and study. See under their separate headings.

'Schermack' Perforation. A vending machine form of 'coils' perforating in use in the U.S.A. from 1909 to 1927, consisting of large and small round holes and (later) a pair of slots. See also: 'Attleboro',' 'Mailometer', etc.

Schleswig-Holstein. Schleswig and Holstein were two duchies south of Denmark, under the Danish crown until 1864. A rebellion against Danish rule broke out in 1848 which was not suppressed until 1851. In November 1850 the revolutionary provisional government issued its own stamps, and these were used until Danish rule was restored in the following year. In the war of 1864, however, Denmark was defeated by Prussia and Austria, and obliged to give up the two duchies. In March of that year the occupying powers issued separate stamps both for Schleswig and for Holstein, followed in 1865 by a combined issue for both territories. By the Convention of Gastein in August 1865 Schleswig was awarded to Prussia, and

Holstein to Austria; and as a result the two duchies again had separate stamps in November of that year. In the war of 1866 Austria was defeated by Prussia, whereupon the latter took over control of both duchies. From November 1866 the stamps of both Schleswig and Holstein could be used in either duchy. Both issues were finally superseded at the beginning of 1868 by the first stamps of the North German Confederation. Area: 5,819 sq. m.; currency: 16 schillings = 1 mark. After the First World War a plebiscite was held in Schleswig, as the result of which the northern part of the province voted to return to Denmark. Special stamps, one set with values in German currency and another with values in Danish currency, were issued for use during the plebiscite period of 1919–20. In October 1920 Denmark issued a set of three commemoratives to mark the recovery of Northern Schleswig.

Schweizer Post-Vaduz. See 'Vaduz-Sevelen'.

Schweizer Reneke. Transvaal village where available stamps were hand-stamped 'Besieged' by British troops during the Boer War 1900–1.

Scinde. District of India. The 'Scinde Dawks' were the first stamps to be used in India; they were issued in July 1852 under the authority of Sir Bartle Frere, Commissioner in Scinde. The small circular embossed design showed the trading mark of the East India Company. They were superseded by the first general issue for India in October 1854.

Scott. One of the two leading catalogues published in the United States. Scott Publications Inc. produce an annual whole-world general catalogue in two columes, also an annual United States specialised catalogue.

Script. A printers' type approximating to handwriting. This is one of the script faces:

Script

Script—C.A., C.C., Royal Cypher, etc. Are British watermarks in which the initials are in a script style or type (see above). See 'Multiple Watermarks', 'C.A.', 'C.C.', 'Royal Cypher', and 'Watermarks', etc.

Scroll Postmark. The so-called 'scroll' type of G.B. pmk. consists of a curved name-panel over-riding the usual c.d.s. The most famous is that of the 'Stamford Mercury', a special journals' canceller authorised by the G.P.O.

Scutari. Town of Albania. Italian stamps were overprinted 'Scutari di Albania' and surcharged with values in Turkish currency for use at the Italian post office there, 1909–16. The town was occupied by Allied forces in 1918–19, when Austrian fiscal stamps were used with an overprint 'Posta Shkodres Shqypnis'.

'Sea Floor, Bahamas'. Special postmark applied to mail 'posted' in the bathysphere at the bottom of the sea in Nassau Marine Garden, 16 August 1939, a souvenir of the Williamson Undersea Expedition.

Seals. Term used to describe adhesive labels of no postal validity, sold to raise money for charity. The letter-seals of Egypt, however, are in a different category. These were genuine postage stamps, first issued in 1932 for use by the British forces in Egypt who enjoyed a concessionary rate of postage on letters to Great Britain; they were replaced in 1936 by the 'Army Post' stamps.

Secret Marks. Identifying and reference marks, many of them almost microscopic in character, abound. They were originally placed there by the artist or engraver for identification and differentiation. Thus the 1873 U.S.A. series, first printed by one company, was reprinted by a rival concern, and tiny amendments and additions were made to the designs— secret marks to identify the new printing. The 1858 set of Naples bears a tiny letter on each stamp in the outer border progressively spelling 's. MASINI', the name, and secret mark, of the engraver, the Bradbury, Wilkinson printings of the 1918–30 George V G.B. high values bear a tiny dot in the top middle margin; and Canadian stamps since 1935 are nearly all dated, with the year in tiny characters that only a magnifying glass will reveal, while the Fifth (1942) Sun Yat Sen issues of China have numerous hidden characters in the design. See also 'Syllabics'.

Sedang. A bogus issue for a mythical postal state in the interior of Annam, Indo-China, made by a French impostor (the self-styled 'King Marie I'), Marie David de Mayréna. Copies turn up from time to time in old collections.

Seebeck. Nicholas Frederick Seebeck collaborated with the Hamilton Bank Note Company of New York to supply (in 1889) certain South American states with most attractive sets of postage stamps free of charge. The authorities concerned—Ecuador, Honduras, Nicaragua, are quoted with Salvador—are stated to have agreed to accept a new issue annually, to demonetize the obsolete set, and to return all the unsold remainders to Seebeck, the agent. In addition, the contractor was authorised to use the original plates to make such reprints as the Company might require to meet the demand of stamp dealers and collectors. The affected issues are said to be: Ecuador 1892–6; Honduras 1890–5; Nicaragua 1890–9; and Salvador 1890–9. These are known as the 'Seebeck' issues and/or reprints.

Segnatasse. (Ital.). Tax, to collect. Postage due.

Seguro Postal. (Span.). Security post. Mexican insured letter stamps are so inscribed.

Seiyun. Kathiri, State of Seiyun. See under 'Aden States'.

Sejm Wilnie. Inscribed on 1922 stamps of Central Lithuania (Litwa Srodkowa) for the opening of the national parliament at Vilna.

Selangor. One of the original federated Malay States, which was issued with inscribed 'Tiger' keytypes in 1891. Its first issues, however, were o/p stamps of the Straits Settlements in 1878. In 1900 used Federated Malay States issues. The Japanese o/p its stamps during the war occupation period 1942–5. Now one of the members of the Malayan Federation (q.v.). Area: 3,150 sq. m.; pop. (1962): 1,221,661; capital: Kuala Lumpur; Straits (Malayan) currency.

SE-TENANT   SEGNATASSE   SEIYUN

Selvedge. Stamp 'edging', or sheet, pane, or gutter margins.

Semi-Postals. Scott's Catalogue classifies all charity or other stamps bearing a surtax in excess of regular postage as semi-postals.

Sen. Japanese currency unit, which from 1952 no longer appears on their stamps. 100 sen = 1 yen.

Senegal. Formerly the oldest French colony in West Africa, with its own stamps 1887–1944, and again since 1960. From 1944 to 1959 Senegal used the stamps of French West Africa. In 1959 the territory joined with French Soudan to form the Mali Federation, but seceded in the following year and since then has been an independent republic within the French Community. Area: 76,119 sq. m.; capital: Dakar; pop. (est. 1960): 3,100,000.

Senegambia and Niger. French West African possessions. Used 'Tablet' keytypes 1930–6. Was then renamed Haut-Sénégal-Niger, and resumed its philatelic career with new keytypes. See under 'Upper Senegal' and 'Niger.'

Separation. The actual separation of individual copies from a mint sheet of modern perforated stamps is correctly done by first folding and firmly creasing along the line of perfs to break the remaining paper fibres in the 'teeth'. Tearing apart is thus attended with little risk of damage to the adjoining stamps.

Serbia (Servia). Former Balkan kingdom; part of Yugoslavia since the end of the First World War. Stamps first issued, 1866. Most of Serbia was occupied during the First World War by Austria, who overprinted Bosnian stamps 'Serbien' for use there. The Serbian administration withdrew to the Greek island of Corfu, where French stamps overprinted 'Postes Serbes' were in use for a time in 1918. After the war Serbian stamps continued to be used until about 1920, when they were replaced by those of Yugoslavia. During the Second World War Serbia was revived as a puppet state under the German occupation 1941–4. Yugoslav stamps were overprinted 'Serbien' in 1941, followed by new definitives in the following year. Area: 36,937 sq. m.; capital: Belgrade; currency: 100 paras = 1 dinar. pop (1910): 2,911,701.

Serbian Occupation of Hungary. Hungarian stamps were overprinted for use in Baranya, a Serbian-occupied district, in 1919. In the same year Hungarian stamps were surcharged with new values for use in Temesvar.

SERBIA   SERPENTINE   SERVICE   SHANGHAI

Serbien. See under 'Serbia' above.

Serif. The short cross-line or finial on the strokes of letters in printers' type. See 'Sans Serif', 'Type', etc.

Serpentine Roulette. (Fr. Percé en serpentine, q.v.). The 1860 issues of Finland are an accentuated example of this type of rouletting.

Serrated Roulette. More correctly known as 'arc' roulette (Fr. Percé en arc). (Would be still more correct if applied to the saw-tooth variety.)

'Service'. Imprint or overprint on stamps utilised by the various government departments of a state. Example: India.

Servicio Official. (Span.). Official Service.

Sesquicentenary. 150th anniversary. Applied to the 1937 Australian set commemorating the foundation of New South Wales, for example.

Se-tenant. Joined together (Fr.); term applied to two or more stamps unseparated. A se-tenant pair is of particular interest when one stamp differs in some material regard—in type, colour, value, overprint, etc.—from the other. Such pairs should always be kept intact.

Set. A set of stamps is a sequence or series of values of like type issued at one time or within a period. The latter may be indeterminate, as a new value may be added after its fellows have been in use for years, as instance the 11d. K.G. VI of G.B. produced in 1948 and added to the 1941 set—which is again the 1938 set in lighter colours.

Set-off. See 'Offset'.

Seychelles. British group of some hundred islands (including the Amirante Archipelago) in the Indian Ocean. Captured from France in 1794 they were first administered from Mauritius, and canceller 'B 64' was in use on stamps of G.B. and Mauritius. It became a separate Crown Colony in 1897 but had its own independent stamps from April 1890—Victorian keytypes suitably inscribed. Area: 156 sq. m.; pop. (1962): 43,750; capital: Victoria on Mahé, the chief island: currency: 100 cents = 1 rupee = 1s. 6d. British.

Shade. In philately, denotes the nuance or tone gradation in a particular basic or pure colour. Strictly speaking, a shade is a degraded or darkened pure colour. A lightened colour or a colour plus white is more correctly a

274

'tint', but the word 'shade' seems to have come to embrace both terms in modern parlance unfortunately—and not in philately alone!

Shanghai. Seaport of China on the Whangpoo, a branch of the Yangtse-Kiang river, a treaty port, and a city with international settlements formerly occupied by the great powers. It had its own municipal or local stamps, typeset imperfs., in 1865. The 1866–9 and 1873 sets were printed in England by Nissen & Parker, and Pemberton once described them 'as weird-looking, as far as the dragon goes, as could be desired'. These municipal issues continued to be produced in various designs until 1898. In 1919–22 the U.S.A. o/p and surcharged its general issues for the use of its Consular offices. Stamps of Hong Kong (overprinted 'China' from 1917) were in use at the British post office in Shanghai until 1922. Shanghai now uses the general issues of China. Currency: 1865, 16 cash = 1 candereen; 1866, 100 cents = 1 Chinese dollar; pop. (1958): 6,900,000.

Shan States. Eastern States of Burma which remained under Japanese Military Government when they set up the puppet Burma government during the war occupation 1942–5. Separate stamps were issued in August 1943, but were o/p for general use throughout the country when these States were incorporated into Burma on 24 December 1943. Area: 56,300 sq. m.; pop. about 1½ million.

Shapes and Sizes of Stamps. The Penny Black of G.B. was so well conceived and planned that it has remained an international standard with little, if any, variation. It measured $\frac{7}{8} \times \frac{3}{4}$ in. (22 mm. × 18½ mm.). G.B. current issues are 29/32 in. × 21/32 in. (23 mm. × 18 mm.). First issues of the U.S.A. were 1 in. × 25/32 in. (25 mm. × 20 mm.), and the 1938 'Presidents' are 1 in. × 29/32 in. (25 mm. × 22 mm.). The rectangular, upright oblong format is popular, economic, and convenient, but there have been interesting departures from the general standard, thus: square, or square-diamond: Newfoundland, Nova Scotia, New Brunswick early classic issues, and many moderns; rhomboid: 1937 Costa Rica, and Tanna Touva of the same year; triangular: 1853 Cape Colony, 1926 South Africa, 1932–3 Lithuania (apex down), 1937 Costa Rica, 1930 air Iceland, Colombia's irregular triangle of 1869 and many others. There have been circular and oval variants, hexagons, octagons, and other geometric shapes; while the upright double-size format is very popular with France for her colonial issues, at home she favours the horizontal oblong. A full selection makes an interesting collection.

Sharjah. Independent sheikhdom of Arabia on the Persian Gulf, in special treaty relationship with Great Britain. Stamps first issued, 1963. Area: 3,000 sq. m.; Currency: 100 naye paise = 1 rupee; pop. (est. 1965): 60,000.

Sheet. The maximum number of stamps printed on one sheet of paper as it comes from the press. Sometimes they are divided into two or four sub-sheets or panes before distribution to post offices. A sheet may contain as few as four stamps (as in the 'Sacred Cows' issue of Bundi) or as many as 480, while a miniature sheet may have only one.

SHIPS ON STAMPS   SHQIPTARE   SIAM

Sheet Watermark. A watermark whose design appears once only on the sheet, each stamp therefore bearing only a small portion of the watermark or none at all. A notable example is the 1854 issue of India, each sheet showing a watermark in the form of the arms of the East India Company.

Shihr and Mukalla. See under 'Aden States'.

Ship Letter. A letter carried by private ship, as distinct from a packet letter, carried either by a ship maintained by the government or by a privately owned ship operating under Post Office contract. The carriage of ship letters was first regulated by an Act of 1660. From the 1760s onward numerous ports in the United Kingdom and overseas used ship letter handstamps of various types on incoming mail. These are keenly collected by specialists. With the introduction of steamships and the growth of the mail contract system, the volume of ship letters began to decline by the middle of the nineteenth century. Some of the handstamps, however, were still in occasional use in the early part of the twentieth century. India letters were a particular type of ship letter, brought in by the East India Company's ships under a special arrangement with that company introduced in 1815. At certain ports distinctive India letter handstamps were applied. These were necessary to distinguish such mail from other ship letters because the postal rates were different. India letter handstamps went out of use when steamers began carrying the Indian mails under contract in the 1840s.

Short set. A set of stamps complete to a specified value only, usually excluding the higher and more expensive values.

Shqiptare. The country known to us as Albania has spelt its name on its stamps in various ways, i.e. Shqiptenia, Shqipterie, Shqipenie, Shqyptare, Shqipni, Shqipnija, Shqiperia, Shqiptare and finally Republika Popullore E. Shquperise.

Shrub Oak Local Post. A modern U.S.A. 2 ¢. local in triangular format introduced by Herman Herst, Jnr., in early 1953. Its status is apparently legal, but it is admittedly an advertising idea.

Shuna. Scottish islet off the Argyllshire coast. In October 1949 the owner produced a stamp-like publicity label, showing a map of Shuna with place names in Gaelic. It is not a local, having no postal validity whatever.

Siam. See under 'Thailand'.

SINGAPORE   SIERRA LEONE   SINKIANG

Siberia. Admiral Kolchak's anti-Bolshevik government, formed at Omsk in 1918 surcharged 'arms' types of Russia in 1918.

Sicily. Large Mediterranean island, a former kingdom which in 1859 issued a set of stamps. They were soon superseded in 1860 by those of Sardinia. Area: 9,935 sq. m.; currency (1859–60): 100 grana = 1 ducat. Now part of Italy.

Sideways Watermark. When the sheet to be printed happens to approximate a square, it is not unusual to find specimens watermarked sideways, due to a sheet having been wrongly 'fed'. In coils (q.v.) of G.B., known to the G.P.O. as 'M' (½d.), 'N' (1d.), 'O' (1½d.), 'P' (2d.), 'S' (2½d.), and 'T' (3d.), all the stamps are so watermarked, being vertically attached for use in stamp-*affixing* (q.v.) machines. See also 'Watermarks'.

Siege of Mafeking. See 'Mafeking'.

Sierra Leone. Former British colony and protectorate in West Africa; since 1961 an independent member of the British Commonwealth. Stamps first issued, 1859. Sierra Leone is noted for the appearance in 1964 of the first 'free-form' issue—self-adhesive stamps in the shape of a map of the territory. Area: 27,925 sq. m.; capital: Freetown; currency: sterling to 1964; thereafter 100 cents = 1 leone; pop. (1963): 2,183,000.

Sievier's Essays. R. W. Sievier submitted interesting machine-engraved (or engine-turned) and embossed designs to the Treasury competition of 1840, which have been preserved, and are known to all keen students of the early stamps of G.B., copies being in existence in specialised collections in various colour combinations.

Signé. (Fr.). Signed. An expert's signature or mark on the back of a stamp attesting to its authenticity.

Silesia. See 'East Silesia' and 'Upper Silesia'.

Silurian, or granite paper. A blue-grey with blue-coloured fibres or particles, which was popular as a notepaper in the nineties and has frequently been used for stamp printing.

Simi, or Symi. See under 'Dodecanese Islands'.

Simplified. In philately the word applies to *Stanley Gibbons' Simplified Catalogue.* published annually, which lists stamps without details of shade, watermark or perforation, and is thus well suited to beginners or thematic collectors. Despite the increasing number of new issues which have to be added every year, the Simplified remains the only catalogue to list all the world's stamps in one volume.

Sin Valor Postal. (Span.). Without postal validity. Poster stamps—notably the Zaragoaz School stamps of 1953—are so inscribed.

Sinaloa. North Mexican province with its own locals 1923–4.

Sind. See 'Scinde'.

Singapore. Island and port at the southern tip of the Malayan peninsula, formerly a British colony and part of the Straits Settlements (q.v.). Malaya B.M.A. (British Military Administration) stamps were used there from 1945 to 1948, when the first stamps for Singapore alone were issued. In 1958 it became an internally self-governing territory known as the State of Singapore. In 1963 Singapore joined the Malaysian Federation but seceded in 1965, becoming an independent member of the British Commonwealth. Area: 224 sq. m.; currency: 100 cents = 1 Malayan dollar; pop. (1961): 1,712,600.

Single Lined. Characters, figures, frames, or circles composed of one stroke or line, are so-called in philately to distinguish them from outline or 'double-lined' (q.v.).

Single Line Perf. Perforating done a line at a time, as distinct from the 'Comb' or 'Harrow' (q.v.). See 'Perforation'.

Sinkiang, or Hsin-chiang. Province of China lying between Mongolia and Tibet, and comprising Chinese Turkestan, Kulja, and Kashgaria. From 1915 to 1945 was issued with stamps of China with o/p in native characters. Area: 550,340 sq. m.; pop.: about 1½ million.

'Sinking Fund'. (Fr. Caisse d'Amortissement). Annual public debt-reducing stamps of France 1927–31.

Sinn Fein 'Labels'. These were stamps issued by the Irish rebels in 1907 as a gesture of defiance to the British authorities. There is evidence of their actual postal use during the 1916 'Easter' Rebellion, and it is stated that postally-cancelled copies exist.

'Sir Codrington' Error. The Battle of Navarino Centenary issue of Greece 1927 had two printings of the 5 drachmai stamps in which Sir Edward Codrington's Christian name was omitted, in ignorance of the British custom: correction was made in the third and final printing. (See page 211).

Sirmoor, or Sirmur: Former feudatory native state of British India, in the Punjab. It had its own internal stamps 1879–1902. Area: 1,198 sq. m.; pop.: 156,026; Indian currency. Now in Himachal Pradesh State, Republic of India.

'Sleeper'. An unsuspected elusive stamp.

Slesvig. (Danish). Schleswig (q.v.).

SLOGANS

Slogan. Originally a war cry (Gaelic) but now applied in philately to the terse, brief, and pithy sentences incorporated in modern machine post-marks, i.e. 'Post Early for Xmas', etc. Their collection is an intriguing sideline of the hobby. The first in use in G.B. was 'Buy National War Bonds Now', during the First World War. See also 'Metered Mail'.

Slovakia (Slovensko). Part of Czechoslovakia, separated from the rest of the country under the German occupation 1939–45, when it had its own stamps. Area: 18,895 sq. m.; capital: Bratislava; currency: 100 heller = 1 krone; pop. (1930): 3,330,885.

Slovenia. Region of Yugoslavia occupied by Italy in 1941, when over-prints were applied to Yugoslav stamps. Slovenia was then annexed by Italy and used Italian stamps until 1943, when it came under German occupation and became known as the Province of Laibach. Italian stamps were overprinted by the Germans for use in Slovenia from 1944, and in the following year some short-lived definitives appeared. Since the end of the Second World War, Slovenia has again been part of Yugo-slavia.

Slovensko, or Slovenska Posta. Slovakia (q.v. above).

'Smiling Boy' Stamp. The famous 1931 design for the Health Stamps of New Zealand, now very elusive items.

Smirne. Italian stamps thus overprinted (and surcharged with values in Turkish currency) were first issued in 1909 for use at the Italian post office in the Turkish city of Smyrna, see below.

Smith & Stephens' City Delivery. Operated in St. Louis, U.S.A., and issued a 'local' stamp.

Smyrna (Smyrne, Smirne). Turkish city where several of the European powers operated post offices in the years prior to the First World War. At the British post office British stamps were used from 1872 with the 'F 87' cancellation, and subsequently stamps of British Levant. Arms-type stamps of Russia were overprinted 'Smyrne' for use at the Russian office from 1909; and Italian stamps overprinted 'Smirne' for use at the Italian office from the same year.

Soaking Off. The removal of surplus adhering paper from used postage stamps by immersion in plain water. Specimens printed in fugitive or

SLOVAKIA   SOBRE PORTE   SOLDIERS'   SOMALI COAST
LETTER STAMPS

'aniline' inks, or stuck to coloured papers, or cancelled with violet ink, should on no account by totally immersed, but should be 'floated off' (q.v.). Salt (sodium chloride) added to the water will slow up any running of colour, and will freshen up the stamps. The coloured linings of airmail envelopes and some brown wrapping papers are particularly prone to staining—not only the attached stamps, but the water also—thus tinting the whole batch. A humidor (q.v.) or sweat-box is the modern and preferred appliance and method for use with mint stamps and those printed in water-soluble inks. See also 'Boiling', 'Cleaning stamps', etc.

Sobre Porte, or Sobre Tasse.   (Span.). Additional postage or tax. Normally implies postage due, but on the 1932 air stamps of Colombia (for instance) it means that extra postage is pre-payable to cover air transit.

Société des Nations.   (Fr.) or S. de N. The League of Nations (q.v.).

'Socked on the nose'.   (U.S.A.). Colloquialism defining a stamp with a centred, legible, and full town and date cancel.

Soldiers' Letter Stamps.   China, France, Germany, Japan, Sweden, and Switzerland have issued special stamps for the use of the armed forces, franking their mail free of charge. See 'F.M.', 'S.F.', 'Crimea', etc.

Solomon Islands.   See 'British Solomon Islands'.

Somalia.   Independent republic of East Africa, formed in 1960 by the union of the former Italian Somaliland and the former British protectorate of Somaliland. The new republic's first stamps of 1960 replaced the separate issues formerly in use under the Italian and British administrations. As an inscription on stamps, however, 'Somalia' and 'Somalia Italiana' can be found on issues of Italian Somaliland from 1916 onwards. See under 'Italian Somaliland' and under 'Somaliland Protectorate'. Area: 246,135 sq. m.; capital: Mogadiscio; currency: 100 centesimi = 1 somalo; pop. over two million.

Somalia Italiana Meriodionale.   Italian Somaliland (q.v.).

Somali Coast.   (Fr. Côte Française de Somalis). See 'French Somali Coast'.

Somaliland Protectorate.   Former British protectorate on the Gulf of Aden, in north-east Africa. When the protectorate was established in

1885, the country was at first administered from Aden as a dependency of India, and Indian stamps were used until 1903. In that year Somaliland's first stamps appeared—a set of British Somaliland overprints on Indian issues—followed by the first definitives in 1904. In 1960 the British protectorate came to an end and the country united with the adjoining territory of Italian Somaliland to form the new independent republic of Somalia (q.v.). Area: 68,000 sq. m.; capital: Berbera; currency: as India until 1951; thereafter 100 cents = 1 East African shilling.

Somerset House. See 'Inland Revenue'.

Sonora. Mexico. Had its own Civil War issues 1913–16.

'Sopron' Overprints. On Hungarian current issues; were made at Sopron, a town about 125 m. west of Buda-Pesth, during an anti-Communist rising in late 1956. Status is uncertain, but genuine postal use is claimed. Stocks were confiscated and invalidated by the Hungarian Directorate of Posts on 26 January 1957.

Soruth (also Sorath). Group of former Indian native states, the only one to issue its own internal stamps being Junagadh, though some of these bore the inscription 'Soruth', under which name they are usually catalogued. The first stamps, believed to have been first issued in 1864, were hand-stamped in water-colours. The values of the 1877 and 1886 issues were expressed in 'annas of a koree', 16 Soruth annas being equal to one koree, and one koree to four annas in Indian currency. Subsequently the name of the region was changed to Sourashtra (from the 1923 issue) and to Saurashtra (q.v.), from 1929.

Soudan. Sudan (q.v.).

Soudan Français. French Soudan (q.v.).

South Africa. A former independent member of the British Commonwealth, South Africa was formed in 1910 by the union of two British colonies—Cape of Good Hope and Natal; and two former Boer republics, Transvaal and Orange Free State. It was known as the Union of South Africa until 1961 when the country left the Commonwealth and became an independent republic. The first stamp of South Africa was a single 2½d. value issued in 1910, but the first definitives did not appear until 1913 and in the intervening period the stamps of the four constituents remained in use. See under 'Inter-Provincials'. South African stamps are noted for the fact that they are either inscribed bilingually in English and Afrikaans, or are printed alternately in these languages throughout the sheet. In the latter case the stamps are best collected in bilingual pairs. Area: 471,445 sq. m.; administrative capital: Pretoria; legislative capital: Cape Town; currency: sterling until 1961; thereafter 100 cents = 1 rand (10s. sterling); pop. (1960): 16,002,797.

South African Republic. For the modern Republic of South Africa, see under 'South Africa' above. The earlier South African Republic (Afrikaans: Zuid Afrikaansche Republiek) was one of the former Boer republics, better known as Transvaal (q.v.), under which name it is usually catalogued.

SOUTH AUSTRALIA	SOUTH ORKNEYS	SOUTH-WEST AFRICA

South Arabian Federation. Formed in February 1959, this Federation comprises most of the territories of the former Western Aden Protectorate, in addition to the Wahidi sultanate from the Eastern Aden Protectorate. Until April 1962 it was known as the Federation of Arab Amirates of the South. In January 1963 the colony of Aden joined the Federation. The first stamps to be inscribed South Arabian Federation were the Red Cross Centenary commemoratives issued later that year. Up to that time the stamps of Aden were used throughout the Federation area. The first definitives appeared in April 1965 and replaced the stamps of Aden. Area: about 60,000 sq. m.; capital: Al Ittihad; pop. (est. 1964): 712,500.

South Australia. Former British colony. Stamps first issued, 1855. In 1901 South Australia was incorporated in the Australian Commonwealth, but the colony's stamps continued in use until the first all-Australian definitives appeared in 1913. Area: 380,070 sq. m.; capital: Adelaide; currency: sterling; pop. (1930): 582,127.

South Bulgaria. Territory originally Eastern Roumelia (q.v.), and which was incorporated into Bulgaria in 1885. It used stamps of Eastern Roumelia o/p from 22 September 1885, to 1886, when Bulgarian general issues superseded. Capital: Philippopolis.

South Georgia. Island in the South Atlantic, a British possession used as a whaling station, formerly part of the Falkland Islands Dependencies. Stamps of the Falkland Islands were used until the first Dependencies issue appeared in 1944. This included a set of overprints for South Georgia. The first definitives for the island were issued in July 1963. Area: 1,450 sq. m.; chief settlement: Grytviken; currency: sterling; pop. (1960): 1,270.

South Korea. See under 'Korea.'

South Lithuania. Under this title are catalogued arms-type stamps of Russia overprinted and surcharged in 1919 during a short-lived Russian occupation of Grodno, a town whose possession was then disputed between Poland and Lithuania. It became part of Poland, but since the Second World War has been in Soviet Russia.

South Moluccas (Malaku Selatan). Large island group in the East Indies, part of Indonesia, where an insurrection against Indonesian rule was reported to have broken out in 1950. In the following year a series of pictorial stamps appeared on the philatelic market, purporting to have been issued by the revolutionary movement. They are considered to be bogus.

South Orkneys. Group of British islands in the Antarctic, formerly part of the Falkland Islands Dependencies whose first issue of 1944 included a set of overprints for the South Orkneys. Since 1963 the islands have formed part of the British Antarctic Territory (q.v.). Area: 240 sq. m.

South Russia.
1. *Kuban Government:* Republic proclaimed 1918 and 'arms' types of Russia surcharged were issued at Ekaterinodar in 1919.
2. *Don Government:* The Don Cossack independent republic proclaimed in 1918 surcharged 'arms' types of Russia in 1919 at Novocherkassk, Rostov, and Taganrog. They were also responsible for the 'Ermak' currency stamp in 1918, which was also valid for postage prepayment.
3. Crimea: 'Arms' types of Russia were surcharged at Sevastopol by a provisional government (set up under German auspices) in January 1919.
4. *General Denikin's Volunteer Army:* Issued a series of imperf. stamps in 1919, which had a short life.
5. *Russian Refugee's Post:* Stamps of Russia, South Russia, Russian Levant, and the Ukraine were o/p and surcharged for use in refugee camps in Turkey and elsewhere after the evacuation of the Crimea in 1921 by General Wrangel's South Russian Volunteer Army.

South Shetlands. Group of British islands in the Antarctic, formerly part of the Falkland Islands Dependencies whose first issue of 1944 included a set of overprints for the South Shetlands. Since 1963 the islands have formed part of the British Antarctic Territory (q.v.). Area: about 1,800 sq. m.

South Viet-Nam. See under 'Viet-Nam'.

South West Africa. Former German colony, mandated to South Africa after the First World War. The first stamps were German issues overprinted 'Deutsch-Sudwest-Afrika' in 1897; German Colonial designs followed in 1900. In 1914–15 the territory was occupied by South African forces, and South African stamps used until 1923. Since that year South West Africa has again had its own stamps. Many of these, however, have been South African stamps overprinted alternately 'South West Africa' and 'Zuidwest Afrika', or simply with the initials 'S.W.A.'. Distinctive definitives were introduced in 1931, inscribed like those of South Africa alternately through the sheet in English and Afrikaans. On issues since 1953 each stamp has been bilingually inscribed. Area: 318,000 sq. m.; capital: Windhoek; currency: German until 1915; thereafter sterling until 1961; since then 100 cents = 1 rand; pop. (1960): 526,004.

Southern Cameroons. See 'Cameroons'.

Southern Nigeria. Former British colony and protectorate in West Africa, previously known as the Niger Coast Protectorate (q.v.). Stamps first issued, 1901. This first issue appeared after the death of Queen Victoria, whose portrait was shown on them, but nevertheless remained in use for two years. In 1906 the colony of Lagos was 'incorporated into Southern Nigeria. Since 1914 Southern Nigeria has formed part of Nigeria (q.v.), and has used the stamps of that country. Area: 90,896 sq. m.; capital: Lagos; currency: sterling; pop. about 8,500,000.

Southern Rhodesia. Self-governing British colony in central Africa, with its own stamps from 1924 to 1954 and again since February 1964. It was part of Rhodesia (q.v.) until 1923. In 1953 it was incorporated into the Central African Federation, using stamps inscribed 'Rhodesia and Nyasaland' from 1954. Although the Federation was dissolved in 1963, its stamps continued in use in Southern Rhodesia until new definitives appeared for that territory in February of the following year. Area: 150,333 sq. m.; capital: Salisbury; currency: sterling; pop. (est. 1962): 3,849,000. In October 1964 the territory was renamed simply 'Rhodesia', the former Northern Rhodesia having taken the name of Zambia, and the first stamps thus inscribed appeared in the following May.

Souvenir sheet. As miniature sheet, but implying some form of commemorative inscription in the sheet margin, and also including certain items of philatelic interest but no postal validity: for example the sheets issued in connection with STAMPEX each year since 1959.

Soviet Union. See under 'Russia'.

'Sower' (French: La Semeuse). Best known and longest-lived French stamp design. Designed by O. Roty and engraved by E. Mouchon, it was first issued in 1903 with a background of horizon and sunset, and redrawn in 1906 with a solid background. After numerous changes of values and colours over the years, it was still in use in the Second World War. It reappeared in a new version in 1961. Poland's 1921 'Peace with Russia' set is also known by this name, as is the 1923 design of Armenia and the 1954 Nebraska Centenary stamp of the U.S.A.

Sowjetische Besatzungs Zone. (Ger.). Soviet Occupation Zone (of Germany). See illustration on page 258.

Space-filler. A stamp not perhaps of the highest quality, but sound and presentable enough to warrant inclusion in a collection. So called from the wish of collectors to fill the old-time printed albums which included a space for every stamp issued.

Spain. (España). South-west European country, formerly a monarchy, and since 1931 a republic. Its first stamps of 1850 were lithographed from transfers of dies engraved by Bartolomeo Coromina, and the 6 ¢. value is sometimes called the 'Penny Black of Spain'. Franco's Nationalist Revolutionary Government have issued stamps since 1936. Area: 194,232 sq. m.; pop. (1960): 30,903,137; capital: Madrid; currency: 1850, 8 cuartos = 1 real; 1867, 1,000 milesimas = 100 centimos = 1 escudo; 1872, 10 céntimos = 1 peseta. See also 'Carlist stamps'.

1903 'SOWER' 1906　　　　SPAIN　　　　SPANDREL

Spandrel. The corner between the central or inner oval, circle, or other frame (not a rectangle), and the outer or main border of the design. The 1897 to 1917 portrait stamps of Canada are examples—the upper spandrels bear the maple leaf or crown and the lower the value in figures. (See illustration above.)

Spanish Guinea (Guinea Española). Spanish colony in West Africa. Stamps first issued, 1902. From 1909 stamps inscribed 'Territorios Españoles del Golfo de Guinea' were issued for use both in mainland Spanish Guinea and in the islands of Fernando Poo and of Elobey, Annobon and Corisco, which previously had their own stamps. Since 1960 the mainland territory has used stamps inscribed Rio Muni, and Fernando Poo has again had its own issues. Area: 10,830 sq. m.; capital: Santa Isabel; currency: Spanish; pop. (1958): 217,000.

Spanish Morocco. Former Spanish protectorate in north-west Africa. Stamps of Spain (without overprint) were used in Spanish post offices throughout Morocco from 1874 until 1903, when Spanish issues were overprinted 'Marreucos' for use there. With the establishment of a Spanish protectorate in the northern part of the country, Spanish post offices elsewhere in Morocco (except in Tangier) were closed, and from 1915 Spanish stamps were overprinted 'Protectorado Español en Maruecos' for use in the Spanish zone. The first definitives followed in 1928. Stamps of Spanish Morocco were withdrawn in 1956 when the territory became part of the newly independent kingdom of Morocco, though a further issue with values in Spanish currency was used in the northern zone until 1958.

Spanish Post Offices in Morocco. See 'Spanish Morocco'.

Spanish West Africa. Africa Occidental Española (Span.). Inscription on joint issues of 1949–51 for use in Ifni and Spanish Sahara.

Spanish (Western) Sahara. Includes Cabo Jubi (Cape Juby), La Aguera, and Rio de Oro—all of which see. First issues were the 1924 'Camel' pictorials. Area: approx. 102,680 sq. m.; pop. (1960): 23,793; capital: El Aaiun; Spanish currency.

Spartanburg. South Carolina. One of the Confederate 'Postmasters'' hand-struck American Civil War stamps was issued here about 1861.

Spaulding's Penny Post. Operated in Buffalo, U.S.A., in 1848.

Special Delivery Stamps. Are of the same general character as Express Letter stamps, and cover the same type of service.

Special Handling Stamps. Secure for the sender an expedited and careful transit handling of the parcels so franked.

Specialist. An advanced and experienced collector who has made an intensive study of the stamps in which he specialises, usually extending to postal history, essays and proofs, covers, varieties, and so on. This somewhat misunderstood term is sometimes wrongly applied to the collector with a limited collection; one is not, for example, automatically a specialist in Canada if it happens that one collects only Canadian stamps!

Specialist Publications and Catalogues. Many highly specialised works of reference are now available to advanced collectors, especially dealing with stamps of the more popular countries and groups. Any collector intending to specialise would be well advised to consult his dealer or local philatelic society for details of the books or catalogues covering his interests. Some well-known specialised volumes, however, are now out of print and difficult to obtain. Many philatelic societies maintain excellent libraries for the use of their members. *The Stamp Lover,* journal of the National Philatelic Society, publishes indices under country headings of specialised articles appearing in the philatelic press.

Specimen. Stamps so o/p (or punch-perforated) are first-printing copies of new issues supplied to the Universal Postal Union for distribution to member-countries for purposes of identification, and for archives; and for distribution on occasion to postmasters for similar reasons. They are often 'remaindered' and thus come on to the market. In the case of high values (and Australia is a case in point) these can be very useful 'space-fillers' and legitimately collected.

Speculation in Stamps. There is a certain satisfaction in having acquired a stamp or set that eventually appreciates to a marked degree, but this often leads to speculation which not only vitiates the hobby and leads to an unhealthy interest in stamp-collecting as a means to a financial end, but unsettles the market upon occasion, and more often than not leads to serious monetary loss. Stamp collecting as a speculative business is no longer a hobby, needs expert knowledge, and wide and long experience, and is 'chancy', even for the expert—the amateur is strongly advised not to dabble.

Speculative Issues. Are stamps for which no adequate postal use or excuse exists, published purely for gain at the expense of the collector. In modern times, San Marino, Roumania, and Spain—to mention only three—have produced issues which have been obviously designed to augment depleted national coffers with monies derived from sales other than for postal franking purposes. See 'Seebeck'.

Spence & Brown. Operators of the Philadelphia Express Post, in the U.S.A., for which local stamps were issued in 1848.

Sperati. Jean de Sperati, modern French forger specialising in lithographed copies of lithoed stamps. Published an apologia in his book, 'Against the Experts'. On 25 July 1952 the Paris Court of Appeal confirmed the sentence imposed upon him by the Seine Tribunal of 2 years imprisonment, fine of 12,000 francs, and damages of 500,000 francs to the Chambre Syndicale des Negociants en Timbres-Poste. He died in April 1957 aged 73. His forgeries are of a high standard of workmanship and not easily detected. The following is a list of countries whose stamps Sperati is known to have forged. The figures indicate the number of different reproductions he is known to have made but, in some cases, he reproduced more than one sheet position of the same stamp.

British Empire: Great Britain (4), Australia (1), Bahamas (2), Barbados (1), Bermuda (1), British Columbia (3), British East Africa (3), British Honduras (2), Cape of Good Hope (1), Ceylon (8), Cyprus (4), Dominica (1), Gibraltar (7), Gold Coast (3), Hong Kong (2), India (5), Lagos (3), Malta (1), Mauritius (4), Montserrat (1), Nevis (3), Newfoundland (12), Papua (1), St. Christopher, St. Lucia (2), Sierra Leone (1), Southern Nigeria (2), Tasmania (1), Tobago (2), Tonga (3), Transvaal (1), Uganda (1), and Western Australia (1).

Foreign: Argentina (3), Buenos Aires (18), Austria (5), Belgium (2), Congo (1), Bolivia (3), Brasil (2), Colombia and States (14), Dominican Republic (5), Finland (1), France (89), Baden (3), Bavaria (10), Bergedorf (1), Bremen (9), Brunswick (2), Hanover (4), Lübeck (1), Mecklenburg-Schwerin (1), Oldenburg (17), Saxony (7), Thurn and Taxis (1) Wurttemberg (2), Greece (3), Guatemala (1), Hungary (3), Modena (2), Naples (3), Neapolitan Provinces (2), Parma (6), Roman States (3), Sardinia (8), Sicily (6), Tuscany (3), Italian Levant (1), Luxembourg (2), Mexico (3), Monaco (1), Panamá (1), Paraguay (1), Peru (2), Persia (2), Mozambique (1), Roumania (5), Wenden (3), Russian Levant (1), San Marino (2), Spain (80), Cuba (3), Elobey (1), Fernando-Poo (1), Philippine Islands (10), Porto Rico (6), Rio de Oro (1), Sweden (7), Switzerland (73), Turkey (9), U.S.A. (5), Confederate States (3), Hawaii (5), and Uruguay (41).

The B.P.A. published a book in September 1954 containing a check list of all the Sperati dies with proofs and specimens of finished stamps and of forged cancellations in a limited edition of 500 copies at £25 per volume.

Spidsbergen. See 'Spitzbergen' below.

Spitzbergen (also Spitsbergen, Spidsbergen). Arctic island, officially part of Norway since 1925 though the first Norwegian post office was opened in 1909. A shipping company issued two local stamps in 1896 to defray the cost of transporting mail to the Norwegian mainland. In 1897–8 Captain W. Bade, master of a ship on the Spitzbergen run, produced labels inscribed 'Arctische Post' and 'Polar Post' which he distributed to his passengers as souvenirs, but they had no postal validity. Various other Spitzbergen labels appeared in the period up to the First World War but these too were valueless for postage and were mementoes intended for sale to tourists either on the island or on board ship. In 1907 a French Arctic expedition on Spitzbergen produced a stamp-like label which was sold in aid of expedition funds. For most of the Second World War Spitzbergen was held by the Free Norwegian Forces, using the stamps of the exiled Norwegian Government in London.

FRANCE U.S.A. JAPAN

SPORTS ON STAMPS

Split. Stamp bisected, quartered, or otherwise 'split' to pay postage to the appropriate proportion of the original face value.

'Spoon' Cancellations. G.B. duplex cancels combining an office number with a named and dated canceller. Introduced at Hull in December 1843, remaining in use for about thirteen years. Nicknamed thus on account of their shape.

Spoorwegen. (Flemish). Trackway, or railroad. By rail. Rail-post parcels stamps of Belgium.

Sports on Stamps. One of the most popular subjects for a thematic collection. Since Greece issued special stamps for the first modern Olympic Games in 1896, almost every type of sporting pastime has been depicted on stamps, and more are added to their number every year. Several books have been published on the subject.

Spray Watermark. The 'Spray of Rose' (to give it its full name) is one of the early G.B. watermarks and depicts a simplified rose bloom on a two-leaved stem—the rose of England, presumably. It first appeared on the 1867 3d. rose of Queen Victoria, and was used until 1873. See also: 'Emblems', 'Crowns', 'Orb', and 'Watermarks'.

'Springbok'. The graceful deer of South Africa was first adopted as a watermark on the 1913 issues of the Union. It was also depicted on the 1926–54 ½d. value.

Spurious Stamps. Description applied to any stamps not genuine in every respect; for example, forgeries, fakes, and bogus items.

Squared Circle Cancellation. Used in Canada from about 1893 to 1910 in about 300 different towns, there are two types, both of which are much sought after by postal historians and collectors of stamps of Canada. (See p. 298.)

Squier & Co.'s City Letter Dispatch. Was a St. Louis, U.S.A., local delivery service operating 1859–60, for which local stamps were issued.

Sri Lanka. (Sinhalese) Ceylon (q.v.).

Srodkowa Litwa. Central Lithuania (q.v.).

Staatsvertrag, 1955. O/p on arms-type stamp of Austria commemorating the signing of the 1955 State treaty ending the Allied military occupation.

Stadt Post Basel. Bâle (or Basle) Town Post. Inscription on the famous Swiss 'Doves' (q.v.) issue of 1845.

Stadt Post Berlin. Berlin City Post. One of the temporary sets issued after the allied occupation, 1945, was so inscribed. Berlin had a local stamp in 1873—one of the many then extant.

Stamboul, Constantinople, or Istanbul. In 1884 the letter 'S' was the G.B. canceller for this Turkish city—the southern half of the former capital. It was in use from 1884 to 1914.

Stamp affixing machines. See 'Affixing Machines, Stamp'.

Stampalia. See under 'Dodecanese Islands'.

'Stamp Collecting'. The only British stamp weekly. Published by Stamp Collecting Limited, at 42 Maiden Lane, Strand, London, W.C.2.

Stamp currency. See 'Money, Stamps as'.

Stamp Dealers are the backbone of stamp-collecting and philately, and most towns of any size in G.B. boast at least one. A dealer of repute will normally be a member of one or more of the recognised dealer-associations: The Philatelic Traders' Society (P.T.S.); or The British Philatelic Association (B.P.A.). Not every responsible dealer trades from accessible business premises, as a large proportion of the business is done by mail-order from private houses.

Stamp Edging. The paper surrounding a sheet of stamps is known in philately as the sheet margin.

STAMPEX. Name given to Britain's National Stamp Exhibition, jointly organised by the National Philatelic Society and the Philatelic Traders' Society, and held in London each March.

Stamp Exchange Clubs and Packets. System of circulating quantities of stamps, either by post or by hand, to a list of members. It is really a misnomer, for the aim is to buy and sell rather than exchange; and the so-called 'packet' is in fact a substantial box containing books in which stamps for sale are mounted and priced. Collectors can be either selling members or buying members or both; they can contribute their own unwanted material to the packet at the same time as buying stamps from others. It is a useful method both of having the opportunity of examining a large amount of philatelic material, and of making purchases in the comfort of one's own home. Some packets are successfully operated as commercial undertakings, the organiser receiving a commission on sales; many more are operated by local philatelic societies, in which case the society's funds benefit from the commission. The latter have a considerable advantage in that being locally based they can usually be circulated by hand, thus saving the costs of registered postage. The usual rule is that each buying member is allowed to keep the packet for up to forty-eight hours; he then sends the packet to the next member on the list, remitting the cost of his purchases direct to the organiser.

Stamp Journals. The world's first periodical to be devoted entirely to stamps was the *Monthly Advertiser* (afterwards the *Stamp Collector's Review and Monthly Advertiser*), founded in December 1862. Although this ran to only nineteen numbers, it was soon followed in February 1863 by the *Stamp Collector's Magazine* which continued for twelve volumes. In the same year *Le Timbre-Poste*, published by J. B. Moens in Brussels, became the first philatelic periodical on the European continent. These pioneers were the first of many. The oldest existing periodical today is the *Philatelic Journal of Great Britain*, with a history going back some seventy years, and now published as an advanced quarterly by Robson Lowe Ltd. The principal commercial journals are *Stamp Collecting* (weekly), *Philatelic Magazine* (fortnightly), and *Stamp Magazine* (monthly). House organs of note include *Gibbons' Stamp Monthly* (Stanley Gibbons Ltd.) and *The Philatelist* (monthly, Robson Lowe Ltd.). Societies' publications include the *London Philatelist* (Royal Philatelic Society of London), *The Stamp Lover* (National Philatelic Society), and *Philately* (British Philatelic Association). In addition numerous other publications are produced by a number of societies, study circles, and dealers.

In the United States the leading publications of general philatelic interest are *Linn's Weekly Stamp News* and *Mekeel's Stamp News*, both weeklies in newspaper format; *Stamps* (weekly) and *Scott's Monthly Journal* are in magazine style. The *American Philatelist* is published by the American Philatelic Society and the *S.P.A. Journal* by the Society of Philatelic Americans; both are monthlies. An advanced publication of note is the *Collectors' Club Philatelist*, published monthly by the Collectors' Club of New York.

'Stamp Magazine'. One of the leading British philatelic periodicals, published monthly by Link House Publications, Croydon.

Stamp Packages. Canadian stamps in small sheets enclosed in transparent plastic envelopes, first sold in this form in 1961. Stamp packages are designed to keep stamps unsoiled and undamaged in pocket or purse, and thus fulfil a similar purpose to booklets.

Stamp Societies. Space does not permit of a list of the very many in operation in the British Isles. A very full list is given in the *Philatelic Societies' Year Book* (published by the B.P.A.). Serious philatelists obviously should be members of their local society or club, for it is by these contacts that the real interest and social value of the hobby is manifest. Beginners and junior members are very welcome, and can learn much from the members of such a fraternity.

Stamp vending machines. Slot machines for the sale of postage stamps, utilising stamps in the roll or 'coil'. See 'Coils'.

Stamps as Money. See 'Money, Stamps as'.

'Standing Helvetia'. Applied to the 1882–1907 definitive designs of

Switzerland to distinguish them from the previous types where this symbolic lady is shown as seated.

Stanley Gibbons. See under 'Gibbons'.

Stanley, H. M. The famous African explorer whom Belgium honoured by portraying him on the 1928 Belgian Congo set, commemorating the fiftieth anniversary of his successful exploration of the Congo River and Basin.

Star and Crescent. The badge of Islam, appears on the stamps of many Moslem countries. A six-pointed Hebrew star was incorrectly used in an overprint by Turkey and hastily corrected. Indian stamps of 1937–43 were o/p with a star and crescent for use in Bahawalpur. Pakistani issues of 1948 showed the moon facing right (decrescent) instead of pointing left. This was corrected in all issues from 1949.

'Stars'. The 1854–7 perforated, line-engraved 1d. and 2d. issues of G.B. with check letters (q.v.) in bottom corners and 'stars' in the upper corners.

Staten Island Express Post. Local delivery service at Staten Island, New York, for which local stamps were issued in 1849.

Stati Parmensi. The Duchy of Parma. See 'Parma'.

Steel Engraving. See 'Line Engraving'. The facing of copper or zinc printing blocks or plates with electro-deposited steel (Fr. Acierage) was largely practised in the early days of stamp printing. Such 'clichés' were often called 'steel engravings'. The modern system is to deposit chromium or nickel on such blocks, to resist wear.

'Steel Helmet' Set. A popular Belgian set issued on 15 July 1919. It shows the late King Albert clad in a steel casque or helmet. Also known as the 'Tin Hat' set.

Stellaland. A temporary Afrikander or Boer Republic in South Africa. It issued a set of 'arms' types on 1 February 1884, but later that year was annexed by G.B., and incorporated in British Bechuanaland. All genuinely used stamps were pen-cancelled. Area about 5,000 sq. m.; capital: Vryburg (q.v.).

Stempel. (Ger.). A stamp. Zeitungstempel were Newspaper or Journal stamps. On Austrian issues 1851–63, and on Imperial Journal stamps 1853–90.

Step and Repeat. A photographic method whereby multiple images are projected, or contact-printed, upon a sensitised plate, cliché, or film, so that each image is in exact relation to its neighbours to form a final printing surface for the production of sheets of stamps.

Stereos. Copies of a process-line, half-tone, or line-engraved block or die, produced by stereotyping. An intermediate matrix, die, or papier-mâché 'flong' is used as a mould into which molten type metal is poured. The resulting stereo may be faced with copper, nickel, or chromium to resist wear. See 'Printing' and allied subjects.

S. Tomé (or Thomé) e Príncipe. St. Thomas and Prince Islands (q.v.).

Stitch Watermark. An occasional, unintentional variety caused by the impress of the stitches joining the 'endless' wire mesh band employed in paper-making.

Stock Book. Stock or duplicate books are obtainable in which loose stamps can be temporarily stored. The normal type consists of stout manila or card pages provided with transparent plastic or tracing linen strips with one edge glued, behind which the stamps are securely held and displayed. A very necessary adjunct for the serious collector.

'Stock Exchange' Forgery. G.B.'s 1/- green stamps, from plates 5 and 6, successfully forged and issued 1870–3 by a telegraph clerk employed at the London Stock Exchange Post Office. First noted by Charles Nissen, a London stamp dealer and expert, in 1898, and later confirmed by a purchase made from a waste-paper dealer by Lewis May, another well-known London dealer, in May 1910. The forger was never brought to justice: he had retired many years before, and proof of the suspect's guilt was almost impossible then to obtain. All are postmarked 'Stock Exchange, E.C.' and dated 1872–3.

Stockholm. Capital city and seaport of Sweden. It had its own local issues in 1856 and 1862, inscribed 'Frimärke Lokalbref' (Prepaid local letter stamp). Pop. (1957): about 800,000.

Stop. A 'full stop' is usually implied (known to printers as a 'period'). Its absence or otherwise on an o/p—for instance—often makes a minor variety. Owing to its small area and fragility, a type 'period' is very liable to snap off during a printing run and escape attention.

'Stormramp/Nederland'. O/p and surcharge on stamps of Suriname in aid of victims of flood damage, Holland, 1953.

Straight Edge. When the outer edge of a sheet of stamps is not perforated, marginal copies will have at least one straight edge—the corner copies having two, at right angles to each other. The early stamps of Canada and the U.S.A. and their modern booklet panes are examples. The *coil* stamps of these countries, and of Sweden, for instance, also show two *opposed* straight edges—these are known as 'imperf. sides', and not as straight edged. The booklet stamps of G.B. and other countries often have one or more inadvertent straight edges due to close trimming by the knife-guillotine in the final making up.

Straits Settlements. Former British colony in Malaya, which included Singapore, Penang, Province Wellesley, the Dindings, Malacca; and the dependencies: Cocos or Keeling Islands, Christmas Island (q.v.), and Labuan. Its first issues were stamps of India o/p with a crown and surcharged in cent values in 1867. Prior to this, stamps of British India postmarked B172 (Singapore), B147 (Penang), and B109 (Malacca) were in use without o/p. Its 1936–41 issues were superscribed 'Malaya', and they were o/p during the Japanese occupation 1942–5. Area: 1,356 sq. m.; pop.: about 1½ million; capital: Singapore; currency: 100 cents = 1 Straits or

Malayan dollar. In 1946 the Colony was dissolved. Penang and Malacca are now in the Federation of Malaya; Labuan was transferred to British North Borneo; Singapore is now a self-governing state, and Christmas Island is now administered by Australia. See 'Singapore', 'Penang', 'Malaya', etc.

Straordinario. (Ital.). Special. The newspaper-tax stamps of Tuscany 1854 were inscribed 'Bollo Straordinario Per Le Poste'. Such journals were for delivery by express messenger.

'Stratosphere' Stamps. Belgium, Poland, and Russia have issued special stamps to commemorate record-breaking stratosphere balloon flights. The 'Piccard' 1932 set of Belgium, Poland's (miniature sheet) 1938, and Russia's Stratostat 'U.S.S.R.' set of 1933.

'Strike'. A hand-stamp impression on cover or stamp.

Stringer & Morton's City Despatch. A local mail service of Baltimore, U.S.A., for which local stamps were issued in 1850.

Strip. Three or more unsevered stamps in a horizontal or vertical row.

Study Circle. A group of collectors who meet or correspond to advance their mutual interest in a particular group of stamps; virtually another name for a small specialised society. Meetings of study circles are frequently arranged in connection with philatelic congresses and exhibitions.

Stuffed cover. A first-day or other special cover which has had a stiffening card inserted to ensure safe passage through the cancelling machine, and in transit.

Su. Overprinted on the SCADTA semi-official airmails of Colombia, these letters indicate that the stamp is a consular overprint sold in Sweden.

Subject Collecting. A popular 'thematic' form of stamp collecting, or 'selecting', in which stamps of various subjects, irrespective of country of origin, colours or values, are selectively collected. Thus, a keen naturalist might concentrate on zoology, and/or botany; a student of heraldry on armorial issues, crests, flags, etc.; while one with a mechanical bent might collect only aeroplanes, railway engines and trains, or mechanically-propelled road vehicles; or bridges, dams, aqueducts and other engineering structures. A nautical collection of shipping both ancient and modern, with or without canoes, small boats and yachts, could attain quite large proportions. Famous personages; monarchs and rulers; musicians and artists; works of art: famous buildings and architecture; churches and cathedrals; old castles and ruins; fish and waterfowl; landscapes; waterfalls and rivers; and many other 'themes' have formed the subject collections of the past, and given great satisfaction and joy to their devotees. See also 'Topicals', and 'Thematics'.

Submarine Mail and Stamps. There have been several authenticated instances of a special philatelic nature, such as the Italian Bordeaux issues (see 'Italia Repubblicana Fascista Base Atlantica'), and the German Aegean Islands service (see 'Inselpost').

Sucré. South American unit of currency. In Ecuador it equals 100 centavos.

Sudan. North African territory until recently jointly administered as a condominium by G.B. and Egypt, but was proclaimed a sovereign independent republic in December 1955. Its first issues were stamps of Egypt o/p in Arabic and English ('Soudan'), on 1 March 1897. The famous 'Camel' series, designed by the late Col. E. A. Stanton, C.M.G., celebrated fifty years of continuous use in 1948. Area of 967,500 sq. m.; pop. (est. 1963): 12,831,000, but there are many nomads; capital: Khartoum; currency: 1,000 milliemes = 100 piastres = 1 pound Egyptian (1E£); 975 milles = £1 British; since 1956; 1,000 milliemes (10 Ryals) = £1S (Sudanese).

Sudan, French. See 'French Soudan'.

Suez Canal. The Suez Canal Company issued a set of stamps in July 1868 which were suppressed in October of the same year. Suez, the seaport at the Red Sea end of the Canal, used canceller 'BO2' on stamps of G.B. from 1860 to 1879.

Suidafrika. (Afrik.). South Africa (q.v.).

Suidwes Afrika. (Afrik.). South-West Africa (q.v.).

Sul Bollettino. (Ital.). Inscription on Italian parcel post stamp, 1914 on. The half that is affixed to the package card.

Sulla Ricevuta. Is inscribed on the (right-hand) portion of the Italian parcel post stamps—the part retained by the sender.

Sullivan's Dispatch Post. A Cincinnati, U.S.A., local post which issued its own local stamps in 1853.

Sultanat d'Anjouan. See 'Anjouan'.

'Sunburst' Postmark. Scarce Hong Kong type, consisting of a circle of long and short radials. Place of use not as yet recorded.

Sunday Delivery Stamps. Bulgaria issued special values 1925–9, and again in 1942, for compulsory use on mail posted on Sundays and public holidays. The funds raised went to charity. Belgium attached labels or tablets to her 1893–1914 stamps which enjoined the postman 'Do Not Deliver On Sunday'—see 'Dominical Labels'.

Sungei Ujong. Former sultanate of Malaya. Stamps of Straits Settlements were overprinted for use there from 1878. Definitives followed in 1891–5 in which the name of the country was abbreviated to 'S. Ujong'. Stamps of Sungei Ujong were withdrawn in 1895 when the territory was incorporated into Negri Sembilan.

Suomi. Finland (q.v.).

Surcharge. An overprint which alters (or in rare cases confirms) the original face value of the stamp. In charity stamps the term is also often

SUOMI   SURCHARGE   SVERIGE

used to denote the amount charged over and above the postal value; in this sense, also known as a surtax.

Surface-Coloured Paper. Paper coloured on one side or surface superficially (sometimes—when glossy—known as enamelled papers), as opposed to paper coloured right through—pulp-dyed in the mass. The 'White-back' stamps (q.v.) are printed on paper of this character.

Surface Printing. Any printing method by which the ink is transferred from the surface of the plate to the paper. In practice the philatelic meaning of 'surface printed' is usually taken to be the same as 'typographed'—i.e. printed by letterpress.

Surinam, or Suriname. Netherlands colony also known as Dutch Guiana. Lies between the British and French Guianas, on the north-east coast of South America. Its first issues were William III definitives of 1873. Area: 55,143 sq. m.; pop. (est. 1957): 225,000; capital Paramaribo; Dutch currency.

Surtax. A value additional to the postal rate on a charity stamp.

Susse Perforation. Applied in 1861 to the imperf. stamps of France. A coarse, p. 7, unofficially used by Susse Frères, stationers and licensed stamp vendors of Paris, as a convenience for their customers.

Sverige. Sweden (q.v. below).

Swart's City Dispatch Post. One of the largest and best known local posts of New York, U.S.A. From 1849 to 1853 it issued a number of 'local' stamps.

Swaziland (Swazieland). British protectorate in southern Africa, lying between Transvaal and Portuguese East Africa. The first stamps were issues of the South African Republic (Transvaal) overprinted 'Swazieland' in October 1889, authorised by a provisional government set up under the joint protection of Great Britain and the South African Republic. In 1894, under a convention, Swaziland was placed under the administration of the Republic. In November of that year the overprints were withdrawn. In 1906 the protectorate was separated from Transvaal and since then has been under the authority of a British High Commissioner. Since 1933 Swaziland has again had its own stamps. Area: 6,705 sq. m.; capital:

SWAZILAND SYRIA SWITZERLAND

Mbabane; currency: sterling until 1961, thereafter 100 cents = 1 rand; pop. (est. 1962): 280,300.

Sweat Box. See 'Humidor'.

Sweden. Sverige. Kingdom of north Europe, and although united under one monarchy with Norway until 1905, has always issued its own stamps, the first of which appeared on 1 July 1855. Area: 158,486 sq. m.; pop. (1960): 7,495,316; capital: Stockholm (q.v.); currency: 1855, 48 skilling banco = 1 rixdaler; 1858, 100 öre = 1 riksdaler; 1878, 100 öre = 1 krona.

Swiss Pioneer (Semi-official) Airmails. Stamps to inaugurate and frank first flight local mails were sold in aid of the Swiss National Military Aviation Fund in 1913. There were local designs for the following twelve centres: Aarau, Basel, Berne, Herisau, Burgdorf, Langnau, Laufen, Liestal, Lugano, Olten, Sion, and Solothurn. The 1933 International Philatelic Congress ruled them to be semi-officials.

Switzerland (Helvetia). Federal republic of central Europe, divided into cantons (provinces). Stamps for internal use were first issued by the cantonal administrations of Zürich (March 1843—the second stamp-issuing authority in the world), Geneva (October 1843), and Basle (1845), The first definitives for the entire country followed in 1850. In philately Switzerland is noted for its annual 'Pro Juventute' charity stamps (of which the first appeared in 1913), for its Soldiers' stamps, and for its Hotel Posts. Area: 15,941 sq. m.; capital: Berne; currency: 100 rappen, now centimes = 1 Swiss franc; pop. (1960): 5,429,061.

Sydney 'Views'. The first issues of New South Wales of January 1850 show what purports to be a view of the capital. As each stamp was engraved separately on the plate, and no less than three artists were engaged on the work, the varieties are many, and they are a philatelic study in themselves.

Syllabics. Japanese numbers, or syllabic-alphabetical characters, the kata kana, were inscribed in minute characters upon the issues of 1874, and were presumably a Japanese system of plate numbering. These 'secret marks' identify this particular issue, and distinguish it from the 1872–3 set of the same designs. See illustration below, also 'Kata kana' and 'Secret marks'.

イ	ロ	ハ	ニ	ホ	ヘ	ト	チ	リ	ヌ	ル	ヲ	
i	ro	ha	ni	ho	he	to	chi	ri	nu	ru	o	
1	2	3	4	5	6	7	8	9	10	11 .	12	
ワ	カ	ヨ	タ	レ	ソ	ツ	子	ナ	ラ	ム		KATA
wa	ka	yo	ta	re	so	tsu	ne	na	ra	mu		KANA
13	14	15	16	17	18	19	20	21	22	23		

Syncopated Perfs.   See 'Interrupted Perfs.'.

Syndicato Condor.   1927 private issues of the Condor Company of Brasil who had a government airmail contract. Stamps so inscribed paid the authorised airmail surtax but have status in few catalogues.

Synoptic.   Term applied to a simplified form of precancel (q.v.) collecting where one specimen of a type or class of stamp only is collected.

Syria (Syrie).   Arab state on the eastern shore of the Mediterranean, formerly part of the Turkish Empire. It was under French Mandate 1919–41 (as an autonomous republic from 1934) and thereafter independent. The first Syrian stamps were French issues overprinted 'T.E.O.' (Territoires Ennemies Occupés) in 1919. 'Syrie' overprints followed in 1920, and the first definitives in 1925. In February 1958 Syria joined with Egypt to form the United Arab Republic, and Syrian stamps at this period were inscribed 'U.A.R.'. This union ended in November 1961, and since then Syria has again been independent under the style of Syrian Arab Republic. Area: 71,210 sq. m.; capital: Damascus; currency: 40 paras = 10 milliemes = 100 centimes = 1 piastre; 100 piastres = 1 Syrian pound; pop. (est. 1962): 5,500,000.

Szechwan.   Province of China on the borders of Tibet, which because of currency depreciation had its own o/p issues of China in 1933–4. It has an area of 218,533 sq. m.; pop. (1953): 62,303,999; capital: Cheng-tu. See also 'Tchongking'.

Szegedin.   The 'Szegedin' issue of Hungary was an anti-Bolshevik provisional government set of o/p Hungarian stamps which appeared when the Bolshevik regime ended in the university city of Szeged in 1919.

Cyrillic

'S' in Cyrillic is the letter 'C', thus:
C.C.C.P. = S.S.S.R., known to us as the U.S.S.R.—the Union of Socialist Soviet Republics.

Modern Greek also uses the 'C' as the equivalent of the English 'S'. The Sigma (Σ) alternates, thus ΕΛΛΑΣ = Hellas (Greece). ΣΑΜΟΥ: Samos (see below).

SAMOS

SQUARED CIRCLE CANCELS:—(Canada 1893 to c 1910).

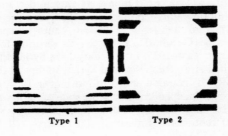

Type 1   Type 2

'T'   'TABLET'   TANGANYIKA   TANGIER

T

'T'. (Fr. Taxe). O/p on a postage stamp, or hand-struck on cover or stamp, indicates postage due, and is affixed or stamped upon insufficiently paid mail. Is recognised internationally as an alternative to stamps specially printed for the purpose. The letter within a circle o/p on stamps of Peru of 1884 indicates a local provisional for Huacho. Tasmanian 'officials' had the letter as an initial punch-perforated in general issues. The 1901–22 'dues' of the Dominican Republic carried the letter in all four corners, but the 1951 design shows the letter superimposed upon an envelope.

T.E.O. (Fr. Territoires Ennemies Occupés). O/p on French stamps for Syria, 1919.

TF. (Afrik.). Telegraaf. O/p on stamps of Orange Free State indicating telegraphic use. See also: 'AT', and 'Telegraph Stamps'.

T.H. Perforated initials on stamps of Hawaii indicate official use, and mean 'Territory of Hawaii'.

T-L. Tonga Royal wedding o/p 1899. T = Taufa'ahau, the groom, and L = Lavinia, the bride.

T.P.O. Travelling Post Office.

T.R.D. Temporary Rubber Datestamp.

T. & T. Or 'T.'nT'. (U.S.A.). Town and type. A form of precancel (q.v.) collecting.

Tab. Coupon, Dominical label (q.v.), or other attachment to a stamp.

'Tablet'. French colonial keytype, a 'Mouchon' (q.v.) design, also known as 'Peace and Navigation' (q.v.).

Tahiti. French island in the Pacific, now part of French Polynesia. Its first stamps were French Colonial keytypes overprinted in 1882. In 1903 a series of Tahiti overprints on stamps of Oceanic Settlements was introduced. The last stamps listed under Tahiti are Red Cross overprints of 1915. Since then the island has used the stamps first of Oceanic Settlements and latterly of French Polynesia.

Taille Douce. (Fr.). Copper plate. In full; gravure en taille douce = copper-plate engraving. In philately, the French equivalent to line-engraving (q.v.) and printing, as applied to stamp production.

Taiwan. Formosa (q.v.).

Takca. (Bulgaria); Taxa (Roumania); or Taxse (Albania) all indicate 'Postage Due'. See 'T' above.

Tanganyika. East African territory formerly a German colony known as German East Africa (q.v.), placed under British mandate after the First World War and now an independent republic within the British Commonwealth. First issues under the British regime were those of Mafia (q.v.), in 1915. In 1916 Nyasaland stamps were overprinted N.F. (standing for Nyasa-Rhodesian Force) for use in the areas taken from the Germans, and in the following year stamps of Kenya overprinted G.E.A. (German East Africa) were introduced. The first Tanganyika definitives followed in 1922. From 1935 to 1961 Tanganyika used the combined issues of Kenya, Uganda, and Tanganyika, but since securing independence has again had its own separate stamps. Area: 361,800 sq. m.; capital: Dar es Salaam; currency: 100 cents = 1 shilling; 20 shillings = £1. (since 1917); pop. (est. 1962): 9,400,000. In 1964 the United Republic of Tanganyika and Zanzibar (also known as Tanzania) was formed, but stamps thus inscribed have at the time of writing been used in Tanganyika only.

Tanger. Tangier, see below. Stamps thus overprinted or inscribed were issued by the French and Spanish authorities for use at the post offices formerly operated by those countries in Tangier.

Tangier (French and Spanish: Tanger). City and port of Morocco, North Africa, which became an international zone in 1912 when the rest of the country was divided into French and Spanish protectorates. Its status was confirmed by a convention in 1924. Britain, France, and Spain (also Germany until 1914) all operated post offices in Tangier, using the same stamps as the respective nations' other post offices in Morocco. French Morocco stamps specifically overprinted for use in Tangier first appeared in 1918, Spanish stamps similarly in 1926, and British stamps in 1927. (The latter are usually catalogued under Morocco Agencies.) In 1948 the Spanish introduced definitives for use in Tangier. The French and Spanish offices were closed in 1956 when Tangier was reincorporated in Morocco and the independence of that country recognised. The British office continued to function until April 1957, finally closing a few weeks after celebrating its centenary with a long series of commemorative overprints. See also under 'Morocco' and 'Morocco Agencies'.

Tannu-Tuva. See under 'Touva'.

Tanzania. See under Tanganyika above.

'Tapling' Collection. Britain's national stamp collection formed by the late Thomas Keay Tapling, a former Vice-President of the Royal Philatelic Society, London, and bequeathed by him on his death in 1891. It is housed in specially constructed cases and cabinets in the King's Library at the British Museum, London. It embraces the £3,000 'Image' collection, and includes among many rarities the 'inverted frame' swan stamp of Western Australia.

'Tapling' Medal. Silver medal awarded for the best paper submitted to the Royal Philatelic Society, London, by a Fellow, Member, or Associate during the two years preceding the date of the award.

'Target' Canceller. Comprising a number of concentric rings, used by Canada, U.S.A., Mauritius, Denmark, and a number of other countries in the early years.

Tartu. See 'Dorpat'.

Tati, or Francistown. District of E. Bechuanaland Protectorate, S. Africa, mining rights of which were exploited by Tati Concessions Limited. Fiscal stamps were issued in 1895 and are found postally used and cancelled, but were not officially valid for prepayment of postage.

Tasa por Cobrar. (Span.). Tax to collect. Postage due.

Tasmania. Large island off the south coast of Australia, a former British colony now part of the Australian Commonwealth. Stamps first issued, 1853. The early issues were inscribed Van Diemen's Land, the former name of the island; the name of Tasmania first appeared on the 1858 issue. In 1899 Tasmania became one of the first British colonies to use large-size pictorial stamps, issuing in that year a series of attractive recess-printed designs showing the scenery of the island. Tasmanian stamps have been obsolete since 1913, when they were replaced by Australian issues. Area: 26,215 sq. m.; capital: Hobart; currency: sterling; pop. (1958): 336,500.

Tassa Gazzette. (Ital.). Newspaper or journal tax. 1859 issues of Modena (q.v.).

Taxa Devida. (Port.). Tax to collect. Postage dues of Brasil, etc.

Taxa de Factagiu. Parcel post stamps of Roumania.

Taxa de Guerra. (Port.). War Tax.

Taxa de Plata. (Lat.). Tax to collect. Postage dues of Roumania.

Taxe Percevoir. (Fr.). Tax to collect. Postage due.

Taxe Perçue. (Fr.). Tax paid. Postage prepaid.

Taylor, Samuel Allan (1838–1913). A notorious producer of bogus stamps, known as 'The Master Grafter' and leader of the 'Boston Gang'. He was at the height of his fraudulent career in the period 1863–70, and for one of his productions, a fictitious U.S. local, used his own portrait in the design! Among his more audacious frauds was to add his own 10 ¢. value to the then current issue of Prince Edward Island, and to produce a stamp for Paraguay at a time when stamps had not been introduced into that country. He was also responsible for the *Stamp Collector's Record*, the first philatelic publication in North America, which appeared for the first time in February 1864 and ran for more than forty numbers.

Tchad (Chad). Former French colony in Central Africa, part of French Congo until 1906, afterwards using stamps of Middle Congo. A set of Middle Congo stamps overprinted for use in Oubangui-Chari and Tchad

TE BETALEN   TELEGRAPH STAMPS   TÊTE-BÊCHE

appeared in 1916; see under 'Oubangui-Chari'. The first stamps for Tchad alone, also overprinted on Middle Congo, were issued in 1922. Stamps of French Equatorial Africa were used in Tchad from 1938 until 1959–62. In 1958 the territory became an autonomous republic within the French Community (Republique du Tchad), and in 1959 began issuing its own stamps once more. Area: 495,624 sq. m.; capital: Fort Lamy; pop. (1959): 2,600,000.

Tchongking, or Chung-king.   Former treaty port of China, in, but independent' of, the province of Szechwan. China's strategic capital 1937–46. Stamps of Indo-China were overprinted for use at the French post office there 1903–22.

Te Betaal.   (Afrik.). To pay. On postage dues of South Africa.

Te Betalen.   (Dutch and Flemish—to pay). On postage dues of Belgium and the Netherlands, etc.

Teese & Co. Penny Post.   A Philadelphia, U.S.A., 'local' of 1852.

Teheran, or Tehran.   Capital of Iran (Persia). Persian issues of 1902 were o/p 'P.L./Teheran' diagonally in red.

'Telegraph Despatch P.O.'.   The inscription on a Philadelphia, U.S.A., 'local' stamp issued in 1848.

Telegraph Stamps.   Stamps issued for the prepayment of telegraphic charges, up to within recent years, were considered as collectable and were bracketed with postage stamps. Nowadays they are usually specially collected or as a sideline. The issues of the G.B. private telegraph companies: Bonelli's, British & Irish Magnetic Telegraph Co., British Telegraph Co., Electric Telegraph Co., National Telephone Co., and many others will be found in old collections, together with the post office emissions of many countries, and G.B.'s military telegraphs of the Victorian era. Telegraph stamps postally used are, however, most desirable items in any modern collection, but in a footnote under Orange Free State (for example) in Gibbons, Part I, will be found: 'Postage stamps overprinted for use as Telegraph stamps and used postally are omitted, as it is impossible to say with certainty which stamps were genuinely used for postal purposes.' The stamps of Spain found cancelled with a punched hole have been telegraphically used. The notorious Stock Exchange forgery of G.B.'s 1/– stamp in 1877 was found exclusively on telegraph forms. See also: 'AT', and 'TF', etc.

Tellico Plains. Tennessee, issued two typeset stamps during the American Civil War.

Temesvar. Former royal 'free' town of Roumania, near Belgrade, now known as Timisoara. It is the capital of the Bánát (q.v.) and Hungarian stamps were o/p for use by the Serbians when they occupied it in 1919, and by the Roumanians who succeeded them. See also 'Bánát-Bácska'.

Tercentenary. 300th Anniversary.

Terres Australes et Antarctiques. French Southern and Antarctic Territories (q.v.).

Territoire de l'Inini. See 'Inini'.

Territoire du Fezzan. See 'Fezzan-Ghadames'.

Territoire du Niger. See 'Niger Territory'.

Territorio de Ifni. See 'Ifni'.

Téte. Portuguese East African district and town on the Zambesi River, and a military station for which was issued a set of o/p stamps in 1913. 'Ceres' keytypes followed in 1914, but were superseded by stamps of Moçambique, which are now in use. Area: 38,768 sq. m.; pop. 419,147.

Tête-Bêche. (Fr.). Head to tail. Stamps printed upside down in relation to each other. Usually collected in pairs, but often in strips of three, with the variety in the centre.

Tetuan. Moroccan town, and the capital of the former Spanish zone. Stamps of Spanish Morocco and of Spain were hand-stamped 'Tetuan' 1908–10.

Thailand. Independent kingdom of south-east Asia, formerly known as Siam. Stamps first issued, 1883. Up to 1940 the English inscriptions gave the old name of Siam. Since then most issues have included the new name, in some cases given as 'Thai'. Thailand continued to issue stamps during the Japanese occupation in the Second World War. At this time the Malayan states of Kedah, Kelantan, Perlis, and Trengganu were ceded to Thailand by the Japanese, and in 1943 a set of occupation stamps appeared for these territories. Area: 198,250 sq. m.; capital: Bangkok; currency: 1883, 32 solots = 16 atts = 8 sios = 4 siks = 1 salung; 1885, 64 atts = 1 tical; 1909–12, 100 satang = 1 tical or baht. (See notation below.) Pop. (est. 1961): 27,180,000.

ၮ ၯ ၰ ၱ ၲ ၳ ၴ ၵ ၶၷ ၸ ၹၺ ၻၼၽ
1 2 3 4 5 6 7 8 10 25 50 100

In 1882–5 stamps of Straits Settlements overprinted 'B' were in use at the former British post office in Bangkok.

Thematic Collecting. The collection and arrangement of stamps by the theme or subject of the design rather than by the country of issue; known in the United States as topical collecting. See also under 'Subject Collecting'.

Theresienstadt. A stamp so inscribed, often found used with a Prague (Praha) cancel, was made obligatory by the German occupation authority in Prague for the franking of parcels sent to the Jewish concentration camp at Terezín (Czech) or Theresienstadt, North Bohemia, during World War II.

Thessaly. (Thessalia). Greek province between Epirus and the Aegean Sea occupied by Turkey in 1898, during which they used a set of octagonal stamps in rich arabesque designs.

Thibet. Tibet (q.v.).

Thies. James H. Thies was a postmaster of St. George's, Bermuda, who followed the example of W. B. Perot and in 1860 produced his own stamps for local use. Now extremely rare, they have recently been accorded catalogue status by Gibbons.

Third Avenue Post. A former local delivery service in New York City, U.S.A., for which local stamps were issued in 1855.

Thomond. Labels thus inscribed appeared on the market in 1962, purporting to be the postage stamps of a principality in Ireland. The principality is non-existent; the stamps are entirely bogus and were the subject of a successful prosecution brought by the Eire Post Office.

Thrace. Formerly Turkish, is now divided between Greece, Bulgaria, and Turkey. During the Allied occupation of 1919 stamps of Bulgaria were o/p 'Thrace Interalliée'. Western Thrace was occupied by Greek forces in October 1919, and Eastern Thrace in July 1920. Greece authorised the use of Bulgarian stamps o/p 'Thrace Occidentale', and later, issues of Greece were o/p (in Greek) 'Administration of Western Thrace'. After the occupation of Eastern Thrace, Greek stamps were o/p (in Greek) 'Administration of Thrace', and Turkish stamps 'High Commission of Thrace'. The area was 89,361 sq. m.

Thule. See under 'Greenland'.

Thuringia. Region of East Germany which had its own short-lived stamp issues under the Russian occupation 1945-6.

Thurn and Taxis. For several centuries the most important postal system on the European continent was operated by the Counts (afterwards Princes) of Thurn and Taxis. From small beginnings in northern Italy in the thirteenth century, the system extended into Austria. In 1505 Franz Taxis signed a contract to organise a postal service throughout the Holy Roman Empire, France, and Spain—at first for official dispatches only, but later for private letters as well. At that time it was an undertaking without precedent, but the Thurn and Taxis post not only honoured its commitments but rapidly extended them, providing the most efficient

THURN & TAXIS   TIBET   'TIGER'   'TIN HAT'

postal service Europe had ever seen. By 1625 the system was employing 20,000 couriers on regular routes over the greater part of western and central Europe. In the eighteenth century the Thurn and Taxis monopoly began to suffer from the growing influence of nationalism; more and more governments expressed the wish to run their own post offices. The Napoleonic wars were a major setback from which the organisation never fully recovered. Even so, in the middle of the nineteenth century it was still operating in large areas of Germany, serving those states which did not possess their own postal administrations. In 1852 the first Thurn and Taxis stamps were issued. Because of currency differences, there were two series —one with values in silbergroschen for use in north Germany, the other with values in kreuzer in the south. This distinction was maintained in succeeding issues up to 30 June 1867, when the surviving rights of the Thurn and Taxis post were bought out by Prussia—a tame ending for an organisation which had pioneered Europe's first public postal service. The stamps of Thurn and Taxis, usually catalogued under German States, are therefore of unique interest as a link with medieval times.

Tibet. (Thibet). Central Asian state lying between India and China, ruled by a Dalai Lama under Chinese overlordship since 1720. Its frontiers were closed to all other foreigners for over 100 years, until the British Mission of 1904 forced a passage through to Lhasa. Indian P.O.s, using British Indian stamps without o/p, were then opened at Lhasa, Gyangtse, Phari-Jong, and Yatung. China deposed the Dalai Lama in 1910 and issued o/p stamps of China in 1911 for their post offices in the towns named above and in Shigatse. The Dalai Lama returned in 1912, the Chinese withdrew, and stamps were then issued by the Tibetan government. On 23 June 1954 the Chinese (Communist) government took over the whole of this postal service. Capital: Lhasa; area: 463,200 sq. m.; pop. (1953): 1,273,969; currency: $6\frac{2}{3}$ trangka = 1 sang.

Tied. A stamp is said to be 'tied' on cover or piece when the postmark or cancellation extends beyond the margins of the copy and is legible on the cover itself, thus proving authenticity. This is particularly necessary in the case of bisects (q.v.).

Tientsin. City and port of China. The name appears as an overprint on Italian stamps, first issued in 1917, for use at the former Italian post office there.

Tierra del Fuego. 'Land of Fire' (Spanish), an island off the southern tip of South America, divided between Argentina and Chile. Julio Popper, a Roumanian engineer, obtained a gold-mining concession from the Argentine Government and arrived in the island in 1890 with a group of supporters. He asserted his authority over the inhabitants by force and became self-styled 'director' of the island. In January 1891 he issued a 10-cents local stamp to pay postage within the island and also to the nearest ports in Argentina and Chile. To complaints that the stamp was illegal, Popper replied that it was a voucher redeemable for small amounts of gold! The stamp appears to have been in use for only a short time; though mint examples are still fairly common, copies used on cover in combination with Argentine or Chilean stamps are exceedingly rare. Amid increasing criticism of his dictatorial attitude, Popper died in Buenos Aires in June 1893.

'Tiger' Keytypes. Two British colonial standard designs for the Federated Malay States. The first, showing a stalking tiger, appeared in 1891; and the second, picturing the head of a snarling beast, in 1895. They were inscribed for use by Negri Sembilan, Pahang, Perak, Selangor, and Sungei Ujong. A combined issue for these states appeared and superseded in 1900, and this again had the tiger as its motif, this time facing right and in full—the now famous and popular 'Tiger' set. The first circular, native issues of Afghanistan, the central motif of which is a crude tiger's head, were known to an older generation also as 'Tigers'.

'Tilleard' Medal. Philatelic award, instituted in memory of the late J. A. Tilleard, M.V.O., first curator of the stamps of King George V of G.B., and a famous philatelist. Is of silver and is awarded by the Royal Philatelic Society, London, for the best display of stamps, essays, reprints, or postal stationery given before the Society by a Fellow, Member, or Associate during the two years preceding the date of the award.

Timbre. (Fr. & Span.). Stamp. **Timbre movil.** Spanish fiscals authorised for postal use 1882–97.

Timbre Complementario. (Span.). Complementary stamp. On postage dues of Mexico.

Timbrologie. (Fr.). The study or science of stamps; i.e. philately.

Timbru. (Roumanian). Stamp.

Timor. Island of the East Indies, the north-eastern half being a Portuguese colony. The first stamps of 1886 were overprints on Macao; Portuguese keytype definitives followed in 1887. Area: 5,763 sq. m.; capital: Dili; currency: Portuguese until 1894; thereafter 100 avos = 1 pataca until 1959; now 100 centavos = 1 escudo; pop. (1960): 517,079. The rest of the island of Timor forms part of Indonesia (formerly Netherlands East Indies).

Tin-Can Mail. Method of conveying mail between ship and shore by means of a buoyant, sealed canister, cast into the sea and retrieved by swimmers or canoes. The most famous example was the Tin-Can Mail operated for many years at Niuafo'ou, a remote island of the Tonga group where there was no suitable quay for a ship to come alongside. It appears to have started by about 1890, but did not become well known until the 1930s. Philatelic mail, bearing special cachets indicating its dispatch by Tin Can, became so large that the natives found difficulty in handling it. The swimmers conveyed outward mail to the ship as well as collecting the inward mail. The system came to an end in 1946 when the population was evacuated following a volcanic eruption. Some of the islanders returned in 1958, and the Tin-Can Mail was revived on one occasion in 1962. Another Tin-Can Mail formerly operated in the Cocos Islands (q.v.). See also under 'St. Kilda'.

'Tin Hat' Set. The King Albert portrait stamps of Belgium, 1919.

Tirane/Kallnuer/1924. (Alb.). Tirana, January 1924. O/p in violet on stamps of Albania commemorates opening of the National Assembly 1924.

Tjenste Frimarke. (Swed.). **Tjeneste Frimaerke.** (Nor.). Official prepaid stamps of Sweden and Norway.

'Tl'. (Magyar: Távolsági levél). Inland letter. 'Tlp' means 'távdsági lev. lap' or inland postcard. O/ps on 1946 inflation stamps of Hungary indicating franking power.

Tlacotalpan. Mexican port, with a local 'Postmasters' ' stamp of about 1856.

Tobago. Island of the British West Indies. Stamps first issued, 1879. Prior to this British stamps were used on overseas mail, cancelled at Scarborough with the 'A 14' marking, 1858–60. Tobago stamps have been obsolete since 1896, when they were superseded by those of Trinidad. Since 1913 the stamps have been inscribed 'Trinidad & Tobago'. Area: 116 sq. m.; chief town: Scarborough; currency: sterling; pop. (1960): 33,333.

Toga. See 'Tonga' below.

Togo (Togoland, Republique du Togo). Territory of West Africa, former German and then French colony, now an independent republic. The first stamps were German issues overprinted in 1897, followed by German Colonial keytypes in 1900. In the early part of the First World War Togc was occupied by French and British forces. Stamps of the German Colonial period were overprinted 'Togo—Anglo-French Occupation' by the British, and 'Togo—Occupation franco-anglaise' by the French. From 1916 the stamps of Gold Coast and of Dahomey were similarly overprinted. After the war the territory was placed under French and British mandate. The smaller British zone was administered as part of Gold Coast, using the stamps of that colony, but the larger French zone was given its own stamps, the first definitives under the French regime appearing in 1924. Following a referendum the British zone united with Ghana (the former Gold Coast) in 1957. In the same year the French zone became a republic, and continues to issue its own stamps. Area of the present republic:

TOGO   TONGA   TRANSJORDAN   TRANSVAAL

22,008 sq. m.; capital: Lomé; pop. (1960): 1,400,000. Total area of the original German colony: 34,934 sq. m.

Tokelau Islands. British group in the southern Pacific Ocean, consisting of five clusters of copra-bearing islets administered by New Zealand. First stamps appeared on 22 June 1948. Area: 4 sq. m.; pop. (1961): 1,960. Also known as the Union Group. N.Z. currency.

Tolima. One of the United States of Colombia, South America, which issued its own stamps 1870–1903. It now uses Colombian.

Toman. Persian currency unit 1885–1933. 10 kran = 1 toman.

Toned Paper. An 'off-white' paper, slightly tinted—usually cream or blue —but not definitely coloured.

Tonga. South Pacific group of islands, sometimes known as the Friendly Islands (as named by Cook in 1773). An independent Polynesian kingdom, under British protection, the responsibility of the Governor of Fiji, by assent of the native ruler. Its first issues bearing the portrait of the native king (George I), appeared in 1886. Area: 270 sq. m.; pop. (1958): about 60,000; Australian currency based on the Tongan pound; capital: Nuku'alofa. See also 'Tin-Can Mail', 'T-L', etc.

Tongs. American name for tweezers (q.v.).

Tonquin, Tongking, or Tonking. See 'Annam and Tonquin'.

'Too Late' Stamps. Late-fee stamps to cover cost of special collection and handling have been issued by several countries, and hand-stamps to explain mail delays have been used by Great Britain, India, Trinidad, and many other countries.

'To Pay'. Higher values of British Postage Due stamps are thus inscribed because they are often used to collect Customs duty on parcels from abroad as well as postal charges.

Topicals. American name for thematic or subject collecting (q.v.).

'Tornese' Naples. The famous re-engraved 1860 issues of Naples; so called from the currency in which they are expressed.

Torn Stamps. A slightly torn specimen, which does not show damage when on the album page, is admissible by many collectors as a temporary space-filler, but the modern philatelist will reject such damaged stamps. The exceptions are the issues of Afghanistan which were cancelled by having a piece torn out by the issuing clerk.

Toscano. (Ital.). Tuscany. See below.

Toughra, or tougra. The triple sign-manual, signature, or paraph of the former Sultan of Turkey. In emblematic theory, the impress of his hand. It appears as a centre-piece on the 1863, 1897–1908 issues of Turkey, and as a later o/p.

Touva (Tannu Tuva). Region of northern Mongolia, formerly a dependency of China, which became an independent state under Russian influence in the 1920s, and issued its first stamps in 1926. In the 1934–6 period sets of pictorials appeared which are generally considered to have been produced mainly for philatelic purposes, and though it appears that on rare occasions they were genuinely used through the post, they are not recognised by the leading catalogues. In 1944 Touva was incorporated into Soviet Russia, and since that date Russian stamps have been in use. Area: 64,000 sq. m.; capital: Kyzyl; currency: Russian; pop. (1944): 65,000.

Town Postmark. Name applied to the named cancellers of G.B. in use 1842–4, to distinguish them from the Maltese Cross and 1844 numbered types.

Trade press. Like other trades, the stamp trade has its own trade press (as distinct from the collector's press), available by subscription to dealers only. In Britain the principal periodicals of this type are the *Philatelic Trader* (fortnightly) and the *Philatelic Exporter* (monthly).

Trans-Caucasian Federation. Comprised Armenia, Russian Azerbaijan, and Georgia—Caucasian states forming an independent soviet republic in 1923. It o/p 'arms' types of royalist Russia, and issued a definitive set. These were all withdrawn in 1924, and stamps of U.S.S.R. substituted. Area: 71,255 sq. m.; pop. about 5,851,000; capital: Tiflis; Russian currency.

Transfer. In lithography the multiple images, each representing one stamp impression, or as a part of a stamp design, are laid down on to the 'stone' in the form of transfers from the original. In so doing, the operator is liable to make certain minor errors in placing, slight creasing, re-transfers, and other variations. Sometimes the transferring is done by means of a soft-textured roller which, if not applied firmly, may result in slight doubling of the image. It is during this process that minor varieties appear. In line-engraving (q.v.) a hardened steel roller or transfer die was used (also known as a transfer roller), which should not be confused with litho transfers. See 'Printing', 'Litho', and allied subjects.

Transjordan. See 'Jordan'.

Transvaal. One of the former Boer republics in South Africa, known as the South African Republic (Zuid Afrikaansche Republiek). Stamps first issued, 1869. In the first British occupation of 1877–82, Republican stamps showing the national coat-of-arms were overprinted 'V.R. Transvaal', followed by a definitive series showing the head of Queen Victoria. From 1883, with the republic restored, republican stamps appeared once more. After the Anglo-Boer War these were superseded by issues of British Colonial type in 1902. Transvaal now uses the stamps of South Africa, (q.v.). Area: 110,450 sq. m.; capital: Pretoria; currency: sterling; pop. (1931): 2,238,271.

Transylvania. European district, which prior to 1918 formed the eastern part of Hungary. In 1919 it passed to Roumania, and occupying troops o/p contemporary Hungarian stamps 'Regatul Romaniei' within a double-lined circle, and surcharged in bani. Area: 24,009 sq. m.; pop. (1948): 3,420,829; Cluj is the chief town.

Trasporto Pacchi in Concessione. Parcels carriage by concession or licence. Special rate for large mail-order firms. Inscribed on new (1953) parcels post stamps of Italy.

Travancore. Former feudatory native state of Madras, British India. It issued its own stamps from 1888 valid for internal use within the State. Area: 7,625 sq. m.; pop: (est. 1948): 6,502,000; capital: Trivandrum; currency: 16 cash = 1 chuckram, 28 chuckrams = 1 rupee.

Travancore-Cochin. Combined local anchel service. First issues July 1949. A transitional measure prior to absorption by Indian government posts in July 1951.

Treasury Competition. In September 1839 the British Treasury offered prizes of £200 and £100 for the best suggestions 'as to the manner in which the projected new postage stamp might best be brought into use'. Over 2,600 entries were received, and four prizes of £100 each were awarded, although none of the suggestions was apparently put into actual use.

'Treasury' Roulette. See 'Gladstone Roulette'.

Treaty Ports. In certain Chinese ports some of the European powers formerly enjoyed treaty privileges. Stamps of Hong Kong used at British post offices in the treaty ports (distinguishable only by the postmarks) are keenly collected by specialists.

Trebizonde (Trebisonde). Russian stamps thus overprinted were first issued in 1909–10 for use at the former Russian post office in the Turkish city of that name.

Trengganu. Federated Malay State lying north of Pahang and east of Kelantan. Its first issues appeared in 1910. Its stamps were o/p during the Japanese occupation 1942–3. Area: about 5,050 sq. m.; pop. (1962): 331,154; capital: Kuala Trengganu; Straits (Malay) currency.

Trentino. District of northern Italy, acquired by Italy from Austria after the First World War; also known as Venezia Tridentina. Austrian stamps were overprinted by the Italians for use in Trentino in November 1918.

'Tretio' Error. Swedish 20 öre stamp which, in 1879, bore 'tretio' (thirty) as its inscribed value. Caused by a worn cliché being replaced by a 30 öre design with altered figures of value—by an oversight the value in words was unaltered.

Triangular Stamps have a definite collector-appeal, and to the junior especially, probably on account of their novelty; the Cape of Good Hope triangulars undoubtedly set the fashion, and today there are many examples—enough to form a considerable specialised collection.

'Trident'. The stylised trident design associated with the Ukraine formed the motif of the various o/ps found on the 'arms' types of Russia in 1918. The designs vary, some are hand-stamped, some are printed, and they are found in various colours. Specialists and catalogue publishers identify many of them and associate them with: Kiev, Odessa, Yekaterinoslav, Kharkov, Poltava, Podolia, Kherson, etc., and they form an absorbing study. They have been extensively forged. See 'Ukraine'.

Trieste. Adriatic city and port, part of Austria until the First World War, thereafter Italian. After the Second World War it was occupied by Allied forces, and in 1947 constituted as the Free Territory of Trieste, divided into two zones. Zone A was administered by the British and Americans, using Italian stamps overprinted 'A.M.G.—F.T.T.' (Allied Military Government, Free Territory of Trieste); Zone B was administered by the Yugoslavs who overprinted Yugoslav stamps 'STT—VUJA' (or Vujna) and also issued distinctive definitive and commemorative stamps for their zone. All Trieste issues have been obsolete since 1954, when Zone A was incorporated into Italy, and Zone B into Yugoslavia. Zone A area: 86 sq. m.; pop. (1951): 270,164. Zone B area: 199 sq. m.; pop. (est. 1949): 70,000. See also under 'Venezia Giulia'.

Trinacria. Ancient name of Sicily (q.v.). Sometimes applied to the 1860 stamps of Naples.

Trinidad. Island of the British West Indies. The famous 'Lady McLeod' local (q.v.), of 1847, was the first stamp ever issued in any British colonial territory, preceding by a few months the Mauritius 'Post Office' stamps; it is also one of the few locals to be listed by Gibbons. The first definitives, which appeared in 1851, were in the well-known 'Britannia' design and are noted for the fact that no face value appeared on them until the design was amended in 1859. From 1896 Trinidad stamps were also used in the neighbouring island of Tobago (q.v.), and since 1913 the stamps have been inscribed 'Trinidad & Tobago'. Total area of the two islands: 1,980 sq. m.; capital: Port of Spain, Trinidad; currency: sterling until 1935; thereafter 100 cents = 1 B.W.I. dollar; pop. (1960): 827,957. In 1962 the islands became an independent member of the British Commonwealth.

Trinidad. South Atlantic Island. James A. Harden-Hickey, a French citizen of Irish descent, and self-styled 'Prince James I of Trinidad', established himself on this lonely isle, and actually issued a set of postage stamps on 1 November 1894, as a preliminary to a postal service. The island was very promptly annexed by G.B., and there is little evidence of valid use of these emissions. It is now Brazilian (as Ilha da Trinidade), has an area of 15 sq. m., and is uninhabited. Not to be confused with Trinidad, B.W.I. (see above).

Trinidad & Tobago. Islands of the British West Indies. See under 'Trinidad' (West Indies) above.

Tripoli. Seaport and capital of Libya, the ancient Oea of the 'Barbary Coast'. Italy o/p stamps 'Tripoli di Barberia' in 1910 for use in its post offices in the (then) Turkish territory, and stamps of Libya were in use after the Italian occupation in 1911–12. In 1927 and 1930 special Tripoli Exhibition stamps appeared. Pop. (1954): 130,238. (Tripoli, *N. Lebanon*, is about 40 miles north of Beirut (Beyrouth) and was occupied by British troops in 1918.)

Tripolitania. Province of Libya (q.v.). During the Italian regime stamps for Tripolitania alone were issued in the 1923–35 period, mostly overprints on current commemorative issues of Italy. During the British occupation after the Second World War, British stamps were overprinted 'B.M.A. Tripolitania' (British Military Administration, subsequently changed to 'B.A.'—British Administration), and surcharged with values in 'M.A.L.' (Military Administration Lire), 1948–51. Otherwise Tripolitania has always used the stamps of Libya. Area: approx. 100,000 sq. m.; capital: Tripoli; pop. (1954): 746,064.

Tristan da Cunha. Remote island in the South Atlantic, about halfway between Cape Town and Buenos Aires, a dependency of the British colony of St. Helena. In years gone by ships visited the island only rarely, and the few letters that were dispatched were usually sent unstamped. In the years preceding the Second World War a number of cases are known of stamps of Great Britain, St. Helena, and South Africa used at Tristan, but no stamps were actually on sale on the island. During and immediately after the war South African stamps were used in greater numbers. In 1946 the islanders petitioned the Colonial Office with a request to be supplied with their own stamps, enclosing with the petition a set of ten suggested designs prepared by a meteorologist stationed on the island. The petition was rejected, but a quantity of the 1d. essay, showing a penguin and the Union Jack, was privately printed and shipped to the island in 1947. This essay was unique in showing not only the normal value in sterling but also a 'local value' expressed as four potatoes! These were used as publicity labels; some were attached to envelopes but as novelties only—they had no postal value. Several years later the Colonial Office appointed an administrator for Tristan, and at the beginning of 1952 the first stamps finally appeared—a set of overprints on the current issue of St. Helena. The first definitives followed in 1954. The early stamps were all expressed in terms of sterling, but in April 1961 a change was made to South African currency, 100 cents = 1 rand. In the following October, as the result of a volcanic eruption, the islanders were evacuated to England, and the issue of Tristan stamps ceased. In 1963 the islanders returned, and in April the current St. Helena stamps were overprinted 'Tristan da Cunha Resettlement' for use

TUNISIA TURKEY TUSCANY

on the island. In 1965 a new series of definitives appeared with values again in sterling. Chief settlement: Edinburgh; pop.: 270.

Tristan Relief. Stamps of Tristan da Cunha with this locally applied overprint were issued by St. Helena in October 1961 with a surcharge intended for the benefit of the refugee Tristan islanders. The issue was unauthorised and was withdrawn on instructions from the Colonial Office in London after only a week's sale. Numbers sold ranged from a mere 527 of the 3d. on 2 ¢. to only 434 of the 1s. on 10 ¢. As a result the set of four stamps has become one of the rarest and most valuable of modern Commonwealth issues.

Trucial States. A group of seven Arab sheikhdoms on the Persian Gulf and Gulf of Oman, in treaty relationship to Great Britain. Stamps thus inscribed, first issued in January 1961, were in fact used only at the British postal agency at Dubai. The stamps were withdrawn when the agency closed in June 1963, since when Dubai (q.v.) has operated its own postal service and issued its own stamps. Since then the other Trucial States have each issued their own stamps; see under 'Abu Dhabi', 'Sharjah', 'Ajman', 'Umm Al Qiwain', 'Ras Al Khaimah', and 'Fujeira'.

Tsingtau. (Tsingtao). See 'Kiautschou'.

Tudor Crown Watermark. The type of crown used in the watermarks of British stamps since 1912, and which was replaced by the St. Edward's crown design types introduced in 1955 (G.B.) and 1956 (Colonial Office).

Tudor Rose Watermark. Alternative and incorrect name for the 'Rosace' (q.v.).

Tumaco. Province of Colombia where typeset provisionals were in use for a short time about 1903.

Tunisia. (Fr. Tunisie). Former French protectorate in North Africa. Became an independent kingdom from 20 March 1956 to 25 July 1957, when it was declared a republic. Its first issues appeared in July 1888. Area: 48,195 sq. m.; pop. (1956): 3,440,999, including 255,232 Europeans; capital: Tunis; currency in Tunisian francs up to 1958; from 1959, 1,000 milliemes = 1 dinar.

Turkey. In the early nineteenth century the Turkish or Ottoman Empire included not only Turkey but much of the Balkans, the Middle East,

Arabia, and parts of North Africa. Gradually nationalist uprisings and pressure of the European powers reduced the area under Turkish control—a process duly reflected in new stamps for the regions concerned. Since 1923 Turkey has been a republic, limited to a small area of Europe and the whole of Asia Minor. From the philatelic point of view, however, it is still usually regarded as one of the European group. The first Turkish stamps appeared in 1863, but for many years the Ottoman Post was considered to be so inefficient that several of the major European powers obtained concessions to operate their own post offices in the major Turkish cities, frequently overprinting their stamps 'Levant' for use there. This system was brought to an end by the First World War. In 1920 the nationalist government at Angora (Ankara) began to overprint Ottoman postage and revenue stamps for postal use, and in 1922 issued its own definitives. These were superseded by the general issues for the whole of Turkey following the establishment of the republic. Area: 301,302 sq. m.; capital: Ankara; currency: 1863, 40 paras = 1 piastre; 1926, 40 paras = 1 grush; 1929, 40 paras = 1 kurus; 1948, 100 kurus = 1 lira; pop. (1960): 27,754,848.

Turk. Postalari. Turkish postal services.

Turks and Caicos Islands. A dependency of Jamaica, in the British West Indies. The two groups were politically separated from the Bahamas in 1900, and the first combined issue then appeared. It depicts the loading of salt at Salt Cay, one of the islands' main industries. The combined area is 166 sq. m.; pop. (1960): 5,716; the seat of government is on Grand Turk; British currency. See 'Turks Islands' above.

Turks Islands. British West Indian group south-east of the Bahamas. From 4 April 1867 to 1900 they had their own issues, but these were superseded by the combined emissions of the Turks and Caicos Islands (q.v. below). Area: 10 sq. m.; pop. about 2,000; capital: Grand Turk; British currency.

Tuscany. Former grand duchy, now part of Italy. Stamps first issued, 1851. In 1859 the reigning grand duke, Leopold II, was driven out by a revolution, and a provisional government set up which in 1860 issued new stamps showing the arms of Savoy. They were superseded by stamps of Sardinia in 1861. Area: 8,800 sq. m.; capital: Florence (Firenze); currency: 60 quattrini = 20 soldi = 12 crazie = 1 lira; 1860, 100 centesimi = 1 lira.

Tweezers. Or stamp 'tongs', as they were at first named, are a very necessary item in the philatelist's kit, as they enable specimens to be handled without danger of soiling and contamination from hot and perspiring fingers. They should be made of hard, springy brass, plated with nickel, chromium, or silver (gold plating was once quite usual!). Avoid the sharp-edged and pointed types—the rounded, spade-end patterns are the most satisfactory. Cheap, lightly plated, or polished steel (unless stainless) should be avoided as they are a potential menace. Use them for *all* handling—dexterity and ease come with practice—and the acquisition of the necessary simple skill will be well repaid.

'Twelve Pence' Black of Canada, 1851–2, was a stamp with the value expressed thus as the shilling had differing rates in various parts of British North America. It is one of the world's rarities. See 'Pence' issues.

Two-coloured Stamps. Or bi-coloured, are normally produced from two distinct sets of plates or dies and printed in two operations, although there are now fast rotary machines that print two or more colours in one working. Perfect registration is very difficult to achieve and to maintain throughout a 'run'. For that reason, the central motif (or 'head' plate in a G.B. colonial keytype, for instance), portrait, or illustration is usually vignetted (shaded off), so that the inevitable deviation or lack of consistent registration is not so pronounced.

'Two Reigns'. Stanley Gibbons' Two Reigns Catalogue (published annually) listed the Commonwealth issues of the reigns of King George VI and Queen Elizabeth II only—in somewhat more detail than appeared in Part I. It was replaced in 1965 by the new 'Elizabethan' catalogue.

Two Sicilies. Name given to the former united kingdoms of Naples and Sicily. Sometimes the stamps of these two Italian states are listed under this heading, but are more usually catalogued separately.

Type. In its major philatelic sense and meaning, a type is a basic design that is typical of a set or series. Thus, catalogue publishers, to obviate needless repetition of an illustration of a design that varies only in colour, value, paper, or perforation from its fellows, will depict one value only and refer to it as 'Type No. ——'. Should minor variations of a key design be deemed necessary to illustrate, such blocks will be given a sub-number and lettered 'Type A', 'Type B', and so on—or they may merely be referred to as of similar 'type'.

Type, Printer's. A slight knowledge of the simple classes of printer's type is useful in identifying overprints, the surcharges especially, and the lettering in stamp designs occasionally, thus:

ROMAN	LARGE CAPITALS SMALL CAPITALS lower case	This is a simplified letter made in many 'faces'.
ITALIC	*LARGE CAPITALS* (or caps). *SMALL CAPITALS* *lower case*	A sloping letter of any 'face'.
SANS SERIF	LARGE CAPITALS SMALL CAPITALS lower case	A simple or 'block' letter without cross strokes (or serifs).

Script	**𝕺𝖑𝖉 𝕰𝖓𝖌𝖑𝖎𝖘𝖍**	Outline
	(Gothic or German)	(or 'double lined')

Typeset. A design made up solely of printer's type, rule, and ornaments, etc., such as are in normal use in an ordinary printer's shop, as distinct from a design drawn and reproduced by one of the many known processes. Overprints and surcharges are usually type-set. See illustration below.

Typewritten Stamps. There are at least two instances of stamp issues produced solely on a typewriter—Uganda 1895, and Long Island 1916; and there is also record of overprints and surcharges having been printed by this means. See 'Uganda' and 'Long Island'. See illustration on opposite page.

Typo: Typography. A philatelic synonym for letterpress or 'surface' printing, i.e. printing from a relief (or process) line, or half-tone block; or from electros or stereos produced from such blocks. See 'Printing'.

Typographically Cancelled. From January 1869 to 31 May 1908 stamps of France were required to be affixed to newspapers in the top right-hand corner, to prepay postage, and to be cancelled by being overprinted by at least four lines of type. 1, 2, and (rarely) 4 centime 'Laureated', and 'Sage' types are the usual stamps found thus cancelled. They are often classified as precancels (q.v.), but are really in a class of their own.

Cyrillic and Greek

'T' is the same as in English. The Greek Tau (T). The THETA (Θ) has a 'th' sound.

TYPESET

AN EXAMPLE FROM
EL SALVADOR

UGANDA

UKRAINE

ULTRAMAR

U

U. Used.

U.A.R. United Arab Republic. Initials found on stamps of Egypt since 1958, and of Syria 1958–61.

U.C. Co. A rare Canadian 'local' of the Upper Columbia Company issued in 1898 to prepay charges on letters carried by steamboat between the towns of Golden and Windermere, on the Columbia River.

U.F. Union Française.

U.N. Force (India) Congo. Indian stamps with this overprint were first issued in 1962 for use by the Indian contingent serving with the United Nations forces in the Congo.

UNTEA. United Nations Temporary Executive Authority. Overprinted on stamps of Netherlands New Guinea 1962, during the temporary U.N. administration of the territory pending its transfer to Indonesia.

U.P.U. Universal Postal Union (q.v.).

U.S. Penny Post. Inscription on two rare Carriers' stamps (q.v.) issued at St. Louis, Missouri, in 1849 and 1857.

U.S.P.O. United States Post Office.

U.S.S.R. See 'Russia'.

U.V. Lamp. Ultra-violet lamp for the detection of fakes and forgeries. See under 'Quartz Lamp'.

U-Boat Post. Unterseeboot Post. A stamp was issued on Hela (q.v.) Peninsula in March 1945 to frank mail sent via submarine from this isolated Danzig base to the unoccupied German ports. It has been forged.

Ubangui. See 'Oubangui-Chari'.

Uganda. Former British protectorate in east Africa; since 1962 an independent member of the British Commonwealth. The first issues of 1895–6 were typewritten productions by a missionary, the Rev. E. Millar. These were followed by typeset provisionals in 1896, and the first definitives in 1898. In 1903 Uganda stamps were superseded by those inscribed East

Africa and Uganda (q.v.), later Kenya and Uganda, and from 1935 to 1962 those of Kenya, Uganda, and Tanganyika. Since independence Uganda has again issued its own stamps. Area: 93,956 sq. m.; capital: Entebbe; currency: 1895, 1,000 cowries = 2 rupees; 1896, 16 annas = 1 rupee; 1962, 100 cents = 1 shilling; pop. (1959): 6,523,628. A cowrie is a small sea-shell which has for centuries served as currency in certain countries bordering the Indian Ocean.

Ukraine. Region of south-west Russia which became temporarily independent following the Russian Revolution. Its first stamps were the Trident (q.v.) overprints applied to arms-type issues of Russia in 1918; later the same year the first definitives appeared. In 1920 certain Ukrainian stamps were overprinted for use by the Ukrainian National army; they are catalogued under Ukrainian Field Post. In 1923 the Ukraine became part of Soviet Russia, and its stamps were replaced by Russian issues. Area 222,600 sq. m.; capital: Kiev; currency: 1918, 100 shagiv = 1 grivni; 2 grivni = 1 rouble; 1923, 100 kopecks = 1 rouble. In 1941 the 'Hitler head' stamps of Germany were overprinted 'Ukraine' for use during the German occupation.

Ukrainian Post. Stamps so inscribed (in Russian only, or in both English and Russian) were said to be 'locals' emanating from the British-controlled Regensburg camp for exiles in captivity awaiting repatriation after the 1939–45 war.

Ultramar. (Span.). Beyond the seas. Stamps of Spain for use in her former oversea dominions—Cuba, Porto Rico, and the Philippines, etc.—were so inscribed.

Umm Al Qiwain. One of the Trucial States of Arabia. Stamps first issued, 1964. Currency: 100 naye paise = 1 rupee.

Un. Unused.

Underprint. A tint or fine repeat design or pattern underlying the main design of a stamp, and usually applied as a security measure to render forgery difficult. Examples are 1869 North German Confederation parcels stamps (with the value in minute letters many times repeated); 1922 Latvian; 1923 Estonian—both of which have a coloured burelé (q.v.) background; and the 'Winchester' security paper used for the 1932 airs of Venezuela. Printed matter on the back of a stamp is sometimes, and incorrectly, called an underprint, but is better described as a backprint.

Ungarn. (Ger.). Hungarian.

Ungummed. Stamps issued by countries with hot, humid climates, or without machine-gumming facilities, such as in China, are often delivered and retailed ungummed, pots of adhesive being sometimes provided at post offices. Such issues are normally noted in a good catalogue. Stamps catalogued, and sold, without gum, but normally supplied as adhesives, are usually mint copies to which some misfortune has happened—they have either been salvaged (as many were in 'blitzed' London), have been badly stored, or in some other manner have been stuck together, soaked

| UNIE VAN ZUID AFRIKA | U.P.U. 75TH ANNIVERSARY | UPPER SILESIA | URUGUAY |

apart, and dried. In the eyes of the modern philatelist such copies have lost prestige and value.

Unie van Zuid Afrika. (Afrikaans). The Union of South Africa. See under 'South Africa'.

Union Française Royaume du Laos. French Union—Kingdom of Laos (Indo-China).

'Union Jack' Re-entry. Occurs on stamp L–K on Plate No. 75 of the 1841 G.B. penny red, Die I, and is a doubling of the top corner 'stars', giving the 'Union Jack' effect. It is a much-sought-after variety.

Union of South Africa. See 'South Africa'.

Union Post. A New York, U.S.A., 'local' of 1846.

Union Postale Universelle. The official (French) name of the Universal Postal Union (q.v.).

Union Square P.O. A local postal service of New York, U.S.A., operating in 1852.

Uniontown, Alabama; **Unionville,** Texas. U.S.A. Confederate 'Postmasters'' issues appeared in these towns during the American Civil War.

Unique Stamps are those of which only one known copy exists. Examples: 1 ¢ British Guiana of 1856, and the 3 skilling yellow of Sweden 1855.

United Arab Republic. A political union formed in February 1958 between Egypt and Syria, but dissolved in 1961. The name is now carried by Egypt alone.

United Nations. Special stamps valid for postage only at the post office of the U.N. headquarters in New York were first issued in 1951. They are unique since every stamp is inscribed in four languages—English, French, Spanish, and Russian. The values, however, are expressed only in U.S. currency.

United States of America. Federal republic of North America, also including Alaska (purchased from Russia in 1867) and Hawaii (q.v.), annexed in 1898. United States stamps are also used in Puerto Rico, the American Virgin Islands (formerly Danish West Indies (q.v.)), Eastern Samoa (see under 'Samoa'), the Pacific island of Guam, and also (since the end of the Second World War) the ex-German islands in the Pacific formerly mandated to Japan. The Canal Zone of Panamá (q.v.) is also leased to the United States, but has its own stamps. During the American Civil War the seceding southern states issued their own stamps under the name of the Confederate States (q.v.). The United States first issued national stamps in July 1847, but these were preceded by a number of postmasters' provisionals of which the first was issued in New York in 1845. Since the 1930s large numbers of commemoratives have appeared, sometimes on seemingly trivial subjects but frequently interesting and always of low face value. Area (including Alaska and Hawaii): 3,615,204 sq. m.; capital: Washington; currency: 100 cents = 1 dollar; pop. (1960): 179,300,000.

United States Post Office in China. United States stamps overprinted 'Shanghai—China' and surcharged with new values were first issued in 1919 for use at the American postal agency in Shanghai. The office was closed and the optd. stamps withdrawn in December 1922. From 1867 to 1919 U.S. stamps were used at the Shanghai office without overprint.

United States of Indonesia. See 'Indonesia'.

'Universal' Cancelling Machines. See 'International Cancelling Machines'.

Universal Colours. See 'Colours, Universal Postal Union'.

Universal Postal Union. The U.P.U. or Union Postale Universelle (its official title) originated and was first organised by Dr. Von Stephan of Germany, who convened the first conference of the General Postal Union (as it was at first named) at Berne on 15 September 1874. It aimed at rationalising international postal co-operation, and is said to be the only such organisation that really functions and works in an international field. Most responsible nations are now members. It was renamed the U.P.U. in 1878. Conferences have been held as follows: Berne 1874, Paris 1878, Lisbon 1885, Vienna 1891, Washington 1897, 25th Anniversary Extraordinary Congress: Berne 1900, Rome 1906, Madrid 1920, Stockholm 1924 (50th Anniv.), London 1929, Cairo 1934, Buenos Aires 1939, Paris 1947, 75th Anniv. with special ceremonies: Berne 1949, Brussels 1952, Canada 1957. For the majority of these, commemorative stamps have been issued. See 'Colours, U.P.U.', 'General Postal Union', etc.

'University College' Sets. Issues to mark the opening of the University College of the West Indies by Princess Alice of Athlone in 1951. Fourteen of the West Indian colonies participated, each issuing two stamps in common designs.

Unpaid-Letter Stamps. The original name for postage 'dues', and now applicable only to hand-struck impressions on mail.

Unused. Term that is normally applied to 'mint' specimens, but is equally applicable to one without gum, or to one that has been through the post and missed cancellation. It can also imply a mint stamp that has been frequently re-mounted, and that can scarcely now deserve that title.

Upper Senegal and Niger. Former French territory in West Africa, previously known as Senegambia and Niger (q.v.). Stamps inscribed 'Haut Sénégal et Niger', first issued in 1906, were replaced in 1921 by those of French Soudan (q.v.).

Upper Silesia. Silesia is a district of Europe which, since 1919, has been divided between Prussia, Czechoslovakia, and Poland. Upper Silesia was the subject of a plebiscite under League of Nations auspices in 1921, and stamps were specially printed for the occasion in 1920. The first was a trilingual set, then followed a definitive series picturing a coal mine, and lettered in French. The 'officials' were German stamps o/p 'C.G.H.S.' (Commission de Gouvernement Haut Silesie). Area: 3,880 sq. m.; pop. (1939): 1,582,225; capital: Oppeln; German (stamp) currency.

Upper Volta. Former French colony of West Africa, formed in 1919 from part of Upper Senegal and Niger. The first stamps were overprints on issues of Upper Senegal and Niger, issued in 1920; the first definitives did not appear until 1928. Stamps of Upper Volta were withdrawn on 1 January 1933, when the territory was divided between Niger, French Soudan, and Ivory Coast. In 1958 Upper Volta was reunited to form a new autonomous republic within the French Community. Since 1959–60 it has again issued its own stamps, inscribed 'Republique de Haute Volta'. Area: 105,803 sq. m.; capital: Onagadougou; pop. (est. 1960): 4,400,000.

Uruguay. South American republic, lying between Brasil and Argentina. Its first issues were the 'Diligencias' which appeared in October 1856 ('diligencia' implies either 'carried by diligence'—the predecessor of the stage-coach—or speed). The 1858 issues which followed were inscribed 'Montevideo' (q.v.) the capital city. It was not until 1 January 1866, that the stamps bore the name of the Republic (Republica Oriental del Uruguay). Area: 72,172 sq. m.; pop. (est. 1957): 2,300,000; capital: Montevideo; currency: 1856, 100 centavos = 1 real; 1864, 1,000 milesimas = 100 centésimos = 1 peso.

Us. Used.

Used. Implies a stamp postally used, normally cancelled, and in fair to good condition—in the absence of any qualification to the contrary.

Used Abroad. Stamps used in places and countries other than their country of origin, are so termed. Their diversity is much wider than at first appears. The list given by Gibbons shows how wide has been the world distribution of the stamps of G.B.—the West Indies alone taking up nearly three pages of the catalogue. France has almost as full a world-wide usage, from the Levant to China; while Spain, Italy, and Russia have had their general issues in use in various parts of the world. Enthusiastic collectors scrutinise all postmarks most carefully in their search for specimens, and new finds are constantly being reported. Entires, showing the whole of the postmarking, are the ideal method of collecting. See Appendix III, 'Hong Kong', etc.

Used on Cover. Implies that the stamp in question is on the original envelope, wrapper, label, postcard, or other 'entire', and that it thus displays all the evidence for the philatelist or postal historian.

Cyrillic

U in Russian is Ю; and a near phonetic to the English 'U' is the У, pronounced 'oo', thus:

УКРАІНСЬКА = Ookrainska = The Ukraine.

Greek:

The upsilon (Υ) has a 'u' sound in some words, and a 'y' in others.

| VALLÉES D'ANDORRE | VAN DIEMEN'S LAND | VATICAN CITY | VENEZIA |

V

'**V**'. = Victory (on stamps of Belgium, Norway, etc.), or Valuable (in catalogue appreciation). Overprinted on the SCADTA semi-official air-mails of Colombia, the capital letter indicates that the stamp is a consular overprint sold in Venezuela.

V.R. Victoria Regina—Queen Victoria.

'**V.R' Essay.** The 1840 G.B. 'penny black' with the letters 'V' and 'R' in the top corners was essayed and proofed as an intended issue for governmental and official use, but the idea was dropped. It is now listed as 'Prepared for use but not issued'.

V.R.I. Victoria Regina Imperatrix—(Empress).

Vaduz—Sevelen. A 'local' stamp was issued by the Vaduz municipal council in 1918 to frank letters from Liechtenstein to Sevelen in Switzerland. Inscribed 'Schweizer Post. Vaduz', it prepaid a messenger charge of 10 heller. It was withdrawn after a few months of use.

Valencia. Province of Spain. 'Carlist' (q.v.) stamps were issued in September 1874. See also 'Catalonia'.

Vallées d'Andorre. (Fr.). Andorra (q.v.).

Valona, or Avalona. Albanian seaport for which Italy o/p and surcharged stamps 1909–16. Now known as Vlonë.

Valparaiso Multada. Early postage dues of Chile.

Valuation of Stamps. Various firms of repute and experience, auctioneers, and stamp dealers, are prepared to undertake the valuation of collections for a fee, for insurance or probate purposes, or with a view to sale. Many dealers are also willing to forego a valuation fee if it also amounts to an offer to purchase, and the offer is accepted by the vendor. It should be added, however, that many other dealers do not undertake valuation work, and material should never be submitted without a preliminary inquiry beforehand.

Values panel. The space on a stamp carrying the declared monetary value.

323

'Van Ackers'. Stamps of Belgium (principally 1.50, 2 and 5 franc values) overprinted '—10%' (minus 10 per cent) in 1946, when an attempt was made to reduce the cost of living by that percentage, under the Premiership of M. Van Acker. Many interesting varieties exist, as all post offices had, at first, to make their own improvised o/ps.

Vancouver Island (Vancouver's Island). Former British colony on the west coast of North America, now part of Canada. In 1860 a 2½d. stamp was issued inscribed 'British Columbia and Vancouver's Island'. In 1865 stamps were issued in decimal currency for use in Vancouver Island alone, but in 1866 British Columbia and Vancouver Island were merged into one territory under the name of British Columbia, the stamps of both being used throughout the combined colony. They were withdrawn in 1871 when the colony joined the Dominion of Canada. Area: 12,408 sq. m.; capital: Victoria.

Van Diemen's Land. Former name of the Australian island known since 1853 as Tasmania (q.v.). Its first stamps appeared on 1 November 1853, and bore the inscription until the first issues of Tasmania made their appearance in January 1858.

Varied perfs. Applied to the special horizontal perforations of the 'coil' stamps of Australia, which consist of larger holes in the centre than at the ends, to facilitate separation.

Varieties. Stamps which in detail differ from the ordinary or normal issue fall within this category, and may be minor or major varieties according to their importance—or merely 'flyspeck' (q.v.) and inconstant variations. Thus a printing variety is one that occurs during a 'run', and is often inconstant; but a plate variety, being due to a defect, flaw, or damage, may be recurring and constant.

Varig Condor Eta. Air stamps of Brasil used (under authority) by private airline companies to prepay extra postage in conjunction with, and additional to, ordinary issues.

Vasco da Gama. A Portuguese keytype is known by that name. It is the 2¼ reis value of the 400th Anniversary commemorative set, which marked this old adventurer's discovery of the route to India. It was first issued in 1898.

Vathy. Town on the Aegean island of Samos (q.v.). French stamps were optd. for use at the former French post office, 1893–1914.

Vatican City. Now a recognised autonomous papal state in Rome, created by treaty with Italy in 1929. Its first stamps under the new regime appeared on 1 August 1929. Area: 108 acres (making it one of the tiniest in the world); pop. (1958): 1,000; Italian currency. See 'Roman States'.

Veglia. Adriatic island. See under 'Fiume'.

Venden. Wenden (q.v.).

Venezia Giulia. Area of north Italy, including the city and seaport of Trieste, acquired from Austria after the First World War. Stamps of Italy and of Austria were overprinted by the Italian regime 1918–19. These were superseded by Italian stamps surcharged with values in new currency, 100 centesimi = 1 corona, for use in all the territory acquired from Austria 1919–22. Thereafter the normal Italian issues were in use. Stamps for Venezia Giulia reappeared after the Second World War, when Italian stamps were overprinted 'A.M.G.—V.G.' (Allied Military Government, Venezia Giulia), 1945–7. At the same period the Yugoslav authorities issued stamps for their zone of occupation (Istria), and these are often catalogued under the same heading. See also under 'Trieste'.

Venezia Tridentina. Region of north Italy, otherwise known as Trentino (q.v.), acquired by Italy from Austria after the First World War. Italian stamps overprinted for use there were first issued in December 1918.

Venezolana. Venezuelan currency unit inscribed on 1863 stamps.

Venezuela. Northern republic of South America. Its first stamps appeared on 1 January 1859. Area: 352,143 sq. m.; pop. (1963): 8,143,629; capital: Caracas; currency: 1859, 100 centavos = 8 reales = 1 peso; 1879, 100 centimos = 1 venezolana (changed in 1880 to 1 bolivar).

Vertical. Upright. As opposed to horizontal—often shortened to 'vert.' when describing a stamp's format (q.v.).

'Vervelle' Variety. Of the 1851 1 f. stamp of France is so named after the original possessor of an ungummed sheet of remainders found in the files of M. Hulot, then government stamp printer. The copies are lighter in colour owing to their not having been gummed, and are a prized rarity among French collectors.

Vichy Administration. Stamps of France and some of the colonies issued during World War II have thus been named and classified in some philatelic quarters. They include the Marechal Pétain portraits and other issues of 'unoccupied' France, and the 1941 special issues of Indo-China.

Victoria. Former British colony, now part of the Australian Common-wealth. The somewhat primitive first issue, which appeared on 3 January 1850, was designed and printed locally, and has become known in philately as the 'half-lengths' (so called after the portrait of Queen Victoria on them). Stamps of Victoria were superseded in 1913 by those of Australia. Area: 87,884 sq. m.; capital: Melbourne; currency: as sterling; pop. (1958): 2,726,400.

Victoria. Texas. Had a typical typeset 'Postmasters'' stamp issued during the American Civil War.

Victoria Land. ½d. and 1d. current stamps of New Zealand were o/p for the use of the members of the Scott Antarctic Expedition 1911–13. 24 stamps of each value went to the personnel of the 'Terra Nova', and the remainders were sold at 5/- each for the 1d., and 25/- for the ½d. A signed guarantee was supplied to each purchaser.

Victorian. Relating to the reign of Queen Victoria. In philately the word is also used as a noun to denote any stamp issued during her reign or bearing her portrait.

VICTORY   VIGNETTE   VOM EMPFÄNGER

Victory Stamps. G.B. issued 45 sets of stamps for the Crown Colonies, and all the Dominions issued Peace commemoratives. France, Belgium, Holland, the U.S.A., Brasil, and China were among other countries issuing special stamps, many of which featured the Churchillian 'V' in one form or another.

Viet-Nam. State of south-east Asia, formerly part of the French territory of Indo-China (q.v.). The name of Viet-Nam first appeared on stamps as an overprint applied to stamps of the French Colonial period in 1945, when the communist nationalists set up a republic. This was recognised by France in 1946, but shortly afterwards fighting broke out between the communists and the French which lasted until 1954. A truce was then arranged and French forces withdrew from the northern part of the country. The territory is now divided into North and South Viet-Nam, each government issuing its own stamps. The area under French control, which continued to use Indo-China stamps until 1951, was a monarchy under Emperor Bao-Dai until 1955; since then, as South Viet-Nam, it has been an independent republic. Area of North Viet-Nam: 77,200 sq. m.; capital: Hanoi; currency: 100 xu = 1 dong (1946 issues, 10 hao = 1 dong); pop. (1958): 15,700,000. Area of South Viet-Nam: 66,263 sq. m.; capital: Saigon; currency: 100 cents = 1 piastre; pop. (est. 1962): 14,200,000.

Vignette. An illustration that shades off at its edges to invisibility. It is a stamp-printer's normal expedient to render less obtrusive the invariable slight lack of true registration in printing bi-coloured stamps, or from two dies or plates. Examples are the centres of the 1907–10 stamps of Papua, and the Silver Jubilees of The Commonwealth. In France the term is used to describe pictorial labels of no postal value.

Vilnius. (Vilna, or Wilna, Lithuania). O/p on 1929 issues of Russia by German occupation troops in 1941.

'Vineta' Bisect. Half of a German 5 pf. green (hand-stamped '3 PF') used in April 1901 on the cruiser *Vineta* as a provisional owing to a shortage of 3 pf. values.

Violet Ink Cancellations. Do not necessarily indicate fiscal (q.v.) use, and reference to a reliable catalogue will instance many such legitimate postal cancellations. Stamps of Straits Settlements, for instance, often bear violet rubber-stamp impressions in addition to normal obliterations. These were put on to letters entrusted to coolies to post, to prevent their being purloined and re-used or sold. The usual ingredient of the ink is methyl-violet, which is particularly sensitive to moistening and 'runs 'on the least provocation, so issues thus cancelled should be carefully 'floated off' (q.v.).

Virgin Islands. Group of Islands in the West Indies, divided between Britain and the United States. First stamps of the British Virgin Islands in the St. Ursula design were issued in 1866. Prior to this, between 1858 and 1860, British stamps were used at Tortola on overseas mail, cancelled with the 'A 13' marking. Virgin Islands stamps were superseded in 1890 by combined issues for the Leeward Islands. Stamps have again been issued since 1899, Leeward Islands issues remaining in use concurrently until 1956. Area: 59 sq. m.; capital: Road Town on Tortola; currency: sterling until 1951–2, then 100 cents = 1 B.W.I. dollar; 1962, 100 cents = 1 U.S. dollar; pop. (1961): 7,338. The American Virgin Islands, formerly the Danish West Indies (q.v.), were acquired from Denmark in 1917; since then they have used United States stamps.

Vojenska Posta. Stamps used by the trans-Siberian Czechoslovak Legion in 1919–20 were so inscribed.

Volkshilfe. (Ger.). Folk's—or People's—Help. Charity stamps.

Volksrust. Fiscal stamps of the South African Republic (q.v.) were o/p 'V.R.I.' in this Transvaal township during the British occupation in March 1902.

Volkstaat Bayern. The People's State of Bavaria.

Voluntary Assistance Stamps. Special reprints of Sweden's 1872 issues were o/p 'Landstormen' and surcharged 5 and 10 öre, bearing franking postal power to the amount of the surcharge only, were published in 1916 to provide a voluntary fund for the purchase of clothing for mobilised reservists.

Vom Empfänger Zahlbar. (Ger.). Payable by Addressee. Inscribed on postage dues of Bavaria, 1862–76, and (Vom Emfänger Einzuziehen) of Danzig, 1921–39.

Von Angeli. Professor Von Angeli, court painter, executed the 1887 Jubilee portrait of Queen Victoria that was the basis of so many designs of contemporary colonial G.B. stamps. The 1892 low values of India are examples (see illustration on next page).

Voor Het Kind. (Dutch). For the Children. On the charity issues of the Netherlands and Colonies.

Voortrekker (Afrik.). Literally, one who goes before. In South African history the Voortrekkers were the settlers of Dutch descent who in 1835–6 travelled northwards from the Cape ('the Great Trek') to establish the Boer republics of Transvaal and Orange Free State. They are commemorated on various South African stamps.

Vryburg. Town of British Bechuanaland, which in November 1899 (during the second Boer War) was temporarily occupied by the Boers, who o/p stamps of the Cape of Good Hope 'Z.A.R.' (Zuid Afrikaansche Republiek) with surcharged new values. British troops retook the town in May 1900 and o/p stamps of the Transvaal 'V.R./Special/Post' sideways in black. The 1½d. green of the Cape of Good Hope (S.G. 59) is also known o/p horizontally, but it is stated to be bogus.

VUJA.S.T.T. O/p on stamps of Yugoslavia for Trieste (former) Zone B. See under 'Trieste'.

Vzorec. (Czech.) Specimen. O/p on copies given to Czechoslovakian officials as favours.

Cyrillic

V is represented by the character 'B', and is often equivalent to the English 'W', thus:

ВЕНДЕНСКАЯ = Vendenskaya = Wenden.

VON ANGELI
A STAMP BEARING
HIS PORTRAIT OF
QUEEN VICTORIA

WALLIS AND   'WAR EFFORT'   WAR TAX
FUTUNA

W

W.f. Wrong fount. An error of typesetting, e.g. in an o/p, when a wrong letter of another style or 'face' appears.

Wadhwan State. Former feudatory native state in the Kathiawar district of Bombay, British India, which published a typeset local, the first issue of which appeared in 1888. It has been obsolete since the nineties. Area: 242 sq. m.; pop.: 69,882; capital: Wadhwan (since 1950 renamed Surendranagar); Indian currency. Now in Saurashtra State, Republic of India.

Wallis and Futuna Islands. Comprises the Wallis Archipelago, Futuna, and Alofi, French Pacific islands north-east of Fiji; and a dependency of New Caledonia. First issues were stamps of New Caledonia o/p 'Iles Wallis et Futuna', in 1920. Total area: 100 sq. m. (Wallis group 40 sq. m.); pop. about 6,250 (Wallis, 4,243, Futuna and Alofi, about 2,000); chief towns: Natu Utu on Wallis, and Sigavé on Futuna; French (C.P.A.) currency.

'Wallpaper'. Philatelic slang for stamps, available in sheets, which have little or no philatelic or monetary value.

Walton & Co.'s City Express. Brooklyn, U.S.A., local mail service for which local stamps were issued in 1846.

Wants, and Want Lists. In building up a collection, a normal method is to send or give details of requirements to a responsible dealer, quoting country, values, colours, catalogue reference numbers, whether mint or used, and the quantity of each item—this is known as a 'Want' list S.G. 'big', 'Two Reigns', or Simplified catalogue numbers; or 'Commonwealth' are usual in G.B., and Scott in America, etc., but provided it is clear what catalogue numbers are quoted, most dealers will accept references to any such known publication. In the case of scarce or elusive items, it is advisable to give a top limit of prices the buyer is prepared to pay. Since catalogue numbers are occasionally changed, it is also helpful to give not only the name of the catalogue but also the edition which is being used to compile the list.

'War Effort' Stamps. Both Canada and the Union of South Africa produced sets of stamps known under this heading. Canada's set first appeared 1 July 1942; South Africa's began to appear piecemeal in 1941, and a second 'Bantam' (q.v.) economy reduced dimensions, set followed in 1942.

War Tax Stamps. The Bahamas, Barbados, Bermuda, British Guiana, British Honduras, Canada, Caymans, Ceylon, Dominica, Falklands, Fiji, Gibraltar, Gilberts, Gold Coast, Grenada, Jamaica, Malta, Montserrat, New Zealand, North Borneo, St. Helena, St. Kitts-Nevis, St. Lucia, St. Vincent, Straits Settlements, and Trengganu (Red Cross surcharges), Trinidad and Tobago, and Turks Islands, all issued war-surcharged stamps during World War I. Spain had them from 1874 to 1877 (Impuesto de Guerra), and again in 1898 during the Spanish-American War.

Waterlow. Waterlow & Sons Ltd., the famous London printing firm. were well known for many years as printers of stamps for many countries, Since 1961, however, the company's stamp printing activities have been taken over by De La Rue.

Watermark. A semi-translucent thinning of the substance of a paper base, reminiscent of the local effect of an application of oil or water. It is usually a device, pattern, or lettering produced by the pressure of wire or brass forms, called 'bits', attached to the dandy roll of a paper-making machine. Philatelists recognise various types of watermarks: 'Simple'—when one device only is designed to be impressed upon each individual stamp; 'Multiple'—when many such devices are visible on each sheet, each stamp bearing more than one impression or parts of the device. 'Sheet'—where one large design or name covers a major portion of the whole sheet of paper, and each stamp receives part of the impression only, or even no trace of it; 'Paper-makers' '—reproducing either the name of the maker (or in some cases that of the stamp contractor or printer), or the trade designation of the paper itself; 'Marginal'—on one or more sheet margins (often the paper-maker's name), and which will appear in part upon marginal copies and due to paper 'shift' and by inadvertence; 'Impressed'—a pseudo watermark applied by a die under pressure after the paper is made; 'Gum' —another false watermark achieved by applying the gum by means of a patterned roller; 'Obverse'—caused by a *thickening* of the paper instead of a thinning, thus making the device appear opaquely instead of semi-transparent; 'False'—an effect brought about by lightly printing (by litho) the required device on the back of the sheet in a pale tint; and 'Pattern'— where wavy lines, grilles, diamond mesh, and other like repeat designs are evenly impressed over the whole sheet. According to the manner in which the sheets are fed to the printing machine, the watermark will be 'normal' (as seen, right way up, from the *front* of the stamp); inverted (upside-down); reversed (wrong way round); inverted and reversed; sideways; or 'Stitch' (q.v.). See under their separate headings.

Watermark Collecting. A specialist collection of curious, interesting, historical, and other watermarks can be made. This may consist not of the actual stamps themselves but of photographic 'contact' prints. The stamp is placed in pressure-contact (in a printing frame, for instance) face up on a sheet of bromide or gaslight paper, and the correct exposure will allow of the watermark being brought out with little or no trace or record of the

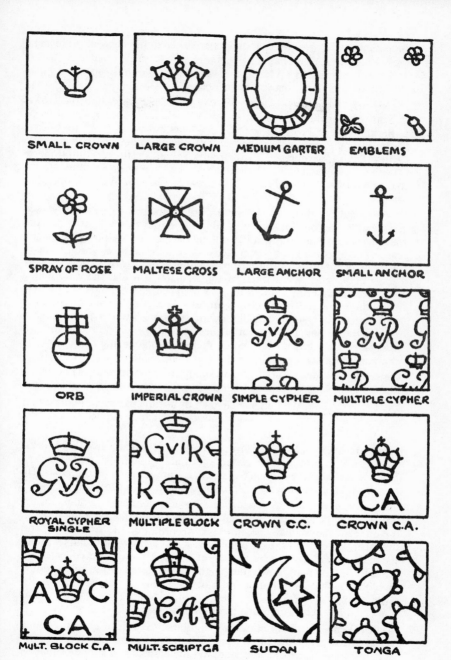

SMALL CROWN   LARGE CROWN   MEDIUM GARTER   EMBLEMS

SPRAY OF ROSE   MALTESE CROSS   LARGE ANCHOR   SMALL ANCHOR

ORB   IMPERIAL CROWN   SIMPLE CYPHER   MULTIPLE CYPHER

ROYAL CYPHER SINGLE   MULTIPLE BLOCK   CROWN C.C.   CROWN C.A.

MULT. BLOCK C.A.   MULT. SCRIPT CA   SUDAN   TONGA

SEE: WATERMARK

stamp design. The print will show the perforations also in detail, and trimmed with a slight margin will be most effectively framed in black. Mounted and written up, such a collection can be most instructive and interesting. See 'Watermark Designs' below.

Watermark Designs. In addition to the small, large, and Imperial crown designs, orb, anchor, emblems, spray of rose, and cypher watermarks of G.B., there have been quatrefoils, crescents, stars (Sudan and India); turtles (Tonga); pineapples (Jamaica); elephants (India and Travancore); castles (Spain); aeroplanes (Luxembourg); shields (Hungary); and many other interesting and quaint designs, all of which have meaning and interest to the philatelist. See 'Emblems', 'St. Edward's Crown', 'Watermarks', etc., above.

Watermark Detection. A watermark not distinguishable at first glance can often be detected either by holding the stamp to the light (when the watermark may show up through the lighter part of the design or in the margin) or by placing the stamp face downward on a black surface. Black trays can be obtained for this purpose. In obstinate cases the application of a drop of benzine to the back of the stamp will reveal the watermark. Although the watermark will also show up if the stamp is soaked in water, this method is not recommended because of the possibility of damaging the design, particularly in the case of modern issues produced by photogravure in which the inks are liable to run if affected by damp. The 'Philatector' is a battery-operated device which employs a set of colour filters to detect the watermark of a stamp placed in it.

'Watersnood' (Inundation). O/p on stamps of the Netherlands on charity issues in aid of the 1953 flood victims.

Way Letter. (U.S.A.). Letters delivered by a route carrier or mailman on his way to a post office were often endorsed or hand-stamped 'Way'. It is also found on ship letters.

Weiner, Jacques. 1945–99. Former designer to the Brussels Stamp Works, and was responsible for the production of all Belgium's stamp designs to 1861. He was also the engraver of the first stamp for the Netherlands. He studied at the London works of Perkins, Bacon & Co. for a time.

Wells, Fargo & Co. American stage-coach company famous in the history of the 'Wild West', which started operations in California in 1852. In April 1861 the company became agents for the Pony Express (q.v.), and subsequently operated similar pony services of their own. Special fees were charged for mail carried by the company, and these were collected by means of the company's own stamps, the earlier issues of 1861–4 including the 'Pony Express' inscription and a design showing a pony rider. Wells, Fargo stamps of subsequent issues continued until 1888. They rank as locals, and are keenly collected by specialists, especially in America.

Wenden (Venden). District of the province of Livonia in Latvia. Though part of Russia until the First World War (and again since 1940), its inhabitants spoke German, and stamps with inscriptions in that language were in use 1863–1901, followed by an issue inscribed in Russian.

West Berlin. The western part of the former German capital, comprising the British, American, and French sectors, has had its own stamps since September 1948. Separate issues have continued even though West Berlin became part of the German Federal Republic in 1951. Pop. (est. 1962): 2,174,000.

West Germany. See under 'Germany', and 'German Federal Republic'.

West Indies Federation. Short-lived federation of various islands of the British West Indies, also known as the British Caribbean Federation. The scheme was abandoned following disagreement among the members. The inauguration of the federation was marked in April 1958 by an omnibus stamp issue, with a common design featuring a map, by all the islands taking part.

West Irian (Irian Barat). Indonesian name for the territory formerly known as Netherlands New Guinea (q.v.), which was ceded to Indonesia in 1963 and since then has used Indonesian stamps optd. 'Irian Barat'. Area: 160,618 sq. m.; capital: Kotabaru (formerly known as Hollandia); currency: 1963, 100 sen = 1 rupiah; pop. (1958): 730,000.

West New Guinea. See under 'Netherlands New Guinea', 'UNTEA', and 'West Irian' above.

West Russia. Stamps of doubtful status were issued by Prince Avalov-Bermondt's government formed at Shavli (or Siauliai) in North Lithuania, in November 1918.

Western Australia. Former British colony in Australia, famous for the 'Black Swan' design featured on so many of its stamp issues. Stamps first issued, 1854. In 1913 stamps of Western Australia were replaced by those of the Australian Commonwealth. Area: 975,920 sq. m.; capital: Perth; pop. (1958): 701,400.

Western Samoa. See 'Samoa'.

Western Thrace. See 'Thrace'.

Western Ukraine. Formerly known as Galicia and once part of Austria, it became temporarily independent as the Western Ukraine in 1919, and used o/p stamps of Austria, etc. It was absorbed by Poland.

Westerveldt's Post. Issued several 'locals' between 1863 and 1865. It operated from Chester, N.Y., U.S.A.

Westtown. A secondary school in Orange County, Pennsylvania, U.S.A., which issued local stamps to prepay letters carried to West Chester, or Street Road, post offices, 1853–70.

Whistler, James Abbott McNeill. American artist. 1834–1903. Painted 'My Mother', reproduced on the 'Mothers' Day' 1934 issue of U.S.A.

White Back. Surface-coated or 'enamelled' paper, in which the base is white. In British Colonial stamps such coloured papers were a war-time (1914–19) substitute for the self-coloured pulp papers usually employed.

333

WENDEN   WINCHESTER   WILDING   WÜRTTEMBERG
              PAPER

The reverse of the stamps printed on these papers is white, hence the descriptive name.

White Russia (Belorussia). Republic of Soviet Russia, adjoining Poland. It printed a series of stamps 1920, for the use of the Ruthenian Army Corps, the postal use and validity of which is in some doubt, and they have also been forged! Now uses the general U.S.S.R. issues. Area: was 48,940 sq. m.; capital: Minsk; Russian currency.

Whitfield King. Formerly a well-known stamp catalogue, published by Whitfield King and Co. of Ipswich, England. It ceased publication in 1952.

Whittley's Express. Was a Chicago, U.S.A., local delivery of 1857–8.

Wilding, Dorothy. Court photographer of London, England, whose portraits of members of the British Royal family have been the bases of design of numerous modern colonial stamps, including 1940 Dominica K.G. VI, 1948 Australia, Elizabeth II, as Princess and Queen, etc.

Williams' City Post. A local letter service of Cincinnati, U.S.A., operating in 1854.

Wilson, Bart., K.C.V.O., Sir John. The present Keeper of Her Majesty the Queen's Philatelic Collections. A philatelist of international fame and author of 'The Royal Philatelic Collection', a magnificent contemporary publication.

'Winchester' Security Paper. An under-printed or pre-patterned paper designed to prevent re-use and forging of stamps and banknotes. Was used for the 1932 airs of Venezuela. See also 'Burelé', 'Safety Paper', 'Forgery', etc.

Windward Islands. Group of islands of the British West Indies, comprising St. Lucia, St. Vincent, Grenada, and also (since 1940) Dominica. Each of these islands has its own stamps and is separately mentioned in this book; but unlike Leeward Islands, there have never been any issues for the group as a whole.

Wing Margin. The gutters (q.v.) of sheets of stamps of G.B. prior to 1880 were perforated down the centre, instead of on either side as in the modern style. This resulted in the central marginal stamps having one wide and exaggerated margin, known as a 'wing' (also colloquially known as 'flappers'). It follows that wing-margined specimens are scarcer than normals, but they were unpopular with collectors of the day on account of their unbalanced appearance, and because they would not fit into the circumscribed spaces provided for them in contemporary albums. They were therefore either rejected, or were cut down to fit into the rectangle; or were cut down and re-perforated. Plating (q.v.) enthusiasts, by reason of their studied knowledge of the check (corner) letters of the stamps of the period, are well on their guard against such manipulated copies. Also known as 'extended' margins.

'Wings For Norway'. An unusual air-combat commemorative issued simultaneously in Norway and in 'Little Norway', Canada, in 1946, as a token of a close liaison during World War II.

Winterhilfe. (Ger.). Winter Help. Charity stamps of Germany and Austria, to aid the poor in winter.

Wmk. Watermark.

Wolmaransstad. Town in the Transvaal occupied by British Forces in June 1900. Stamps of the Transvaal were o/p 'Cancelled/V-R-I'.

Wood & Co. City Despatch. Local delivery service, privately operated in Baltimore, U.S.A., for which local stamps were issued in 1856–7.

'Woodblock'. The 1861 locally-produced triangular stamps of the Cape of Good Hope. Owing to their crudity, it was assumed they were wood engravings, when as a matter of fact they were engraved on steel by C. J. Roberts, a local craftsman. They were an emergency issue to meet the postal needs of the community pending the arrival of delayed supplies from England.

Woon, or won. South Korean currency unit (converted to hwan since 1953). 100 cheun = 1 woon.

World Refugee Year. In 1960 more than seventy countries issued special stamps in honour of World Refugee Year, devoting part of the proceeds to W.R.Y. funds.

'Wotton-under-Edge' Postmark. This little town of Gloucestershire won philatelic renown because the local postmaster, for some unknown reason, filed three horizontal and three vertical cuts across the face of the 'Maltese cross' canceller, thus creating a recognisable (and desirable) postmark variety in the 1840s.

Wove Paper. A machine-made paper with a finely netted texture due to contact of the wet pulp with the wire gauze mesh of the paper-making machine belt. It is a book paper much used for stamp production, especially for the mass-produced moderns. See also 'Paper', 'Laid', etc.

Wreck or 'Crash' Covers. Covers salvaged from mail recovered from shipwrecks, trans-ocean mail-planes, etc., are often given cachets or official labels explanatory of their (often) sea-soaked condition, thus linking the exhibit with the disaster, and of special interest to the philatelist.

Writing-up. Is the embellishment of a page or collection by the addition of hand or typewritten data concerning and descriptive of the stamps displayed. The name of the country of origin, date of issue, reason or occasion—if commemorative or unusual—designer, engraver; printer; paper; printing process; perforation, and even details of the persons, places, or incidents shown on the stamps themselves, are all facts that may be thus inscribed. Enlarged detail (either hand-drawn or photographically reproduced), and maps, may accompany such writing-up, and each specimen may be outlined with an indian ink frame, or mounted upon a rectangle of black paper, but over-elaboration should be avoided at all costs. Essentials are: a balanced, uncrowded arrangement, neat hand-written or typed lettering or script (in black preferably), and all essential facts given. See 'Arrangement', 'Mounting', etc.

Württemberg. Former South German independent kingdom issuing its own stamps from 1851 to 1 April 1920, when it transferred its postal rights to the Reichpost for the sum of 225 million marks and now uses stamps of Germany. Area: 7,530 sq. m.; pop. about 2½ million; capital: Stuttgart; currency: 1851, 60 kreuzer = 1 gulden; 1875, 100 pfennige = 1 mark.

Wyman. W. Wyman of Boston, U.S.A., issued a local stamp to frank mail carried to and from New York, and elsewhere, in 1844.

Wyon, William. 1795–1851. Engraver of Seals to Queen Victoria, and to the Royal Academy. Designer of the 'Wyon' medal, prototype for the 1840 1d. black of G.B.

The letter 'W' is absent from Cyrillic and Greek.

The Letter 'Y'.

Cyrillic

The Cyrillic У is normally sounded as 'oo', thus:—

УКРАЇНСЬКА: Ookraineska = Ukraine (q.v.).

See opposite page.

Greek

The Upsilon (Υ) has a 'y' sound—as in English, or occasionally 'u'.

'YACHT'
KEYTYPE

YEMEN

YUNNAN

Y

'Y'. (Span. Ynterior). The local Havana issue of Spain for Cuba and for Puerto Rico was thus o/p in 1857.

'Yacht' Keytype. German colonial stamps picturing the *Hohenzollern*, yacht of Kaiser Wilhelm. There were two stamp designs: one of upright format showing the ship almost head on; the other horizontal, picturing her steaming broadside on. They were issued, suitably inscribed for each colony, 1900–15.

Yca. Peru. In April and May 1884 used two control o/ps on stamps of Arequipa (q.v.). Now known as Ica.

Yctab. (Mont.). Constitution.

Yemen. Independent state of south-west Arabia, part of the Ottoman Empire until 1918; thereafter an imamate (monarchy) until 1962 when a revolution occurred and a republic was set up. The ruling Imam, however, succeeded in escaping and in rallying his followers in the remoter parts of the country. As the monarchists counter-attacked, stocks of stamps fell into their hands and were overprinted 'Free Yemen Fights for God, Imam and Country'. At the time of writing the rival republican and monarchist regimes are each issuing their stamps as civil war continues. Stamps first issued, 1926. Area: 75,270 sq. m.; capital: Sana'a; currency: 40 bogaches = 1 imadi (since 1951, ahmadi); pop. about 4,500,000.

Yen. Japanese currency unit. 100 sen = 1 yen.

Ying Yang. The Chinese symbol of all created things. Appears as a watermark in stamps of China and in Korean stamp designs.

Yugoslavia (Jugoslavia, Jugoslavija). Independent state of south-eastern Europe, formed after the First World War by the union of the former kingdoms of Serbia and Montenegro with the former Austrian provinces of Bosnia and Herzegovina (q.v.), Croatia, Slovenia, and Dalmatia. King Peter I of Serbia became first king of Yugoslavia, which was known as the Kingdom of the Serbs, Croats, and Slovenes until the present title was officially adopted in 1929. The first stamps appeared in 1918, the early issues including separate stamps for Bosnia, for Croatia, and for Slovenia, as different currencies were circulating there. The first unified definitives for the whole country followed in 1921.

In the Second World War Yugoslavia was occupied by German forces, who set up separate puppet governments for Croatia, Serbia and Montenegro, each of which issued its own stamps until the end of the war. Slovenia (the province of Ljubljana or Laibach) was occupied by the Italians who issued occupation stamps in 1941 including 'Co.Ci.' overprints on Yugoslav stamps, standing for 'Commissariato Civile', and thereafter annexed it to Italy. In 1944, however, Slovenia was occupied by the Germans, who issued further occupation stamps including a set of pictorials inscribed 'Provinz Laibach'. Meanwhile the Yugoslav Government-in-exile in London also produced its own stamps 1943–5 for use by members of the Yugoslav Merchant Navy working with the Allies. By the end of 1944 the Yugoslav partisans led by Marshal Tito had driven the Germans from most of the country, and established a provisional government which re-commenced issuing stamps for all Yugoslavia. In 1945 a republic replaced the monarchy. Area: 98,725 sq. m.; capital: Belgrade; currency: 1918, 100 heller = 1 krone (Bosnia), 100 filir = 1 kruna (Crotia), 100 vinar = 1 krona (Slovenia); 1920, 100 para = 1 dinar; pop. (1961): 18,549,291.

Yunnan. Province of South-West China, for which stamps of China were o/p in Chinese between 1926 and 1934, owing to differences in the value of the dollar in other parts of China. Area: 146,718 sq. m.; pop. (est. 1955): 14,472,737; capital: Kunming; Chinese currency.

Yunnan-Sen, or Yunnan-fou. Stamps of French Indo-China were o/p for use in the French postal agency of Yunnan (now Kunming) from 1903 to 1922, when the office closed down.

Yvert et Tellier-Champion Catalogue. Re-titled Yvert & Tellier in 1955 (after the death of Theodore Champion). The leading French stamp publication, published by Yvert & Tellier, 37 Rue des Jacobins, Amiens, France.

Z

'Z'-Grill. A type of embossed security grill (given Gibbons' Catalogue recognition for the first time in 1948) on the 1861–6 stamps of the U.S.A. They are distinguished in having the tips of the points appearing as short horizontal ridges, instead of vertical.

Z.A.R. (Afrik.). Zuid Afrikaansche Republiek = South African Republic. See under 'Transvaal'.

Zambezia. Province of Portuguese East Africa, formerly administered by the Zambesia Company. Inscribed Portuguese colonial stamps were in use 1894–1914. Up to 1922 used Quelimane issues; now uses stamps of Moçambique.

Zambia. Name adopted by the former British protectorate of Northern Rhodesia (q.v.) on becoming an independent member of the Commonwealth in October 1964, when the first stamps were issued bearing the new name.

Zangezur. A district on the confines of Armenia and Azerbaijan. Russian 'arms' types were surcharged in late 1919 for use as provisionals.

Zante. See under 'Ionian Islands'.

Zanzibar. Former British protectorate comprising the islands of Zanzibar and Pemba off the coast of Tanganyika; an independent member of the British Commonwealth since December 1963 and a sultanate until January 1964, when a republic was established. An Indian post office was opened there in 1875, using Indian stamps without overprint until 1895. In the latter year Zanzibar's own first stamps appeared, consisting of overprints on Indian issues. These were followed by the first definitives in 1896. The 'Uhuru' set of December 1963 was both the first under independence and the last under the sultanate. First issues of the republic consisted of the earlier stamps overprinted 'JAMHURI 1964'. In July 1964 the United Republic of Tanganyika and Zanzibar (Tanzania) was formed, but at the time of writing stamps thus inscribed have been circulated in Tanganyika only, and Zanzibar continues to issue its own stamps. Area: 1,026 sq. m.; currency: as India until 1908, thereafter 100 cents = 1 rupee; 1936, 100 cents = 1 shilling; pop. (1959): 304,000. See also under 'French Post Office in Zanzibar'.

Zara. Dalmatian seaport ceded to Italy by Austria after the 1914–18 War. Now known as Zadar (Yugoslavia). Germany o/p stamps of Italy in 1943 'Deutsche besetzung Zara' (German occupation Zara). Pop. (1952): 14,847.

339

ZEPPELIN STAMPS   ZANZIBAR   ZUID AFRIKAANSCHE
REPUBLIEK

Zarska Bulgarska Posta. Stamps thus inscribed are completely bogus labels purporting to be issued by a non-existent 'Royal Bulgarian Post', distributed from Buenos Aires and Madrid in 1964.

Zegelregt. (Afrik.: Stamp duty). Inscription on fiscal stamp o/p for use in the Transvaal, August 1895.

Zeitung. (Ger.). Newspaper or journal. Zeitung stempel = newspaper or journal stamp.

Zelaya. Province of Nicaragua, for which contemporary issues were specially o/p 1904–8. Gibbons' says: 'The stamps o/p were used in the Bluefields district of the province on the Atlantic coast. The reason given was that silver currency in that district was worth 50 ¢ to the peso, instead of paper worth 25 ¢ elsewhere in Nicaragua'.

Zemstvos. Russian Government locals, authorised by Imperial edict on 3 September 1870, calling upon local assemblies to establish postal services within their jurisdiction to augment the general post. Nearly 150 rural districts issued 'locals' ranging from simple hand-struck impressions to elaborate hand-coloured issues (e.g. 'Tikhivin'). They were current, in many instances, for over 20 years.

, **Zentraler Kurierdienst.** See 'Courier Mail'.

Zeppelin Stamps. Stamps franking mail actually airborne by the German 'Graf Zeppelin', and other rigid airships, or celebrating Zeppelin flights and visits to the countries of Europe and America, form an interesting series in great popular demand. The 1928 and 1934 airs, and the 'Hindenburg' dirigible 1926 stamps, emanated from Germany, while in America they commemorated the 1930 Pan-American flight with three stamps. Italy followed suit with a home issue, and one for Cirenaica and for Tripolitania, in 1933. Egypt showed the airship the same year in the International Aviation Congress set; while Greece, also in 1933, issued three airs showing the dirigible, this time over the Acropolis; and it was depicted by Liechtenstein as crossing the Alps on the air stamps of 1931. Paraguay did homage in her 1933 air set, and Russia paid the ship the compliment of two sets in 1931. These Zeppelin stamps have been taken at random, and as typical of how easily a fashion in stamp designs can be set and followed.

Zieber's Dispatch. A Pittsburgh, U.S.A., local stamp was in use in 1852.

Zig-Zag Roulette. (Fr. Percé en pointes). Results in sharp pointed teeth along the edges of the stamps. Example: La Guaira 1864; and (percé en pointes de couleur) in black on the Queensland 1899 penny stamps. See 'Roulette' and 'Percé'.

Zinco. A process line block on zinc. The negative is printed down on to the sensitised metal, acid-etched into relief, and mounted type-high. From the original a number of electros or stereos (clichés) can be made to make up the number requisite to print a sheet of stamps by the 'typo' or 'surface' method. See 'Line Block', 'Typography', 'Surface Printing', etc.

Zuid Afrikaansche Republiek (Afrikaans). South African Republic. See under 'Transvaal'.

Zuid Afrika. South Africa (q.v.).

Zuid-West Afrika. South-West Africa (q.v.).

Zulassungsmarke. (Ger.). Concession stamp. Inscription on German Forces special stamp authorised in 1943 for the free franking of parcels of 2 kg. maximum weight, addressed to the fighting services.

Zulia. Two stamps (5 ¢. deep purple and 10 ¢. vermilion) were prepared for use for a still-born new South American state in 1904 under revolutionary General Rafael Parra of Venezuela. The revolt collapsed before they could be issued.

Zululand. District of Natal, South Africa. The British broke the power of the Zulu kings and annexed the territory in 1887. It had its own Crown Colony issues from the 1888 o/p stamps of G.B. to the Queen Victoria keytypes of 1894–6, the issue of which ceased on 30 June 1898, when it was absorbed into Natal (q.v.). Area: 10,427 sq. m.; pop. about 260,000.

Zumstein Europa Katalog. The Zumstein catalogues, which include one for Switzerland and Liechtenstein, are published by Zumstein & Co., Marktgasse 50, Berne, Switzerland.

Zürich. Canton of Switzerland which issued its now famous 'Figures' stamps in March 1843—the very first Swiss stamps (and actually the second authority in the world to adopt pre-paid adhesives), but with local (cantonal) franking power only.

Greek

The Zeta (Z) used as in English.

APPENDIX

APPENDIX I

PERFORATION GAUGE

Back and front of a typical commercially printed gauge are pictured on the pages below, and opposite.

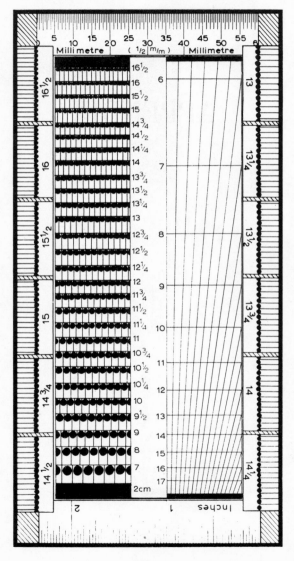

342

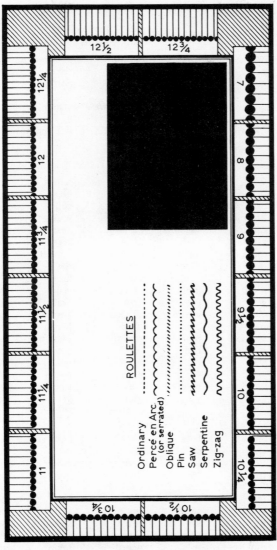

Reproduced by permission of Messrs. Wallace Brothers, Philatelists, Bournemouth.

The following brief glossary of foreign words may be of help in referring

GENERAL POSTAL TERMS

English	Swedish	Danish	Dutch	German	French
Letter	brev	brev	brief	brief	lettre
Letter-box	brevlada	brefkasse	brievenbus	briefkasten	boîte aux lettres
Paper	papper	papir	papier	papier	papier
Parcel	paket	pakke	pakje	paket	paquet
Postage	porto	porto	porto	porto	port
Post office	postkontor	posthus	postkantoor	postamt	bureau de poste
Postage stamp	frimarke	frimaerke	postzegel	briefmarke	timbre-poste

APPERTAINING TO COLOUR

English	Swedish	Danish	Dutch	German	French
Black	svart	sort	zwart	schwarz	noir
Blue	bla	blaa	blauw	blau	bleu
Bright	ljus	lys	helder	hell	vif
Brown	brun	brun	bruin	braun	brun
Chestnut	castanje	kastanie	kastanje	kastanie	marron
Clear	klar	klar	klaar	klar	clair
Dark	mörk	mørk	donker	dunkel	foncé
Deep	djup	dyb	diep	tief	foncé
Flat	flat	flad	vlak	flach	terne
Green	grön	grøn	groen	grün	vert
Grey	gra	graa	grijs	grau	gris
Lemon	citron	citron	citroen	zitrone	citron
Pale	blek	bleg	bleek	bleich	pâle
Plum	plommon	blomme	pruim	pflaume	prune
Red	röd	rød	rood	rot	rouge
Rich	rik	rig	rijk	reich	rich
Warm	varm	varm	warm	warm	chaud
White	vit	hvid	wit	weiss	blanc
Yellow	gul	gul	geel	gelb	jaune

APPERTAINING TO NUMBERS AND VALUES

English	Swedish	Danish	Dutch	German	French
Half	en halv	halv	helft	halb	demi
One	en	en	een	ein	un
Two	tva	to	twee	zwei	deux
Three	tre	tre	drie	drei	trois
Four	fyra	fire	vier	vier	quatre
Five	fem	fem	vijf	fünf	cinq
Six	sex	seks	zes	sechs	six
Seven	sju	syv	zeven	sieben	sept
Eight	atta	otte	acht	acht	huit
Nine	nio	ni	negen	neun	neuf
Ten	tio	ti	tien	zehn	dix
Twelve	tolv	tolv	twaalf	zwölf	douze
Fifteen	femton	femten	vijftien	funfzehn	quinze
Twenty	tjugo	tyve	twintig	zwanzig	vingt
Fifty	femtie	halvtres	vijftig	fünfzig	cinquante
Hundred	hundra	hundrede	honderd	hundert	cent

to Continental stamp catalogues and literature

Spanish	Portuguese	Italian	Russian	Russian (Phonetically)
carta	carta	lettera	ПИСЬМО	peesmo
buzón el correo	caixa do correio	buca delle lattere	ПОЧТОВЫЙ ЯЩИК	pochtovee yasheek
papel	papel	carta	БУМАГА	boomaga
paquete	pacote	pacco	ПАКЕТ	packet
franqueo	porte	affranca-túra	ПОЧТА	pochta
casa de correos	correio	ufficio postale	ПОЧТОВАЯ-КОНТОРА	pochttovaya kantora
sello de correo	selo	franco-bollo	ПОЧТОВАЯ МАРКА	pochttovaya marka

negro	preto	nero	ЧЕРНЫЙ	chernee
azul	azul	azzurro	СИНИЙ	sinnee
subido	fervente	lucido	СВЕТДЫЙ	svetlyee
bruno	bruno	bruno	КОРИЧНЕВЫЙ	korcihnyavee
castaña	castanha	castagno	КАШТАН	kashtan
claro	claro	chiaro	ЯСНЫЙ	yessnee
obscuro	escuro	oscuro	ТЕМНЫЙ	tyemnie
profundo	profundo	profondo	ГЛУБОКИЙ	gloobokie
llano	plano	piano	КВАРТИРА	kvarteera
verde	verde	verde	ЗЕЛЕНЫЙ	zhelyenie
gris	cinzento	grigio	СЕРЫЙ	syerie
limón	limao	limone	ЛИМОН	leemon
pálido	palido	pallido	БЛЕДНЫЙ	blyednie
ciruela	ameixa	susina	СЛИВА	sleeva
rojo	vermelho	rosso	КРАСНЫЙ	krasnee
rico	rico	ricco	БОГАТЫЙ	bogatee
caliente	quente	caldo	ТЕЛПЫЙ	telpee
blanco	blanco	bianco	БЕЛЫЙ	byelee
amarillo	amarelo	giallo	ЖЕЛТЫЙ	zholtee

medio	meio	mezzo	ПОЛОВИНА	poloveenya
uno	um	uno	ОДИН	odyeen
dos	dois	due	ДВА	dva
tres	tres	tre	ТРИ	tree
cuatro	quatro	quattro	ЧЕТЫРЕ	cheteerie
cinco	cinco	cinque	ПЯТЬ	pyat
seis	seis	sei	ЩЕСТЬ	schest
siete	sete	sette	СЕМЬ	sem
ocho	oito	otto	ВОСЕМЬ	vosem
neuve	nove	nove	ДЕВЯТЬ	davyet
diez	dez	dieci	ДЕСЯТЬ	dasyit
doce	doze	dodici	ДВЕНАДЦАТЬ	dva-nadsit
quince	quinze	quindici	ПЯТНАДЦАТЬ	pyat-nadsit
viente	vinte	venti	ДВЕДЦАТЬ	dva-tsit
cincuenta	cinquenta	cinquanta	ПЯТДЕСЯТЬ	peedisat
ciento	cem	cento	СТО	stoe

STAMPS OF GREAT BRITAIN 'USED ABROAD'

Numeral Cancellations

NUMERALS (with or without index letters) used as post office means of identification are in use all over the world, and where they are incorporated in postmarks indicating usage of stamps in places other than their country of origin they have a particular interest for collectors. In the period between 1857 and 1881 (in particular) the following numbered cancellations were in use by British postal agencies and offices in various parts of the world, in many cases preceding the issue of regular stamps for the places and countries affected. Such numbered postmarkings upon general issues of Great Britain are therefore of especial interest to stamp collectors and to postal historians:

No.	Used at	No.	Used at
A01	Kingston, Jamaica.	A10	Kingstown, St. Vincent, Windward Is.
A02	St. John's, Antigua, B.W.I.		
A03	Georgetown, or Demerara, British Guiana.	A11	Castries, St. Lucia, Windward Is.
		A12	Basseterre, St. Christopher, Leeward Is.
A04	New Amsterdam, or Berbice, British Guiana.		
		A13	Tortola, Virgin Is.
A05	Nassau, Bahamas.	A14	Scarborough, Tobago, B.W.I.
A06	British Honduras.	A15	St. George, Grenada, B.W.I.
A07	Dominica, B.W.I.	A18	English Harbour, Antigua, B.W.I.
A08	Montserrat, Leeward Is.	A25	Malta.
A09	Nevis, Leeward Is.	A26	Gibraltar.

Numbers A27 to A78 were issued to the following post offices then in existence in Jamaica:

No.	Used at	No.	Used at
A27	Alexandria, Middlesex.	A51	Lucea, Cornwall.
A28	Annotta Bay, Middlesex.	A52	Manchioneal, Surrey.
A29	Bath, Surrey.	A53	Mandeville, Middlesex.
A30	Black River, St. Elizabeth.	A54	May Hill (near Spur Tree).
A31	Brown's Town, Middlesex.	A55	Mile Gully, Middlesex.
A32	Bluff Bay, Surrey.	A56	Moneague, Middlesex.
A33	Chapleton, Middlesex.	A57	Montego Bay, Cornwall.
A35	Clarendon, Middlesex.	A58	Montpelier, Cornwall.
A36	Dry Harbour, Middlesex..	A59	Morant Bay, Surrey.
A37	Duncans, Cornwall.	A60	Ochos Rios, Middlesex.
A38	Ewarton, Middlesex.	A61	Old Harbour, Middlesex.
A39	Falmouth, Cornwall.	A62	Golden Grove, Surrey.
A40	Flint River, Cornwall.	A63	Pear Tree Grove.
A41	Gayle, Cornwall.	A64	Port Antonio, Surrey.
A42	Golden Spring, Surrey.	A65	Port Morant, Surrey.
A43	Gordon Town, Surrey.	A66	Port Maria, Middlesex.
A44	Goshen, Cornwall.	A67	Port Royal, Middlesex.

No.	Used at	No.	Used at
A45	Grange Hill, Cornwall.	A68	Porus, Middlesex.
A46	Green Island, Cornwall.	A69	Ramble, Cornwall.
A47	Highgate, Middlesex.	A70	Rio Bueno, Middlesex.
A48	Hope Bay, Surrey.	A71	Linstead, Middlesex.
A49	Lilliput, Cornwall.	A72	Yallahs, Surrey.
A50	Little River, Cornwall.	A73	St. Ann's Bay, Middlesex.
A74	Salt Gut (near Ora Cabess), Middlesex.	C60	La Guayra (or Guaira), Venezuela.
A75	Savanna-la-Mar, Cornwall.	C61	Puerto Rico (Porto Rico), West Indies.
A76	Spanish Town, Middlesex.	C62	Santa Marta, Colombia.
A77	Stewart Town, Cornwall.	C63	Tampico, Mexico.
A78	The Alley, Middlesex.	C65	Cartagena, Colombia.
		C79	British mailboat.
A80 to A99	Were allotted to British mail boats.	C81	Bahia, Brasil.
		C82	Pernambuco, Brasil.
B01	Alexandria, Egypt.	C83	Rio de Janeiro, Brasil.
B02	Suez, Egypt.	C86	Porto Plata, Dominican Republic.
B03,	B12, B56 and B57 Other mail boats.	C87	San Domingo, Dominican Republic.
B32	Buenos Aires, Argentina.	C88	Santiago de Cuba.
B53	Mauritius.	D22	Cuidad Bolivar (formerly Angostura), Venezuela.
B54	The Seychelles.		
B62	Hong Kong.	D26	Spanish mail packet (St. Thomas, Virgin Islands).
C	Constantinople (now Istanbul).		
C28	Montevideo, Uruguay.	D47	Cyprus.
C30	Valparaiso, Chile.	D48	Cyprus—Army Headquarters.
C35	Panama.	D74	Pisco, Ica, Peru.
C36	Arica, Chile.	D87	Iquique, Chile.
C37	Caldera, Chile.	E53	Port au Prince, Haïtï.
C38	Callao, Peru.	E88	Aspinwall, Colon, Colombia.
C39	Cobija, Antofagasta, Chile.	F69	Savanilla, Bolivar, Colombia.
C40	Coquimbo, Chile.	F83	Arroyo, Porto Rico, West Indies.
C41	Guayaquil, Ecuador.	F84	Aguadilla, Porto Rico, West Indies.
C42	Islay, Arequipa, Peru.	F85	Mayaguez, Porto Rico, West Indies.
C43	Payta, Peru.		
C51	St. Thomas (then Danish West Indies).	F87	Smyrna (now Izmir), Turkey.
		F88	Ponce, Porto Rico, West Indies.
C56	Cartagena, Colombia.	G	Gibraltar.
C57	Greytown, Nicaragua.	G06	Geyrouth, Syria.
C58	Havana, Cuba.	M	Malta.
C59	Jacmel, Haïtï.	S	Stamboul, Turkey.

The following numbers without a prefixed initial are also of interest to the specialist and postal historian:

No.	Used at	No.	Used at
247	Fernando Pó (or Poo), Gulf of Guinea.	965	Alderney, Channel Islands.
		969	Nicosia, Cyprus.
324	Guernsey, Channel Islands.	974	Kyrenia, Cyprus.
409	Jersey, Channel Islands.	975	Limassol, Cyprus.
582	Naguabo, Porto Rico, West Indies.	981	Paphos, Cyprus.
942	Larnaca, Cyprus.	982	Famagusta, Cyprus.

Such numeral cancellations should be collected 'on cover' or at least 'on piece', but rarities are still valuable if a clear strike is obtained upon a stamp.

French stamp catalogues list similar 'used abroad' cancellations—all of interest to the collector of the stamps of France—especially the earlier issues.

STAMP RECOGNITION

ONE of the difficulties of the beginner, and even at times of the advanced collector, is to identify accurately stamps which do not carry the names of the countries of origin in Western European lettering.

The following pages illustrate many of these difficult stamps, and where a general 'clue' by which initial recognition can be made is possible, this is given. Thus, for example, many Chinese stamps bear the sun emblem with twelve rays; Japanese issues have as a central motif (or, placed at the top) the sixteen-petalled chrysanthemum; and Manchurian designs usually incorporate the stylised orchid. These are but three specific instances, others are given with the stamp recognitions.

Cyrillic* (Russian, Yugoslavian, Bulgarian, etc.) inscriptions are a frequent cause of trouble, but careful study of their characteristics soon enables the student to pick them out. Arabic is admittedly most difficult, but most of the nations conform to the rules of the Universal Postal Union, and display either the name of the country in recognisable Western symbols, or state their coinage in recognisable terms, and once these are mastered, future recognition is easy.

Russia, for example, uses kopecks and rubles, but in the very confusing and similar designs of Finland, the monetary units are penni and markka. Where a Japanese stamp will show the value in either sen, yen, or en, Chinese issues will give cents and dollars, and Manchurian values will be in fen and yen. Currency clues are perhaps more valuable than any, and these illustrations, used in conjunction with the notes accompanying them, and the references within the body of this work, especially the monetary appendix, should enable the collector to make rapid recognition of any stamp without further difficulty.

* See the Cyrillic Alphabet given on page 88.

These are, all four of them, stamps of Japan. The clue is the chrysanthemum emblem in the centre (or centre top) of the stamp. The values are expressed in 'sen', 'yen', or en.

Here, again, are all Japanese issues, but only two (Nos. 5 and 7) show the national emblem. No. 6 is one of the very first of Japan's stamps and there are no real clues. In the latest issues there is a tendency to drop the chrysanthemum emblem altogether, and there is no Western lettering by which to check. There are, however, certain intangible elements in these designs which the student will learn to associate with Japanese modern issues.

These are Chinese issues, as identified by the 'risen sun' emblem with its 12 rays, but as the first was issued only in Formosa (No. 10), and will be found catalogued only under that head, it is easy to see where confusion can arise. Here are few clues as there is little or no Western lettering.

The first three of these (Nos. 13, 14, and 15) are Manchurian. The clues are the values in 'fen' and in No. 14, the 'orchid' emblem. No. 16 is Persian (Iranian). Both Persia and Egypt (among others) use the official U.P.U. language (French) for any Western words. The 'Ch.' (for chahi) is the values clue, and the heraldic lion *passant* with scimitar—the Persian national crest—can just be seen as the central motif of the stamp, underneath the surcharge.

The first two are Serbian. (In many old albums it will be found named 'Servia'.) No. 17 depicts King Peter I. The coinage is expressed in paras, a monetary unit in use in many former Turkish countries, and therefore apt to confuse. No. 19 is Swiss and is a 'postage due' stamp, identifiable by the emblem of the country —the white (Geneva) cross on a red ground—found in many stamps of Switzerland. No. 20 is also a 'due' but of the Netherlands or Holland. Identical designs were used by Curaçao, and the catalogue must be consulted to confirm identification.

21 **22** **23** **24**

No. 21 is an 'official' stamp of Germany. The Gothic lettering and the word 'dienst' (meaning 'service') help in recognition. No. 22, however, though also German, is specifically from Württemberg, and it is a 'Municipal service' stamp. The value in pfennig is a useful clue—the catalogue will do the rest. The last two (Nos. 23 and 24) are from Yugoslavia. If you look up either 'Drz (ava)', 'Hrvatska', or 'S.H.S.' in the encyclopaedic section, you will have identified them both easily.

25 **26** **27** **28**

The typically Greek letters should enable these to be quickly found, once their significance is realised, although No. 28 is allocated only to Epirus (most of which is now in Albania) and to the town of Moscopolis, now named Voskopoje (by Zumstein). As it is not listed by Gibbons (although Scott, Yvert and Zumstein recognise it) this stamp usually causes trouble. No. 25 is a Greek charity issue; No. 26 is one of the earliest, and No. 27 shows the Corinth Canal, but the major clues are the lettering and the coinage (lepta and drachmai).

29 **30** **31** **32** **33**

'Indian States'! Yes, the first four are, anyway, but the fifth is from Nepal, which although once listed with them, is really an independent country. No. 29 is lettered 'Orcha' and will be found (with slightly different spelling) under the state named. No. 30 is from Nawanagar; Nos. 31 and 32 are Hyderabad or Deccan issues, and (as has been said) No. 33 is Nepalese. It is almost impossible to identify these without an adequately illustrated catalogue.

17 18 19 20

21 22 23 24

25 26 27 28

29 30 31 32 33

These are all Russian stamps, but No. 34 is from White Russia, No. 35 is Czarist in origin, and No. 36 is an early Soviet stamp. The coinage symbols are the clue —and the Cyrillic inscriptions.

37   38   39   40   41

All of Russian 'parentage', but whereas No. 37 is correctly Russian, No. 38 (the same stamp overprinted and surcharged) rightly belongs to the Far Eastern Republic; and whereas No. 40 is Russian, yet No. 41, in the same colour and almost exactly the same design, is Finnish, when Finland was under Russian rule —the monetary unit is 'pen' (penni) instead of in kopecks, and that is the clue. No. 39 is also Russian.

42   43   44   45

Nos. 42 and 43 are also from Finland. The first is one of the early 'serpentine' rouletted issues (a good clue); while No. 43 is one you will not find in Gibbons— it is a stamp issued for the use of the military. No. 44 is Finnish also by reason of its value—it is expressed in Markka instead of in roubles; but No. 35, although the value is also in roubles, will be found listed in Gibbons Part I, under 'Batum (British Occupation)'.

46   47   48

The Ukraine issued the first two of these stamps (Nos. 46 and 47). The clues are again the monetary units, which are not in kopecks and roubles as they would be were they truly Russian (U.S.S.R.) stamps. No. 48 is from Armenia. The lettering is often mistaken for Amharic (Ethiopian) which it resembles. The clue is the letter 'Z' which is the Armenian monogram (repeated in this design).

49   **50**   **51**

No. 49 hails from Azerbaijan (the Russian republic, not the Persian district of similar name). No. 50 was issued by the Trans-Caucasian Republic before it joined the Soviet Union; while No. 51 is titled 'Epirus', but is actually spurious and without any official status.

52   **53**   **54**   **55**

Are all stamps with links with Austria. The first two are journal or newspaper stamps of that country; No. 54 is Austria's earliest design, but this, inscribed in 'centes' instead of 'kreuzer', was issued for use in Austrian Italy. A similar subtlety exists in regard to No. 55, which is also an Austrian 'early', but had it been valued in 'soldi' (Sld. instead of kr.) it also would be found under a new heading: 'Austrian P.O.s in the Turkish Empire'.

56   **57**   **58**

No. 56, although also Austrian, was issued for Bosnia and Herzegovina, under which heading it will be found. No. 57 is an Austrian Imperial Journal stamp. No. 58 is one of the Cervantes commemoratives issued by Spain in 1905, and depicts an episode from 'Don Quixote'.

59   **60**   **61**   **62**

These have all a Spanish origin. No. 59 is an early stamp of Spain; No. 60 is Spanish Colonial issued for use in both Cuba and in Puerto Rico; No. 61 is one of Spain's 'Baby' set; but No. 62 is a printed papers' stamp intended for use in the Philippines.

49

50

51

52

53

54

55

56

57

58

59

60

61

62

63   **64**   **65**   **66**

The first two specimens are Indian native states: No. 63 from Jammu and Kashmir (Cashmere); and No. 64 from Bhopal. No. 65 is a modern Nepal stamp; while No. 66 is one of the notorious 'Free India' stamps prepared for the conquest of India by the Nazi-German government in 1942. They were never issued and few catalogues list them.

67   **68**   **69**   **70**

No. 67 is clearly entitled 'Republica Dominicana'—but often causes confusion. It is listed under the Dominican Republic. No. 68 is a 'borderline' stamp not listed by Gibbons. It is a semi-private issue made by the Condor airline operating in Brasil. No. 69 is the famous issue of the 'Pacific Steam Navigation Company' that was used to test the first postal service in Peru and which will be found listed under this latter country. The 'Instruccion' stamp belongs to Venezuela, being a stamp originally issued to raise funds for the education of the masses, but which was authorised for normal postal use.

71   **72**   **73**   **74**

The Roman States—now the Vatican, whose arms are shown—claims No. 71. No. 72 is one of the early stamps of Denmark. No. 73 is from Albania—variously inscribed: Shqiptare, Shqiptenia, Shqipni, etc. The qind or qint is the monetary unit of recognition. No. 74 is a portrait of King William III of Holland as shown on the first stamps of the Netherlands. A similar portrait, but facing left, appears on the first issues of Luxembourg of which he was also the Grand Duke.

75   **76**   **77**   **78**   **79**

Switzerland issued this first stamp to commemorate the 25th anniversary of the U.P.U.; No. 76 was a German-occupied Alsace Lorraine stamp of 1870; No. 77 was issued by Austria for use in Bosnia and Herzegovina, but surcharged (as the specimen), was used in the 1918 Austrian Occupation of Italy—it is valued in centesimi. No. 78 is an early Brasilian stamp (this is actually a forged copy); and No. 79 is a French colonial for the former Indian Settlements.

63   64   65   66

67   68   69   70

71   72   73   74

75   76   77   78   79

The cross of Geneva displayed on the shield should identify this (No. 80) stamp as Swiss, and the title 'Helvetia' confirms this. No. 81 is from Estonia; No. 82 from Sweden; and No. 83 is from Schleswig and is one of the set of plebiscite stamps issued in 1920. These are all four fully titled stamps but with strange spellings.

84   85   86   87

Nos. 84 and 85 came from Liechtenstein—the second one is a 'due'. No. 86 is also a postage due, but from Danzig. In common with many stamps from here it shows the Danzig city arms. No. 87 is a relic of the German occupation of Poland, identifiable by the 'Zloty' value printed in the top left corner, and the 'General Gouvernement' inscription.

88   89   90   91

No. 88 is Lithuanian; No. 89 is another 'due' of Switzerland; No. 90 is for Central Lithuania, which is often identified as Polish. No. 91 is one of the stamps of autonomous Crete, before its union with Greece.

92   93   94   95

Lebanon is correct for stamp No. 92—one of the Arabic countries, as also are the Egyptian (who account for Nos. 93 and 94) and Afghan (No. 95) countries. No. 93 is one of the older issues of Egypt, and the Pyramid and Sphinx makes recognition easy.

96   **97**   **98**

All three of these are Turkish, and although the crescent and star appear also on the stamps of Egypt, Pakistan, and other eastern countries, it is the accepted emblem for Turkey and a useful clue.

99   **100**   **101**

Nos. 99 and 101 are classed as 'locals' and will not be found listed in many catalogues as they have been reprinted many times and their validity in any event was doubtful and within a very circumscribed area. The first was for use on the Danube and Black Sea Railway in conjunction with the Kustendjie (Constanza) Harbour Company at the sea end of the Danube. The second one (No. 101) served a similar purpose, and both were issued when Turkey was overlord. No. 100 is a regular Turkish issue.

102   **103**   **104**

No. 102 is also a general issue of Turkey; and No. 104 is a charity stamp from the same country. No. 103, however, is listed under Saudi-Arabia, although it was actually issued in Hejaz before the latter was absorbed (with Nejd) into the new state.

105   **106**   **107**   **108**

No. 105 is Turkish and is overprinted for use as a 'printed papers' stamp, No. 106 is also from Turkey. No. 107 is an early issue from Abyssinia, now more generally known and listed as Ethiopia: while No. 108 is Persian (Iranian).

Both Nos. 109 and 111 are from Thailand—formerly known as Siam. No. 110 is one of the pictorial issues of Touva, or Tanna Touva—now more generally listed under North Mongolia. This stamp is one of a series not listed by Gibbons, and it is certain that many of these stamps serve no real postal duty, but are made for the collector.

112   113   114   115

Persia claims the first two of these (Nos. 112 and 113). The first is entitled 'Poste Persane', and the other bears the lion emblem of the country. Nos. 114 and 115 are from Georgia (La Georgie).

116   117   118   119

All four are stamps of Montenegro, now part of Yugoslavia. The name of the country is in Cyrillic—Monte, a mountain; Negro, black = The black Mountain. No. 118 is one of the 'definitives' of 1907: and No. 119 is a 1907 postage due.

120   121   122   123

The first three of these stamps are Bulgarian. No. 122 gives the name of the country in Cyrillic very clearly and is a clue worthy of a little study and memorising. No. 123 is from Wenden, now a town and province of Latvia (Livonia) but will be found catalogued under Russia, under whose regime it was issued.

STAMP CURRENCY GUIDE

In many countries currency is not freely convertible. Official rates of exchange may be unrealistic, and this makes it difficult in some cases to determine true values. The list below, therefore, is intended only as a very general guide to collectors who wish to calculate the face value of their stamps in terms of sterling or U.S. dollars. It applies, of course, only to new and comparatively recent issues. Collectors should bear in mind that the values of most currencies have fluctuated widely over the years since stamps were first issued. Inflation and revaluation continue to affect certain currencies, and the list should be treated with reserve.

Stamp-issuing authority	Currency expressed on stamps	Approx. value in Sterling £ s. d.			U.S. dollars $ ¢.
ADEN	E. African shilling = 100 cents	1	0		0·14
AFGHÁNISTAN	Afgháni = 100 puls		2		0·02½
ALBANIA	Lek = 100 qintars		1¾		0·02
ANDORRA	French and Spanish currencies				
ANTIGUA	B.W.I. dollar = 100 cents	4	2		0·58½
ARGENTINA	Peso = 100 centavos (much depreciated in recent years)		0½		0·00½
ARMENIA	Rouble = 100 kopecks (1923)		4		0·05
AUSTRALIA	Australian £	16	0		2·24
AUSTRIA	Schilling = 100 groschen		3¼		0·04
BAHRAIN	Rupee = 100 naye paise	1	6		0·21
BARBADOS	B.W.I. dollar = 100 cents	4	2		0·58½
BASUTOLAND AND BECHUANALAND	Rand = 100 cents	10	0		1·40
BELGIUM	Franc = 100 centimes		1¾		0·02
BOLIVIA	Peso = 100 cents = 1,000 old bolivianos		7¼		0·08½
BRASIL	Cruzeiro = 100 centavos		7¼		0·08½
BRITISH GUIANA	B.W.I. dollar = 100 cents	4	2		0·58½
BRITISH HONDURAS	Br. Honduras dollar = 100 cents	5	0		0·70
BRITISH SOLOMON IS.	Australian £	16	0		2·24
BRUNEI	Malayan dollar = 100 cents	2	4		0·33
BULGARIA	Lev = 100 stotinki (upvalued in 1962)	6	1		0·85½
BURMA	Kyat = 100 pyas	1	6		0·21
CAMBODIA	Reil = 100 sen		2½		0·03

Stamp-issuing authority	Currency expressed on stamps	Sterling £ s. d.	Approx. value in U.S. dollars $ ¢.
CANADA	Canadian dollar = 100 cents	6 7½	0·93
CEYLON	Rupee = 100 cents	1 6	0·21
CHILE	Escudo = 100 centesimos or condores = 1,000 old pesos	2 2¾	0·30
CHINA	Yuan or dollar = 10 chiao = 10 fen	2 10¾	0·41
COCOS IS.	Australian £	16 0	2·24
COLOMBIA	Peso = 100 centavos	8½	0·10
CONGO	Congolese franc, formerly at par with Belgian franc, now much depreciated		
COSTA RICA	Colon = 100 centimos	1 1	0·15½
CUBA	Peso = 100 centavos	7 2	1·00
CYPRUS	Cyprus £ = 1,000 mils	1 0 0	2·80
CZECHOSLOVAKIA	Koruna = 100 haleru	1 0¾	0·15
DENMARK	Krone = 100 öre	1 0½	0·15
DOMINICA	B.W.I. dollar = 100 cents	4 2	0·58½
DOMINICAN REPUBLIC	Peso = 100 centavos	7 2	1·00
ECUADOR	Sucré = 100 centavos	4½	0·05½
EGYPT	Egyptian pound = 1,000 mills	16 4¾	2·30
ETHIOPIA	Ethiopian dollar = 100 cents	2 10	0·40
FIJI	Fijian £	18 0	2·52
FINLAND	Markka = 100 pennis	2 3	0·32
FRANCE	Franc = 100 centimes (= 100 old francs)	1 5½	0·20½
GERMANY (EAST)	Ost-Mark = 100 pfennig	3 2½	0·43½
GERMANY (WEST)	Deutsche-Mark = 100 pfennig	1 9½	0·25
GHANA	Cedi = 100 pesewa	8 4	1·19
GILBERT & ELLICE ISLANDS	Australian £	16 0	2·24
GREECE	Drachma = 100 lepta	2¾	0·03½
GRENADA	B.W.I. dollar = 100 cents	4 2	0·58½
GUATEMALA	Quetzal = 100 centavos	7 2	1·00
HAITI	Gourde = 100 centimes	1 5	0·20
HONDURAS	Lempira = 100 centavos	3 7	0·50
HONG KONG	Hong Kong dollar = 100 cents	1 3	0·17½
HUNGARY	Forint = 100 filler	7½	0·09
ICELAND	Krona = 100 aurar	2	0·02½
INDIA	Rupee = 100 paise	1 6	0·21
INDONESIA	Rupiah = 100 sen	2	0·02½
IRAQ	Dinar = 1,000 fils	1 0 0	2·80
IRELAND (EIRE)	Irish £	1 0 0	2·80
ISRAEL	Israeli pound = 100 agorot	2 4½	0·33½
ITALY	Lira = 100 centesimi	1 2	0·16½
JAPAN	Yen = 100 sen	2 0	0·28
JORDAN	Dinar = 1,000 fils	1 0 0	2·80
KENYA	E. African shilling = 100 cents	1 0	0·14
KOREA (SOUTH)	Hwan = 100 won	3½	0·04½
KUWAIT	Dinar = 1,000 fils	1 0 0	2·80

Stamp-issuing authority	Currency expressed on stamps	Sterling £ s. d.	U.S. dollars $ ¢.
LEBANON	Lebanese pound = 100 piastres	2 4	0·33
LIBERIA	Dollar = 100 cents	7 2	1·00
LIBYA	Libyan pound = 1,000 mils	1 0 0	2·80
LIECHTENSTEIN	Franc = 100 rappen	1 8	0·23½
LUXEMBURG	Franc = 100 centimes	1¾	0·02
MACAO	Pataca or dollar = 100 avos	1 4¾	0·06
MALAYA AND MALAYSIA	Malayan dollar = 100 cents or sen	2 4	0·33
MALDIVE ISLANDS	Rupee = 100 larees	1 6	0·21
MAURITIUS	Rupee = 100 cents	1 6	0·21
MEXICO	Peso = 100 centavos	7	0·08½
MONACO	French currency		
MONGOLIA	Tugrik = 100 mongo	1 9½	0·25½
MONTSERRAT	B.W.I. dollar = 100 cents	4 2	0·58½
MOROCCO	Dirham = 100 francs	1 5	0·20
NAURU	Australian £	16 0	2·24
NEPAL	Rupee = 100 pice	11¼	0·13
NETHERLANDS	Gulden, guilder or florin = 100 cents	1 11¾	0·28
NETHERLANDS ANTILLES	Gulden = 100 cents	3 9¾	0·53
NEW HEBRIDES	Gold franc = 100 centimes	2 4	0·33
NICARAGUA	Cordoba = 100 centavos	1 0	0·14
NORFOLK ISLAND	Australian £	16 0	2·24
NORTH BORNEO (SABAH)	Malayan dollar = 100 cents	2 4	0·33
NORWAY	Krone = 100 öre	1 0	0·14
PAKISTAN	Rupee = 100 paise	1 6	0·21
PANAMA	Balboa = 100 cents	7 2	1·00
PAPUA & NEW GUINEA	Australian £	16 0	2·24
PARAGUAY	Guarani = 100 centimos	6¾	0·08
PERSIA (IRAN)	Rial = 100 dinars	1	0·01
PERU	Sol = 100 centavos	3¼	0·04
PHILIPPINES	Peso = 100 centavos	1 10	0·26
POLAND	Zloty = 1,000 groszy	1 9½	0·25½
PORTUGAL	Escudo = 100 centavos	3	0·04
ROUMANIA	Leu = 100 bani	1 2½	0·17
RUSSIA (U.S.S.R.)	Rouble = 100 kopecks	7 11¼	1·13
SABAH	Malayan dollar = 100 cents	2 4	0·33
ST. CHRISTOPHER, NEVIS & ANGUILLA: ST. LUCIA AND ST. VINCENT	B.W.I. dollar = 100 cents	4 2	0·58½
SALVADOR	Colon = 100 centavos	2 10	0·40
SARAWAK	Malayan dollar = 100 cents	2 4	0·33
SAUDI ARABIA	Riyal = 11 piastres	1 7	0·22½
SEYCHELLES	Rupee = 100 cents	1 6	0·21
SIERRA LEONE	Leone = 100 cents	10 0	1·40

Stamp-issuing authority	Currency expressed on stamps	Approx. value in Sterling £ s. d.	U.S. dollars $ ¢.
SINGAPORE	Malayan dollar = 100 cents	2 4	0·33
SOMALIA	Somalo = 100 centesimi	1 0	0·14
SOUTH AFRICA AND SOUTH WEST AFRICA	Rand = 100 cents	10 0	1·40
SPAIN	Peseta = 100 centimos	1½	0·02
SUDAN	Sudanese pound = 100 piastres = 1,000 mils	1 0 6	2·87
SURINAM	Gulden = 100 cents	3 9¾	0·53
SWAZILAND	Rand = 100 cents	10 0	1·40
SWEDEN	Krone = 100 öre	1 4½	0·19½
SWITZERLAND	Franc = 100 rappen or centimes	1 8	0·23½
SYRIA	Syrian pound = 100 piastres	1 9¾	0·25½
TANZANIA & TANGANYIKA	E. African shilling = 100 cents	1 0	0·14
THAILAND (SIAM)	Baht = 100 satang	4	0·05
TIMOR	Tapaca or dollar = 100 avos	1 7	0·22½
TONGA	Tonga £	16 0	2·24
TRINIDAD & TOBAGO	B.W.I. dollar = 100 cents	4 2	0·58½
TUNISIA	Dinar = 1,000 milliemes	17 2	2·40½
TURKEY	Lira = 100 kurus	9½	0·11
UGANDA	E. African shilling = 100 cents	1 0	0·14
UNITED STATES	Dollar = 100 cents	7 2	1·00
URUGUAY	Peso = 100 centesimos	4½	0·05½
VATICAN CITY	Italian currency		
VENEZUELA	Bolivar = 100 centimos	1 7	0·22½
VIET-NAM	Dong or piastre = 100 cents	2½	0·03
VIRGIN ISLANDS (BRITISH)	U.S. dollar = 100 cents (since December 1962; previously B.W.I. dollar)	7 2	1·00
YUGOSLAVIA	Dinar = 100 paras	11½	0·13½
ZANZIBAR	E. African shilling = 100 cents	1 0	0·14

NOTES

The list above includes most of the world's currencies which are likely to be encountered by collectors and whose approximate value can be ascertained with some degree of reliability.

Colonial territories in general use the same currency as the mother country; certain exceptions are noted in the list. Many British colonies issue stamps with values in sterling, and have therefore been omitted from the table, as have certain newly independent members of the British Commonwealth, such as Malawi, and Zambia, which continue to use currency in British notation at par with sterling.

Except for Christmas Island which uses the Malayan dollar, countries of the Australian group use currency in British notation, but the Australian £ is worth only 16s. sterling. It should be noted that this does not apply to the New Zealand group. Countries using the Australian £ are noted individually in the list.

The Malayan dollar is in use throughout all the Malayan states and in the rest of Malaysia. The British West Indian dollar is in use throughout the B.W.I. group, except Jamaica, Cayman Islands, and Turks and Caicos, which continue to use sterling, and British Honduras, which has its own dollar.

In the French group the C.F.A. and C.F.P. francs may be noted. The former (Communauté Française d'Afrique) was equivalent to two old French Metropolitan francs; the latter (Communauté Française du Pacifique) to five old French Metropolitan francs.

NOTES: Additions and Amendments

NOTES: Additions and Amendments